MEDIEVAL ITALY

MEDIEVAL ITALY

CONSTRAINTS AND CREATIVITY

Marvin B. Becker

INDIANA UNIVERSITY PRESS

Bloomington

Manufactured in the United States of America

Library of Congress Cataloging in Publication Data

Becker, Marvin B.
Medieval Italy.

Bibliography: p.
Includes index.
1. Italy—Civilization—476–1268   2. Italy—
Religious life and customs.   I. Title.
DG443.B42   945   80-8376
ISBN 0-253-15294-1   AACR2
1 2 3 4 5 85 84 83 82 81

Always to Betty

CONTENTS

ACKNOWLEDGMENTS

I wish to pay scholarly homage to the works and ideas of several historians whose assistance and insights have aided in my investigations. The numerous monographs and articles of Giovanni Miccoli, cited in my bibliography, provided indispensable scaffolding for researches into the relationship between church and society in medieval Italy. His work remains fundamental for all who would explore the boundaries between spiritual life and social change. My study of wills and pious benefactions confirms, and perhaps extends, certain of his interpretations. I am also indebted to F. Edward Cranz, whose numerous papers (many of which are unpublished) contributed to my appreciation for the historical importance of linguistic and epistemological questions. His approach to intellectual history, with its sensitivity to the relationship between word and thing, can, in my opinion, be utilized effectively by historians analyzing economic and social change. Indeed, it is possible to connect structural analysis with linguistic philosophy in the interest of deepening our understanding of intellectual activity. Roberto Lopez's writings on urban commercial life in the later Middle Ages are models of a combination of sturdy empiricism with a quest for theory. The many studies of Philip J. Jones on Tuscan economic history, and the many years of good talk, enhanced my respect for relationships between agricultural history and patterns of settlement. Donald Weinstein, in conversation and writings, challenged me to come to terms with the linkages between economic progress and spiritual change. My esteemed colleague Charles Trinkaus, like Weinstein, taught me that religious and social modes of thought often occupied the same space. And, literally, credit must be given to Richard Goldthwaite, with whom I have discussed problems of indebtedness these many years.

Finally, I should point out that in my footnotes, I have cited English translations of sources wherever possible, my reason being that they may be consulted more readily by the reader.

MEDIEVAL ITALY

Introduction

THE PRESENT VOLUME stems from a series of questions about
the social, economic, and religious history of Florence. It is a working
backwards of themes I first confronted in the Florentine archives when
examining documents of the fourteenth and fifteenth centuries. I felt a
deep dissatisfaction with the state of knowledge pertaining to some
leading questions. Without reaching back into earlier history, it seemed
to me, our views of the texture of Florentine society and communal
economics would remain bland. The need for nuance was essential if
we were to generate new hypotheses. A reading of the records of the
legislative debates held before the signory prompted me to perceive a
very high order of cooperation and a deep and abiding sense of community. What was striking was public confidence, and I became persuaded that that trust was engendered by faith in the durability of the
Republic's elaborate credit structure. I was delighted to discover that
the principal chronicler of the 1350s, Matteo Villani, an official with
authority over the funded communal debt, shared my opinion: "Faith
more useful than anything else, is of great assistance in supplying the
needs of the republic." What he had in mind was, of course, public
credit. Numerous other Florentines understood the nexus between the
survival of the political community and the availability of loan money.
Indeed, it was evident that Florence in particular and the Italian city-
states in general played a role on the European stage far out of proportion to their size simply because they were so precocious in matters of
public finance. The question was how to explain this remarkable, almost magical, phenomenon. It was all psychology, and the state could
never hope to amortize the principal. Yet the Florentines were reckoned
to be the shrewdest businessmen in Europe; the pope had referred to
them as the "fifth element." It would be essential to trace back the rise

of that mentality. How did the abstract ties of credit gain primacy? What part did religion play in these developments? Certainly, preachers were commanding figures in the Trecento debates on public indebtedness. Finally, there was the impressive fact that interest rates were declining, and this fact suggested something important about social change.[1]

Immediately after the Black Death a list of all the affluent citizens of the city was drawn up. The document is astonishing, for it speaks to the question that, in my opinion, was at the very center of social organization. For each ward of the city we have the individual named and the amount indicated for which he could post security.[2] Surety, or bond, was a common practice, with communal courts operating on the principle of collective liability. *Mallevadore* was posted by officeholders, artisans, magnates, magistrates, recruiters of mercenaries, the night watch, vendors of foodstuffs, and others. This surety was proffered to guarantee the fulfillment of contracts or the commitment to shun violence or to cover possible shortages in accounts. The list of *mallevadore* rates of 1351 ranged from a high of two thousand florins to a low of twenty florins. Everyone who was anybody in the city was included, with the amount designated for which he could assume responsibility. Citizens summoned to court could then call upon their fellows to offer appropriate guarantees. Karl Marx once spoke of the funded communal debt as a magic wand that contributed to the creation of the state. The mechanism of surety was the magic wand creating the web of everyday life. The more closely one examines fourteenth- and fifteenth-century Florentine society, the more central becomes the question of surety. Bond posted, like so many other financial transactions, was conducted by a type of ghost money; no cash was actually paid. One had a standing in the community, and a certain value was fixed to it. This was a variation on the practice of offsetting, whereby credits were transferred from one account book to another. Indeed, the communal treasury (*camera del comune*) was just such a repository. On every level, from the most exalted to the most humble, credit was the lifeblood of the commune, and in the fifteenth century Florentine civic humanists, such as Leonardo Bruni Aretino, Poggio Bracciolini, and Matteo Palmieri, so described it. It would not be a coarse exaggeration to caption the economy of Florence as Florentine-a-Card. Liquidity was low, and the expansion of both public and private economy depended upon the negotiability of commercial paper and the communal debt.[3]

It would have been possible to follow a more direct route if the documents of the fourteenth and fifteenth centuries spoke only to matters of sophisticated finance, but there is other evidence that speaks to the question of the durability of an archaic culture. Agricultural loans were rather like favors and could be regarded as gifts rather than debts. The landlord (*ospite*) expected to receive presents and gestures of homage from tenants. He was the patron, protector, and godparent of the tenant. This was not wage labor and clearly had its distant roots in the complex world of the gift culture. As one searches through the debris of the fourteenth and thirteenth centuries, one finds much that does not fit the model so carefully crafted by generations of Renaissance historians. Documents indicating that Lombard laws were still followed in matters of marriage, land sales, and family custom abound for particular regions of Tuscany. As one moves back through time, one can observe that many of the ancient ways became attenuated, taking an increasingly symbolic form. Not so with the vendetta, or blood feud! Money was left in the will of a Florentine of the early fourteenth century to anyone who would avenge his death. To stimulate the appetite for blood feud, the dead were left unwashed and placed on their biers lying in their blood. The commune sought to reduce the chance of vendetta by scheduling funerals at eventide and limiting the number attending. Over the fourteenth century the obligation of vendetta vied with the desire of merchants, artisans, and even nobles to be free of this onerous custom. In matters of religion we find that the practice of public penance for such grave crimes as murder, while unusual, did persist through the thirteenth century. Last, Germanic rites and Lombard ceremonies were in evidence in the outer reaches of the countryside through the fourteenth century.[4]

One observes two sets of linkages: the first based on credit (abstract ties) and the other on the gift (literal bonds)—*pace* Marcel Mauss. They coexisted in fourteenth- and fifteenth-century Florence, but the balance had shifted. The movement was clearly toward credit, and perhaps the most telling instance of this shift can be noted in the transformation of marital arrangements. Surely, nothing is more fundamental to social organization than the institution of marriage. In an earlier time the dowry was conceived of as a gift and was rendered in a transaction characteristic of numerous other negotiations in the form of gift and countergift. This, then, was an exchange between the two households. In the communal age, beginning with the twelfth century, the dowry was well on the way to becoming a special form of credit conceded by the wife's family. It was this credit that was destined to guarantee the formation and maintenance of the family nucleus and that was subject to revocation under certain conditions by women and kinfolk. If restoration was ordered, payment was to be made with interest and penalties. In the diaries and memorials of fourteenth- and fifteenth-century Florentine merchants, matrimonial contracts of family members were listed with the exact amount of the dowry. This was, in substance, a credit-debit relationship: the *dos aestimata* was registered as a contract, with the husband and his heirs designated as debtors. The Germanic system of gifts, making for an equilibrium between families, was replaced by a credit structure, the viability of which was dependent upon the communal government and the courts.[5]

The prosperity of the city was built upon a banking establishment virtually unregulated and taking enormous risks. Although the city's financiers were organized into a guild, this was no controlled activity. The word *guild*, in fact, is a misnomer by any medieval standard. These banking houses were free and competitive, doing international finance. At the heart of the Florentine economy were the risk-taking bankers and public creditors. The word *risk* sums up, better than any other, the nature of the historical change. To appreciate the transformation from an archaic and primitive society, characterized by dependence upon literal ties, such as gifts, oaths, and pledges, to one featuring the abstract ties of credit and risk taking requires a journey back to the ninth and tenth centuries. The structure and politics of tenth-century society were grounded on the display of wealth and the exchange of treasure. These were the transactions that riveted the consciousness of contemporary chroniclers. How different these were from the perceptions of society by the Florentine historians of the fourteenth century—Giovanni, Matteo, and Filippo Villani. One has but to peruse texts of an earlier time (the ninth and tenth centuries) to observe the changes in perception. The political world described in *Gesta Berengarii*, the *Antapodosis* of Liutprand of Cremona, the *Historia* of Andrea da Bergamo, and the polemical writings of Auxilius and Vulgarius, along with a variety of other sources, presents a bold picture of a society governed by blood money and fierce, narrow loyalties. Justice was archaic, with its customary, fluid, and epic characteristics. Bonds were constructed from solemn procedures and lavish ceremony. Hospitality, tribute, and immunity were vital linkages, and dependence on kin was quintessential to survival.[6]

To compare these ancient texts with the writings of such Tuscan chroniclers as Compagni, Stefani, and the Villanis is to realize that the world of the social observer had altered radically. No longer was it possible to write the history of Florence by simply recounting the annals of great families. Moreover, the materials of recent Florentine experience were refractory and could not be subsumed under traditional schemata, such as the regimes of emperors or the reign of popes. Historical experience broke out of the tidy receptacles in which it had been placed with such exquisite care. We note that in Milan the episcopal chronicle was to be converted into a communal history. In Genoa the first chronicle to be authored by a layman (Caffaro) was also the first historical narrative to make credit a fundamental topic of discourse. By the twelfth century, policy, or the absence thereof, was determined by very different strategies and mechanisms.

Risk taking implied less dependence on narrow allegiances and kinship ties. Alternate principles of merit and money were competing with blood ties. Loyalty flowed increasingly inward toward the conjugal center of the family and outward toward the state. Clan and *consorteria* affiliations weakened. In territorial states, such as Florence, communal governments attacked the power of aristocratic kinship; indeed, kinship as a principle of political organization went into eclipse. The rights of women were circumscribed and confined to a particular piece of property. Under the old system of the *quarta* or *tertia*, women participated in a wide range of family transactions. In the Florence of the thirteenth and fourteenth centuries the rights of kin were limited and communal ownership of property less significant. In the Arno city we can observe the transformation of family businesses into more impersonal networks. The rise of banks, insurance plans, credit systems, and communal charities made possible more autonomous life-styles. Florentine last wills and testaments demonstrate that far fewer bequests were being made to distant relatives during the later Middle Ages than hitherto. Pious benefactions also provide valuable evidence of the decline of family solidarity. The emancipation of sons, partable inheritance, the extension of limited liability, and the decline of joint penal responsibility were increasingly prominent in the records of law courts and the cartularies of notaries. In late-fourteenth-century Florence the officials with authority over the funded communal debt served as guardians for orphan children, and in 1425, with the foundation of the *Monte delle Doti*, the government created a credit institution serving as a type of insurance bank in which deposits were made by families so that their daughters might be guaranteed a dowry and so that they might be assured of progeny.[7]

With society emerging from traditional solidarities, yet with archaic forms still more than vestiges, tensions abounded. At Borgo San Sepolcro the local religious confraternity designated as sacred particular areas in which it met. There the membership of the small-town sodality was to preserve the pure gift culture. Relationships and exchanges were to be predicated on the gift rather than money. Soon, however, these archaic strategies were abandoned when it became necessary to give a close accounting of the charitable activities and financial responsibilities

of the lay brothers. We observe in miniature how the old unities receded before the new exigencies. In this instance more stringent organ-
izational forms were required to ensure the continuity of the fraternity.
An even more dramatic example of the complexities confronting ancient practices is to be found in the life of the religious confraternities
of Florence. During Holy Week one of the lay brothers, acting in imitation of Christ, would wash the feet of his brethren. By the sixteenth
century it was becoming so difficult to recruit an aristocratic Florentine
to play so humble a role that the ritual was generally omitted.[8]

Perhaps tensions ran deepest in the lives of the most privileged: in
Florence, as in so many other north and central Italian cities, this meant
the nobility and the commercial classes. This urban patriciate, involved
in business investment and the world of credit, was gradually redefining
its relationship with man and God. In the early fourteenth century the
guild of bankers (Cambio) required its members to participate in a
ritual whereby they pardoned each other for any usury they may have
exacted from one another. It is the hypothesis of this book that religion
followed the exchange system in many of its particulars. (Scholarly
impulse and sinful nature almost prompted me to entitle the present
volume *God: From Gift Giver to Partner*; instead, I decided to save
that title for the sequel to this study since a much greater exposition of
social history in the fifteenth century is necessary.) Again, in examining
evidence of Florentine commercial life in the thirteenth and fourteenth
centuries, one is struck by the rise of a type of business civilization
whose literary forms of expression were not determined by the university, princely court, or monastic centers. Among the earliest nonpoetic,
nondramatic, nonartistic uses of the vernacular are those evidenced in
fragments of account books dated 1211. Parenthetically, the merchant
stands as a strong progenitor of a laic culture. The economic historian
Roberto Lopez makes an effective comparison between the eleventh-
century physicians of Salerno, "intelligent yet illiterate," and their literate merchant contemporaries. If one follows these merchant ledgers,
one soon discovers that a special account had been set up for the "Lord
God." God was to become a partner in the business enterprise, and
there was no cynicism when the Alberti Company began its books with
the invocation "In the Name of God and Profit." A merchant of Prato,
Francesco di Marco Datini, was urged to close his account with God
and did so in a splendid burst of charity with the foundation of the
Ospedale di S. Maria de' Poveri del Ceppo in Pistoia. The Medici were
to say, part in jest, part in earnest, "Only have patience with me, my
Lord, and I will return it all to you." Account books acknowledge the
merchant as God's debtor, who is seeking a just settlement with the

supreme creator. The overwhelming impression conveyed by diaries and family memorials is that of an author who would keep all things in order so that if he were to die unexpectedly, it would be easy to make a final reckoning. Lorenzo de' Medici's memorial to his son records his charities, taxes, and building expenses together; they were an inordinate source of pride. Every time a contract was drawn up, money was to be set aside; this was "denaro di Dio." The converse was the evolution of a simple lawsuit for nonpayment of debt into an indictment for gross immorality or even heresy. In guild life the penalty for bankruptcy was Draconian: not only was the good name of the *arte* injured, but a wound was inflicted on God, and this might induce Him to punish an entire city. At the end of the thirteenth century, merchant bankrupts were likened to rebels who could be killed with impunity. In cases of bankruptcy, the poor, for whom money from dividends had been set aside and who until then were partners in the company, now became creditors. They, of course, were "God's poor," and the monies owed them, after liquidation, were paid to confraternities, mendicant orders, or the bishop's fisc.

The fourteenth-century chronicler Giovanni Villani, himself a member of a banking company, spoke confidently of the commercial houses of the Bardi, Peruzzi, and Accaiauoli as "the pillars of Christianity." He commenced his chronicle in the same spirit as did the Florentine diarists:

> In the name of Our Lord Jesus Christ and His Holy Mother, the Virgin Mary and all the Holy Court of Paradise, through their grace and mercy may we be granted the blessings of health and wealth, on sea as on land, and may our wealth and children be multiplied. Amen.

The impulse for writing the chronicle was a mixture of civic pride and religious devotion. Villani tells us that he was constantly nurtured by acts of piety. It was on a visit to Rome, in the Jubilee Year of 1300, that he vowed to undertake a history of his native city, which, although "daughter of Rome," gave every indication of surpassing the mother. On that pilgrimage he placed himself in the arms of God "in the hope of which" he would perform his civic duty: "And so that our work be more praiseworthy and better, I ask the help of our Lord Jesus Christ, in whose name every work has a good beginning, a good middle and a good end."[9]

I

Such a partnership with the deity carried both burdens and blessings. God was personal and to be found in the piazzas and streets of the city. At the various sites of commercial and public transactions were mounted sacred images intended to curb violent behavior and blasphemous language. The great edifice and center of guild activities in Florence in the late thirteenth century was Or San Michele—part grain market, part church. Here the image of the Madonna worked miracles on behalf of the underprivileged; her fame attracted pilgrims to the city center from all Tuscany. Lauds were sung by laity, and a religious company was formed. The captaincy of this assemblage devolved upon the most eminent of the urban patriciate. Their prime responsibility was to distribute alms. By the first part of the fourteenth century the captains were administering the medieval equivalent of a food-stamp program to those who could not afford to pay the escalating price of grain. In time of famine the communes of Tuscany disgraced themselves in the eyes of God and the nations by expelling all beggars. Not so the Florentine republic, which received and fed Christ's poor. A grain dealer and diarist of events in the grim famine year of 1329 recorded the almost Dantesque suffering of the poor and their understandable proclivity for violence. The captains of Or San Michele and the city's officials provided grain. The chronicler Giovanni Villani was one of these officials and tells us that sixty thousand florins was spent to sustain *il popolo*. In no other Tuscan city did wealthy citizens behave so charitably. Because of their piety and reverence God saw fit to protect and save Florence from "the danger of furor and rebellion."[10]

The individual's conscience concerning the rights and wrongs of daily living was made anxious, and the temptation to commit the sin of usury filled him with dread. In the case of Villani, his moral odyssey was marked by mounting guilt and despair. What began on the upbeat ended in disillusionment with a community whose inordinate desires brought tyranny and bankruptcy. The partnership with God entailed deep religious responsibilities. Indeed, fourteenth-century Florentines were increasingly sensitive to personal spiritual obligations and increasingly attracted to penitential societies, flagellant confraternities, the restitution of usury, and the construction of private chapels. A very different relationship prevailed between the individual and his maker than that which had obtained in an earlier age. The spiritual life had been realized more as a matter of external zeal than interior striving. God was remote, and His majesty inspired awe and obedience. Pious benefactions were made in the form of gifts to a distant God whose favor might be gained through lavish display and elaborate ceremony. The formula was stated boldly: give in this life so that you might receive a hundredfold in the life to come. Latter-day benefactions were consummated in quite a different spirit, with the emphasis on personal responsibility. In the most economically precocious region of Europe claims of conscience were not easily settled. As D. Weinstein and R. Bell will demonstrate, in their soon-to-be-published monograph *Saints and Society: The Two Worlds of Western Christendom 1000–1700*, the need for the play of the supernatural intensified in direct proportion to secular progress. The attraction of the sacred was strong, but so, too, were the claims of the everyday world. No easy outcome was in prospect in the contest between the world and the spirit. The lives of Tuscan saints of the thirteenth and fourteenth centuries poignantly dramatize this struggle. Nowhere in the hagiography of late medieval Europe do we find a greater expression given to that ambiguous zone between secular impulse and material interests on the one side and the claims of the spirit on the other. From the conversion of Ubaldo Adimari in the thirteenth century to the spiritual battles of Giovanni Colombini and St. Catherine of Siena in the next century, we observe a glorification of the transcendent that did not disvalue the attractions of the world.

Earlier, the nexus between God and man took a material form, replicating, as it did, ties existing in the secular world. The lack of confidence in the durability of human bonds resonated in the realm of the spirit. Behind social life loomed uncontrollable forces and physical contrasts. Claims to human dignity were, in the words of the French medievalist Marc Bloch, "a piece of eschatological eloquence" without any prospect of historical realization. Documents of the early Middle Ages confirm the stark observation that spirituality was concentrated on the Benedictines and their convents. Beyond the walls of the monastery all was in aimless flux. When a donor entrusted his soul to the ministrations of monks conducting a ceaseless round of prayers, he was in fact attempting to stay the chaos and brighten the impending shadows. God resembled a tribal chieftain to be placated only by gift and ritual. The benefactor was vicarious and passive, with saintly intercessors and priestly mediators designated to represent the sinner at the last judgment. Penance was a debt, and the monastery provided the surest way of making restitution. If penance was harsh, then the well-to-do could hire surrogates.[11]

Behind the documents of these unstable times was a consummate lack of confidence in the power of such abstractions as human sociability, love, and credit. This was a world of scarcity, in which commodities and labor were in short supply; money did not enjoy ample public trust. No strong political community existed to guarantee its value; therefore, fiduciary coinage was bound to collapse. The impulse toward making all relationships literal and concrete was commanding. What was to alter gradually was faith in the durability of human arrangements and the power of sentiment. Man was, in the words of the poet Dante, "companionable." We note that even in the face of such catastrophes as the Black Death, within less than a decade donors and testators were displaying a renewed faith in the effectiveness of earthly arrangements. Further, over the next century and a half, despite the continued incidence of the plague, pious benefactions and testaments demonstrated a psychic robustness and faith in civic values. The *Consulte e Pratiche* (records of the advisory councils to the government) reveal the extent of the unwavering commitment to political solutions to social questions. Not until the late fifteenth century did this confidence begin to ebb. Discussions were not conducted in an atmosphere of anxiety. Even in moments of extreme crisis speakers remained resolute and free of guilt. In these debates Florence was perceived as the beneficiary of God's favor.

If we compare these documents with charters of the ninth and tenth centuries, carrying numerous penal clauses and curses directed against all who would threaten the intent of donor or testator, then we have evidence of a monumental change. By the same token, the use of magic to endorse public arrangements in the earlier period was commonplace. Even the most trivial agreements would not hold without divine sanction. We shall trace gradual changes as trust was restored to the civic realm. Of course, the veneration of relics continued, but they ceased to serve as palpable signs of public authority. In Italy the decline of vivid interest in the "translations" and theft of relics coincided precisely with the first stage of commercial and economic revival. During the same interval the papacy rejected the title "Vicar of St. Peter" in favor of "Vicar of Christ." The new claim indicated that the uniqueness of papal authority no longer rested on the presence of St. Peter's body in Rome. Magic and the supernatural continued as a force in public life, but the ebb and flow was away from the civic realm toward regions that might be described as private and domestic. No longer were they to be invoked so frequently to endorse petty obligations and daily negotiations. The major preoccupation of influential Tuscan religious personalities and humanist writers was the social dimension of religion. The emphasis was upon piety, and the holy was located in social relations. Charity was divested of its universal and theological elements. The Florentine chancellor Coluccio Salutati, in the late fourteenth century, was to speculate on the question of whether the civilization of his day could rival those of Greece and Rome. His response was predicated upon a conception of civic virtue grounded on Christian charity. The associative impulse depended upon the ability of men and women to act piously, responding to the holy as the quintessential element in human relationships. In an earlier age charity was more often expressed in ritual acts, and piety was not the foremost component of a Christian community.[12]

Humanists from Petrarch and Coluccio Salutati to Ficino and Pico della Mirandola would perceive that the greatness of antiquity lay in a vigorous pursuit of glory by pagan citizens. Christian fortitude derived not from the desire for fame but from hope for immortality. Without the Incarnation, Petrarch was to state, "*humanitas* would have lain sick and torpid forever." No longer was Christ God's gift to man or a ransom paid to Lucifer for man's salvation; he was a companion and partner. Indeed, Florentine art in the Quattrocento was dedicated to lending form to this reassuring proposition. The spiritualities were now democratized. The miraculous was to be found in the ordinary, and its utility was psychological rather than economic and political. Yet, one must be careful not to accept a glossy view of human potential and achievement. If Dante argued for the "companionable" in human nature, he was just as convinced of man's proclivity for evil. If Donatello lent dignity to the laic quest for salvation, he also dramatized the high spiritual cost of such an odyssey. How to endure both truths? No such problematic view would emerge from a reading of an earlier literature and poetry. Only gradually would the dualism of a Paul the Deacon or Liutprand of Cremona be stilled and the new problematic view surface. The tenth-century churchman Raterio of Verona was the author of the *Praeloquia*, the first autobiography in early medieval Italy. In it he expressed, above all things, the desire to be pure and that the world should be stable and orderly. So bifurcated was his vision that he could not communicate it to the reader. This would-be reformer, like his fellow churchman Attone di Vercelli, lived in a world of jarring contrasts and was unable to formulate any coherent program. Only in subsequent centuries would such coherence be possible.

Of course, literature holds a privileged position, having a greater capacity to achieve formal lucidity: such a privilege belongs to art, not life. Caution as to the cultural weight we wish to assign the new literary genre, the Tuscan *novella*, is required. Still, it is evident that this genre, so well developed in Florence during the fourteenth and fifteenth centuries, contains social perceptions of the first magnitude. In Boccaccio, Sacchetti, and the rest we observe the remarkable mix of social classes. Indeed, it is difficult to make distinctions based on rank or ceremonial identity. In the *novella* materials from diverse strata of medieval experience (the fabliau, the romance, and the lyric) were combined into a fictional whole and crafted into works of great explanatory power. A vision of life was projected whereby competition between men and women, noble and nouveau, young and old was creative. These contests brought out the very best in individuals and social classes. The resolution of conflict did not necessitate a final verdict or decisive victory. The orders must live together without seeking reparation for ancient grievances. Rivalries could be harmlessly resolved through wit; compulsive behavior could be diffused with jokes and clever repartee. Extravagant expectations, the quest for vengeance, and zeal for omnipotence gave way to the creative game of competition.[13]

A noble creation was the projection of a vision of social space in which classes and individuals met in the certainty of their common humanity. The instinctual life could be consonant with the human enterprise. If social harmony was possible, it was not based on any final or ultimate knowledge. From the opening tale of the *Decameron* we are introduced to a world dominated by spiritual paradox. The capacity of characters to tolerate the radical disjunction between human knowledge and eternal truths is a measure of intelligence in this literary world. It is a hypothesis of this book that the ability to endure this separation was to increase over the centuries. The rise of fifteenth-century science represents something of a culmination of this talent for sustaining ambiguity. At one and the same time theoreticians, such as Leon Battista Alberti, could acknowledge the full force of a self-created order and conduct a passionate quest for the eternal mathematical order. Needless to say, Alberti's genius for paradox was unparalleled.

The four centuries under review here were times of phenomenal growth. Individuals were able to take risks with some assurance of success. Social change transpired in a benevolent atmosphere, and it is possible to argue that the best of merchant culture could be fused with the ideals of chivalry. Of course the *Decameron* presented a world of plenty; even the plague could not diminish its generous view of human nature. Feelings—even instincts—could be expressed without threatening the sense of community. The play of energy, even at its lustiest, did not need to have fatal repercussions. The distance between this imaginatively rendered world and that of an earlier time is as between two stars. So fragile were the bonds of affection and loyalty that they always had to be confirmed by an exchange of oaths, gifts, and pledges. The enemy was passion, and its play in the historical world was certain to bring down the kingdom. It must be confined to the free spaces of fantasy. The *Waltarius*, a representative work of that distant archaic society, portrayed a hero having no need of companions or society. This is a drama without history; proof of the hero's force comes only through combat.

II

Many facets of civilization in north and central Italy were prompted by a commitment to understanding historical development. The communal chronicle was itself the most dynamic literary form in eleventh- and twelfth-century Italy; historical writing was far more advanced in Italy than in any other area of western Europe. The same historical consciousness found a different vocabulary in the communal arts. The collective and choral expressions of an urban society created a space for civility and public action rather than for contemplation. History involved knowledge of the present and responsibility to the past. Deprived of its immutable character, it was to encompass the details of everyday life. The cathedral presented a vernacular chronicle in which popular notions of collective life triumphed over a more elevated and solemn idiom. Popular narrative tastes became a rich resource for architect, sculptor, and painter. A hallmark of Tuscan art was the moral seriousness with which these narratives were presented by a Nicola Pisano or a Giotto. As early as the first years of the twelfth century we observe that a sculptor, in this case Wiligelmo at the cathedral in Modena, related the story of Genesis as an irregular sequence of events. The figures are no longer housed in "a world of uniform measure." Space is not immobile; contrasts and contradiction abound. The new style had exceptional expressive power as composition moved away from a rhythmic and courtly language. In the next generation Niccolò, a pupil of Wiligelmo, working at Piacenza, Ferrara, and Verona, liberated sculpture from the architectural structure.[14]

The excellence of art was judged increasingly on the quality of craftsmanship, not the value of the precious materials used. Sculpture was released from its role of decoration. How different from the appreciation of materials by the peoples of an earlier, archaic time! The love of pomp and the production of larger and more sumptuous objects encouraged a rich ornamentation. The appreciation of luxurious materials, guaranteed to strike the senses immediately, was most appealing. The capacity of matter to reflect and transmit light was particularly prized; the enameler's skill in embellishing sacred articles was much in vogue. Chalices became larger and more elegant, altarpieces, like the paliotto in San Ambrogio, Milan, were richly decorated, and the covers of ecclesiastical manuscripts were encrusted with gold, ivory, and precious stones. Filigree work and the use of gems demonstrated an ever-higher level of skill as devotion to the relic intensified. This appreciation for the materials suggests an elevation of the tactile sense over the visual. Indeed, the miraculous was rendered tactile, and the power of the hand of God was manifested directly on earth.

Just as vital was the tendency of artists of the earlier Middle Ages to flatten forms. Figures were portrayed in isolation, no longer set in relation to each other. The antique notion of space lost its hold, and the impulse to endow figures with weight and substance atrophied. Moreover, the relief, so favored by the ancients, lost its power to communicate. Figures hovered one above the other; in fact, they existed as signs to be understood like writing on the wall or in folios of a manuscript. The world of earthly appearances signified little as the artist lost interest in representing depth; the third dimension was ignored. In each instance the connection between the symbol and what it represented was an identity: the space between object and image was conflated. The world was either a liturgy in which it was sufficient to pronounce the words in order to satisfy the realities or was one in which ideas existed exclusively in objects. In the latter case the word could not be separated from the thing, whereas in the former the body could not be separated from the spirit. The human figure lost mimetic significance. In the allegories and symbolism of the early Middle Ages each phenomenon was studied above all for its spiritual and moral significance. One searched directly in the phenomenon not for the physical causes but for the understanding that the phenomenon itself could provide. Nature was a book written by God, and the causes were to be found in "the will of God." The attacks on "vain curiosity" were fierce. Nature did not have its own consistency or autonomy. The physical world either dissolved into a set of symbols or existed in its stark concreteness. Claude Lévi-Strauss has suggested that the "untamed thinker" (*sauvage*) widened the notion of relevance so that galaxies of meaning emerged.

The sense men made of their lives was not inappropriate to the way they lived. Just as they were reluctant to endow nature with greater autonomy, so they were unwilling to venture far beyond regulated markets. In the early Middle Ages, there were timid intervals of growth when modest increases of trade and goods encouraged individuals to reject traditional structures and narrow allegiances in order to claim greater independence. Such periods were exceptional, and, for the most part, exchange was highly regulated and elaborately ritualized. Legislation was aimed at maintaining prices and wages and ameliorating scarcity. Markets were public and conformed almost classically to Fernand Braudel's notions of those eye-to-eye "transparent exchanges." Merchants were under episcopal or royal protection. The main problems of economic life stemmed from a dearth of goods and labor. Precious metals were in ample supply but were hoarded, only to accumulate in the form of ornaments, bullion, and coins. How the exchange system was freed from rules and rituals is the stuff of the present monograph. How a countermarket or private market emerged, released from regulation and control, is also a prime question. A world of unequal exchanges, where capital and credit could be readily moved to gain maximum advantage, was in place in the cities of north and central Italy. Nowhere was the state more securely in the power of a moneyed elite than in Florence. Nowhere was a moneyed elite freer to take risks than in Florence. In an earlier time such a figure as the Milanese merchant Semplicianus, who made gifts to the monastery of Nonantola, was exceptional. By the thirteenth century, however, Tuscany, Liguria, and Lombardy were peopled with merchants and bankers who not only made gifts to the Church but executed public policy. How many halting steps were required between the eighth and thirteenth centuries before such a commercial civilization could take shape and coexist with—even rival—an older, archaic culture? Documentation surviving for the earlier centuries in the Lucca and Florence regions pertains principally to land deals. Before 1000 exchange and donations accounted for approximately 80 to 85 percent of all transactions; after this date sales increased until, by the second half of the twelfth century, they accounted for more than 75 percent of all transactions. In other words, the prevalence of donation and exchange, so evident in an earlier time, was now rivalled and overturned by a vigorous commercial economy. Those essential features of an archaic economy were receding. By 1427 over 75 percent of the lands of the Tuscan countryside (*contado*) was owned by Florentine citizens.[15]

III

The fact of growth is undeniable. Some 8,000 settlements have been identified for medieval Italy; of them, 700 were pre-Roman and 2,000 Roman, and there were approximately 225 for the eighth century, 262 for the ninth, 552 for the tenth, 945 for the eleventh, and 1,014 for the twelfth. The population has been estimated at four and one-half million for the year 700, rising to five and one-half million in the mid-tenth century and peaking in the thirteenth at about ten million. Of course all these figures are but approximations, yet they do represent a great leap forward. Although the fact of growth is undeniable, one cannot be satisfied with a stark empirical approach. Opportunities increased substantially beginning with the second half of the tenth century, and the individual had reason to believe that his life prospects were much improved. The climate for investment and mobility did brighten. Evidence mounts for markets, tolls, transport, and merchant activity in north and central Italy over the tenth century; still, one senses deeper rhythms at work in economic and social life. Everyday transactions were endorsed less often by ritual and the force of the supernatural. Ordinary relationships were less likely to be governed by what the historian Georges Duby terms "the necessary generosities." Now exchange could more aptly be spoken of as *trade*; traditional symbolism attending negotiations became less essential. Commemoration records disclose a greater emphasis on family rather than estate or office, suggesting the individual's growing independence from the insignia of rank or status. The language of politics, formerly so liturgical, was now responding to the new legal science, in which logic and precise verbal distinctions were calculated to resolve disputes. How to explain these changes? Surely, cultural change is no mere response to an external demand but is in accordance with the internal consistency of the human mind.[16]

Never had such dramatic increases in population occurred; never had the movement toward urbanization and land recovery been so active. Population increases were registered at a time when little change could be observed in the mortality rate. If we follow Marc Bloch, we can opine that a larger percentage of the population married, with more households forming on newly reclaimed lands. Certainly, reclamation and colonization were prominent features of tenth- and eleventh-century life, but so too were dreams. It is fascinating to recall that the first heretic of the new age was the Italian grammarian Vilgardus of Ravenna. The Cluniac chronicler who tells us his story narrates that the heretic was visited in a dream by Virgil, Juvenal, and Horace. They assured him that his admiration for their works would gain him eternal fame. It was then that the heretic "began to preach many things contrary to the faith." Vilgardus's fall was attributed to the Italian fascination with pagan learning. Another grammarian of the following generation, Anselm of Besate, was embittered when he was "shunned as a demoniac, almost as a heretic" by contemporaries because he conducted secular studies. Disturbed by dreams, he tells us that he imagined himself in heaven, where he was the object of a battle for his allegiance between the shades of his saved ancestors and three beauteous virgins symbolizing logic, rhetoric, and grammar. The struggle of Anselm to rehabilitate an ancient secular culture in the domain of the dream suggests something of the ensuing drama. Escape from censorship and repression was, of course, the function of dreams. In the literature of the eleventh and twelfth centuries the realm of the dream was to expand as conflict between the claims of old and new intensified. The dreams of laity acquired the status of a literary genre, but what of their more mundane aspirations? What of the tenants of the cathedral church of Lucca at the end of the tenth century who were released from labor services and payment in kind in return for money rents? Now that they were freer to dispose of their own energies, would their work be more productive?

What theory can we offer that does not opt exclusively for either the earth bound or the domain of dreams? My preference is for the general theory of the human mind as having "a natural adaptation to imagining correct theories of some kinds"—what the American philosopher Charles Sanders Peirce labeled the "principle of abduction." Peirce regarded "abduction" as fixing a limit on admissible hypotheses; it was a type of instinct developed over the course of evolution. Noam Chomsky put Peirce's notions to good use, arguing that scientific creativity depends on both an intrinsic property of mind and social and economic conditions. Cultural variation and human nature are not incompatible ideas. Behind the first lies the second—a unified abstract structure controlling specific variations. How can we explain the interaction between those properties of mind and social and economic conditions? To illustrate, one might compare the last moments before death of the learned Venerable Bede of the eighth century with eleventh-century St. Anselm of Aosta. Bede had only one fear on his deathbed: that he would be unable to complete his translation of the Gospel of St. John the Evangelist into Anglo-Saxon. St. Anselm was troubled by his repeated failure to resolve the metaphysical problem that had engaged him for so long; he would have more time to meditate on the origin of the soul. Until the last moment, so his biographer Eadmer tells us, the saint's penetrating mind searched for God on the very summits of the Alps. How different were the images of heroic deeds![17]

Can one explore the zone between brute fact and dream? When Nietzsche stated, "I am afraid we shall not get rid of God until we get rid of grammar," he was asserting a proposition essential to this book. For the philosopher this impossibility indicated that error had fixed itself to human thought and indeed is biologically valuable. For the historian it is historically valuable since, at least for medieval Italy, the relationship between God, grammar, and exchange was at the center of consciousness. Surely, it affected the subject/object dichotomy. As Dante was to observe, language sustained by faith achieves its full sense. Grammar is the ground on which the split between words and

things, characteristic of the fallen world, is healed and a correct interpretation is envisioned. The poet's own writings suggest that as prospects for communal unity became less mechanical, self-consciousness
about language became more acute. Such was the case for many thinkers. But all this would have to be qualified beyond the historical or
metaphysical endurance of even the most patient reader. As Judge
Learned Hand once suggested to a too-talkative lawyer: "Some concession must be made to the brevity of human life."[18]

1

Religion and Social Change
From Archaic to Communal Society

THE TERM *takeoff* has been applied to the economy and society of western Europe in the eleventh and twelfth centuries. For Italy— the most precocious of all European regions—economic and social historians have amply chronicled this quantum leap. Economic indicators, such as population growth, technological advance, and urbanization, have been carefully investigated for these revolutionary centuries: the advance was indeed startling. The eleventh and twelfth centuries have been justly compared with those of Neolithic times (fifth millennium B.C.) and the Industrial Revolution of the early modern age. These three eras have been called responsible for a massive transformation of the patterns of settlement and dramatic mutations in the tempo of everyday life. For the medieval period the towns of north and central Italy, with their burgeoning business and banking activities, have been depicted as experiencing nothing short of a commercial revolution. At the base of this economic renaissance was a renewal of confidence in abstract ties and relationships.[1]

Recent studies of the Italian urban scene in the later Middle Ages have argued persuasively that at the very heart of this transformation was an exponential increase in credit and the circulation of money. Economic historians have observed that from the fifth to the eleventh century virtually no substantial mechanisms existed for facilitating the transformation of savings into investment. Those who saved either invested directly or hoarded. Loans were made chiefly for the purpose of consumption; consequently, the economy suffered from the deflationary effects of hoarding and inadequate investment. Contractual arrangements were very rare; barter was a widespread practice. In land transactions the price was calculated in money but often paid in kind. So, too, were tax imposts. Gold money, perhaps because it was being hoarded, was gradually disvalued until it was abandoned in Carolingian Italy. The coinage of small money almost ceased in most parts of Italy except for the Byzantine territories. Even there, between the sixth and eighth centuries, symbolic money (*tessere*) was substituted on the great estates of popes and bishops. In the West, between the fifth and eighth centuries, the minting of bronze coins (*follis*) for small exchanges and then the minting of gold coins for international trade had ceased. The coins in circulation had a very high value and therefore could not be used for everyday transactions. Barter and exchange were the key to the economy, with purchases intermittent. Agreements of eighth-century Italian landowners featured payments of bacon and grain for plots of land. A minter of Lucca who could procure cash more readily than most gave a horse in part payment for a debt. Trade tended to be in necessities, such as salt and iron, or in certain luxury cloths. Merchants were too few to be separated readily from other *laboratores*.[2]

With a small population living on the land, with local commerce tending to be in large measure through barter, and with little division of labor or accumulation of capital, a constant monetary inflation existed with a minimal circulation of money. Barbarian kings struck gold currency not for business transactions but because they wished to imitate the Roman emperors. The coin was a symbol of order and of "stable and divine values" rather than a medium of exchange. Further, this was a society in which distinctions between trade on the one side and war plunder and robbery on the other were surely writ in sand. In many particulars this society resembled the gift culture familiar to the anthropologist. People placed confidence principally in primary ties of obligation. They had little faith in abstractions; seldom did they judge abstractions sufficient for constituting effective social bonding. In this archaic world it was rare to find individuals pursuing a middle path between deep trust and total mistrust. The power of the gift to secure goodwill was a supreme article of faith. As we have noted, contractual arrangements were rare, and it was difficult for contemporaries to sustain a belief in the binding force of judicial abstraction. The *launegeld*, or countergift, had become a regular feature of daily transactions. Men and women of the eighth and ninth centuries did not readily subscribe to the conception of a gratuitous donation. As we shall observe, this distrust held even in religious matters. The exchange of goods was not a mechanical transaction but a moral one; even during the later period *launegeld* persisted as a mechanism for endorsing the sale of property. In economically advanced regions, such as twelfth-century Tuscany, the countergift remained a feature of economic and social exchange, but, as we shall see, its value was becoming increasingly symbolic.[3]

Throughout the earlier period the upper classes considered the exchange of gifts quintessential to maintaining political cohesion. Moreover, they celebrated personal virtues over ethical abstractions, such as the idea of justice. Each individual had a concrete value predicated on his or her position in the society: a price was fixed for the dead as well as for the living. In cases of personal injury, payment went to the nearest kin, with damages assessed according to a rigid scale of penalties. Composition or payments made to avert blood feuds were codified scrupulously. When the price was too great, resort to the judgment of God through the ordeal or judicial duel was legally prescribed. Placing an economic evaluation on individuals was, of course, quite unclassical and foreign to the Roman Republic. Families inherited the sacred duty of avenging injury done to kinfolk, living or dead. Only through the payment of blood money (*wergeld* or *guidrigildo*) could one avert feud and vengeance (*fida-inimicitia*).[4]

A necessary material rapport existed between the person and the object. The need to concretize relationships between men and their possessions (*gewere*) had its analogue in such practices as *mundium*, in which wardship over women and minors, held by the father or guardian, was transferred to the husband only after payment of the brides gift. This was a world where women, gifts, pledges, and oaths were exchanged in a manner well understood by the anthropologist studying primitive and archaic societies. Guarantees were required for fulfilling daily obligations, with agreements sealed by the exchange of sacred tokens or pledges. Frequently the pledge, or *wadia*, was equal in value to the debt incurred; the oath was sacred, of course, and a personal guarantee was required for those going surety. Indeed, the law itself was personal rather than territorial; the right to legislate was inherent in the person of the king. The conception of *Heil*, or *virtus*, included a belief in divine power operating through royal and saintly figures. The king, by exercising his *Heil*, gave protection to pilgrims and merchants. The onset of catastrophes or strokes of misfortune was seen as an indication that once-powerful figures had forfeited divine favor. The surest signs of *virtus* were to be found at shrines of the popular miracle-working saints. Relics were used to validate public arrangements, and this widespread custom was testimony to the fragility of ties between individuals. Numerous witnesses were required to confirm the import of commonplace obligations. Maximum publicity was given to pious acts since the notion of initiating a transaction, which was a pure gift, had only a modest hold on the imagination of the people of this archaic age. Of course it was difficult to alienate property: this act required the acquiescence of numerous kinfolk.[5]

This literal exchange system had its ready analogue in religious ritual and practice. Preeminent was the idea of making a literal exchange with the deity. Gifts to churches, pious foundations, or monasteries brought *launegeld* in the form of prayer. People believed it literally true that one gave in this life in order to receive a hundredfold in the next. Documents from the eighth and ninth centuries convey a sensibility very close to a material conception of salvation. Gifts had the power to gain the goodwill of the unseen and hostile forces governing the universe; favors to monks and clergy could forestall a divine vendetta and were similar to the payment of *guidrigildo*. It was not to the justice of God that one usually appealed but to His omnipotence and mercy. He was a great chieftain, and gifts were likely to increase His largesse. Had not Christ gone surety when He came to earth, taking human form in order to save mankind from Tartarus? Christ was God's gift, and He shed His blood for our redemption. He was a lonely and distant figure, and His voice could be heard in benefactions and donations of the time telling all that His Father had prepared a kingdom for them from the very beginning. Surely the last judgment, when the Savior would come to mete out punishment to those lacking charity, was imminent. In these documents (*chartae dotis*) the eternal fires of hell were described vividly—but so, too, was the angelic choir. Death could signify being removed from light into darkness or bearing a heavy yoke.[6]

Sin, for the most part, was undifferentiated and generalized—a great weight. One did not know the transgressions for which one might stand condemned. In order to merit eternal salvation it was necessary "to meditate on the weight of our sins." Little could be done by the individual to influence his final salvation beyond giving alms or making provision for prayers to be said. Charity was formal and ritualistic, neatly fitting "the mold of the gift economy." Bequests to the poor might involve few individuals, and, not surprisingly, the figure *twelve* was a favorite. The injunction "Give to the poor so that you might have treasure in heaven" became formulaic. Children were offered to monasteries as gifts to God; this was the Lord of the Old Testament, omnipotent and full of wrath, a figure to be placated. Because the last judgment was imminent and punitive, fear was intense. No God of love this taker of gifts! Individuals were powerless, requiring the direct intervention of the supernatural to ensure salvation. One could do little to change one's spiritual fate while in exile in this vale of tears. Life was a pilgrimage, and human frailty required an army of monks and saints to battle against Satan and his minions. Grace was instantaneous, and slight effort was expended in describing the merits or spiritual worth of the individual.

Benefactions tended to be ancestral and retrospective, voicing little confidence in the future. Concern for one's forebears took precedence over provision for one's progeny. History and historical sensibility played almost no role in the thoughts of donors, benefactors, and testators. Since the fate of mankind seemed so bleak and human arrangements so precarious, little energy was expended in projecting the present into the future. Sensibilities remained tribal and archaic, whereas historical consciousness appeared static and frozen. As we shall observe, a new awareness was to emerge in the twelfth century, when individuals grew more confident that despite flux and instability, the future would be like the present; no amount of buffeting would cause radical historical discontinuity. In the earlier period, however, trust was placed in neither kin, progeny, nor institution but in holy places. Patrimony was offered to the monastery so that battle might be waged against those malignant forces determined to frustrate humanity's quest for salvation. Benedictine convents were organized communally to undertake such spiritual warfare. Even the saints were seldom individualized and, with the exception of Peter, Paul, and Michael, were a collectivity, a heavenly host. It was to sacred places (*sacris locis*) rather than to holy men that one bestowed gifts, for "just as liquid extinguishes the funeral pyre, so alms purge sin."[7]

I

With little confidence in the effectiveness of human institutions to make the volition of donor, benefactor, or testator prevail, the document itself became an object of veneration. Placed on the altar and validated by clergy and numerous witnesses, wills and donations were sacred in themselves. The document was iconic—a transparent medium, crystal-like, through which the power of the divine could be apprehended directly. The imagery was Biblical and vivid, with the voices of saints heard in chorus with heavenly angels. The splendor of lights and pleasing fragrances excited the human heart to experience the glow of the Holy Spirit. The single most important guide to the faithful was the word of God, and this they could hear plainly telling them to meditate on Holy Scripture, where it is written that all sins will be forgiven if they heed the voice of Christ: Sell all that you possess and give it to the poor.[8]

As we have noted, religious remedies were extreme: Forget your people and your fatherland; go into exile or undertake a pilgrimage. Is not life itself exile from your true father and from your true fatherland? Heroic virtues were necessary for gaining eternal life. Donors and testators did not have a strong sense of human dignity and worth, nor did they express substantial appreciation for the possibility of human achievement. Death was a kind of limbo; the idea of purgatory had limited appeal, as did the conception of the treasury of merits. Therefore, the possibility of spiritual intervention between the moment of death and the onset of the last judgment remained slight. Relatives and friends did not work for the salvation of others; wives and children were not considered effective intermediaries. Death was in fact a form of sleep, and little could be done by the living to aid the soul of the dead in making the felicitous transit to paradise. Alms and gifts were the best hope of donors and testators seeking to be liberated from a "second death." Personal immortality had only a modest purchase on human imagination. The memory of the individual and his progeny was likely to survive only if it was rooted in the consciousness of a clan or a people (*gens*). Honor and glory pertained to the collectivity rather than to the individual. Death was seen as a conclusive separation from temporal life; the soul of the deceased was in God's hands, and not much could be done to influence divine judgment beyond proffering gifts. Few believed that the actions of one's heirs and survivors could modify the spiritual destiny of an individual soul. Donors and testators left funds for a tomb and specified the place of burial but were not overly concerned with elaborate funerals or commissioning numerous prayers and masses. The mass for the dead was an "occasional collective ritual," and few instructions were left for the salvation of an individual soul.[9]

We observe, then, that men and women were prone to believe that God was influenced by considerations of equity and mercy as little as were fellow mortals. Furthermore, the bonds between the individual and his God were concrete and literal, very like the exchange system here on earth, predicated on palpable and tangible transactions. In matters spiritual, as well as in affairs temporal, little place existed for the play of abstraction. Symbols tended to be perceived directly, and the relationship between word and image or word and thing interlocked. Just as donations and testaments were iconic, allowing the divine to shine through, and just as the Holy Book was very like a relic, the *charta*, or document, had symbolic value. Indeed, the *charta* was equivalent to the material exchanged or objects sold. The notary, or scribe, was not passive but rather an active participant in what has been described as a "laic liturgy." Witnesses assumed responsibility to corroborate the truth of the document in any future juridical contest. The *charta* in Italy during the early Middle Ages was not proof in itself. Not until the eleventh century did the document generally become dispositive rather than probative. Complex ritual and symbolism were invoked to endorse the ordinary negotiations of men and women living in a world where trust in abstract arrangements was seldom ample. Ritual and symbolism were required to authenticate quotidian relationships. The ties of obligation and duty were rendered corporeal and material by a series of magical gestures. For example, pledges and pawns were exchanged along with the transfer of a wood baton, a tree branch, or a handful of earth. At first the passage was from debtor to guarantor (*fideiussor*) to creditor; only later did the pledge or pawn pass directly from debtor to creditor.[10]

The number of instances in which ties of obligation were lent concrete form could readily be multiplied. Creditors acknowledged their debts *per lignum et chartam*, and it is difficult to distinguish a pawn from a document as a source of obligation. The notion that writing in itself could be a cause of obligation was tenuous at best. This, then, was a world of narrow tribal loyalties, demanding kinship ties and exacting primary allegiances. The individual was encadred in a literal world where the materiality of bonds was immediate and certain. In part this archaic society represented a response to the precariousness of existence and the frailty of abstract ties. In such a universe the realm of religious practice came to resemble a world of secular activity, where goods, services, courtesies, and ceremonies were exchanged in order to gain goodwill and secure loyalties. In both the spiritual and temporal spheres we observe an absence of trust and confidence; this resulted in conflating the distance between an act or gesture and its symbolic representation. We see manifestations of this mentality in many forms of cultural expression. For example, linguistic transformations disclose that tendencies toward a symbolism highly attentive to tangible objects and the physical world were gaining strength. The need was to render material the many manifestations of the human will. Strenuous effort was exerted in making contracts corporeal in order to validate juridical relations. The Lombard language offered a textured vocabulary for fixing the boundaries of property and conveying the status of ownership. In quotidian transactions, symbols, tokens, and signs provided physical confirmation of the validity of agreements. Markings on houses at each corner established the extent of the property. When the walls of a city were demolished, the life of the city was over, although bishop and inhabitants continued to dwell there. One cannot review the history of early medieval Italian law without appreciating the power lent to "judicial folklore." The quintessential requirement was to give palpable form to human volition.[11]

II

In the eleventh and twelfth centuries we observe a dialectic at work. Perhaps citing an incident will clarify the change: many citizens of Milan became incensed over the behavior of a certain prominent cleric, who refused to dress in luxurious clothes and furs, preferring instead to walk the city in rags and tatters. Yet others acclaimed this holy man when he appeared in pauper's garb as vicar of the bishop. The crowd perceived him and a reforming monk from Vallombrosa as "angels of God" when they took the pulpit of the cathedral. A contemporary Milanese chronicler opined that much of their popular success resulted from their rejection of proper clothes and food. Some citizens, the chronicler observed, did upbraid the clerics for failing to wear skins of ermine and vair, display ornaments, or eat delicate food. Would not the city be disgraced in the eyes of pilgrims and strangers if these clerics took the poor Christ as their model? But the idea of voluntary poverty was gaining appeal, and holy men and reformers did catch the popular imagination.[12]

About this time an attack against wealth, pomp, and ostentation surfaced in Tuscany. A particularly valuable source of this conflict, the "Matilda Gospels," presents visual evidence of a new attitude toward wealth. The illuminations of this eleventh-century manuscript show money changers on the steps of the temple of the Lord. They are identified as first- and second-rank nobles (*capitanei* and *valvassori*) hawking ecclesiastical properties. Christ is portrayed as driving these money changers and *venditores ecclesiarum* from the holy precincts. Matilda of Canossa and her mother, Countess Beatrice of Lorraine, gave shelter to the Milanese reformers in the 1060s when they were driven from the city by the German emperor. Close ties existed between Milanese Patarines and the Tuscan Vallombrosans.[13]

The idea of poverty had broad appeal, and the effects of religious ferment could be discerned throughout the orders of society—from the noble to the merchant to the landed peasant. The reform movements of the eleventh and twelfth centuries were popular in that the various classes participated, but at their beginnings leadership rested, for the most part, with the nobility. What was at issue was nothing less than a vision of restructuring society, and this vision, in turn, had grave social and economic consequences. In Milan and Florence the attack against wealth, pomp, and display was in fact a challenge to those symbols of prestige and power most certain to command obedience. In the archaic world of the ninth and tenth centuries, ostentation and display were the instruments of government.[14]

The holy man was at the cutting edge of social change, advancing new possibilities for the relationship between the human and the divine. Of course, these prospects had their analogue in the changing character of quotidian social and economic arrangements. In Tuscany we observe the beginnings of a harsh critique of the world of gift culture at mid-eleventh century. A bitter campaign launched by Giovanni Gualberto and other Florentine reformers was mounted against ecclesiastical institutions accepting gifts in return for spiritual benefits. These Florentine monks and clerics attacked this nefarious practice, rejecting the widely held and time-honored idea that wealth was a sign of divine favor and a proper means of gaining salvation. If we survey pious benefactions and donations over these years, we perceive a significant modification of this traditional attitude. In the ninth and tenth centuries the sensibilities informing large-scale bequests were markedly familial, with the donor reserving private rights and personal control. This was the spirit that found ample expression in the benefactions of the great Tuscan noble houses. Moreover, prayers and other spiritual aids were considered a direct compensation for the gift itself, as was salvation. Starting in the very late tenth century we find Tuscan nobles making grants to monasteries with fewer reservations. Such eminent figures as Count Ugo of Tuscany and his mother, Willa, were probably in contact with the leading holy men of the age, Nilo of Rossano (ca. 910–1005) and Romualdo of Ravenna (ca. 950–1027). These two saintly figures brought new religious fervor to the region. The marchesa Willa, in her donation to the monks of the Badia fiorentina, omitted the customary reservation of *dominatio*. The absence of the traditional clause indicated the extent to which nobles were eager to trust their souls to the ministrations of devout monks, who would storm the skies with prayer. This corps of angelic men was freed from temporal obligation to the donor; they could elect an abbot not in consultation with a Tuscan noble house but in accord with the holy rule of St. Benedict. In the next century this family went to elaborate lengths when making grants to avoid the taint of simony. The great monasteries of Tuscany were to be freer from the world of power, arms, and gifts; they would demonstrate their spiritual authority from a vantage point beyond the narrow limits

of concrete obligation. Separate from customary defenders and pro-
tectors, these monks projected an ideal of more ample and open social
space.[15]

As we have noted, the holy man Giovanni Gualberto attacked the
notion of gift and countergift with great spiritual urgency. Challenges
to the idea that prayer offered up by monks and clerics for donors and
benefactors was a type of *launegeld* were central to the Tuscan reform
movement. Supported in their holy work by Peter Damiani, whose
letter to the bishop of Florence exhorted him to reject these criminous
gifts from any man, the Tuscan holy men conducted a fiery crusade
against the simoniac clerics. In Damiani's letter he tells of a priest who
was the confessor of the Tuscan noble Ildebrando della Gherardesca.
Ildebrando gloried in his castles, manors, and courts, which were as
numerous as the days of the year. The priest had served this rapacious
noble well, but one day he had a vision: covered with sores, he met St.
Benedict, and the saint explained that the sores were an affliction caused
by the priest's acceptance of gifts and alms that were cursed, the fruits
of robbery and usurpation. The saint led the priest into a deep valley,
where hot waters ran; there the priest saw figures being boiled like fish
in the steamy liquid. The flower of the Tuscan nobility were crying out
in agony for their sins and performing useless acts of penance. On the
banks, awaiting their turn to be immersed, were men of terrible visage.
Leading the way were the Tuscan nobles, first among whom was Ildebrando della Gherardesca.[16]

Changing trends in motivation are discernible in pious benefactions
of the Tuscan elite in the eleventh century. Legacies and bequests
tended to go to eccelesiastical bodies subscribing to voluntary poverty
and practicing the common life. Diatribes were directed against rich
and powerful monasteries indulging in pomp and luxury. The idea of
poverty was being transferred from individual to collective life. The
critique of wealth was extended to the papacy itself, which was now
perceived as being distanced from the pauperistic ideals of the time
when the Apostles walked the earth. Giovanni Gualberto, soon to be
recognized as a *civic saint*, was lauded by the Florentines for his rejection of riches and espousal of voluntary pauperism. The saint was regarded as Christlike for the care tendered to the poor and infirm at his
monastery at Vallombrosa. However, the Vallombrosans were not permitted to deviate from the Rule in order to aid the poor unless conditions were exceptional. They were to have faith in the beneficence of
divine providence, which could provide for all earthly needs. The general attitude of eleventh-century Tuscan reformers toward poverty did

not involve the conception of conquering it through material assistance; rather, the holy man was called upon to console the poor and even share their plight.[17]

III

The challenge of the reformers and their allies was directed against a system of values and social relationships structurally dependent upon the gift and literal exchange. Pomp, wealth, and display commanded respect and obedience and were the anchor of human arrangements. They were also links to the divine, for money and gifts were exchanged for benefices, prayers, and spiritual advantage. The growing belief that relationships among individuals and between the individual and God could be predicated upon more abstract ties was an innovation of great import. Accompanying this gradual transformation was an increasing emphasis on interiority and the subjective. Pious bequests in eleventh-century Tuscany disclose a marked increase in concern for the internal, spiritual state of donor and testator. Many hoped to be saved *per spiritum compunctionis*, and the analogue to this accent on interiority was the projection of a different image of God. In the eleventh and twelfth centuries the focus was more on God's mercy, love, and redemptive powers than on His wrath. A secure place was accorded the term *misericordia* in the benefactions of the twelfth century. Christ was perceived as an effective intercessor intent upon redeeming mankind through divine love. A coercive and punitive religious mentality was slowly being divested of its tight hold. No longer was Judgment Day conceived of so exclusively as a time of cruel punishment; the idea of spiritual rewards was achieving wider appeal. The possibility of gaining celestial justice was enhanced as men acquired greater confidence in that greatest of all human abstractions, earthly justice. Expressions of anxiety about retribution by a punishing and angry God lost much dramatic force. Fear as a motive for pious actions was in decline and love of God on the rise. The Virgin Mary became a more familiar figure and the emblem of divine solicitude for humankind.[18]

A very different sense of sin was revealed in testaments and benefactions of eleventh- and twelfth-century Tuscany. Documents of an earlier time portrayed the stain of sin as an undifferentiated burden weighing heavily upon humans; donors and testators were dreadfully oppressed by this "weight of sin." Beginning in the later period, however, we notice a shift from this harsh view toward a different form of representation in which transgressions were particularized. Furthermore, remedies for sin were lightened; a more optimistic concept of the penitential was also taking root. In part this change was the result of the fact that individuals could know their sins: that had not always been the case. Harsh penalties, such as exile, long and dangerous pilgrimages, and strict ascetic renunciation, were now giving way to the milder remedies of specific acts of charity. By the late eleventh century the foundation of hospitals had become a growth industry in the region of Tuscany. Meanwhile, the practice of penance grew more personal, with individuals fulfilling the obligation rather than commissioning or even hiring others to perform this onerous task.[19]

An extension of human feeling and concern was also evidenced in Tuscan documents of the eleventh and twelfth centuries. Formerly, wills and benefactions were marked by a deep ancestral bias; loyalties and allegiances tended to be narrow and strictly defined. Piety was expressed most frequently toward forebears rather than progeny or even contemporaries. Blood ties rendered the notion of gratuitous bequests difficult to sustain; relatives could and did challenge the conveyance of property. The practice of "cursing" was a regular feature of early bequests, with donors importuning the wrath of God and malevolence of Satan against anyone seeking to thwart their intent. Penal clauses were also standard in charters of every type. The idea that property should be allowed to move outside the narrow circle of blood ties was hotly disputed. Neither donor nor testator displayed much confidence in affective ties: the cursing of kinfolk and the lengths to which individuals would go to berate all who might seek to baffle their wishes suggest that little regard was lent to the power of love and affection. Indeed, in those earlier times, trust in one's intimates was secured by oaths, threats, and pledges.[20]

In the eleventh and twelfth centuries benefactors and testators tended to reach beyond the world of narrow obligation. These were centuries in which collective Christian interests found a fullness of expression that was to be altogether novel. Impulses toward association with a community of souls gave voice to generalized and universal concerns transcending the strict limits of former times. Sensibilities became increasingly future oriented, and this change, in turn, prompted a view of history wherein ages to come were perceived as differing little from the present. A sense of historical continuity gained force, and the living felt a deepened obligation to progeny. Confidence in the power of human volition also mounted, and for the first time in the eleventh and twelfth centuries we find wills that are true contracts of alienation with the right of usufruct. Donors and testators could dispose of landed proper-

ties more readily without resorting to the prayers and curses once regularly directed against Judases who might subvert their intent. Over
these centuries the role of executor was much strengthened so that the
wishes of donors and testators might triumph. Bequests were considered irrevocable, and the testator was to achieve greater freedom of
action.[21]

IV

This movement toward release from an archaic world structured on
networks of primary obligation was clearly reflected in the slackening
of blood ties. Once again this loosening of bonds was dramatized by
the holy man, who solemnly and publicly disavowed the once-sacred
duty of pursuing the blood feud. Kinsmen had inherited the duty of
revenge. The two most influential religious figures in Tuscany in the
eleventh century, Romualdo and Gualberto, both vociferously renounced
this time-honored tradition, refusing to settle family scores in the
bloody, tribal way. Religious reformers and spiritual leaders from
Damiani to St. Francis challenged that bedrock of aristocratic insensitivity, the payment of composition for settling violent crimes. Holy men
were the most relentless critics of these tribal practices. As we shall
observe, they were to propose very different networks of relationships
based on empathy, compassion, and love; their trust was increasingly
invested in the power of abstract ties.[22]

At the very base of social arrangements was, of course, marriage and
the family. During these times the institution of marriage came to be
viewed quite differently by leading clerics. In an earlier day, before the
great revision of canon law, a celebrated master offered a theological
argument to support the notion that it was necessary to have physical
consummation for matrimony to be regarded as insoluble and valid.
Only in a consummated marriage could the sacrament be realized, for
was not marriage a concrete manifestation of the union between Christ
and the Church? Therefore, matrimonial ties were not valid without
incarnation. Within less than a century, however, the nuptial ritual, like
so many other rites, was being transferred from a world of literal exchange and concrete forms to one where symbolism and abstraction prevailed. In the eleventh and twelfth centuries the sacramental character
of marriage was solemnized. No longer was it necessary to provide
proof of consummation; indeed, canonical thought emphasized the
spiritual dimension of the union. The sacred character of marriage was
vigorously upheld against ecclesiastical concubinage and clandestine

union. The religious intervention of the priest was prescribed, and the Church challenged the easier sexual mores of an earlier time. Canon law was intruding into many areas of private life once cordoned off by tribal practice.[23]

We see an enormous enrichment of the vocabulary pertaining to marriage in particular and family life in general. Language in the eleventh and twelfth centuries was acquiring a greater capacity to express the psychology of these relationships. The clergy was playing a leading role in elevating the dignity of the marital state, and the *ordo conjugatorum* was now seen as being capable of leading a life pleasing in the sight of God. Traditional monastic hostility gave way to more sympathetic understanding. In the late eleventh century in north and central Italy we observe a growing conviction that conjugal ties were not a barrier to participation in spiritual activities. This changing attitude was reflected in sermons elevating the worth of the laic condition. Previously, clerics had advocated abstinence from the conjugal act on holy days, but by the eleventh and twelfth centuries marital relations were not singled out as sinful acts polluting religious holy days. As we shall see, new avenues of authentic Christian life were being opened to men and women who continued to live within the family circle.[24]

In these centuries the power of human affection and the durability of familial ties was to be highlighted in unprecedented ways: in wills and pious benefactions we observe a resurgence of confidence in the strength of family concerns. Husbands appeared to be interacting more profoundly with wives and children. As we have noted, wills were no longer focused exclusively on the ancestral. A greater trust was evolving in supportive, contemporary networks. We have already seen the decline in provisos of *chartae*, donations, and wills, whereby donor and testator set up penal clauses against kinsmen who might thwart their intent. Similarly, we observed a decline in clauses containing threats and religious imprecations against relatives who would subvert a benefactor's will. This new confidence gave donors and testators a sense of security. Benefactions to monasteries in twelfth-century Tuscany indicate a gradual transformation: formerly they had been centers of clan activity; now the principle of lineage worked to challenge traditional ties of kinship. Burial privileges, the right of *dominatio*, and the duty of *defensio* were reserved solely for male heirs.[25]

The assertion of the agnatic principle was an important feature of the attempt to prevent fragmentation of patrimony by an extensive division between collateral lines. The strengthening of family ties elevated the legal position of the husband, but above all it buttressed the contractual base of marriage. Not only was the idea of marriage as a sacrament becoming the rule and gaining moral prestige, but contractual relationships were replacing traditional, more literal bonds. For example, the dowry, or jointure, was governed by a very different spirit: it was becoming a real contract. The glossators from Martinus to Plancentinus regarded it as irreversible. Formal guarantees of women's rights over the dowry were affirmed, and the widow was free to dispose of it. She stood more independent of her own kin.

If the sacral and contractual base of marriage was gaining, so, too, was the repression of such marginal liaisons as concubinage, bigamy, and the clandestine union. As the *ordo conjugatorum* achieved higher status, chastity was idealized. The denunciation of illegitimacy, ecclesiastical concubinage, and adultery had a great impact on the mores of Tuscan laity and clergy in the eleventh and twelfth centuries. Grounds for repudiation and annulment were strictly delimited. Ecclesiastical prohibitions extended the forbidden degree of relationship for marriage between kin. In notarial documents of the early twelfth century we see the rich vocabulary pertaining to the marital relationship. The older language contained elaborate terms concerning the extended family. Whether such extended families did exist is not the point at issue: instead, our interest lies in changing perceptions. During the eleventh and twelfth centuries notaries regarded the conjugal family as the basic social unit. Notarial formulas came into vogue for guaranteeing legitimacy and thereby ensuring descent through lineage; in this way the social function of the conjugal family was buttressed.[26]

Again wills and pious benefactions suggest an intensification of bonds of affection and familial intimacy. As parents and kin relinquished all rights over the bride, she drew closer to her husband. He, in turn, came to rely on his wife, and we observe in the Tuscan last will and testament that the widow acquired greater authority and responsibility. We find a gradual increase in provisions stating that when wives become executors of patrimony, they should remain in the "widowed condition." Anxiety was great, of course, about second marriages and the loss of patrimony for children. What was surfacing now, however, was the husband's desire to have his widow exercise her spiritual duty. As the idea of purgatory gained wider acceptance in the twelfth century, widows became highly valued as spiritual intercessors. Careful distinctions must be made between the various conditions under which women functioned: surely, widows were among the most favored—at least materially—of all the members of their sex. By the thirteenth century, Tuscan poets from Forese Donati to Dante Alighieri were prizing the widow for her "devout prayers" and remembrances of her departed spouse. Spiritual acts by the widow aided the passage of her husband's soul through purgatory to paradise.[27]

V

The desire to believe in the durability of human relationships and the power of abstract and emotive bonds was a hallmark of the new cultural and social forms. Increased confidence in contractual relationships was undergirded by a growing trust in the effectiveness of new types of association. Mechanical forms of solidarity were much less prominent; this fact was most evident in the expansion of credit, and nowhere in western Europe was its use more widespread than in north and central Italy. As we have already observed, from the fifth to the eleventh century few financial mechanisms existed for facilitating the transformation of savings into investment. Those who saved either invested directly or hoarded: loans were made chiefly for purposes of consumption, and the economy suffered from the deflationary effects of hoarding and inadequate amounts of productive investment. Economic historians have contrasted the takeoff of the eleventh century in the city-states of north and central Italy with the world of Greece and Rome. Their findings permit us to extend these observations even further and say that the city-states of antiquity lacked credit mechanisms. With a few minor exceptions, such as the sea loan, ancient cities of the Mediterranean world had only the most rudimentary credit mechanisms. Therefore, with this comparison in mind, urbanization in medieval Italy appears even more striking.[28]

The traditional argument that the "economic renaissance" of the eleventh and twelfth centuries was keyed by the release of treasure hoards from the Church has been effectively disputed. The expansion of credit has been reckoned to be of much greater significance for the takeoff in north and central Italy. In earlier times we find very few notices in documents of *cambiatores, prestatores,* and other specialists in credit. By the eleventh and twelfth centuries, however, we find such references on the rise. We also observe that the document of indebtedness was losing its penitential character; so, too, the *wadia,* or pawn guaranteeing restitution, was no longer prominent. The idea of *fideiussione* was extended beyond the ambience of personal guarantees. Exactly at this time the language of economic transaction was acquiring a varied and subtle vocabulary. Accounting procedures were becoming more sophisticated, and new associative forms of economic organization were evolving. Credit and partnership agreements permitted risks to be shared, thus reducing hoarding and deflationary pressure. All of this suggests a greater confidence in the effectiveness of institutions and trust in one's fellows.[29]

Private acts multiplied during the tenth century with a regularity that cannot easily be imputed to chance. Recourse to notaries for private contracts, marriage agreements, and wills was becoming commonplace. The use of parchment instead of papyrus indicated a new interest in the conservation of documents. Contracts were being substituted for ritual gestures; the courts tended to move toward written proof (*probatio per scripta*). After the tenth century it was rare to find a defendant who did not have written title. The *charta* was becoming a means of juridical proof, as in Roman law. No longer was the consigning of *chartae* equivalent to the material exchange of objects sold, nor was the document perceived as the cause of obligation without a careful investigation of the parties' intent. In the older world the document was not only proof of the judicial act but represented it—and almost personified it. Witnesses assumed responsibility in future judicial contests for corroborating the truth of the document, which was still not proof in itself. Now, in the eleventh and twelfth centuries, the document, redacted according to proper legal norms by a qualified person, could stand as an independent element of proof. The notary was becoming an active party in the task of authentication as his prestige was enhanced and the document accorded *fides publica*.[30]

The study of Roman law projected a vision of legal order more stable and autonomous. In earlier times justice drew much of its effectiveness from the adhesion of both parties to the decision, with very few tried *in absentia*. By the eleventh century, however, the justice of technicalities was rivaling that of treaties and agreements. Courts were not so strongly committed to arranging concord between plaintiff and defendant. Indeed, they were moving from the open air of the *placitum* (called that because it pleased both parties) into the closed space of the tribunal. In business, as in law, the shift was away from voluntary or amiable transactions ruled by the principle of *convenienta*, which had resulted in pacts or agreements, toward more impartial legal norms. Justice had not been possible without publicity or solemnity. Indeed, it had been necessary to call a *concursus populi* in order to endorse a verdict. The public solemnity of the courts paralleled private negotiations, in which straws, tree limbs, batons, or *launegeld* passed from hand to hand in order to sanction the most ordinary transaction.[31]

In associative life, too, palpable expressions were de rigueur. For example, the very building in which minters practiced their craft was part and parcel of guild collective life; fraternal ties were expressed through the very proprietorship of the structure itself. Comparable tendencies were evident in religious confraternities. Originally they were cultic organizations bound together by stern, pious obligations to a particular place of worship and a special object of veneration. Their confraternal life was expressed through concrete and literal actions. The same was true of other forms of the religious guild. Priests were bound together by vows of mutual assistance so they might find support within the narrow confines of their orders when old or infirm. Gradually, however, sodalities became associations of a mixed character, with priests and laymen mingling. Indeed, they were to draw their membership from all classes, becoming the most democratic of medieval institutions. By the thirteenth century these religious bodies were bound together by the most abstract of all bonds—affection, love, and charity. Confraternities were creating networks of concern very different from those of blood, cult, and even profession.[32]

Canon law in eleventh- and twelfth-century Italy was much influenced by theological developments. This science was to work toward spiritualizing material relationships; in so doing its practitioners were to utilize a figurative and highly emotive language. The transformation was most evident in the substitution of the patient investigation of intention for the crude application of a fixed and codified penitential system. The shift was away from the idea of penance as being materially understood toward a subjective view based on contrition and the human heart. The conception of interiority was challenging earlier notions of culpability. The valuation of an act in all its concreteness was being undermined by rising psychological concerns. Emphasis was placed upon consent at the expense of solemn ritual. The oath was regarded as an inviolable promise able to save an agreement from formal defects. In penal law canonists demonstrated a talent for enlarging the body of terms to express a greater awareness of the idea of intention while qualifying the concept of ignorance and error.[33]

Germanic law had less interest in the abstract and subjective and depended on the corporality of relations. It was difficult to postulate ideal entities distinct from the collectivity or to dispense with material and formal proof. As we have seen, the notion of giving something away without receiving something in return was far from commonplace. Moreover, when bequests were made to hospitals and convents, they became part of the patrimonial mass, belonging to the saint presiding spiritually over the institution; procurators of charitable foundations were, then, administrators of celestial property. Even the mass commissioned for the salvation of souls entered into the patrimony of the church. By the eleventh and twelfth centuries, however, canonists were beginning to regard pious foundations as corporations with a legal life of their own: the concept of the juridical person was taking form. The doctrine of *perpetus necessitas* elaborated on the idea of the continuity of practical needs and the natural persistence of things. Confidence in the durability of pious foundations was marked. Donations did not require maximum publicity or solemnization by intricate ritual, nor was it necessary that charitable institutions be protected by arms or the *virtus* of a powerful saint.[34]

VI

The impulse toward philanthropy and spirituality was heightened in eleventh-century Tuscany. A nadir in pious benefactions appears to have been reached in the mid-ninth century, but after that the recovery was dramatic. In the diocese of Lucca, between 824 and 1008, only four donations for care of the poor and infirm were recorded, whereas between 1008 and 1100, twenty-two gifts were registered. A similar pattern can be discerned for Florence and its environs: in the ninth century only three bequests were recorded for the establishment of pious foundations, and none were noted in the tenth century before the year 978. For the next thirty years, however, we have information concerning nineteen new foundations, and this number equals the total for the preceding two hundred years. Of course this renaissance of philanthropy was no simple occurrence, nor is there any easy explanation for it, but we find that it did coincide with the economic recovery of north and central Italy. Further, these developments transpired only shortly after the last great invasions by Hungarians and Saracens in the first part of the tenth century. Identical patterns, documented even more amply, can be observed for other regions of Italy.[35]

Again, returning to wills and benefactions, we observe that in earlier times the sense of charity was very limited; generally it was formulaic and even ritualistic. Seldom was it linked to collective ideals, with *caritas* often extended to friends and kinsmen. The impulse was sporadic and emotional involvements narrow. Alms giving, as we have noted, blended very well into the mold of a gift economy: one bestowed goods on the poor in order to gain God's favor in this world and salvation in the next. By the eleventh century in Tuscany, however, we observe a deepening and extension of charitable sentiment. Empathy for the plight of the poor was matched by a vital concern for human suffering. In the religious realm and the arts the focus was on the life of the Savior, with particular regard for His passion. A keener sensitivity to the human qualities of the suffering Christ was being displayed;

the stern figure of Christ the judge—prone to punish, rather than save, men—was losing its monopoly on the artistic imagination.[36]

In Tuscany during the eleventh and twelfth centuries a chain of hospitals was established, and their fame spread throughout Europe. These institutions were founded at Lucca, Altopascio, and Fucecchio and across the two branches of the Arno before the hills of San Miniato. This boom in hospital construction continued over the next two centuries, with Florence, Arezzo, Pisa, and Siena becoming leading centers. In Florence, poor relief and the construction of hospitals were accompanied by attitudinal change, with laity committing themselves to sharing the suffering of the impoverished and infirm. Wills and pious benefactions reveal that increasing numbers of Florentines were entering a life of Christian charitable service. Donors and benefactors were less satisfied with a passive or remote role, preferring to act out their philanthropic commitments. As we shall see, the possibilities open to laity were increasing during these eras; they were able to lead a life pleasing in the sight of God without entering a religious order or placing themselves in opposition to the hieratic church. The impact of lay piety was to be so strong in shaping the culture of Tuscany that St. Francis and Franciscanism were to gain great acceptance in this region; so, too, was his teaching that happiness was not synonymous with riches and that wealth was not a source of joy among men. Francis, the follower of the naked Christ, preached that the cardinal sin was indifference to the misfortunes of others, and Tuscans responded dramatically.[37]

A belief in the power of such abstractions as love and charity found its analogue in the institutional and social life of eleventh- and twelfth-century Italy. As we shall observe, ties of affection were increasingly acknowledged as a base for marriage. We have already mentioned that wills and benefactions were demonstrating more generalized concerns. A new social vision was proving more attractive; the classes and orders of medieval Italian cities were drawing closer. Collective values predicated upon cooperation between the orders were finding ready spokesmen. This cooperation was based upon the growing authority of communal imperatives. The great cities of north and central Italy were themselves patrician creations and not products of revolutionary conditions. In fact, the antithesis was true: their society and government were products of an internal transformation of the feudal world. The nobility participated in the life of the commune from its inception and were a driving force. It was the surpluses from agriculture that served as an economic base for the phenomenal urban growth. When these cities expanded and conquered the countryside, feudatories submitted but retained their privileges. The immunities and exemptions of the local aristocracy were held in high regard; of course, they were not to be tampered with by a consular aristocracy composed mainly of landed proprietors.[38]

In such centers as Florence we see nobility and burghers blending so that new families, such as the Caponsachi, Giuochi, Lamberti, and Ughi, joined the Visdomini, Uberti, Sichelmi, and Suarizzi nobles as the ruling cadre of the city. Even the use of such terms as *old-line nobles* can be somewhat misleading. Tuscany, for the most part, was dominated by nouveau families; even the pedigree of so exalted a figure as Countess Matilda of Tuscany was abbreviated. The founder of that line, a certain Adalberto-Atto, first appears in a charter of 958; he had no connection with an older Lombard or Frankish nobility but was a property owner with sizable resources—a type of middling landlord. The secret of his success lay in castle building, and this in turn allowed the settlement of vast tracts of land. By constructing fortresses and giving protection to agricultural colonists, this lord, like so many others of his time, was able to bring wealth to his house and gain political eminence. This same pattern of economic expansion can be documented for Lombardy and the region around Rome. The new lord acquired several vassals, and they, in turn, rose in society along with their chief. In the case of Adalberto-Atto, he was to win the favor of Emperor Otto I, and, in only a few short years (962), he acquired the title of count, thus arriving at the pinnacle of a new feudal aristocracy along with his *fideles*. The feudal nobility and urban patriciate of the tenth and eleventh centuries had no strong ties to an older aristocracy. The decline of Lombardic and Frankish lords was a consequence of extravagant marriage settlements and the excessive partition of lands. What we witness, then, is the circulation of elites—an internal transformation of the feudal world, not a revolutionary change.[39]

In cities we perceive that the main thrust was toward the inclusion of second-line nobles (*valvassores*) into feudal society. Similarly, when citizenry struggled "pro libertate acquirenda," they were battling to be included in the world of feudal hierarchy. The city itself was to be integrated within the feudal system. In general, town governments demonstrated a scrupulous regard for customary laws and liberties. For the most part, the consular aristocracy ruling the towns of the eleventh century rose from the ranks of great landed proprietors, many of whom now resided in the town. Differences between rural and urban branches of the same family were often obscure, and this was to be the case in Florence with the Buondelmonti, Compiobesi, Da Quona, Ricasoli, and others. The blend of old viscontal nobility and commercial families included the Amadei and Donati, from trade, and the Firidolfi, Uberti, and Ubaldini, of noble lineage. Indeed, for the nobility the twelfth and thirteenth centuries represented something of a golden age: they were not displaced from public life; instead, they participated in it vigorously. Through legal studies they qualified as jurists and administrators; their status favored their selection as ambassadors and diplomats and their election to town councils. Finally, their prowess at arms placed them at the head of communal armies.[40]

As early as the first part of the eleventh century we notice a growing conception of the mutuality of the orders. The call to arms, as recorded in contemporary chronicles, brought rustics and city folk together as well as knights and burghers. On many different levels we observe early instances of cooperation between social classes. In Milan alliances were made between burghers and second-line nobles, while at the same time popular political movements were surfacing in Florence. The term *popular* can be used effectively if we agree that representatives of all orders of society were included; the constitutive element was no longer the *potentiores*, a military caste. Exactly at this time the term *popolo fiorentino* was first recorded in the documents. The earliest stirrings of Florentine citizen life were linked with religious reform movements. Giovanni Gualberto, Florence's most saintly son and a leading reformer of the second half of the eleventh century, was himself the subject of a contemporary panegyric taking the form of a civic laud. This celebration of heroism possessed a high charge of spirituality.[41]

VII

Sentiments of mutuality found their greatest and most explicit expression in the religious life of the eleventh-century community. In Lucca, the Holy Cross, long an object of veneration, became a symbol of the pacification of the town during those times. In Milan, Ariberto was to transform the *carroccio* into a symbol both civic and spiritual. To the south, in Umbria, St. Ubaldo was being recognized as a citizen-patriot whose civic concerns were surpassed only by his religious zeal. The call for peace among the orders was voiced by spiritual leaders in many an Italian town. On the lunette of the Church of San Zeno in Verona, the sculptured figure of the town's patron saint was depicted in the act of benediction: on either side were assembled the citizenry; on his right were the knights and on his left, the foot soldiers. All were fully armed, and the saint was presenting *il popolo* with a standard worthy of being defended.[42]

The mutuality of the orders, the civic concern of holy men, and the movement toward reform of the church were closely connected. The direction of change was away from a society whose structural base was tribal and archaic. The older world had been easier and more relaxed, accepting in practice ecclesiastical concubinage, the marriage of priests, lay domination over church property, and the fragmentation of benefices. Documents from tenth-century Tuscany indicate that wives and children of clergy received material support and attained social prestige. Ecclesiastical concubinage allowed the continuity of the clerical presence on the land. Meanwhile, properties of the bishop were passing into the hands of great secular lords. The buying and selling of ecclesiastical offices, lay investiture, and clerics with family ties were part and parcel of the old system. When the reformers challenged these practices, they were depriving many of support and social standing— not the least of whom were the wives and children of clergy. Again a social structure based upon literal ties of obligation was being called into question. Church organization and social organization were finding different models. In the case of the former, ideals of ecclesiastical liberty and immunity were gaining ground. Attacks against clerical marriage and concubinage were part of a general spiritualization of the bonds of Christian society.[43]

In the great struggles against ecclesiastical concubinage, simony, and lay investiture, laity were active participants. More conscious of their spiritual worth, they sought to play a more active role in church matters. The movement toward a communital religious life included meetings of laity with clergy, discussion of religious questions, common prayer, and processions by *il popolo* to the various churches to honor the memory of saints. During these times prayers were offered for the peace and salvation of the Church, for the conversion of her enemies, and, indeed, for many other "useful purposes." Cooperation among the orders for the reform of church and society was fundamental to the success of the Gregorian movement. For the first time, then, in medieval Italian history we observe the sustained and large-scale participation of laity in spiritual life. In Tuscany the call to laity was not the traditional one of seeking to imitate the monk. Asceticism in late-tenth- and early-eleventh-century Tuscany did not spring solely from a desire for mortification but also from a feeling for life. The harsh ascetic ideal, so inspirational to many in the past, had been an exercise in endurance with no relief and little hope; the aim had been voluntary annihilation of individuality. We find new ideals of a positive and liberating nature rivaling these traditional goals inspired by hatred of the world. These ideals included self-knowledge and the possibility of following a calling other than that prescribed by a rigid society. The canonical movement in Tuscany broke the boundary lines between the role of priest and monk. The most influential of the new monasteries was that of the Vallombrosans, who regarded their houses not as islands of peace and prayer far from the tumult of civil society but as launching pads for activity and reform of the world. A new motive for the foundation of monasteries evidenced itself in eleventh-century Tuscany; monasticism was no longer considered so generally a retreat and flight from the world but rather an opportunity to gain another perspective on things temporal. Asceticism conferred a new dimension on existence and experience.[44]

Christian life came to demand strenuous effort; Giovanni Gualberto laid upon his followers the sacred charge to bring the Christian truth to the masses. Religious energies broke the bounds of refined and aristocratic spirituality. Reformers had much less feeling for the exigencies of power, rank, and wealth. Limited, closed, and tragic perspectives on life and survival in this world were being converted into youthful enthusiasm. What had its origins as the private affliction of a penitential sinner seemed now to be opening out to embrace a new religious mission—nothing less than a spiritual regeneration of the world. The elevation and elaboration of the pastoral role were principal features of eleventh-century Italian hagiography and theology. The evangelical impulse to Christianize the temporal world was celebrated with exceptional zeal.[45]

Breaking the barriers of aristocratic spirituality, religious sentiment was democratized and no longer so subservient to the instruments of worldly power. North and central Italy proved to be hospitable to the idealism of religious reformers. The new Eucharistic doctrine popularized by the Gregorians was as concerned with the reform of the inner life of the believer as with the external structure of the Church. In each instance the direction of change was toward greater autonomy and purity. In politics this led to the formulation of a program of ecclesiastical liberties allowing the sustained application of rational dialectics and legal theory. Reform of the inner life led to the self-examination and elevation of the goal of self-knowledge. This psychological search placed a high value on the power of emotion. Mortification, the traditional form of expiation, lost some of its force in the face of this quest for interiority. Confidence was enhanced in the spiritual efficacy of confession and forgiveness: remission of sin was to come through contrition.[46]

Greater reliance was placed on human intention and the effectiveness of moral intervention in spiritual matters. As we have noted, benefactions and wills allow us to trace aspects of this transformation. Documents, which once portrayed life as a pilgrimage and death as a departure from light into shadow, expressed the essence of a radical pessimism wherein little could be done by donor or testator to earn salvation. Individual merit counted for little; penance was harsh, and emphasis was placed on the difficulty of leading a life in this world pleasing in the sight of God. Moral life for laity was a form of combat, and they were called upon to display aristocratic and heroic virtues. Sin was generalized and the possibility of remission slight and unforeseeable. But starting in the eleventh and twelfth centuries the accent was on spiritual striving and the ability of laity to achieve grace. Moreover, God's mercy was no longer regarded exclusively as the countergift rendered in return for the gift. The relationship between man and God was now more likely to be predicated on abstract, rather than literal, considerations. For the will-making population, salvation was something to be earned.[47]

VIII

The renewal of confidence also extended to individuals' ability to relate their personal quest for salvation with more generalized and global purposes. Again we observe that donors and testators had customarily requested that they be remembered in the monks' prayers or be buried in the abbey cemetery. Tuscan benefactors asked to be received into the monastic community and therefore be part of an ongoing and *eternal* community. In the twelfth and early thirteenth centuries we begin to see that individuals were less satisfied with this passive role. No longer were they content merely to have their names included in necrologies or inscribed in the matriculae of the living and the dead. Over the centuries Tuscan necrologies became mere records of burial sites as more active forms of spirituality achieved greater expression.

We have already considered the expansion of the charitable impulse, which displayed extraordinary concern for the spiritual well-being of the Christian community. Indeed, collective purposes were being taken up by Tuscan testators and benefactors with an enthusiasm hitherto unknown. Global enterprises, such as the crusades, and laic religious activities, such as pilgrimages, were particular favorites. Bequests to the papal treasury and to churches throughout Christendom, east as well as west, suggest an emerging cosmopolitanism. The spiritual destiny of the individual was increasingly attached to the fate of the larger Christian society, with greater empathy shown for the needs of the community. Bequests to lay confraternities were soon to vie with legacies to monasteries. Gifts of property to hospitals were accompanied by pledges to serve the poor and sick. Personal involvement in works of charity was becoming a leading feature of twelfth- and early-thirteenth-century spirituality. Less anonymous and more assertive, donors and testators were finding enhanced possibilities for a life of Christian service in this world. Meanwhile, Tuscan notaries strived ever harder to clarify the intention of donor or testator. Obscurity of language was the cardinal sin in a notarized document. The desire to make human volition prevail led to the lively battle against *obscuritas pactorum*, including the renunciation of archaic techniques and the acceptance of systematic forms and chronologies. Notaries of the thirteenth century expressed incomprehension at the vagueness of earlier contractual arrangements.[48]

In a world where intention was central and the individual exposed to judgment, human traits were more sharply delineated and the person more likely to be lent a spiritual biography. As we have observed, the sense of sin was particularized, while at the same time remedies for transgressions were moderated and rendered subjective. The emphasis was on interiority and contrition rather than satisfaction of a code morality as prescribed in the earlier penitential books. The power of love and repentance counted for much more, and the boundaries of the forum of conscience were extended. Once again the subjective and the abstract challenged a literal and public system of punishment. At this time the first large-scale restitutions of usury were being made in Tuscany, and the first sizable groups of Florentines were commencing to undertake voluntary penance. Hitherto, the tendency had been for penitents to be branded as public sinners and condemned to harsh punishment, frequently involving humiliation before the community. These sentences could be satisfied by kinsmen, heirs, or clerics, but someone in this impersonal system was required to perform a dramatic or wrenching gesture. In the twelfth century the diagnosis of sin became more radical and harsh, but the remedies were more moderate, involving, as they did, the human heart. Just as telling was the changing conception of conversion. In previous eras *metanoia*, or conversion, generally implied renouncing the laic condition and taking religious vows; in ninth- and tenth-century Tuscany the laic condition was perceived negatively and ranked at the bottom of the spiritual hierarchy. It would be rare to find a contemporary view of spirituality advancing an optimistic assessment of the religious possibilities inherent in the laic condition. To live beyond the world of orders was to exist in the shadows of Christianity. Elevation of a monastic perspective on the *ordo coniugatorum* was a hallmark of tenth-century Tuscan religious life. Slowly, however, a more favorable line of argument took hold: the idea of conversion assumed an easier and livelier connotation. No longer was it quintessential for those experiencing *metanoia,* or spiritual rebirth, to reject the round of everyday activities: they could now hope to live a life pleasing in the sight of God while still honoring their terrestrial obligations.[49]

IX

Religious impulses were unfolding to encompass and sanctify larger expanses of temporal experience. Nowhere was this extension more apparent than in relations between the sexes. In the second decade of the eleventh century a very influential *collectio canonum* was assembled, and if we judge from the number of surviving manuscripts and collections derived from it, it was well known to Italian contemporaries. In schematic form it anticipated the more elaborate responses to be made in the following century, when a sacramental theology on marriage reached full expression. In the early-eleventh-century Italian work we see apt comparisons made between the "marriage bond" and the "sacrament of regeneration." The marriage bond endured as a sacrament and could be severed only by death: husband and wife had equal dignity and worth. Earlier collections had less confidence in the durability of this abstract and sacred basis for union. In the eleventh and twelfth centuries, however, the notion of spiritual union was gaining ground against the necessity of having "union of the flesh" in order to make a true marriage. The rites of marriage were being spiritualized and the ceremony coming under the aegis of the Church. Soon it was contended that husband and wife could make spiritual progress and be reborn in Christ after death.[50]

Formerly, it was exceptional for clergy to counsel programs of moral comportment according to the customs and habits of laity (*more laicorum vivere*). When such advice was given, it was generally intended for the nobility. Models of moral betterment were aristocratic and heroic. The imagery of these tracts was that of combat and struggle, and the terrain on which laity might experience spiritual improvement was lofty and hard. Beginning in the eleventh century, however, laity were achieving a more textured consciousness of the possibilities open to ordinary men and women for achieving higher levels of spiritual perfection. Popular movements, such as the Patarine, disputed the idea of the efficacy of ritual alone. In Florence and Milan in the eleventh century, religious commitment required greater intellectual understanding on the part of laity. They were exhorted to seek Scriptural justification as a basis for claims of conscience. Spiritual understanding was considered more often when people discussed the preconditions for the effective sacrament. Laity in these two cities were implicated in fierce contests against sinful priests who robbed the sacraments of their efficacy. It was merit, not hieratic position, that determined the effectiveness of the sacraments. Laity established a common life with clergy, and it was at this moment that the first lay saints were created in an endorsement of the new-found dignity of laic life. In Florence, religious sodalities, lay confraternities, and third-order movements were to shape cultural life over the next two centuries. Wills and benefactions suggest something of the vigor and scope of lay piety as increasing numbers of men and women dedicated their lives and property to serving Christ. No longer so passive or vicarious in attitude, this laity commenced to exercise direct control over philanthropic and even cultic activities.[51]

Particularly noticeable were the many women participating in religious life during the twelfth and thirteenth centuries. Numerous among them were married women and widows, whose status had been much enhanced through developments in civil and canon law. Turning away from traditional and negative perspectives featuring the human proclivity for adultery, fornication, and incest, canonists and jurists now focused on the family as the nucleus of associative life. Religious reflection on marriage expressed itself in language more responsive to the social role of women; simultaneously, we find Tuscan female saints imbued with human virtues and confronting costly personal choices. No longer were they so exclusively wonder-working icons; even their social status was democratized somewhat. Less and less was the married condition regarded as a barrier to sanctity.[52]

X

Florentine literary culture was demonstrating greater sensitivity toward laic spiritual aspirations. Indeed, the first significant composition by a Florentine who was to be viewed as the progenitor of the Tuscan literary renaissance—Arrigo da Settimello—was a work of consolation created to minister to the troubled laic conscience. At one time students of Italian literature believed that Bologna was the cradle for the rise of the vernacular in Italy. Today scholars give primacy to Florence instead, and in no other part of Italy was vernacular prose literature to compare with that of thirteenth-century Florence. Moreover, when moral treatises were written in Latin for the elevation of laity, they were soon translated into Italian by Tuscans. Florence was also the center for the translation of the Latin classics. This is not to suggest that the Arno city was the most advanced or sophisticated intellectual center in north or central Italy: indeed, it was not comparable to Padua or Milan and in

many areas of cultural life was something of a backwater. The manuscript tradition demonstrates that great religious texts, such as the *Fioretti*, survived mainly in Florentine copies, and so, too, did vernacular
translations, sermons, and works of spiritual counsel. The primacy of
Florence was demonstrated in not its advanced ideas but the popularization of a pious and moral literature directed toward a spiritually and
civic-minded laity.[53]

In former times peasants, merchants, and artisans were reduced to
the functions of their roles within the social order. Even so progressive
a thinker as Raterio, the tenth-century bishop of Verona who perceived
that gradations in society were not founded on any immutable decree
of divine providence chaining the individual eternally to his destiny,
still offered only the vaguest of spiritual ideals to laity. As we have
observed, these ideals were most often addressed to nobles and largely
negative on the subject of marriage. In thirteenth-century Florence,
however, a very different vision of spiritual possibilities was in the offing: from the first writings of Arrigo to Brunetto Latini and Dante,
exquisite sympathy was displayed for the vicissitudes of the laic condition. Awareness of the higher truths that philosophy gave to man would
foster an autonomy of spirit over which fortune could not exercise its
tyrannical domination. To buttress the dignity and worth of the laic
condition was a remarkable feature of Florentine culture. As has been
noted, the conversion experience was presented as a possibility to be
realized within the round of everyday life; it was not necessary to enter
religious orders to experience *metanoia*. Spiritual opportunities for laity
were much enriched. Dante was to give literary support to the blessed-
ness of terrestrial life, and his was to be but one of the many esthetic
attempts to validate the activities of those remaining in this world yet
hoping to find favor in the sight of God. One has but to gaze at the
art of Giotto's age to appreciate the new and positive spiritual value
accorded to the religious aspirations of townspeople.[54]

What had been in progress over the eleventh and twelfth centuries
was little short of a monumental effort to sacralize the terrestrial world.
This attempt entailed finding supports for those moving outside the
traditional cadres of archaic society to take up broader allegiances. At
the base of this transformation was a renewed confidence that a world
beyond hierarchy and vows could be effectively colonized. Gradually,
individuals became conscious of the possibility that abstract ties might
prove sustaining. Intent, consent, and volition were accorded new primacy in civil and canon law. In an earlier age, when human relations
required validation through tangible and visible signs, it appears that
trust in one's fellows was at a nadir. Insecurity and lack of faith in

social possibilities was also a leading feature of spiritual relationships in the archaic world. In art, literature, and documents of public and private life, word and image were interlocked: the symbol and that which it symbolized tended to mesh. The ubiquitous symbolism of the period was calculated to convey an idea in tangible form.[55]

For human volition to prevail, even in ordinary transactions, it had been essential to call upon the forces of the supernatural. The power of human institutions and the durability of human arrangements were so negligible that it was felt necessary to invoke the divine. In everyday relations, symbols and rituals were explicitly designed to strengthen social ties. In art the symbolic content was perceived directly in the image itself. The presence of Christ was realized in an act of faith or in an object belonging to Him. This was a Christ far distanced from the historical Jesus. The Redeemer was not to be portrayed as human but rather as a figure severe and rigid, with great, dilated eyes, in all His hieratic grandeur. Sacred texts were identified with the blood and body of Christ; the single guide the faithful possessed was the word of God, allowing the possibility of direct communion. In art and literature, references to the life and death of Christ and His miracles were not presented to the public as a model for human comportment. In the most splendid of Italian churches narrative scenes of His life were placed almost out of view. The word of God transmitted through the Bible was the sign of the saving presence of Christ. The resources of culture sought to evoke in viewer and listener the unshakable conviction that they were in the presence of a report that literally and faithfully represented the acts and words of the Savior.[56]

Just as a material sense of salvation had strength, so, too, a concrete sense of the ties of obligation and mechanics of exchange gained general acceptance. Just as the sacred was made tangible, so, too, the juridical relationship between men and objects was one of fact. Contracts were becoming corporeal and material, thus lending stability to human arrangements. In a famous passage of Paul the Deacon's *History of the Lombards* we have a description of the meeting of the great chiefs of Lomello after the death of King Autari: Agilulphus and Theudelindam exchanged the kiss of fidelity, a pledge giving definition to precise duties and juridical obligations (*wadiata et osculata*). How different was this kiss from the chaste and mutually reverent exchange at the imperial Roman betrothal of Constantine! In the Roman world the kiss was spiritual and gentle, suggesting the meeting of two souls. In the Lombard world it was a material expression of legal arrangements, serving as a warrant for the durability of human relationships. Not surprisingly, one discovers that the ritual for breaking family ties under Lombard law involved the snapping of four sticks, which were then thrown into each of the corners of the room: how different from the solemn, contractual ritual of the antique world.[57]

Ordinary negotiations of everyday life required the solemn consignment or exchange of tokens or objects. That pawns or pledges were given implied the execution of a contract. Symbols of investiture, such as pieces of wood, blades of grass, or pieces of vine stock, accompanied ordinary transactions; these gestures validated acts ranging from the sale of property to the taking of a bride. The tendency was to resort to procedures establishing a direct connection between word-thing and word-image. At the level of conceptualization the tie existed between being and knowing. The ideal was to achieve an identity between sign and referent, between the epistemological and the ontological. The reduction of subjective mediation between being and knowing was the ideal, and this quest for an exact correspondence was itself a consequence of an underlying lack of trust in the capacity of individuals to create effective connections between subject and object. This archaic civilization bears a marked resemblance to that described by Claude Lévi-Strauss in his *La pensée sauvage* and prefigured in earlier anthropological studies by Frazer and Mauss. What is central to the mentality is a concrete logic in which data of the empirical world were arranged without reducing the number of discrete elements. The assumption in this archaic world had been that connections between data must make a kind of sense—to be, in the language of Frazer, "sympathetic." According to Lévi-Strauss, who is close to Frazer on this point and others, the connections were formulated at the level of perception in concrete terms—that is, close to what was seized by the senses. This description suggests a mentality in opposition to the abstraction of science. Without attempting a detailed analysis of the various levels of early medieval culture, we can propose that thinking by analogy held a privileged position. Here we discover an emphasis on a type of sympathy generating ideals, visions, and vital perceptions not readily reducible to formal logic or experimental verification. Furthermore, this analogical thinking was predicated on the assumption that an object may be subject to laws completely independent of our existence. The intrusion of personal and psychic factors would be perceived as weakening the connection between objects; this nexus should exist independent of the human psyche.[58]

Our investigations have led us to suggest that in the archaic society of early medieval Italy a whole series of images of concrete symbols was generated in which what was being symbolized and the symbol itself merged. On the level of daily social and economic life similar correspondences were in evidence. In the eleventh and twelfth centuries a dramatic change ensued: the language of business activity no longer required such literal exposition; in the courts, merchant consent was sufficient to create obligation. Contracts were considered valid, and the need for formalities and solemn rituals diminished. To put it slightly differently, the search for likenesses, correspondences, and congruences was no longer pursued with such intensity. As formalism receded, the metaphors of quotidian activity were relaxed: individuals were now more confident about the prospect of finding similarities in those building blocks of quotidian life that appeared mismatched at first glance; therefore, the possibilities of reaching agreement on moral and intellectual grounds, rather than through the exchange of pledges, were much enhanced. Meanwhile, jurists and canonists were becoming aware of the fictional use of symbols, and self-consciousness about the role of ritual was expanded.[59]

If we agree with the anthropologists that human thought is basically social and public and, therefore, that its natural habitat is the courtyard, the marketplace, and the town square, then we are in a position to suggest that the growing authority of abstractions was a response to a heightened appreciation that it was indeed possible to move toward modes of thought and imagination more distanced from sensory perception. Greater trust in impersonal mechanisms, institutions, and exchange transactions tended to release the mind from an unequivocal commitment to the literal and concrete. No longer was it so vital for men to exchange gifts, oaths, women, or pledges; now it was possible to enjoy the benefits of associative life through the complex and vicarious mechanisms of partnership, credit, and insurance. Agreements and contracts were no longer as likely to be endorsed by oath takers or countersigners as by the full faith and credit of an individual.

Here again Lévi-Strauss provides us with suitable generalizations for appreciating the structural significance of this transformation. At the base was a gradual alteration of an exchange system. At least, in this instance, his emphasis on the positive features of exchange assists us in following the transformation. Unlike Freud, he regards exchange as that which sets man apart from nature: for him, exchange is at the heart of culture. Freud, of course, would see culture as a result of the imposition of restraints on free sexual activity, which in turn generates fear and guilt. Lévi-Strauss's views of this type of transition lend emphasis to creative forms of behavior rather than to the harsh adaptations suggested by Freud.[60]

Certainly, the takeoff led to greater confidence and optimism. Economic surpluses from agriculture provided a material base for expansion and urbanization. The legitimation of political power and the rise of impersonal institutions encouraged people to loosen rudimentary bonds. Moving out of the primary arrangements of the tribal and archaic society permitted greater freedom. However, there was a paradoxical, almost Augustinian, turn: freedom was experienced under the aegis of renewed authority. An age of venturesomeness and risk taking, unmatched for vibrancy since the Roman world of the second century A.D., was in the making. It may well be that Lévi-Strauss has aided us in appreciating the new role of abstraction and the renewed confidence in the mediating power of mind, but it was the ancient and medieval historians who understood that this freedom was possible only under the law. These memorialists and chroniclers expressed a point of view that might serve as a happy corrective to that of current thinkers, with their dualities opposing culture and nature, freedom and authority.

XI

In the eighth and ninth centuries the ideal of spiritual liberty was remote, if not inaccessible. When the soul was the subject of literary analysis, it was portrayed as a field of battle rather than an active force. The Christian life was described as an implacable struggle requiring enormous effort. Sanctity was a virtue acquired through heredity; the mechanism was divine predestination. The will of man could effect little change. It is of the greatest interest to recall that one of the very rare theological problems to excite controversy in the ninth century involved precisely the question of predestination. The heated debate revolved around a view of predestination even more pessimistic than St. Augustine's. Bleak interpretations of the teachings of Augustine were exchanged. Fears were aroused that God had predestined man to sin and damnation. It was as if the Lord did not will the salvation of all men or that Christ had not died for all humankind. Support for this stark perspective was widespread. Even though it was ultimately condemned, the more articulate personalities of the time found it exceedingly difficult to conceive of the role of human freedom and abundance of grace.[61]

The sacrament of the mass during those centuries was seen as a gift made by God, who descended from on high even unto earth. A rare liturgical tract from this period, Amalarius's *De ecclesiasticis officiis*, ventures a symbolic interpretation of the successive phases of ceremony, ornaments, and instruments of religious cult. They were related to various Biblical episodes by subtle analogies; the entire ceremony was placed under the rubric of commemorative allegory on the life of Jesus. This lonely effort, however, was soon roundly condemned at a church synod. Described as the "civilization of the liturgy," religion tended to be identified with cult. Still, the winds of change and reform did blow. Under that commanding figure Benedict of Aniane, ninth-century monasticism was to undergo a dramatic change. The liturgical life of the convent was elaborated and enriched at the expense of apostolic activity. How different were these reforms to be from those of the eleventh and twelfth centuries! Ritual signs tended to multiply and were externalized. At the moment of the confiteor the priest struck his breast: such gestures as the extension of arms during the reading of the canon testified to direct communication with God, as did the kissing of the altar and the making of numerous signs of the cross during mass.[62]

Certainly, ritual was the leading trait of spiritual life during this epoch. Laity no longer took an active part in the affairs of cult: placed in the nave of the church and separated from the sacristy by the altar and choir, they had a role that grew increasingly passive. The priest celebrating the mass turned his back on the congregation when addressing God in their name. At the beginning of the eighth century the priest offered the Eucharistic sacrifice to heaven while chanting "qui tibi offerunt hoc sacrificum laudis"; soon it would be considered necessary to add the formula "vel pro quibus tibi offerimus." Indeed, the celebration of the Eucharist was growing more infrequent. Laity were also becoming less accustomed to praying in private and were rarely invited to pray in common. Italian ascetic treatises of the eighth century counseling laity did not dwell on taking communion but focused on mortification of the flesh and fasting: evils of this world were to be shunned, and this meant ascetic denial of things of the flesh and matter. Sin was externalized, only to be held at bay by strict discipline. The cultivation of interiority had limited value, and the religious impulse tended to be practical and externalized. When spirituality found social expression, it was through good works and moral comportment. Religious texts presented a description of a very concrete and practical rapport between man and God. Harsh penance was imposed, but reparation could be converted into fines or gifts of money. The materialistic character of these practices has already been mentioned. Alms, too, remained a ritual act; between benefactor and poor there was little communication, with charity frequently dispensed by great lords through such intermediaries as chaplains and abbots of monasteries. In addition, wealth was perceived as a sign of God's favor, enhancing, as it did, the spiritual opportunities of the rich. Through the gift the poor were obligated to pray for the soul of the benefactor.[63]

If the literal prevailed on the level of everyday life, the world of high culture was characterized by lofty and overarching speculation.

Such towering figures as John Scotus Erigena (ca. 810–77) aimed at nothing less than a total understanding of the world. He saw nature as a mirror of God Himself, calling it a "theophany"—a revelation of God through His creation. Perhaps it would be excessive to say that Erigena's science harbored totalitarian ambitions, seeking, as it did, to understand the totality. The highest form of intellectual activity sought to explain everything objectively, and if this high purpose could not be achieved, then nothing would be rendered intelligible. Nature for Erigena was the name "for all things that are, and in a certain sense are not." His understanding of nature stemmed not from physics but from theology and was an extension of similar notions from Gregory of Nyssa, Maximus the Confessor, and the pseudo-Dionysius. The role he assigned reason and his contemplation of an intelligible world beyond physical reality were original but without influence in his time.[64]

Again Lévi-Strauss comes to mind. An archaic society, decentralized politically and kin oriented, grounds its social life on material bonds while conducting an intellectual inquiry in which nature is all things that are and are not. The power of abstraction on the level of everyday activity was slight, but on the plane of theoretical and scientific investigation its force was cosmic, overarching, and transcendent. Perhaps the most telling examples of scientific research in the earlier period involved commentaries on Scripture. The seventh and eighth centuries have been described as "alogical," with dialectic virtually abandoned. One must wait until the ninth century to recover dialectic, but it would be two centuries before scholars recognized its significance and learned to handle it as an effective tool for discovering meaning. In the eighth century, when Paul the Deacon portrayed Gregory the Great composing his commentaries, the saint was listening intently to a dove perched on his shoulder with its bill to his ear. The tenth century was without any important Biblical commentaries or compilations. Even in Carolingian times, when sensibilities were less mechanical and more critical, the Evangelists were ordinarily represented by artists as writing at the dictation of the Holy Spirit or an angel.[65]

The privileged place of the meeting of conscience with God was the Bible; God was present in the Scriptures with a physical reality. Citations and recollections of Biblical texts were abundant in the writings of clerics. It is difficult to separate those charged with a personal spirit from those conveying the spirit of the sacred text. Subtle exegesis prospered but frequently slid toward an allegorism that quickly dissolved into a rich but incoherent symbolism. The Scriptures could become supercharged with symbolism, making the commentaries difficult to decipher; this was also true in the realm of ceremony, which, when overelaborated, lost the ability to communicate its symbolic content effectively. The great reforms of the tenth century undertaken by Cluniacs further emphasized liturgy at the expense of Biblical studies. Tenth-century literary talent ran to drama and liturgical poetry. Sermons and meditations focused on the emotional and dramatic in the Gospels. Their method has been described as "exclamatory"—a series of "pious ejaculations" inserted into the liturgy.[66]

The impulse to conjoin knowledge and the knower, to fuse word and image, found its ultimate expression in the philosophy of Erigena. His radical commitment to Platonism was articulated in *De divisione naturae*. He advanced the epigram "The knowledge of what is, is what is" (*Cognitio eorum que sunt, eo quae sunt est*). He gave classical traditions of thought a most radical summation in a graceful effort to make the knower one with what he knows. If we turn to the eleventh and twelfth centuries, a stark dichotomy is evident between word and image, the knower and the known. Very different classical traditions were drawn upon and even reconstituted by advanced thinkers; of course it is commonplace to observe that Aristotle and dialectic were in the springtime of their heady influence. A dichotomy between a universe of meanings and a universe of things was surfacing in what has recently been described as a revolutionary reorganization of categories of thought and expression. No longer was the conjunction between knower and known to be so commanding philosophically; instead we will discover separation, rather than union, between knower and known.[67]

The principal philosophic tradition of the early Middle Ages was of course Neoplatonic and Augustinian, with intellect conjoined to being or form. Furthermore, St. Augustine treated reason as a type of vision: "Hence reason is a vision [*aspectus*] of the mind, while reasoning [*ratiocinatio*] is the search of reason, that is the movement of such vision through what are to be seen" (*De quantitate animae*, book 27, chapter 53). Vision and seeing are crucial for Augustine, shaping even the pattern of an argument: "There is this good and that good. Remove the this and the that, and *see* if you can, the good itself. Thus you will *see* God, not good by any other good, but the good of every other good" (*De Trinitate*, book 8, chapter 3, section 4).

Augustine advanced his case by compelling the vision of the listener to concur with that of the speaker. In the late eleventh century a radically different perspective was proposed and accepted: a division between word and image. Moreover, that unity guaranteed through *seeing* was now rejected. A sharp line was fixed between what is in "intellect" and what is in "thing," or reality. Mind and reason were understood in a new way by major thinkers from St. Anselm of Aosta to St. Thomas of Aquino. The transit from the single realm to the two separate realms of intellect and things has recently been described as a movement from "aggregate order to a systematic universe."[68]

This revolution was an expression of structural transformation in the exchange system of society. As confidence grew in the power of abstraction, it became possible to tolerate a separation between word and thing. It appears that the changing character of crucial social and economic transactions at the everyday level had its impact on high culture. Perhaps it would not be amiss to compare this era with that of the Greek city-states in the seventh and sixth centuries B.C. There too we observe the decline of an archaic and tribal world and the energetic expansion of urban life. There too we note the rise of Greek science and see an exponential increase in abstract transactions and new forms of associative life. The parallels are striking. The two great intellectual and social revolutions of the premodern Western world bear a marked resemblance. It may be that the phenomenon we are investigating has certain cyclical features; it also may be that what Lévi-Strauss has observed in his oeuvres pertains to historical and literate peoples as well as to primitive ones. Moreover, there is some self-consciousness about these tranformations among leading contemporaries. No single figure was closer to the cutting edge of change in the eleventh century than St. Anselm; he established the philosophical agenda for hundreds of years to come. Breaking with the theory of knowledge as vision and dissociating word from image were for him a costly and even tragic choice. At the moment of his greatest intellectual victory, after just having established his celebrated ontological proof of the existence of God, he uttered a *cri de coeur*: "If, O my soul, you have found God, why is it that you do not feel or experience [*sentis*] Him? Why, O Lord God, does not my soul feel or experience you, if it has found you?"[69]

Indeed, this tension was to persist, finding expression in the works of many thinkers eager to accept the new science but reluctant to lose the old unities. Again, one is reminded of the dilemma of Greek thought in the age of Plato. Yet another dimension of the multilayers of culture can readily be adduced from Plato. At the core of his speculations on society and politics were the many definitions of the nature of justice. If one follows Socrates's questioning of his opponents, we perceive that a succession of ideas of justice was advanced. From the *Dialogues* it becomes apparent that the arguments proceed from archaic notions that justice was merely a simple form of restitution to more complex definitions rooted in the democratic-commercial world of the Greek city-state. Though we shall be examining the top layer of social and economic activity in the Italian city-states of the late Middle Ages, archaic and tribal practices endured. What is relevant here, however, is not this obvious fact but a more subtle matter. Just as Anselm was conscious of the price to be paid, so various other medieval thinkers were keenly aware of the persistence of the claims of older ideals and forms. Therefore, we must not cling too closely to even the most illuminating strategies of Lévi-Strauss and the structuralists without weighing the possibility of moral intervention by individuals acutely conscious of the tolls exacted by change. Likewise, we must not disvalue the contemporary appreciation of the multitextured world of social experience.

XII

A primary intellectual preoccupation of the eleventh and twelfth centuries was the status and nature of such general terms as *man* and *animal*. What was the relationship between *genera* and *species* to individuals? Were such words as *man* and *animal* simply mental constructs, or did they have an existence (things) in reality? The debate between nominalists and realists over universals concerned no less a problem than the nature of reality. The tools were logic and dialectic. The first issue to rivet intellectual attention was the strident debate over the sacrament of the Eucharist. Did the bread and wine really change into the body and blood of Our Lord? If the accidents (properties) of matter remain the same, then so too must the substance: therefore, bread and wine are only symbols of Christ. This debate on transubstantiation was not initiated by a heresiarch but by a writer exercising "strenuous vigilance in understanding and expounding Scripture."[70]

In the eleventh century Berengarius made a precise correlation between baptism and the Eucharist. The visible elements—water in the first instance and bread and wine in the second—became the visible sign of an invisible grace. Yet the bread remained bread and the wine remained wine, just as the water remained water. "The invisible Body and Blood cannot be called *sacramentum*; they are *res sacramenti.*" In denying what later came to be known as transubstantiation—a substantial change of the bread and wine into the body and blood of Christ— Berengarius was to use the new science of dialectics effectively. His most formidable opponent, Lanfranc of Pavia, founder of the influential school at Bec (1043), was equally convinced that the rigorous use of dialectic could demolish this pernicious view of the Holy Sacrifice. Indeed, the most sacred of all Christian mysteries was amenable to logical investigation. Also important is that the explanatory power of traditional concepts and symbols was strained in the arguments of both Berengarius and his opponents.[71]

The Eucharistic controversies of the early ninth century had focused on the arguments of Paschasius Radbertus, who stressed the reality of the body of Christ in the Holy Sacrifice. The body of Our Lord in the Eucharist was indeed identical to the historical body of Christ. Paschasius's interpretation was literalist and materialist: he identified the Eucharistic sacramental body with the physical body and historical person of Jesus. His pupil Ratramnus challenged this interpretation and in its stead centered on the "mystery aspect" of the Eucharist against the materialistic view. In his *De corpore et sanguine domini*, composed about 856, Ratramnus maintained the objective reality of the external species against Paschasius, for whom species or appearances had no objective reality. For Ratramnus the bread and wine were not merely "external appearances." At the heart of the controversy was a "coarse" theory pervasive among the faithful of the ninth century. This theory, recently described as "grossolana," featured the materialistic, or symbolic, aspects of the Eucharist. As in the argument between Paschasius and Ratramnus, the tendency was to stress the concrete, or mystery, aspect of the Holy Sacrifice. The domain of theological discourse did not seem too remote from the world of everyday transactions; in both realms, connections between word and image were fleeting and tenuous. Confidence in the power of mind and thought, like trust in abstraction, did not prove durable.[72]

XIII

When Henry James offered this comment on human experience, he was not being overly fastidious:

> Experience is never limited, and it is never complete; it is an immense sensibility, a kind of huge spider's web of the silken threads suspended in the chambers of consciousness and catching every airborne particle in its tissue. It is the very atmosphere of the mind.

The complexity of the question of the role of social experience in shaping intellectual forays into the nature of reality requires us to be even more circumspect than the ironic Henry James. That ideas and norms are rooted in social relations does not imply that mental activity is a mere epiphenomenon. Belief derives much of its prestige from its social relevance, but culture is as much a cognitive phenomenon as a material one. In each field of intellectual endeavor, from Biblical exegesis to canon law to dialectic to the liberal arts to science to theology and logic, new prospects and confident appraisals of opportunity were resolutely advanced by leading eleventh-century thinkers. The anticipatory and venturesome mind was lured by the promise of a springtime to come. Networks of economic roots encouraged the flowering of tender shoots of intersubjective meaning. The deep structure of this imaginative world nurtured a heterogeneous garden of new plants. As society entered an era in which easier and more spontaneous social forms gained cohesion, so these plants blossomed. (Contemporary writers on language incorporated many metaphors from the world of flowers and plants into titles of their treatises.)[73]

New impulses toward systematization and science were evident in writings of eleventh-century Italian authors dealing with themes as varied as mysticism, medicine, grammar, and law. Roman law had a vital attraction for Italians, but until the eleventh century it was applied in a fragmentary way, with tradition and custom generally preeminent. At that time the beginnings of investigations into the doctrinal dimension of law made its application increasingly programmatic. The scope of dialectic was considerably expanded and began to invade the study of the *trivium* of the liberal arts. An appetite for formal perfection enhanced the dignity of language; rhetoricians worked purposively to confer honor on the language arts. Exact rules governed the composition of a letter or speech, the study of language was to be elevated into a science, and new forms of musical notation were invented. A monk from Farfa (Gregorio di Catino) and another from Monte Casino (Leone d'Ostia) classified and ordered documents for the purpose of providing an exact historical account. Confidence in logic was extravagant by the standards of an earlier time. Methodological efforts were intensified to find reasons for faith.[74]

As social arrangements relaxed, traditional patterns of thought lost some of their hold. Writers were less wedded to analogy and not so distanced from making abstract and logical connections. It was more important to verify what one thought through logical demonstration than to resort to experience or an inner vision. Making others *see* the truth of their condition was now matched by appeals to forms of reasoning both necessary and universal. An earlier age lacked procedures for maintaining distance between the immediate knowledge of things and their ultimate meaning. Enormous affection was displayed for what was solid and palpable, and it was depicted in lively colored language. In later times new voyagers, spiritually minded men and women, were to leave the luxuriant but narrowly colonized shores for wider and rougher seas.

2

Challenges in the Eleventh Century

IF OUR SEARCH has merit, then the eleventh and twelfth centuries in north and central Italy marked the beginnings of a sustained effort to project single codes and formal theories. Concrete logic was losing some of its effectiveness, and the power of more abstract modes of perception and thought were gaining wider acceptance. No longer was it considered essential to fix a direct relationship between word and image or express with such immediacy the symbolic content of thought and gesture. In the courts the ordeal and the judicial duel were resorted to less frequently and sometimes with perplexing results. The crisis of civil power and authority, described by the historian Giorgio Falco, places the nadir of public life in the late ninth and early tenth centuries. Certainly the invasions of the Hungarians and Moslems contributed to the dissolution of social and economic life. However, with the recovery in the late tenth century, more impartial procedures were slowly to achieve wider acceptance. It was now possible to conceptualize abstract relationships and looser ties more readily *Obsequia* (or dependence) and other incapacities no longer went unchallenged. In city and countryside (*contado*) taxation and the use of mercenaries were making inroads into personal service. The effect of urban policy, conscious or not, was to separate landlordship from lordship. Credit operations by city-states would soon lead to establishment of the funded debt as citizen borrowing and lending assumed grand proportions. In earlier times only an indeterminate number of holdings were based on written contracts, with a large class of tenants on the land by custom. Even in the written agreement obligations were defined as "the custom of the place" (*consuetudo in ipso loco*). We observe an increase in the use of contracts between ordinary individuals treating such mundane matters as sharecropping and artisan apprenticeship. This tendency to fix in writ-

59

ing the accustomed norms also extended to feudal arrangements. By the early twelfth century communes were declaring that rights and privileges would not be recognized unless they were reduced to writing. By the middle of the century communal statutes were being codified and the regulation of urban and rural life explicated in detail.[1]

In the eleventh century we find wills that are true contracts of alienation with the right of usufruct. Penal clauses were disappearing as donors and testators were able to dispose of property more freely. As we have noted, bequests and legacies no longer required divine intervention for implementation; trust in the effectiveness of contemporary institutions and legal procedures allowed donors and testators to rely upon the written word. Everywhere, new forms of associative life were gaining strength: at mid-eleventh century the inhabitants of such cities as Genoa were acting collectively in defense of the juridical rights of their town. New solidarities were emerging in a society aptly termed "communal." In the *contado* at mid-eleventh century, associations of knights and burgesses formed the first Tuscan rural communes. *Mezzadria* was spreading rapidly in twelfth-century Tuscany and was defined by contemporaries as a form of partnership (*societas*) in which landlord and tenant collaborated in farming. At the top of urban society we observe the formation of aggregations of patrician lineage with the rise of the *consorteria,* whereas at the middling level solidarity was being derived from occupation and institutionalized in newly established guilds. In Florence the number of artisan corporations peaked in the late thirteenth century, when scores of occupations were grouped into *arti.* Horizontal ties between citizens were strengthened by the newly formed lay confraternities. Criminal procedures and elaborate legal codes were promulgated to contain the violence of the overmighty. *Wergeld* and composition had been keystones of the archaic legal system; now they were challenged by the intervention of communal officials in the quarrels and vendettas of magnates. Even modest occupations of artisans and craftsmen were to receive their own sets of rules. Town governments acted to regulate life in the *contado*, supervising marketing and limiting manufacturing. Communal regimes enacted provisions designed to control the price and quality of certain goods and services in the interest of the common good. Indeed, the expression *bene comune* was in wide usage by the thirteenth century, suggesting the strength of collective imperatives.[2]

The oldest statutes we know of are those of Genoa for 1143 and Pisa for 1162, but the principle of representation had authority since the end of the eleventh century. Consuls were being chosen regularly to deal with civic matters—from maintenance of public works to conservation of communal property, establishment of markets, direction of land reclamation, and recruitment of soldiers. Of course, collective action was no innovation, for it reached far back into the history of medieval Italy: villagers acted in concert in defense of the commons and in matters pertaining to parish life. Custom and mutual necessities of farming produced joint action, and the village assembly (*conventus ante ecclesiam fabula inter vicinos*) was the place for decisions. But organized and purposive self-government took hold only in the late tenth century and burgeoned in the eleventh. Collective franchises were granted by bishops, emperors, and lords, freeing inhabitants from the obligation of particular services and removing restrictions on migration or marriage. Ties of neighborhood were being formalized and alliances of rural communes established in the twelfth century. Meanwhile, these communes were gradually relaxing certain primitive restraints: in time the requirement that individuals selling property or withdrawing from the neighborhood be obligated to pay money fines (composition) lost considerable force. Again we note mechanical solidarities being challenged. The *ius prelationis* was designed to keep land under village control, but over the centuries discriminatory provisions against foreigners (outsiders) were to disappear in many regions. The term *forensis* would become exceptional and was to be replaced by *persona alterius*. Charters were making it easier to alienate property. Reciprocal accords were being drawn up between rural communes as the power of credit eroded tendencies toward self-sufficiency and isolation. The community was increasingly defined as being composed of all who submitted to *onera communis*. In Bologna and Florence in the thirteenth century, peasants were emancipated so that they might resume the "perfect and perpetual liberty to which every individual is entitled in paradise." The more mundane implication of this action by the benevolent Bolognese government was that serfs could be inscribed on communal tax rolls. In Florence the *vinculum fidelitatis* (the authority of the seigneur) was shattered in order to render peasants liable for imposts and subject to communal justice. The movement of society in urban centers and their environs was from corporeal bonds of personal obligation to the more abstract territorial ties. In the countryside collective agreements for founding new settlements rendered relationships between tenant and lord corporate and communal; as villages acquired political rights, communities were converted into communes.[3]

Resonances of these changes were felt in the domain of high culture —the liberal arts, theology, and the sciences. The relaxation of archaic ties appears to have favored an exploration of the possibilities for abstraction in intellectual, as well as social and economic, life. An interest in and appreciation of the mediating power of thought was a prominent feature of eleventh- and twelfth-century cultural activity. Arrangements once perceived as direct and unmediated were now more likely to be regarded as creations of the human mind. In the early Middle Ages divine causality played a commanding role, and physical phenomena were considered the immediate expression of moral and religious imperatives. Now, between God the creator and each physical event there was a series of causes. These secondary causes acquired their own autonomy, becoming the object of scientific and philosophical investigation. What was being challenged was a unity that had a reality and existence prior to any distinction the mind might make between sign and referent, knowledge and being, or God and nature. If we define philosophy as the *consciousness of consciousness*, then the eleventh and twelfth centuries can be viewed as times of revolutionary transformation: no longer was the relationship between word and thing so likely to be regarded as unmediated. As social bonds relaxed, the realm of discourse expanded. Parenthetically, because nature was not so prone to be reduced to the will of God (*voluntas Dei*), events in the physical and social universe had greater autonomy and consistency.[4]

I

In the time of Alcuin and the Carolingian renaissance, dialectic was being recovered, and the ability to handle logical problems was much improved over that of previous centuries. So, too, were certain technical rhetorical skills: it was possible to consider permutations of the syllogism as well as make subtle definitions of a variety of terms, such as *accident, substance, genus,* and *species.* For the most part, however, such strategies were used for the purpose of Biblical exegesis. Leading medievalists, such as Georges Duby and Renée Doehaerd, have recently argued that the eleventh and twelfth centuries were no revolution but a renewal and amplification of cultural and economic impulses at work in Carolingian times. It is certainly possible to agree that the transition from Carolingian times to the Renaissance of the eleventh and twelfth centuries was no quantum leap. Surely there were continuities in intellectual life: many of the questions discussed by eleventh-century thinkers had an ancient and honorable pedigree. However, they were being dealt with more broadly and with greater assurance. Furthermore, the movement in the eleventh century was distanced from Alcuin's dream that the study of Scripture could be enriched through an appreciation for tropes, classical stylistics, and "that dialectic and rhetoric invented by the Greeks." Elementary treatises on the *quadrivium* housing the

De nuptis of Martianus Capella were slowly to be displaced by Greek and Arabic scientific writings from Spain, Italy, and southern France and were to include Galen, Ptolemy, Albumasar, Avicenna, Alfarghani, and Alfarabi. By the end of the twelfth century Aristotle was to join these select authors. Polemics were conducted against those "Latin doctors" who had impeded the cultural progress of Europe for so long.[5]

Studies of intellectual life in Pavia argue persuasively that this new assurance and range surfaced over little more than a generation, just after the year 1000. Questions once debated by a few specialists behind cloistered walls or among restricted courtly circles were now being discussed by an interested public throughout the towns of north Italy. Pavia was one of several influential centers of this revivified intellectual activity. Trade had been intense there, with foreign merchants regularly vending their wares and a mint providing coinage, necessary for interregional exchange. The *Honorantiae Civitatis Papiae* is a unique source allowing us to glimpse details of the historical transformation at Pavia. Referring to the 920s, this document, composed in the first decades of the eleventh century, is a memorial and restrospective glorification of an economic past. Like other sources, it voices a historical awareness of separation from a royal, ducal, and episcopal past. The *Honorantiae* celebrates the trade of the early tenth century, when Pavia was visited regularly by many rich merchants (*multi divites negotiatores*) from Amalfi, Gaeta, Salerno, Venice, and the north of Europe. Protesting against a change in customs tolls, the author describes a world in which Pavia's artisans, craftsmen, and merchants were organized into *ministeria*, or special departments under the jurisdiction of the royal treasury. Lombard kings and German emperors had favored this type of organization: in return for a formal grant of a monopoly, members made contributions in money, kind, and service to the *camera*. For example, fishermen provided a fixed amount of their catch annually and, on the occasion of a royal visit to Pavia, were obliged to cooperate with the boatmen to equip vessels for royal use. The collective responsibility for providing the lord with certain services reduced his dependency on the market. On the other side, economic privileges and protection reduced risks for the producers of goods and services. In the tenth century this old regime of guild privilege was protected by a landed knightly order profiting from the urban demand for food. The prosperity of the town and the preeminence of its merchants were tightly bound to royal patronage.[6]

By the eleventh century such a system appeared rigid and inappropriate. The rights of the royal *camera* were being dissipated and alienated. Citizen anger led to a rebellion against the German emperor in

1024 and the destruction of the symbol of his authority—the palace (*palatium*). Chancellory personnel were freed for different intellectual tasks. These *notarii sacri palatii* were to be essential to conducting the business of communal and civic life in Pavia. In addition to the start of a separation between culture and royal power, we observe the erosion of the nexus between trade and royal patronage. The ties of an archaic society were being called into question and increasingly viewed as anomalous. It is significant that within little more than a generation, we observe the formation of a vocabulary and legal language in the north Italian cities (of which Pavia was a leader) that was to revolutionize Italian education. Eleventh-century Pavia, which experienced the transition from a highly developed archaic economy to one of greater competition and a freer market, was also to be a locale for the evolution of a technical vocabulary whose twists and turns—*sed contra e converso* or *tu autem oppones*—were ultimately to shape the language of such advanced thinkers as Abelard. Derived from texts of the *trivium,* this vocabulary, in its particulars, was traditional but, when taken as a whole, was new. We can trace the origins of the terms back to Boethius, but when the terms were assembled, their meaning was altered, and they constituted the beginnings of a new language, that of the scholastics.[7]

In Pavia we find the earliest glosses of the *moderni,* appearing about 1020. The *Expositiones* (the apparatus to the Lombard code) presented records of cases and memorable disputes dealing with ways in which the law should be interpreted in a given situation. Within fifty years the laws were to be rearranged and systematized study begun. Lanfranc of Pavia, later to become archbishop of Canterbury and one of the most forceful debaters of the age, was alleged to have challenged older legal procedures that relied on custom and oath taking. Indeed, the fields of law, grammar, and rhetoric were undergoing a remarkable series of revisions. Society was manifesting very practical needs, and these exigencies were being experienced at the most fundamental level—that of language. In the law the *moderni* were intent upon studying cases and explaining difficult words; in grammar they compiled lists of esoteric and ambiguous words. The *Vocabularium* of Papias, a very successful work of exposition of the ancient grammar of Priscan, was much studied at Pavia in the 1050s. The rhetorical arts flourished there and also in Milan with Anselm of Besate, Sigefredo, Bonifilio, Guglielmo, and others systematically exploring this antique discipline. Teachers of rhetoric in Carolingian times found Cicero's *Topics* and Alcuin's *Rhetoric* sufficient for their purpose. Writers borrowed stylistic techniques from *De inven-*

tione and *Ad Herennium*, but the first serious attempt to master both of these texts, with the assistance of ancient commentaries, was made by Anselm of Besate. Again, the exposition of the texts highlighted specific examples demonstrating how rhetorical strategies might operate in particular situations. In all these fields—law, grammar, and rhetoric— the stated intention was to deal with problems of practical life. Within the context of practical life the objective was to educate men who could argue effectively on legal questions and civic matters.

Foreign observers of the north Italian scene in the eleventh and twelfth centuries were struck, and sometimes appalled, by the magnetic effect of public life on high-born aristocrats and affluent commoners. The attraction of legal and business careers evidenced itself in the multiplication of urban-based notaries and the enhancement of their status. The notary was attaining the character of public official, and soon communal legislation would invest him with voluntary jurisdiction. Confidence was growing in the efficacy of impersonal norms and the authority of impartial institutions. Recent scholarship has documented the presence of a certain Pepo, or Pepone, a teacher of law at Bologna between 1172 and 1176. At first what he taught was displeasing to the princes because it disvalued ancient custom; only later, as knowledge of the science of law spread, did it gain royal approval. As in business negotiations and credit transactions, the rise of public trust can be seen readily in the flourishing civic world of north and central Italy in the eleventh and twelfth centuries. The Ciceronian principle of the necessary connection between eloquence and its civic utility was extended to include all the arts, liberal and mechanical. Roman law had its center first in Ravenna, then in Bologna; among its early practitioners were laymen, and they explicated this law in a professional manner in the service of the commune.[8]

II

In theology, too, we observe an increase in professionalism and impersonal forms of argument. The language and rhetoric deployed so brilliantly by Peter Damiani at mid-eleventh century was both inspired and passionate, working through a series of dramatic progressions stemming from an ascetic tradition. Antithesis was frequently used to make bold contrasts; inspiration, rather than clarification and isolation of ideas, was Damiani's highest rhetorical purpose. The human drama was perceived as being realized in paradoxes without end. Damiani's talent for lyricism was unrivalled among letter writers of his time. He por-

trayed the terrible tension between the contemplative science of the
spirit and the secular science of the world. Yet, while rejecting the glo-
ries of eloquence, he sought to reconcile an errant people to the Church
through the triumphs of Roman oratory. Having little imagination for
the abstract, he remained deeply attached to the concrete and to singular
situations. It was necessary to verify what one thought not through logical demonstration but within the context of experience. Further, this living experience was to be translated into a vision of what one believed.
Lively colored thought, free of all formalisms and agilely following the
contours and movements of a singular situation, was Damiani's stylistic
forte. Ideally, it was a mystical sensibility that would render the mysteries of creation transparent rather than opaque. Reasoning by analogy,
Damiani had few strategies for moving from diversity to the unity of
things. The distance between the immediate knowledge of things and
their ultimate meaning was as vast as the space between two stars. In the
preceding century the leading rhetorician and chronicler, Liutprand of
Cremona, who had studied at Pavia, followed an opposite strategy with
his "artificial eloquence." Again we perceive the attraction for concreteness at the one extreme and abstraction at the other without high regard
for intermediary procedures.[9]

It is difficult to know what Damiani meant by "rational argument,"
but by the end of the century, with Anselm of Aosta, a concerted methodological effort would be made to find reasons for faith. Anselm's
language was more impersonal and scholastic and its appeal less emotional; the emphasis was on logic and reason. A return to the sources in
both Biblical and juridical studies was widespread, with Latin acquiring
greater potential as a language of analysis. As quotidian forms became
more abstract and social relations more relaxed, confidence in the resources of language strengthened. Strategies of thought were more
likely to be dedicated to tasks of mediation. Questions about the relationship between matter and form were becoming more central to discourse in the second half of the eleventh century. This fact suggests
that more reliance was placed on metaphysical concepts as tools for explicating philosophical and theological issues. When St. Anselm developed his philosophical position, making a basic separation between
mind and what was being thought, he was giving ample intellectual
dimension to a profound transformation with roots in *ordinary* life. He
called into question the coexistence of knowing and being. This irreducible distinction between thought and thinker was to be the beginning of a revolution that has been called as significant for the eleventh
century as the Cartesian revolution was for the seventeenth. Soon it

would be argued that all thought and knowledge must be subsumed under the notion of similitude, or likeness to something typically outside the mind.[10]

Lanfranc of Pavia, under whom Anselm had studied, went further than any previous writer in explaining the Eucharist in language borrowed from the science of logic. He described change in the Eucharistic elements in terms of the Aristotelian categories of substance and accident. His polemic with Berengar was the first victory of Aristotelian philosophy in a matter of general thought and widespread interest. Attention was riveted on the relationship between words and the reality they express, between logical necessity and necessary being, and between the order of discourse and that of nature (*ordo disserendi et ordo naturae*). Heroic and sustained attempts were undertaken to extract from the definition of the word something about the reality it represented. Intellectual processes were characterized by Herculean efforts to deduce from grammatical structure alone fundamental truths about the nature of reality.[11]

St. Anselm stood at the beginning of a movement that focused upon the coherence-creating power of the human mind. The quest for mediating concepts was a prime cultural imperative, and the seat of these concepts was in the mind. Self-consciousness about dualities increased as literal bonds and concrete ties were attenuated. Dichotomies between object-subject, form-content, matter-spirit, faith-reason, and sacred-profane were heightened, but so, too, was the confidence that these dualities could be overcome through the correct use of abstraction. In his *De Grammatica*, St. Anselm proved to be a logician of great power, raising, in an apparently casual manner, the main logical problems that were to occupy the next generations of thinkers: the relation between substance and accidents, between words and the things they represent, between the formal shape of an argument and its verbal expression, and, finally, between dialectic and grammar. The disciplines of grammar and logic were applied to a serious discussion of theology as strategies of rational inquiry were extended to the mysteries of faith.[12]

With Anselm of Besate, who taught at Pavia in the mid-eleventh century, we discern an extravagant effort to transcend the concrete. He tells us that he dreamed he was in the heavens with saints who considered him to be one of them and that the personified figure of Dialectic called upon him to return to earth because that esteemed science had disappeared from this world. His was a dramatic, bizarre attempt to surpass the literalness of an archaic society in an ascent guided by pure reason. The problem of the abyss between action and being, between the world of the senses and that of the spirit, had once been the province of isolated thinkers, such as Gottschalk and Erigena. This was now the domain of the educated. Man, a rational being, created by God in His image, rises to divinity not through the senses and certainly not through their annihilation but through the exercise of reason. Needless to say, such felicitous visions were not always held securely. Anselm was also troubled in his dreams, believing himself to be in heaven and the object of a vigorous contest between the spirits of his saved ancestors and three beautiful virgins representing Grammar, Logic, and Rhetoric. The three won the day—or night. This Italian grammarian complained bitterly that his contemporaries shunned him as a "demoniac —almost a heretic." Indeed, the first convicted heretic of the central Middle Ages was Vilgardus, who came from the thriving legal center of Ravenna and who was said to have been visited in a dream by Virgil, Horace, and Juvenal. The Roman poets promised him fame equal to their own were he to dedicate himself to their writings. The Cluniac chronicler Ralph Glaber ascribed the arrogant Vilgardus's fall to the typical Italian preference for secular over religious learning. Vilgardus's erudite contemporary Gerbert of Aurillac, soon to ascend the papal throne as Sylvester II, was likewise judged to be a magician and may have been the prototype of the Faust legend. No matter how audacious the proposition that secular learning had value, it was to find defenders among the eloquent clergy.[13]

To his contemporaries Lanfranc of Pavia sparkled as a dialectician, going further than anyone else in explaining the Eucharist in a language appropriated from logic. He was the first to describe purposively and clearly the change in the Eucharistic elements in terms of the Aristotelian categories of substance and accidents. Attempts to deduce from grammatical structure alone a truth about the nature of sacramental reality were to be at the very heart of the fierce intellectual disputes of the late eleventh century. St. Anselm's famous argument for the existence of God was a special case of one of these problems. It was a vibrant attempt to deduce from the definition of the word something of the reality it expressed. All of this suggests important features of the intellectual processes of the times. On the one side we have a separation between the word and that which it signifies: consciousness of separation and loosening of literal bonds was apparent; so, too, was the penchant for abstraction. On the other side we have renewed confidence in the mediating power of mind to find likeness in apparent dissimilarity. Furthermore, we notice the growth of a trust in secular knowledge and the beginning of a feeling that a harmonious synthesis could be achieved between the sacred and the profane. In the twelfth and thirteenth centuries those having the most profound experiences in new types of religious communities were to shape the cultural imperatives of the emerging university community.[14]

III

On his deathbed St. Anselm reflected on the problem of the origin of the soul and expressed deep uncertainty that anyone would be able to solve it after he was gone. The tone of his discourse was personal and human; he was not preoccupied with his own salvation but with the problem of the knowledge of God. He had challenged traditional theories of the incarnation, which harshly limited the prospect of salvation; these older views gave dominion over nature and the supernatural to the devil. Man had voluntarily submitted to the devil and his empire of death when committing the primal sin. The order and justice of the devil's empire was not to be broken by any arbitrary exercise of power —not even by omnipotent God. This conception of the incarnation posited a view of forgiveness as an affront to justice. In certain essentials it epitomized traditional social and economic arrangements, with their strict, literal, and narrow ties sustained by harsh, coercive injunctions. Great was the price that men had struggled to pay for their sins, and for many, reparation was hopeless. Anselm rejected the notion that the devil possessed a just power over man or that man must spend his life satisfying the claims of God and the devil. For him the significance of the incarnation lay in the life of Jesus and in renewing man's love for God. Anselm's confidence in God's mercy was consonant with his strong espousal of ideas of friendship and his belief in the power of bonds of affection. Yet, as we shall see, while excluding the devil, Anselm placed a great burden on the individual in the contest for salvation. For him the spiritual risks of the laic condition were appalling.[15]

The harsher, older conviction that God had sent Christ to earth and through His sacrifice man was ransomed from the empire of death was now being challenged by a very different perspective on the Creation as well as on the Incarnation. God had taken human form in the incarnation and later transformed wine and bread mystically into His blood and body. In so doing He divinized, or sanctified, human nature and the natural universe. More precisely, He vindicated and redeemed for future renewal what was left of goodness in creation. If Christ assumed human form and lived on earth, then creation must have been worth saving despite man's many crimes and sins. The incarnational-creational perspective was espoused by church-reforming supporters of Pope Gregory VII with single-minded resolve. Intent upon conquering the world for Christ, these reformers sought to render more Christian the entire terrestrial world—a world to be organized according to Christian law and theology. Wide areas of natural life were absorbed into the supernatural world of redemption. Taking this stance into account permits us to appreciate more deeply the basis for twelfth-century humanism and naturalism. The energies behind these developments were, of course, religious.[16]

From the mid-eleventh century to the early thirteenth century doctrine worked to define the real presence of the incarnate Christ on the altar in the Eucharistic sacrament under the term *transubstantiation*. Increasingly we notice explicit assertions of the real presence of Christ in the Eucharist being celebrated on earth. Spiritual energies could be gained from that ever-to-be-repeated renewal of the incarnation and its redemptive power. One point was absolutely clear, however: such figures as St. Anselm held out very little hope for laity. Despite his confidence in God's mercy, Anselm pictured the spiritual plight of laity as being unbelievably oppressed. Man was steeped in original sin and unable to redeem himself by his own efforts; because of the depth of his depravity, he could make no sacrifice great enough. All who lived outside the monastery dwelled in the shadows, and Anselm accepted the unique virtue of taking monastic vows. Shortly before his death he advised Matilda of Tuscany to flee the spiritual perils of secular life and enter a convent.[17]

Anselm had repudiated the older theology of atonement, in which the devil, through a compact with God, was entitled to the souls of all sinners. The weight of man's sins, both his own and his forebears', was so heavy that for the individual soul there was no salvation outside the Church. Gregory VII had stimulated the enthusiasm of laity, declaring that as to the goal of Christian perfection, one *ordo* was not superior, nor should it prevail over another: all were on the same plane. Each starts from the same place, and day by day one realizes the design that God has entrusted to each in life's contest to render more or less perfect one's spiritual experience. Yet against this we have Gregory's fear that laity will abuse ecclesiastical liberty and that it is dangerous to detach the faithful from the *ordo ecclesiae*.[18]

Peter Damiani's writings and career (1007–72) illustrate the caution of the past and promise of the future. He was to tell the prefect of Rome: "Your place is precisely in the heart of the world where there are being built two cities ignorant of one another's existence: with a layman's means you must help to build the City of God." He was even to reproach this prefect for spending too much time in prayer: "To render justice, is that not prayer?" Then he would add: "Defend the liberties of the Church: fight for Her; punish those who oppress the poor. Keep firm the balance of equity. Forget your personal worries always in order to watch over the State." Most exemplary was the charity of a certain citizen of Ravenna who fed the population during times of famine. Indeed, following the hard road of Christian duty and practicing the precepts of the Gospel brought spiritual health to laity. In Damiani's letters we see a passionate concern for the spiritual well-being of laity desirous of achieving perfection. His empathy was strong for *idiotae ignarique scripture* wishing to insert themselves in the divine economy of salvation. Just as he was fearful of reliance upon reason and the "secular sciences," so he was anxious about the baleful consequences of any excessive autonomy for laity. His vision of their spiritual capacity was restricted, rooted as it was in a monastic ambiance. His insistence on personal responsibility for salvation led to the reform of preaching and prayer, but his apprehension about human frailty and his knowledge of the temptations of the world always remained alert. That he would limit a monastic tradition, appropriating unto itself the only form of spiritual perfection, and would maintain that for the various orders of Christian society there are different paths did not hinder him from regarding eremitic-monastic experience as the best way of achieving the Christian presence in this world. Furthermore, because monks were detached from things of this world (*mortui mundi*), they were rightly entrusted with the care of souls. To follow the path of poverty and penitence, great piety was required. In the search for God, recourse to the sacraments and the protection of Our Lady were necessary. In a century when sacramental practice was neglected, Damiani recommended frequent confession and daily communion: "For when He sees your lips red with the blood of Christ, the devil will shrink back." The more involved men became with society, the more treacherous would be their spiritual odyssey. His *Liber Gomarrhianus* is a stunning tribute to the evils infesting the secular world, recording in detail the countless pitfalls and risks. There is logic in that he was the first great proponent of voluntary flagellation with his *De laude flagellarum*, which stirred such controversy and enthusiasm among the Florentines.[19]

IV

Holy men from north and central Italy both sponsored and were anxious about laic participation in the great reform movements of the eleventh century. Damiani attributed to Romualdo, his spiritual forebear, the remark that he desired to convert the entire world into a hermitage ("volebat totum mundum in eremum convertere"). This was no traditional call for the monasticization of society, nor was it the usual summons to laity to imitate monks. Romualdo's message expressed more than the notion of a fundamental incompatibility between Christian truths and the values of contemporary society. He was indicating the inadequacy of the institutions of his day for realizing the highest religious purposes. Damiani, too, was lacerated by his zeal to reform the world and his desire to withdraw from it. Traditional Benedictine monasticism was insufficient for achieving these contradictory ends. What was needed was a hard search for another road so that the spiritually minded could give full witness to the Christianization of society. Damiani was to substitute the ideal of *penuria* for the Benedictine conception of *sufficientia*. Poverty was perceived by reformers as the virtue most essential to restoring Christian values and converting to a more nearly perfect life. Meanwhile, an inner and active struggle was prescribed: the will was not to be stabilized and subjected, as in the traditional Benedictine teachings. Damiani, in his fifty-fourth sermon, would proclaim:

> There are barriers between us and those against whom we are always in battle array; no ramparts to isolate them from us, and no deep rivers flow between us and them. They are always with us because they dwell in the depths of the soul.

How was the enemy to be overcome? Through penance, poverty, and prayer. These were the instruments of our search for God. What was counseled was not the customary resistance to evil but the fierce attack. No longer could the sinner be described as a member of a group, as was traditional in the Benedictine vision; instead, he was particularized, and the steps in his transformation ran as follows: "self-knowledge, grief, confession, persuasion of guilt, acquiescence in judgment, suffering of punishment, love of punishment."[20]

In north and central Italy a mild critique of the life of the Cluniac monks was in progress. In 1056 St. Anselm had considered taking vows at Cluny but chose Bec instead; his objection to Cluny was that excessive choir activity would leave him too little time for private meditation and prayer. Peter Damiani, though an admirer of the piety and discipline at Cluny, had gently chided the monks for excessive devotion to refectory and choir. At Camaldoli, near Arezzo, and Vallombrosa, near Florence, communal conceptions of monasticism were scuttled in favor of individual prayer and meditation. Romualdo had left a Cluniac monastery, intending to restore the austere and solitary life of the desert fathers. The monument to his intentions was Camaldoli. The Florentine Giovanni Gualberto was at first a Cluniac monk and later a brother at

Camaldoli; from there he moved to Vallombrosa, where he established his monastery. Traditional Benedictine religious communities had not allowed individual monks scope for study, prayer, and voluntary acts of asceticism. Damiani had spent formative years at Camaldoli and Vallombrosa; when writing the life of Romualdo, founder of the eremitic movements in Italy, he was to convey a radically new spirit. Instead of describing his hero's solitary war against evil spirits and demons, characteristic of an earlier hagiographic literature, Damiani allows us to hear the rush of fresh springs, the sweetness of solitude, and the unimpeded converse wth God. Damiani tells us that Romualdo preached against simoniacs, advocated a free rapport between the hermit and the world, and favored the common life for clergy: "Therefore the saintly man founded numerous presbyteries and taught the clergy to live secularly according to the customs of laity together in a community." He maintained social contacts at all levels, desiring to associate laity with his experience. Chosen groups of elected souls united by solid ties of friendship best expressed his spiritual ideal, *privilegium amoris*. Never was it possible for him to fix his choices in precise formulas or imprison his contradictory experience in traditional forms. He stood free of existing ecclesiastical institutions. Again, Romualdo's invitation to laity, recorded in the *Vita* by Damiani, was not the traditional call to imitate monks. His message revealed fundamental contradictions: the new monasticism insisted on radical alternatives and dilemmas—Christ or the world—rather than compromise or conciliation.[21]

Until the eleventh century few would have contended that the idea of Christian perfection could be realized outside the walls of the cloister. The canonical movement, with its eremitic ideals, broke the rigid conception of *ordines*, with its priest-monk model. The concept of religious life was broadened to extend from the monastery to the lay world with the formation of rejuvenated groups of lay canons. Appeals were made to the ideal of a primitive apostolic community in which laity and clergy lived together. No longer was the life of spiritual perfection to be the exclusive preserve of monks and clerics. What was crucial was not membership in an *ordo* but the way in which one lived (*modo vivendi*). In the mid-tenth century, Raterio, bishop of Verona, was aware of social change and extreme mobility in the city. He took an evolutionary view of social gradations: society was not founded on any immutable decree of divine providence chaining man to his destiny. His was a very Roman, almost laic, view of the social condition. When he wrote on spiritual matters, however, even so advanced a thinker as Raterio could offer only vague and abstract ideas about the religious aspirations of laity. Christianity was not realizable in the secular world, and the model for piety must be the monk. A century later the spiritual status of laity had changed, and laity were participating vigorously in the world of religious reform. No longer did they live impoverished Christian lives outside the cloister, as Raterio had contended; instead, they were acquiring greater spiritual dignity. In Umbria, Tuscany, and Lombardy an ecclesiastical hierarchy, once little mindful of its pastoral obligation, was preaching to its flock with exceptional ardor. In Florence the Vallombrosans were accused of forgetting the traditional monastic commitments to the exemplary and prophetic in favor of making direct and revolutionary appeals to laity.[22]

V

Andrea da Strumi, later to withdraw to Vallombrosa, was the biographer of the deacon Arialdo da Carimate, who, more than any other figure, was at the heart of the spiritual revolution in Lombardy at mid-eleventh century. Preaching in the countryside of Varese near Milan, this son of a small, landed proprietor assembled a group of clergy who embraced the common life (*vita comune*), combining the regular life of the monk and its penitential practices with the preaching and ministering of sacraments of the secular cleric. From their center at the Church of the Holy Trinity, these "sons of the canonical order" (*filii ordinis canonici*) exhorted laity to assume an active role in the struggle against the simoniac and concubinary priests. This church, now the center for dissidents (later to be referred to as "Patarines"), had been founded by Benedetto Rozza, a prominent moneyer, and it remained under the patronage of his family. Another moneyer, Nazario, assisted Arialdo and his followers with financial support. Andrea da Strumi attributed the following observation to Nazario when welcoming Arialdo to his home: "Lord Arialdo, not only the learned but the unlettered realize that the things you say are useful and true." Laity were being urged to have recourse to Scripture, from which they could learn the message of Christ, rather than to follow the example and teachings of the corrupt clergy of Milan. The laity responded to the promptings of Arialdo and his followers by establishing a common life with the reformers. In these early days of the Patarine movement Arialdo gladly accepted Nazario's invitation to enter his house and conduct the *vita comunitaria* with his family and neighbors.[23]

Supporters of Arialdo included great nobles, knights, moneyers, merchants, lawyers, judges, and notaries. Andrea da Strumi tells us that "one household was entirely faithful [pro-Patarine]; the next entirely faithless; in a third the mother believed with one son, while the father disbelieved with another. The whole city was thrown into disorder by this confusion and strife." Indeed, we find knights and many lesser folk supporting the Patarines ("multi de populo minore"), whereas the detested archbishop was backed by "pars nobilium ac de populo multi." Assembling behind the papal banner, under which the Patarines fought, were "the youth of the city from both the people and nobility." These descriptions by Milanese chroniclers indicate that theories of social class and class conflict have limited explanatory power. The second-line nobles of Milan had achieved an awareness of their strength as an order when they battled to obtain imperial guarantees of the inheritability of their fiefs from Conrad II in 1037 (*Constitutio de feudis*). Such a victory permitted them to be securely ensconced in a world of more durable arrangements. The mark of the Patarine movement was not the class antagonism of first- and second-line nobles but rather the mutuality and cooperation among the various orders at the top of medieval society. This was a time when notaries, merchants, artisans, and judges were acquiring land in the Milanese *contado* and influence in the city. Among leading supporters of the Patarines was the wealthy Anselmo of Baggio, soon to be bishop of Lucca (1057) and later Pope Alexander II (1062). Arialdo's first two allies were Landolfo Cotta, a notary of the Church, and his brother Erlembaldo, both first-line Milanese nobles (*capitanei*). When Erlembaldo first proposed entering a monastery, Arialdo exhorted him to remain at his sacred post, doing battle for the *true* Catholic faith. He promised that if Erlembaldo remained in the world, he would become "more powerful with God" (*potiorem apud deum*). Citizenry of Milan, a mix of judges, merchants, moneyers, notaries, and first- and second-line nobles, were soon captained by Erlembaldo, who received the papal banner of St. Peter from Alexander II. He was to be the first lay person exercising the metier of knight to be canonized in medieval Europe. A new type of saint came into being in the second half of the eleventh century. This heroic figure battled for the faith in a war judged to be an *opus sanctum* and was deemed worthy of being consecrated by a special liturgy. At this moment lay spirituality was finding new forms of expression in pilgrimage, warfare, and crusading. Within another century the Italians would have the first merchant saint of Europe as the laic condition achieved greater spiritual regard.[24]

In Florence and Milan deep challenges were being directed against the structure of church and society. The Arno city came under the influence of the reformed monasteries of Vallombrosa and Camaldoli. Forces for change were nurtured inside Florence, but revolution in Tuscany was neither so abrupt nor so violent as that in Lombardy and Milan. The effects, however, were comparable. A heightened sense of community was evidenced in the common prayers of laity and clergy, in the frequent discussion of religious questions, and in liturgical practices, recitations, processions, and preaching. From their beginnings, the Patarines had refused to participate in holy offices celebrated by unworthy priests or to receive sacraments from them. This refusal implied more than active involvement by laity in a war to extirpate evil from the Church: the birth of a new consciousness among the populace was being expressed by its zeal for judging the dignity and spiritual worth of clergy. Faith was more personal and evangelical teaching more immediate. Both revolutions were popular in the sense that a military caste was not the sole or primary constitutive element. As we have observed, the term *popolo fiorentino* first came into use during the mid-eleventh century, and of course it signified a growing conception of the mutuality of the orders. Laity from all segments of society were participating in civic and religious life. The evangelical spirit and the preaching of the gospel were directed toward conversion of the masses; this was not consonant with an older view, which regarded the rigid division of society as inviolate. Aspirations for spiritual renewal were not essentially ecclesiastical. The times had passed when church hierarchy had little pastoral obligation. Indeed, Christian virtues and duties were increasingly pastoral rather than contemplative and monastic. Eleventh-century hagiography was beginning to celebrate the preaching clergy from the Latium to Umbria to Tuscany to Lombardy.[25]

What was transpiring in the life of the Church, in both Florence and Milan, was a chipping away of the very cement of society. The wealth of the Church allowed bishop and archbishop to command society. Through gifts and enfiefment the nobility was bound. The disposition of cathedral lands gave status and power to a network of vassals connected by solid ties of obligation. The cathedral chapter was the preserve of an ecclesiastical hierarchy. From the episcopacy stemmed the protection of merchants, markets, and privileges, giving the trader an advantageous place in society. The episcopal court provided judges, notaries, and advocates with lucrative business. Fixed tariffs for church offices, including ordination, and for every benefice was "the expression of a carefully articulated system for the amicable distribution of land and wealth among members of an established order." In Florence, and even more so in Milan, the marriage of clergy worked to consolidate society further. In 1057, when Arialdo attacked concubinary and married deacons and priests in his *Phytacium de castitate*, he provoked a popular revolution and a liturgical crisis. Opposition was particularly strong to dispersion, alienation, and subinfeudation of ecclesiastical jurisdiction and property. Only secondarily did the reluctance of the Milanese to pay tithes appear to be a factor in the revolt.[26]

The lesser nobles had attacked this system in order to improve their position in it; they were not intent upon undermining that network of literal bonds constituting its foundation. The first self-conscious assault emanated from religious reformers during the mid-eleventh century, when they cast into doubt the traditional nexus between salvation and wealth. They denounced the notion of spiritual gift and countergift while roundly condemning lay investiture and the buying and selling of church office. Their attack against ecclesiastical concubinage and clerical marriage provoked deep disturbances in customary social arrangements. (Of course, the tradition of the Ambrosian Church of Milan allowed just such relationships.) The zeal of religious reformers threatened the idea of a society bound together by wealth, pomp, and ostentation. Preaching renunciation of the oath, the vendetta, and the practice of composition, they were encouraging the populace to reject narrow primary blood ties. Their views on consanguinity and ecclesiastical marriage were also favorable to the loosening of social constraints. So, too, was the invective launched against monasteries for accepting gifts that would bind them to the religious ambitions of powerful clans. In the earlier world of the tenth century the practice of simony was never mentioned by contemporaries, with but a few vituperative exceptions, and on the whole seems to have been quite acceptable. Such reformers as Raterio of Verona and Atto of Vercelli were anomalies in their own time and therefore had little impact. Only with the eleventh century did such practices as simony assume a menacing form in the minds of the spiritually involved. The Pistoian author of the *Vita* of Giovanni Gualberto advises his readers that the nefarious practice of simony was "pullulating in Tuscany in the Saint's youth." What had gone almost unnoticed, and therefore seldom recorded, now became a major preoccupation. Those opposing the reformers were well aware of the risks in attacking time-honored links and ties.[27]

In challenging traditional arrangements and primary bonds, reformers themselves stepped outside the rigid structure of Benedictine monasticism. They stood as uncompromising foes of worldly power, elevating purity of intention to an operational principle. Yet, they had little practical concern with what might effectively serve to hold society together. Reformers were harsh critics of military action by popes and kings; the most articulate and thoughtful of their number were seriously troubled by the use of coercion. The Patarines and their leadership polemicized against usages and traditions introduced late in the history of Christianity. In general, their ready formula was a return to the purity of apostolic days through an imitation of the life of Christ. The *Vita apostolica* called for chastity, poverty, prayer, and the performance of manual labor. The laity had been invested with a sense of spiritual dignity, but at the price of challenging contemporary values and standards. Among the followers of the reformers in Florence and Siena were many caught up in the welter of contradictions. Resorting to coercion, military reprisal, the use of mercenaries, and even bribes, the leader of the Patarines, Erlembaldo, with the banner of St. Peter fixed to his lance, was now an awesome and brutal general. To achieve the loftiest of objectives it was necessary for him to don armor over his hair shirt: "He now subdued the city by the sword and by gold and by many and diverse oaths; none of the nobles could withstand him." The monastic reformers of Florence would also be obliged to give up their resolute opposition to donations and gifts. The heroic challenge of reformers was based on an appeal to voluntary poverty and a recognition of the corrupt influence of wealth on society and church, but they had no adequate vision of how to manage the tempestuous present. Gregorians summoned the people to judge and discipline the church hierarchy; they were to resist the concubinary priests "even by force if necessary." Yet, never had the need for asserting the authority of Rome been more compelling. At a moment when the spiritual powers of the priest were exalted, laity were exhorted to participate vigorously in the renewal of the Church. Finally, the irony of history worked to render most prosperous many new religious foundations dedicated to the ideal of apostolic poverty. Such houses used the labor of lay brothers (*conversi*) during a period in which labor services (*corvées*) were declining. The prosperity of these foundations contrasted dramatically with the austerity of the lives of devoted monks and canons.[28]

The tragic contradiction between the teaching of a traditional faith and the general direction taken by society was blatant; so, too, was the sense that the message of Christ could not be used to serve the instruments of this world. The laity of north and central Italy were coming to rank poverty and asceticism as major Christian virtues. The radical advocacy of voluntary poverty was in itself a recognition that wealth, in the early archaic society of Italy, had been a reward for virtue and brave deeds. Wealth bore those heroic connotations so characteristic of a gift culture: in Carolingian times wealth came primarily from warfare. A mystical predilection for poverty was an emerging fact in the history of Western spirituality. Until the eleventh century, wealth was generally viewed as a sign of divine favor and poverty considered to be punishment. Certainly, poverty was no sign of election. In the eleventh century it became clear to Italian townsmen and nobles that profit was seldom the outcome of heroic military ventures or the generosity of warlords. Money was no longer the reward for epic deeds but earned through patience and astuteness. Gold and jewels had lost those qualities of moral virtue celebrated by an archaic society. The propensity for ostentation and wastefulness in the aristocratic life-style came under attack, as did the display of ecclesiastical riches. Townsmen and nobles were more likely to associate the ideal of perfection with the notion of poverty.[29]

The advanced economies of the Italian cities of the eleventh and twelfth centuries were fueled by money and credit. This "commercial revolution" challenged a literal world of concrete ties on which social relations were based. The direction of change in economic life was perceived as rapidly separating townsmen from the purity of the early Christian message. Reformers appealed to their audience by correctly emphasizing the radical disjunction between an apostolic past and a corrupt present. Their answer to this dilemma was to accent the tragic contradictions and exhort their listeners to reject the logic of the quotidian world in favor of a return to the poverty of apostolic times. Moreover, laity were to take spiritual direction from the words and example of Christ rather than from the teachings of a degenerate clergy who trafficked in the buying and selling of church offices. Sacraments administered by this debased clergy would prove inefficacious in any case.[30]

VI

Gregory VII expressed the new spirit very succinctly when he wrote, "The Lord said my name is not *custom*; my name is *truth*." Indeed, custom was found inadequate in many areas of experience by eleventh-century Italians. Nothing short of a return to the sources would satisfy Latin stylists, teachers of law, hermits, and, of course, religious reformers. In intellectual and religious life time-honored practices were judged defective. A sense of disjunction led Irnerius and the glossators of Bologna to work at restoring Roman law. The same impulse prompted Latinists to choose Cicero and Virgil over Macrobius and Lactantius. Monks desired to return to the primitive Rule of St. Benedict; hermits abandoned the enclosed life of the monastic community in great numbers in order to recover the experience of the desert fathers. In literature, law, and religion the mood was one of seeking to recover a lost heritage. The program most certain to prompt the masses to act was restoring the purity of the primitive Christian Church. Such a challenge found its greatest expression in the changing nature of daily transactions. The documents of eleventh- and twelfth-century Tuscany reveal that an archaic civilization was on the decline. Particularly telling was the loss of primacy of the practice of gift and countergift. This is not to suggest that this type of exchange disappeared; it continued, in fact, over subsequent centuries. With the eleventh century, however, it is clear that this hallmark of gift culture was on the decline and that this type of concrete exchange was in the process of becoming a symbolic act. As we have observed, the basic meaning of riches had been rule or power rather than wealth. To be poor meant to be without power, and to be rich meant to be favored by God. At precisely this time religious reformers attacked the ideology of gift culture, with its literal bonds. In Tuscany the monks of Vallombrosa and Camaldoli preached effectively against religious practices associated with gift and countergift.[31]

In the eleventh century a multitude of literal ties that had operated to ensure interrelatedness were becoming old-fashioned and losing primacy. We observe that in such centers as Bologna notaries continued to add to instruments for the transfer of goods a special clause testifying to the execution of the *traditio* (exchange), not of the *charta* but of the property. This procedure was followed well into the eleventh century; according to Lombard law such contracts were only obligatory, and the material consignment of property was required. By 1060, however, a break was already discernible, and we observe contracts departing from the age-old form. Not only did the notary employ an elegant curial hand instead of the rude cursive of his predecessors, but he demonstrated that the authenticity of the document stemmed not from the signatures of witnesses but from public certification by the notary that the document expressed the will of the parties. Again, if we peruse Tuscan documents, it soon becomes clear that the eleventh and twelfth centuries were indeed the locale for the decline of formal legal relations whereby an obligation was to be realized in something tangible. The use of *mund, wadia, launegeld, wergeld,* and the *morgengabe* was either likely to fall into disuse or find symbolic forms of expression. Composition and the judicial duel were resorted to, of course, but were being countered by ideas of law, territorial rather than personal. By the time of the Camaldolese monk Gratian, at mid-twelfth century, discussions of the topic of the ordeal involved the meticulous listing of arguments pro and con; those in favor were all Germanic, whereas those opposed were frequently from the new, revived Roman law.[32]

Religious reformers attacked a system of closely knit ties of obligation based on an amiable distribution of lands and women among members of the established order. Church property itself was, of course, a principal ingredient in holding together this yeasty mix. Most of the writings of clerics on the time-honored theme of despising the world (*contemptus mundi*) detailed the struggle against simoniacs, defined as those tied too closely to things of this world. At the heart of the Gregorian struggle was lay investiture. The more austere monks rejected closure as an obstacle to religious expression and Christian charity. The word *rule* was no longer exclusively an expression of "une attitude concrète" or an exact definition of a prescribed way of life. The Benedictine ideal of stability was put in jeopardy, and the importance of following the vocation of the Apostles was staunchly reasserted. Papal leadership encouraged breaking the domination of the private seigneurial church (*Eigenkirche*) so that the care of souls moved beyond those familiar constraints. From Nicholas II to Gregory VII a relentless war was waged to free the papacy from imperial tutelage. In the attendant ideological controversy aspirations toward juridical universality and a world law, not limited to a single nation or a single order (feudatories or clerics), were expressed by both papal and imperial supporters. Roman law was no longer so easily conceived of as a law of a particular Latin people or the Church.[33]

Indeed, from new conceptions of the mass to new ideas of penance the materialistic character of spirituality was undergoing a revision at the hands of reforming clergy. From a concern for intention and consent to the elevation of the spiritual dignity of marriage, churchmen were tipping the balance toward a society no longer structurally bound together by the exchange of women. Holy men themselves were dramatizing the movement away from narrow structures toward broader allegiances. In the lives of saints Romualdo and Giovanni Gualberto, the rejection of strict ties of clan obligation and vendetta was highlighted. Spiritual life itself was increasingly depicted as incessant combat, with struggle against temptation becoming the centerpiece. The lives of saints reveal how many ways Satan had of thwarting aspirations for perfection. When encadrement was weakest and custom losing force, spiritual life was most likely to resemble a contest against the powers of evil. The harshest penance and severest punishment were to be endured by the *conversi*, or lay brothers. After all, they were farthest from the world of orders and hierarchy and therefore bereft of supports: their disencadrement held the most risk.[34]

St. Romualdo (died 1027) was a most influential figure in restoring the solitary way of the desert fathers. Eremitic life had begun to flourish in western Europe in the early eleventh century after a hiatus of almost seven hundred years. Although the Egyptian saints had continued to exercise their fascination over the minds of devout men and women, they had inspired no substantial movement in the West. When the prior Rudolfo set forth the customs of Camaldoli in 1080, he praised "the life that purges the mind and clears the conscience, purifies reason, creates wisdom, sharpens the intelligence, leads to God." Among the authorities cited for this statement were Moses, John the Baptist, Christ, St. Benedict, and St. Romualdo. The daring of Romualdo in renouncing the security of the Benedictine community lent him a grandeur felt by biographers from Damiani to the early humanists. The idea of the holy was linked to the example of the Egyptian saints, who battled against evil and temptation, having renounced ties of community to engage in solitary struggle. No writings of Romualdo survive, and the *Life* by Damiani is the best source of his ideas. Damiani addresses his contemporaries fully aware of their desire to have him rehearse the numerous miracles Romualdo performed. Instead, the author states his intention to report the conversations and actions of his spiritual mentor. Romualdo's grandeur was expressed in his struggles and actions, not in miracles. So vivid were they in the mind of Damiani that the world projected comes alive.[35]

The spiritual crisis of Romualdo was initiated by the contest between his father and a distant kinsman, resulting in the latter's violent death. Although not involved, the son entered a monastery to do penance for his father's sin. Damiani's conversion experience did not come from rejection of the blood feud but was triggered by the offer, acceptance, and subsequent refusal of a gift. Well educated in Faenza and Parma, he took up the career of teacher and achieved fame and fortune in just a few years. Giovanni di Lodi, his biographer and companion during his later years, describes the crisis of this sensitive young man, who, at the pinnacle of worldly success, found himself wracked by excruciating spiritual torment. At precisely this time he chanced to meet two hermits from Fonte Avellana who told him about St. Romualdo. So grateful was the young man for the spiritual enlightenment that he offered them a silver vase. When they refused the gift, Damiani did not take offense, as would have been customary, but came to understand that the two hermits were "truly free and happy." Shortly thereafter he entered the monastery of Fonte Avellana. Later in life he experienced yet another crisis when, on a diplomatic mission to Milan for the pope dealing with the Patarine question, he was offered a gift. When Damiani refused it, the donor, an abbot, stated that he was not attempting to influence him. Damiani contended that there was no need for clerics to exchange gifts, as was the custom among laity. Finally, however, the abbot won him over by saying that the gift should be used for some lofty religious purpose. Upon returning to Fonte Avellana, Damiani became emotionally distraught. In the evening, upon attempting to recite psalms, he grew dizzy and felt that his innards were infested with vermin. The gift was returned and the solemn vow taken to reject all future offerings.[36]

Giovanni Gualberto, from a noble family with a brave military history, was raised in the Florentine *contado*. During his youth a kinsman was slain, and the name of the murderer was soon known to all. The obligation of vendetta was sacred, of course, if family honor was to be upheld. Giovanni was the first of his clan to encounter the dastardly villain, and the culprit was without weapons. Standing before Gualberto with arms outstretched in the form of a cross, the fiend awaited a death blow. It chanced to be Good Friday, and Giovanni did not deliver the death blow; instead he sought spiritual refuge in the monastery of San Miniato to meditate upon his terrible dilemma: in performing this Christian act of forgiveness he was bringing dishonor upon himself and his clan. He poured out his anguished heart to the crucifix in his cell and was overjoyed to receive a sign of approbation. Immediately he requested entry into the monastery, and the brothers welcomed this holy man.[37]

The drama of the loosening of the literal ties and bonds of an archaic society entailed grave psychic and material risks. From Gualberto to Francis of Assisi, Umbrian and Tuscan saints were to gain assurance from the crucifix for their renunciation of wealth and clan obligation. This was to become an exhilarating theme for late medieval artists and patrons in those regions. Eremiticism and voluntary poverty were now perceived as quintessential to holy life. Embracing the apostolic life exposed the individual to the vagaries of chance. Most vulnerable were those renouncing the claims of clan and honor or rejecting the culture of gift and countergift.[38]

VII

In his *De contemptu saeculi*, Damiani confessed to the reader that for him God was food and raiment and that it sufficed for man to trust in Our Heavenly Father and His promise for sustenance and support. One must look for God, who is love, and in order to discover Him we must respond to Him with love. Conceptions of love and devotion were gaining spiritual endorsement, and Damiani was one of the earliest collectors of accounts of miracles performed by the Virgin Mary. Recent scholarship, from Peter Brown to Richard Southern, has examined deftly the significance of changes in the idea of the miraculous. Before the eleventh century miracle stories were associated with the physical remains of a particular saint; through these remains was channeled the *virtus* of the saint's spiritual power, which communicated itself to the physical world. The relics of the saint connected the believer with an unseen world; the body of the patron saint protected the property of the sanctuary, doing vengeance against those who would desecrate it.

The Virgin played only a minor role in these miraculous interventions devoutly recorded by hagiographers. Since her body had been borne directly to heaven, the problem of relics and physical remains proved formidable for those in search of evidence of divine intercession. In addition, the miracles of the Blessed Virgin were of a different type: they were directed principally to individuals and were personal, supportive, and concerned, for the most part, with those who had transgressed or overstepped the bounds. She was to become guarantor for those inner resources required by individuals facing horrendous obstacles. With her divine aid the individual was to find that spiritual strength allowing him to move beyond the strict confines of kinship, vows, or tribal vengeance. She introduced him to a morally ambiguous zone where the hard certainties of the group no longer prevailed. Frequently, she supported the individual against the strict claims of primal obligation; her miracles were those of inspiration and guidance, aimed at salvation of the individual soul.[39]

Damiani was associated with the earliest collection of these miracles, and St. Anselm was identified with the most influential form of this popular literature; the latter returned to Italy as an exile from England in 1098. In the foothills of the Alps, at the monastery of St. Michael of Chiusa, he spent Good Friday and Easter with his nephew, a young monk also named Anselm. This was the start of a warm association, ending only with the death of the famed archbishop in 1109. The young Anselm was to die (1148), rich in years and honor, as abbot of Bury St. Edmund's. He had been a devoted champion of the most sophisticated form of veneration of the Virgin—celebration of the Holy Day of her conception. He has also been given principal credit for gathering stories about Mary that were to form the basis for all subsequent collections over the next century. The three personages contributing most to this new literature speaking so directly to laity emerged from a milieu where separation between the physical and spiritual could be most readily imagined. No longer was it essential that the holy always be communicated through relics and remains.[40]

Religion in the later Middle Ages has been characterized as giving primacy to the sense of sight rather than of touch, as in an earlier time. Spiritual benefits and cures had been transmitted by direct contact with the holy. The number of saints had multiplied in response to the demand for temporal grace in return for gifts. Faith in the *virtus* of the local saint was often greater than trust in the powers of Christ. In the eleventh century, however, Damiani and Anselm made eloquent claims for the interior and personal. Greater effort was expended to find Christ in moral life; saints were more likely to be models for constructing a spiritual life. Christ and the Holy Family were being endowed with an anecdotal history having direct moral application. Sanctity was no longer so likely to be regarded as immutable. Hagiographers were less prone to present the saint as mysteriously destined for an exalted state. The fidelity with which the saint observed divine law was less a palpable manifestation of his election by God than a result of his spiritual struggle in the ascent toward perfection. The miraculous power of saints could very readily be subordinated to their charitable deeds and ascetic impulses. Faith and good works were gaining ground over the miraculous: of course the miraculous had value, but for the first time signs of the sacred would be ambiguous. With the pontificate of Innocent III (1198–1216), miracles performed by saints were to be certified by credible witnesses and confirmed by a holy life.[41]

VIII

As we have observed, the extension of credit and the increased use of the contract were prominent features of the takeoff in the towns of north and central Italy in the eleventh and twelfth centuries. In Genoa, Pisa, Venice, and a bit later in Florence, new legal strategies for raising capital and creating partnerships were coming into vogue. In the matter of credit we note something of a historical irony: the Church insisted that loans were sinful unless granted "in a spirit of charity and without interest." Therefore, straight loans at high interest rates, "most of which look like usurious consumption credit rather than commercial investments," were in fact discouraged. By regarding straight loans as illicit, the Church was encouraging the formulation of new options for profit sharing and risk taking. Because of the paucity of documents it is possible only to suggest that the incidence of straight loans in relation to more abstract economic transactions was on the decline from the archaic through the commercial period. Not surprisingly, the bonds of partnership were grafted onto family ties, as evidenced in the *fraterna* agreements in Venice. By the twelfth century, however, more flexible contractual arrangements were being entered into and the contributions of outsiders welcomed. These changes were manifested in the rise of the *compagnia*, the *commenda*, deposit banking, fiduciary money, and letters of credit. In the new practices and organization of business activity risks were minimized, whereas opportunities for cooperation and profit were enhanced: partnership arrangements were more durable, and the prototype of the bill of exchange (*instrumentum ex cambi*) was to appear. Credit was granted by permitting depositors to make overdrafts, and payment was made by bank transfer. Merchants were conducting business by correspondence rather than through personal contact. In Florence merchant law (*ius mercatorum*) moved away from solemn procedures toward informality and trust in the validation of exchange and insurance arrangements. The leading features of these changes were predicated on the willingness of individuals to venture far beyond the literal ties of an archaic society and have confidence in an abstract basis for joint action. Such a world could emerge only with the erosion of the literal dimension of public acts. One example of this transformation is seen in the system of exchange. In the older world the value of money was determined by its weight; thus, a pound was made up of 240 silver pennies. However, in the Italian commune of the eleventh and twelfth centuries, money was to have an extrinsic, as well as intrinsic, value—the worth accorded it by the government mint.[42]

A discussion of the miracles of the Virgin in conjunction with the miracles of coinage and credit can raise questions in the mind of even the most kindly disposed reader. Yet these two developments are not so disparate: each rewarded risk taking and the individual's stepping outside the bounds of traditional security; each required that the believer have confidence in the efficacy of abstract ties. The willingness to take chances, both materially and spiritually, was fundamental to the commercial revolution of towns in north and central Italy. It is clear that veneration of the physical remains of saints did not cease, nor was trade in relics to be abandoned. Similarly, even in the most economically precocious regions of north and central Italy, literal ties and concrete obligations continued to provide security and support for the many. For example, among the poor and middling citizenry, dowry and counterdowry continued to be exchanged, with their value roughly equal. Ties between tenant and landlord still carried the imprint of a gift culture; even in the fifteenth century it was not easy to distinguish between loans and gifts. Nobles were violent, and communal governments still relied on payment of composition and a modified system of *wergeld*. Yet the direction of change was toward a more impersonal law and a stricter justice against nobles of the city.[43]

Disagreement existed in the area of property rights. The Camaldolese monk Gratian resolutely asserted that in this imperfect world choice is often costly. Of course, the possession of all things in common was sacred according to divine and natural law, but in this life we are

obliged to select property rights over and against the greater evils of an-
archy and violence, likely to ensue if those rights were abolished. Ample
documentation survives for the monastery of Passignano, founded by
the Vallombrosans in the Florentine *contado*. From the time of Giovanni Gualberto we can observe the tangled web of seigneurial and
property rights on the one hand and common privileges and obligations
on the other. Throughout the twelfth and thirteenth centuries the tension between security and the needs of the collectivity was in dramatic
conflict with venturesomeness and economic autonomy. Furthermore,
risk taking and the new social freedoms were exacting a high psychic
toll. The claims of conscience were particularly devastating in that gray
area of economic transaction labeled "usurious."[44]

A sense of loss matched that of gain. Damiani, recently described as
a man of the new age, was also a man of the former age. It would be
misleading to characterize him as belonging to the new commercial
world. However, few were more keenly aware of the transformation;
it invaded his language and echoed the life of Po Valley towns:

> Oh storehouse of celestial merchants, in which are found the finest
> of those wares for whom the land of the living is prepared. Felicitous
> marketplace, where earthly wares are exchanged for heavenly ones and
> eternal things for the transitory. Oh sanctified market, where eternal
> life is offered for sale and may be purchased by any man, no matter
> how little he owns; where a little bodily pain can purchase the com-
> pany of heaven and a few scattered tears gain eternal joy; where we
> put away worldly possessions and come into the patrimony of our
> heavenly inheritance.

This grandiloquent passage occurs in his tract *In Praise of Eremitic
Life*. He was preoccupied with the "filthy sins" of avarice and simony
and stood as the dedicated champion of voluntary poverty. No more
resolute foe of the religion of gift and countergift can be found than
this enemy of a spirituality so charged with materialism. Although he
was at one with so much of the reformers' program, his sense of loss
had deep historical roots. He understood the issues all too well and was
torn by them. He recognized how much Italy had changed, mourning the
loss of the justice and graciousness of the rule of the German emperor
Otto III. His most exquisite awareness of the disjunction between past
and present was in the area of Scriptural studies. There he perceived
with alarm the growing separation of the divine word from the truth
of the senses. The Scriptures were the privileged place of the meeting
of the individual conscience with God. This conjunction was being
threatened by the new, professionalized education available to men of

the Italian towns. The perfidious dialecticians, with their vain appeals to science and reason, were an offense in the sight of omnipotent God. Their reasoning was exterior to reality; Damiani appreciated the threat to the unity of word and thing. His passion for the concrete was insatiable and his distrust of rational arguments monumental. What was crucial to him was the attention lent the divine word and the close observation of things. Therefore, he rejected material ties at the spiritual level while holding fast to the concrete, literal, and tactile at the level of epistemology.[45]

IX

Although prayers were no longer so apt to be described as "counter-gifts" paid by monks in return for donations, votive offerings continued to be popular. Although lay investiture was on the decline and the most progressive feudatories of Tuscany were renouncing dominion over monasteries and churches, the patronage of *potentes* survived. The old images did not lose their power and continued to be resurrected in artistic programs prompted by sentiments of conscious archaism. The spiritual world certainly retained deep roots in the past, but in twelfth-century Tuscany we find less evidence of the practice of *translatio*. This once-prominent feature of religious life, recorded so solemnly in monastic chronicles, told of transporting relics of a patron saint to the boundaries of a property in order to protect it from usurpation. Clearly, the area of vengeance and "unmodified human rigor" had shrunk; no longer was it necessary to invoke divine power in order to coerce men into respecting the imperatives of community. The imagery of the façades and porches—even the inscriptions—of town cathedrals in north Italy called upon citizenry to maintain public peace. The symbolism and language of these exhortations were Biblical and allegorical, making their appeal through the example of individuals in effective human terms.[46]

Such theologians as St. Anselm were to speak movingly of the human character of Christ and His sufferings; emphasis was upon compassion and contrition rather than harsh judgment. The autobiographical and personal note was intoned more frequently:

> I recognize and give you thanks, Oh Lord, that you have created in me this image of you, that I may remember you, think of you, love you. But this image has been so worn away by the withering action of my vices, so obscured by the smoke of my sins, that it cannot do what it was made to do unless you renew and reform it. Oh Lord, I do not try to penetrate your way to understand your truth, which my

heart believes and loves. For I do not seem to understand in order that I may believe, but I believe in order that I may understand. For this, too, I believe: since 'unless I believe, I shall not understand.'

Anselm had understood that it was necessary for God to be incarnate and participate in the human condition so that humanity might be saved. Faith in the force of love and emotion was strengthened; more trust was placed in the curative powers of the miraculous in diseases of the mind and body. This prevailing sentiment of compassion and tenderness was light-years away from the fantasy world of Lombard times. If one turns to the writings of Paul the Deacon, one finds the play of imagination given full autonomy: insights and images break the texture of the chronicle to shine like jewels in the decorative arts of the period. Paul's *Historia Langobardorum* stands as a sublime exaltation of youthful physical and spiritual vigor. Behind all of this lurks a sense of foreboding and tragedy, but the instinctive certainty that audacity can capture the prize continues to glow. Love of youth, beauty, bravery, and that joy transfiguring those who triumph by daring deeds was projected against the backdrop of events only dimly perceived on a distant screen. How different were attitudes toward the creations of the popular imagination in the twelfth century! Carolingian epics of the deeds of Roland and Oliver were subject to a single rational system, with logic used to explicate that which, at least superficially, might appear to be merely fantastic or emotive. On the portal of the Porta della Pescheria of the Duomo at Modena we discover a new iconography for the Arthurian legend, with its concern for order and narrative detail.[47]

The triumph of narrative principles and the use of logic to explicate the emotional and fantastic are evidence of the appeal of the "economy of a single code." The ornate, extravagant, and splendid style of pre-Romanesque times was abandoned in favor of a more controlled decorative vocabulary. The heroic age of Lombard sculpture, with its neat and sharp cuts and lines charged with emotion, was passing. This had not been a period of grave decline or tired survival but was marked by the birth of a harsh and violent figurative language. The dialogue was between plane and line; naturalistic detail tended to be eliminated and dynamic values brought to the fore. Whereas geometric schemes constrained the brusque linearity, geometric design contributed less. By the eleventh century, however, a new sense of architectural arrangement was apparent in the construction of the great cathedrals of north and central Italy. Sculptors created organic forms that contained the worlds of nature and man. A controlled tension prevailed between the freedom of the human figure and the rigidity of the framework. A harmony was being attained between decorative function and the naturalistic character of figures, animals, and plants. A close examination of the capitals of the crypt of San Michele Maggiore in Pavia and the Church of San Savino in Piacenza discloses the way in which earlier medieval decorative strategies were combined with a three-dimensional style to indicate new spatial possibilities. The decorative dialogue between line and plane, so charged with emotion and governed by principles of interchangeability and ambivalence, was losing something of its hold on the artistic imagination. No longer were the forms of natural species continuously evolving from man to animal, from animal to man, and from animal to plant. Kaleidoscopic effects and ambiguity of form had lent dramatic power to the object. Violent expressionism and emotionally charged symbolism required that the ambiance be subordinated to the object; the intermingling of images and signs was translated into geometry and decoration, with a concentration upon linear, rather than plastic, values. Classical revivals were just that: problems involving a rational definition of the relationship between object and ambiance or a concern for a unifying interpretation of space were not an esthetic preoccupation. The finest monument to this ambition was San Miniato in Florence, begun about 1018 and completed in 1063. The design, with its careful geometry, simplicity, and serenity, was a prime example of discriminating borrowing from antiquity. It was here that the troubled Giovanni Gualberto came to seek spiritual direction.[48]

The cathedrals—pride of the cities, born from communal enterprise, those great monuments to collective energies—were most hospitable to the new stylistic impulses. In the late eleventh and twelfth centuries north Italian sculptors commenced to demonstrate a consciousness of plasticity and devised aesthetic strategies for portraying the spiritual force of the human personality. The power of art to represent this plasticity was accompanied by a maturation of interest in the interior life of the figure; statuary once limited to figures in relief and treated ornamentally was now invested with latent energy and placed in carefully defined space. With the sculptor Wiligelmo and his school in Modena in the early twelfth century, we see the working out of a symbolic rapport between figure and space: a heightened consciousness of narrative possibilities in rendering scenes from the Old Testament and a Herculean effort to achieve an iconographic coherence between pulpit and altar. An intimate animation of figures and a solemnity of narrative allowed the portrayal of effective human contact on the plane of spirituality. Within less than a generation we observe the development of a more complex and organic iconography coupled with a subtlety of modeling that made the work of the sculptor Niccolò at Ferrara an example for artists interested in moving away from traditional depictions of the human body. Drapery no longer followed a formal calligraphy; bodily movement was being expressed. Similar observations could be made for the bronze door of St. Zeno at Verona, as well as for its portal; the portal at Nonantola and the cathedral facade at Cremona are also vivid examples. The greatest expression was to appear at the close of the century in the work of Benedetto Antelami, whose sense of plasticity and ability to dramatize inner feelings can be appreciated in his *Deposition* (1178) in the right transept of the Duomo at Parma. The possibilities for effective human contact were monumentalized: the life of the Savior was chronicled through the portrayal of the Redeemer's human works; intimate deeds of mercy were presented in summary but expressive fashion in the baptistery at Parma. Over the course of the century, from Wiligelmo to Benedetto Antelami, we can witness the formation of a new vocabulary for describing interiority and spiritual contact. At the same time a greater realization of aesthetic tactics was on the rise, calculated to abstract and subordinate detail to a vision of the whole. Finally, sculptural decoration was now routinely assimilated into architectural schemes: the style was at once more severe and synthetic.[49]

Liturgy and didactic writings were finding their visual equivalent in complex allegory: exploration of the concordance between the Old and New Testament led to remarkable intellectual invention. For the first time, in the baptistery at Parma, the six works of mercy were connected with the Last Judgment. On the north porch spandrels of the Cathedral at Piacenza we have the bearded St. John the Baptist appearing for the first time as a preacher. This portrayal would soon become a favorite of the sculptor Niccolò, and in his mature work we see it on the porch spandrels of the cathedrals at Ferrara (1135) and Verona (1138) as well as on the Church of St. Zeno (1139), also in Verona. Cathedral and pilgrimage churches were most hospitable to the imagery appealing to laity. The centrality of preaching was apparent, as was the symbolism depicting life as a contest between good and evil. The awareness of the spiritual plight of laity was straightforward and their proclivity for sin presented in clear narrative programs. The psychology of the alternation of hope and despair was vividly communicated; so, too, were the beguiling temptations of everyday life. A comparable development can be discerned in the sculptured calendars of the months describing the various seasonal occupations and labors. On the façades of the cathedrals at Ferrara, Modena, and Lucca we notice how thoroughly the sculptor penetrated into the daily life and routine of peasant

and worker. A new idiom was being coined—a "volgare illustre"—
and this vernacular conferred an exceptional dignity on a world of
earthly burdens and spiritual opportunities. This popular vocabulary
made an appeal markedly different from that of the classical revival of
Carolingian and Ottonian times, with their aristocratic and courtly commitments. Its directness and easy accessibility set it off from the highly
intellectualized preoccupations of the great monastic centers of artistic
patronage.[50]

X

Peter Damiani, writing just after the mid-eleventh century, made detailed observations on the transformation most fundamental to an appreciation of the forces of social change. This acute observer saw quite correctly that by "modern custom" estates were being divided among many
cultivators, and this practice he contrasted with "ancient custom," where
such division and fragmentation were not commonplace. Indeed, evidence from surviving charters bears out his analysis. He was witness
to an energetic movement of colonization and land reclamation having
its beginnings in north and central Italy in the late tenth century. Needless to say, his delineation of a society on the move contained some
stern reservations. He was to argue that the effect of leasing to new
families and the impact of social mobility were to elevate merchants,
petty artisans, and rustics, whom he frequently referred to as "ditch
diggers," to positions of prestige and power. In towns and villages dissension among leading citizens (*primores*) provided an opportunity for
lesser folk, who now spoke up at public assemblies on vital matters of
common concern, from the election of clergy and the partition of
church property to the levying of militia and the defense of the community. These nouveaux folk soon migrated to the cities, where they
became involved in the business of the courts and communal councils.
The reorganization of patterns of habitation and land use was transforming Italian society and its values. The powerful landlords, lay and
ecclesiastical, of north and central Italy who were promoting this change
were responsible, in Damiani's view, for the loss of amity and concord
pervasive in the first years of the century. No longer did they cultivate
land directly but extorted money from peasants to whom the farms
were rented. Nobility prospered "de rapinis pauperum," and arrogant
new men achieved high places. Leases and charters do support the conclusion that in the eleventh century great landlords colonized new land
and exploited old estates; in the process the excess labor supply was
forced to move to the cities.[51]

Again the Vallombrosan monastery of Passignano, so central to religious reform in Tuscany, with its thousands of charters and leases, provides us with an opportunity to examine in some detail the migrations transforming north and central Italy in the eleventh and twelfth centuries. Located in the southern region of the Florentine countryside (*contado*), close to the much-traveled route between the Valdelsa and the upper valley of the Arno, this heavily forested area was to be the center for extensive land reclamation and settlement. Here we observe in miniature the rise of a complex village society, with its new, communal structures working to systematize the rights and responsibilities of the inhabitants. Under ecclesiastical and secular lordship, *castra*, or fortified villages, were regularly being established throughout Tuscany. Similar foundations are well documented for Lombardy and the Sabine and Latium districts around Rome. In the Florentine *contado*, which ran sixty miles or so to the north and south and thirty miles to the east and west, we observe a boom in the creation of new, fortified settlements. By a rough count only 2 are mentioned in the documents as existing before 900. Before 1000 only 11 are noted, but within the next fifty years, 52 more were added. In the interval between 1050 and 1100 the figure reached 130. In a survey of 1376 (a bit selective) the Florentine *contado* is described as having as many *castra* as village hamlets.

These *castra* contained a diversified population, and, without presenting an idyllic picture of life in these communities, one can suggest that a fair degree of equality existed among the inhabitants. In those settlements under the lordship of Passignano we have a population composed of middling immigrants distanced from landless peasants and feudal nobles. The change from "antique practices" to "modern customs," as recorded by Damiani for the Arezzo zone, whereby estates were divided into properties occupied by separate households, bringing people together in a new setting, was distressing to some but highly beneficial to others. Villages were planned: houses constructed on a thoroughfare, space provided for a square, a church with a bell tower erected, and walls with gates raised. Arranged around these nucleated centers were arable and nonarable lands, over which the lord, in this case the monastery, exercised new types of jurisdiction. These centers of production, the fortified villages, were the creation of risk-taking immigrants and ambitious lords willing to enter into new arrangements. This relationship brought together complex, even contradictory, tendencies: on the one hand, community interdependence and cooperation was indispensable; on the other, hereditary tenants enjoyed considerable economic freedom. Into this mix must be placed the persistence of feudal rights and obligations. They restricted activity while providing protection and assurance. Finally, as we have noted, revolutionary changes were achieved in an economic environment favorable to avaricious landlords and ambitious middling folk. It was cooperation between landlord, tenant, and merchant that would make possible the reclamation and settlement of Tuscan lands in the eleventh and twelfth centuries. The rights of great landlords, prosperous tenants, and feudal nobles were respected and upheld when tested in the tribunals of Florence. Almost from the start the success of this movement allowed nobles to invest in trade and traders to buy land.[52]

The survival of the *castrum* depended upon maintaining a delicate ecological balance. The number of inhabitants in rural fortified villages generally did not exceed two or three hundred. There was great concern about such life-and-death subjects as an excess of cattle: if newcomers brought their livestock into the village, then the common pasture would be depleted. Similar anxieties were voiced over fishing rights and the communal woods. There were gardens immediately adjacent to the walls and vegetable patches a bit beyond; then followed orchards, vineyards, the dry grain fields, groves of olives, and, finally, the summer pastures above and the winter pastures below. With modest productivity, controls were essential; in fact, villages failed and were abandoned when the fine equation between population and land resources was undone. The dynamics of internal colonization and land reclamation required planning on an unprecedented scale. Urban centers depended upon immigration to replace population, and in Tuscany and Lombardy the towns were perhaps more numerous than those of any other region in western Europe. More critical, however, was that as the population increased, the grain supply of the *contado* was in high demand and the supply frequently short. It has been estimated that by the late thirteenth century, even with full productivity in Tuscany, the Florentine government was compelled to import better than 60 percent of its grain.[53]

Inhabitants of new towns and villages assumed responsibility for public charges: they looked to maintenance of walls, bridges, and roads, assessed taxes, and provided for the common defense. Out of this communal experience were to come those statutes and provisions fixing agricultural and collective life in minute detail. Formal enactments regulating the use of woods, pastures, commons, and ponds were established and times for sowing, reaping, and harvesting announced. Redaction of these laws governing the work of inhabitants of the rural Tuscan commune proceeded apace in the thirteenth and fourteenth centuries; the talent for codification found its most textured expression in these enactments. The appetite for corporate responsibility did not diminish the authority of ecclesiastical or secular overlords. Independent in economic matters, hereditary tenants of the monastery of Passignano sold lands and houses but continued to respect the prerogatives of the abbot. In microcosm the rural commune was emblematic of a society on the move, willing to take risks while trusting in cooperative undertakings. The economic historian Philip J. Jones speaks of an agricultural system in which the customary and individualistic disputed for primacy on the soil of medieval Italy.[54]

A general relaxation of the conditions of tenure and the bonds of service has been well documented for these pivotal centuries. The excessive rigidity of large country estates was modified, and well-to-do peasants were transformed into villagers. Castral ties were loosened, and in their stead family bonds and *consorteria* connections were strengthened. As we have seen, the vocabulary for delineating *consorteria* arrangements was enriched. In these permanent settlements the holdings of rural artisans and peasants tended to pass in fixed lines of succession governed by contractual obligation. Among rural nobility lines of succession were also established, and common surnames were employed more widely as lineage became more cohesive. The family was becoming the fiscal unit for purposes of taxation and representation. Assemblies of the heads of families administered affairs of vital concern; out of the coexistence of private and collective rights and properties emerged the economic solidarity of the fortified village.[55]

Equally important to an understanding of these changes is an investigation of practices that were losing their commanding position in the rural and urban commune. As has been noted on several occasions, gift and countergift were not so likely to be recorded in the documents of the eleventh and twelfth centuries. Similarly, we find that the *quarta* of Lombard law and the *tercia* of Frankish law, whereby wives were given an active interest in apportioning their husbands' property, were gradually falling into disuse, to be replaced by the dowry system. The expansion of Roman legal forms led to the wider adoption of the testament and the breaking of immutable rules of the customary inheritance. With the testament we observe that the relationship between family and property was subject to constant revision; the authority of the parental group was much reduced. In areas closest to the commercial town, patrimony was least likely to pass to customary heirs, with the testator freer to alienate property. The practice of *mund* and its strict operation was also on the decline, as was the exchange of pledges and pawns equal to the value of loan and credit. Notaries and the notarized document were achieving wider currency as credit dealings competed effectively with traditional practices. Indeed, if one were to identify the single greatest export from the new hamlets and villages under the jurisdiction of the abbot of Passignano, it might well have been the notary. Of the sixteen families whose genealogy we can reconstruct and who were to become Florentine citizens, eighteen were notaries; only two families failed to provide a member of this prestigious profession. Identical conclusions can be drawn from other rural communes and towns, and by the late thirteenth century the number of notaries and judges matriculated in that prominent guild totalled almost seven hundred. They were to be at the center of the dissemination of a laic and civic culture responsive to new political imperatives and enhancing the power of corporatism and statutory law. In their hands legal language was to attain that confidence allowing the triumph of such abstractions as the theory of representation, principles of agency, and the juridical personality of corporate bodies. Governments, guilds, and business organizations were soon to have a legal life of their own.[56]

XI

Just before the beginnings of the commune in Florence in the eleventh century we can discern activity in the parishes. The revitalization of parish life was a leading feature of the takeoff in the cities and countryside of Tuscany. In the ninth and tenth centuries little distinction had been made between the way in which a parish priest held his church and leasing arrangements by which land was ceded to a lay person. Clerical duties were regarded rather like the work required of tenants. A priest's obligation to hold religious services in the church could be entrusted to another cleric; bishops treated baptismal churches as if they were private property. By the close of the ninth century, bishops were bestowing parish lands to vassals as benefices. Parochial property and tithes were alienated by the bishop of Lucca, passing into the hands of a newly formed nobility—the Rolandinghi, Corvaresi, and the lords of Vaccoli, Montemagno, and Ripafratta. In the *contado* of Lucca, Pisa, Arezzo, and Florence we see land-hungry magnates acquiring parish churches and tithes. A network of private and personal relations bound churchmen and feudatories. Ecclesiastical estates were being parcelled out among vassals in return for valuable services. Italian chroniclers described in splendid detail a world in which bishops and *nobiles* were linked by gifts, benefices, service, and marriage.[57]

From the vantage point of the eleventh and twelfth centuries this world seemed corrupt beyond redemption: priests spawned bastards, took brides, or cared more for their mistresses than for Mother Church.

Church property was inheritable, and Tuscan bishops regularly alienated ecclesiastical holdings to laity. Feudatories were invested with hospices and benefices belonging to the cathedral chapter. What prevailed and was to be attacked so fiercely by reformers of the eleventh century as sinful and corrupt, however, was nothing more than a complex system of relationships whereby society achieved cohesion through gift and literal exchange. Few tenth-century figures challenged or even questioned these arrangements: Bishop Raterio of Verona was the exception, and even he felt it necessary to state that had he attempted to enforce clerical celibacy in his diocese, he would have been left without clergy. But within a century the climate of opinion was to be radically changed. In his elegant, poetic biography of Countess Matilda of Tuscany, *Vita Mathildis*, the monk Donizo related how utterly demoralizing to the people was the sale of parish lands to laymen and priests. It is not difficult to trace these transactions and discover how prevalent they were, for they lent structure to a tightly knit and intimate society.[58]

The issue on which reformers of the eleventh and twelfth centuries spent abundant energy and talent involved nothing short of a projection of a vision of the world. Already in Carolingian times there had been spokesmen for this vision, but their reforms proved ephemeral. What monks and priests were saying was not entirely novel: Christian reformers had always resisted the interpenetration of the sacred and the profane. This resistance generally found a few able spokesmen, and there even were glorious historical moments when it crystallized. But now, in the eleventh and twelfth centuries, the drama was to be played out on a wide stage, and the consequences were as unforeseen as they were lasting. To the reforming clergy of this later time and to their loyal supporters, the root of all evil was to be found in that sinful mix of sacred and secular things. Previously, the consciences of particular individuals were occasionally troubled by this mingling, but for the most part the effects were perceived as innocuous and perhaps even beneficial to society and the Church. Now the legitimacy of this mix was sternly challenged, as were the myriad transactions lending society its coherence. Fundamental social arrangements were cast in doubt and time-honored practices placed under the dread charge of simony. Damiani provides us with a vivid account of a typical Italian bishop, attended by lancers and shield bearers, who, having given away church lands, had to have recourse to the patrimony and tithes of the parish church; these too he sacrificed in order to gain the support of laity. His exercise in liberality took bread from the poor and discouraged rural parishioners from fulfilling Christian obligations. All were culpable:

the priest who paid the bishop for a rural parish (*plebs agrorum*) and the lay aristocracy who converted grants of ecclesiastical property into hereditary tenure. Damiani goes on to say:

> There are bishops who hand over parish churches to laymen; such prelates sin the more grievously in that they are committing the sacrilege of profaning sacred things; and to those whom they seem to benefit they dispense mortal poison. For to divert tithes to laymen, is not this to give them a poison of which they will die? Add further that just cause is given to the parishioners of such churches for withdrawing their obedience from their mother churches and not paying them their due tribute of tithes.[59]

Evidence from parish churches in the territories of Arezzo, Florence, and Pistoia discloses in detail how they were bestowed by bishops as prebends with the right of unrestricted alienation. An archdeacon might give the church as a benefice to a layman, provided that he pay rent to the bishop. Frequently assigned to nobility (*milites*), properties and tithes went to strengthen local bonds between laity and clergy. Without these exchanges it was apparent to many that society would lose cohesion. Indeed, precisely these arguments were later to be made by those fearing the social effects of condemning ecclesiastical marriage. The patient and incomplete task of recovering church property became the subject of historical exposition, and in the late eleventh century a protracted account was given of procedures lasting over a century. This narrative delved into details of the intermingling of secular and sacred interests going back to the mid-ninth century. The post-Carolingian period saw bishops trying to ensure the continuity of priest and holy office in the parish through grants of church lands and long-term leases. Expansion and economic growth favored reform since the possibility of envisioning a society held together by more abstract ties was gaining credence. Lay investiture and even spiritual intervention of laity for reform of the Church were condemned and assurance given that free from secular influence the Church could fill its pastoral role. The ideal of institutions effectively ministering to social problems without recourse to narrow allegiances and literal ties had captured the imaginations of reformers and their adherents.[60]

3

Lay Piety

WE DETECT NUMEROUS changes in Tuscan bequests and pious benefactions of the eleventh and twelfth centuries. After 1000 the number of donations increased dramatically: in the fifty-year period after the 980s, donations to churches and monasteries in the Lucca region were three times as frequent as in the half century from 930 to 980. In fact, if one pursues this investigation in order to determine the nadir, it will be located in that chaotic interval between the Saracen and Hungarian invasions in the ninth century, when only seven churches were founded. In contrast to this, the half century after 1030 was one of substantial increase: bequests and donations were five times more numerous than during the preceding fifty years. Nor was this the peak: regular increases in benefactions were registered over the next century. Similar patterns can be detected for such monasteries as Passignano: from 884 to 1010 only four donations were received, from 1011 to 1040 the number was seven, from 1041 to 1070 it was seventeen, and from 1071 to 1100 it was thirty-six. An approximation of the percentages of gifts suggests that for Tuscany the figure for the eleventh century stood over five times that for the ninth and tenth centuries. Indeed, we are at the threshold of a spiritual and philanthropic revolution. Tuscan documents from the eighth to the eleventh century disclose little interest in pastoral care, obeying in this, as in so much else, the imperatives of monastic piety. It was not until the eleventh century that the pastoral ministry became a preoccupation for the charitably minded.[1]

After the year 1000, donations and bequests by lesser folk cascaded forth, and these benefactions remained a persistent feature of Tuscan spiritual life. In an earlier time small proprietors had surrendered their land and independence "out of poverty, fear, and piety"; now the impulse focused on piety. Also in an earlier time, gifts to monasteries and churches were most likely to originate with leading comital families. Large tracts of land, and even entire estates, were bestowed on monasteries; frequently the religious foundations were headed by the benefactor's noble kinfolk. Churches were constructed on the territory of the founder and quite independent of the bishop's will. Religious donations and political aggrandizement went hand in glove; the right of heirs to nominate priests was explicitly stated. With the eleventh century the world of benevolence was democratized, and lesser folk were able to participate more in pious activities. Of course the nobility continued to play a prominent role in the life of the Tuscan church, but they, in turn, relinquished certain prerogatives in the face of Gregorian reform. Harbingers of this change were already evident in the philanthropic behavior of newly affluent merchants, judges, and notaries over the eleventh century. Grants were smaller; works of philanthropy and benefaction were undertaken in greater numbers by prosperous cultivators, artisans, and merchants. Improved economic conditions strengthened the patrimonial base of middling Tuscan families so that it was now possible for land to be donated without bringing financial ruin to the donor's family. In the ninth century, when land was given to the Church by small proprietors, it was often returned to the donor through a long-term leasing arrangement. Although this practice did persist and many gifts were camouflaged land exchanges, the clear and compelling conclusion to be drawn is that donations and bequests of the eleventh and twelfth centuries, by both magnates and small landholders, were freer of restraints and less likely to assert the economic interest of the benefactor.[2]

The spirit of these Tuscan pious benefactions of the eleventh and twelfth centuries also discloses a gradual decline in the primacy of what has hitherto been described as a "material sense of salvation." Religious reformers were constantly attacking the practice of gift giving to monasteries in return for prayers (*launegeld*). Upon hearing that a wealthy Tuscan had entered a Vallombrosan monastery in the traditional Benedictine way, by donating his patrimony, Giovanni Gualberto proceeded directly to the place, requested the charter of donation, tore it into shreds, and trampled on it. Departing in a rage, he invoked the vengeance of God; instantly the monastery burst into flame, but the holy man did not even look back. The idea of voluntary poverty was proving particularly attractive, and donations to regular canons professing the common life were favored by charitable Tuscans of the eleventh century. The very notion of charity and philanthropy was undergoing radical revision. Part of the attraction of the canons was their "sense of responsibility for the edification of their fellow men." Despite certain similarities, canons and monks differed in their attitudes toward the apostolate: in the centuries to follow, monastic life, as a quest for personal sanctification, became less prized as combat for the faith and service to one's neighbors became sacred Christian duties.[3]

In an earlier time the ritual elements of the charitable act predominated over its social features. Bequests made to the poor were often benefactions to particular monks, who were designated "Christ's paupers." Charity itself was closely associated with liturgy. Lombard nobles, when endowing convents, prescribed that twelve paupers be fed one day each week and that during Easter they each be provided with a hot bath. *Caritas* was frequently a sentiment limited to kinsmen and friends of the benefactor. When extended to strangers, it bore a mystical aura: monasteries received them as if each stranger were Jesus Christ. A certain number of paupers were sheltered and fed meat, wine, and bread by the sacristan when large donations were forthcoming. In the early Middle Ages faith entered into a relationship with the supernatural through gesture, with liturgy playing the fundamental role. Alms giving was most likely to occur at solemn moments in the Christian calendar: the great abbeys would then feed the crowd of paupers, and largesse was most often exhibited on the day of the patron saint or upon the death of a monk. Hospitals established by the Lombard nobility, of course, remained in the hands of the founding families, who chose the rector.[4]

In comparison with the ninth and tenth centuries gifts for charitable works in the diocese of Lucca in the eleventh century increased almost sixfold. Middling folk participated enthusiastically in eleemosynary activity, with hospitals and alms houses proliferating throughout Tuscany. Quantitative studies of twelfth-century Lombardy also disclose that all classes of society engaged vigorously in performing good works. The amelioration of human suffering came to be viewed as a human preoccupation as well as a divine concern. A chain of hospitals, leproseries, and xenodochia were being constructed along the rapidly expanding network of roads in Tuscany. A charitable revolution accompanied what has been appropriately described as a road-building revolution. At Lucca, Altopascio, and Fucecchio and across two branches of the Arno to the hills of San Miniato we find these pious foundations ministering to the weary traveler, the poor, the aged, the sick, and the infirm. San Jacopo of Altopascio was soon to become the model hospital for western Europe and spawned sister institutions in foreign parts. In the principal cities of Tuscany—Arezzo, Lucca, Pisa, Florence, and Siena—hospital construction was to become a growth industry. As we shall observe, service in these institutions was to be a spiritual activity singularly appealing to the middling and upper echelons of lay society. When the chronicler Giovanni Villani presented his statistical survey of his beloved city of Florence, covering the biennium 1336–38, he proudly called attention to her hospitals, with a thousand beds for the care of the poor, sick, and infirm. This figure was approached by Arezzo, whose number of hospitals had increased from fourteen to twenty-six over the thirteenth century; by Pisa, whose number was augmented from eleven to twenty-seven; and by Florence herself, whose increase was from fifteen to thirty. We lack information on the size of these hospitals for this period, but in terms of the number of foundations, Lucca was most precocious and first on the scene. Siena, though experiencing a doubling of number over the course of the thirteenth century, had fewer but may have been more advanced in terms of rational organization.[5]

I

The reforming work of Florentine bishops, particularly Gherardo (soon to be Pope Nicholas II), just before the Lateran synod of 1059 was directed toward strengthening rural parish life. The reforming bishop of Lucca and soon-to-become Pope Alexander II prohibited his episcopal successors from granting benefices to lay lords. Church lands were to be leased to tenant farmers or worked by laborers. He did exclude from this prohibition properties already conceded to secular lords, but on balance the recovery of church lands improved dramatically. Country churches were being rebuilt and income from legacies and pious benefactions assigned to maintenance and staffing. As the rural parish commenced to assume a distinct physiognomy with definite boundaries, parochial organization became the beneficiary of new attention. The first stone parish churches appeared in the countryside of Tuscany shortly after 1000, the earlier wood structures having disappeared without a trace. The vitality of country life was evidenced in the increase of land prices: in Lombardy and Tuscany they rose 400 to 500 percent from the mid-tenth to early eleventh century. Over the next hundred years they were to double in districts around Milan and Lucca, affecting all land—arable, waste, and wood. The demographic increase and changing patterns of settlement, as we have noted, were hallmarks of these centuries: in rural Tuscany the number of *castra* founded in the twelfth century may well have exceeded two hundred. Market towns and unwalled centers of trade were likewise on the upswing. The number of parishes multiplied, becoming ever more responsive to the pastoral needs (*cura animarum*) of a growing population moving into recently established village communities, many of which were founded by the commune for strategic reasons. The vast ecclesiastical districts of the early Middle Ages were now replaced by smaller and more compact territorial units; these organic structures of encadrement were better suited to administering to a more collectivized life-style. At the center of this transformation were such reformers as Gherardo, Damiani, Giovanni Gualberto, and the Gregorians, vigorously championing the recovery of parochial revenues usurped in times past by great lords and even lesser folk. Again, people from middling, as well as lower, ranks of society were responsive to appeals. Commencing at mid-eleventh century, the restitution of tithes and rights of parish churches is well documented for the dioceses of Lucca and Pistoia. We have evidence of spectacular deathbed repentances by powerful nobles as well as the small-scale restitution of portions of tithes by minor landholders. This recovery was aided by the extinction of such feudal dynasties as the Cadolinghi and the death without heirs of Countess Matilda of Tuscany in 1113. Conflicts ensued between the noble clan of Alberti and the German emperors for territories of the countess, and when Henry V, last of the Salic line, died, imperial power was dissipated in civil war between pretenders. The strength of the great Tuscan feudatories and the authority of the emperor were attenuated.[6]

Throughout the lands of Tuscany the reorganization of parish life worked to strengthen the social base of the rural communes. In the city of Florence the twenty-four parishes of the four quarters, with their chaplains and vicars, became the focus of citizen life. Statutes of rural communes required each family to send one member to participate in religious processions and assist in ceremonies. Within the *castra*, whose basic unit was the family, a discipline emerged supportive of the household, headed by husband and wife. Elevation of the role of the family, strict censure of illegitimacy, and condemnation of ecclesiastical concubinage were manifestations of successful intervention by the reforming church in matters once regarded as clan or tribal prerogatives. A recent statistical analysis indicates a sharp decline after the mid-eleventh century in the number of references in documents explicitly designating sons of priests or their bastards. Whereas this type of investigation bristles with difficulties, still the percentage reduction suggests that reformers were affecting social behavior. The decrease in the period 1040 to 1071, as compared with the interval 1011 to 1040, was roughly 75 percent; from 1071 to 1110 we have another diminution, of more than 33 percent. At the same time we find harsher views being voiced on the subject of bastardy, and again a recent study of the Latium and Sabine regions around Rome concluded that control of the village population and the requirements of revitalized collective life were at the core of this sterner regimen. The household was the unit of colonization and as such was to be buttressed by efforts to enforce stricter Christian norms. In surveys and tax registers the family hearth was to be the basic unit.[7]

The growth of the population and colonization were accompanied by enhanced feelings of mutuality and interdependence. In the twelfth century the technical term for reclamation, *bonum facere*, appears in charters. The decline of labor services and rural slavery, along with an increase in agricultural specialization, stimulated the need for cooperation. Collective contracts between landlords and peasant communities evolved into communal rural statutes, and they, in turn, regulated the details of village life in the interest of the community's survival. Bonds of amity between villages were strengthened by periodic religious reunions. The right of sanctuary was guaranteed at the shrine of the patron saint of the village confederation. Representatives of leading families from different hamlets were summoned to assist at the commemorative masses on saints' days. Rural codes were soon to require offerings of wine, wax, candles, bread, honey, milk, and cheese at Easter and on the day of the Nativity. Increasingly, the parish church was being named the beneficiary by will-making parishioners; time and money were donated for the repair and maintenance of the stonework, walls, and facade. Chapels were constructed, towers erected, and new bells cast. Numerous bequests were made for the dowries of young girls of the parish as well as for the support of widows and orphans. New urban money was also being channeled into rural settlements through legacies to confraternities and charitable sodalities. Townsmen did not sever ties with their natal parishes; in wills and benefactions they continued to be responsive to the needs of "Christ's poor" while instructing executors and heirs to commission commemorative masses for their souls and to hire villagers to follow their biers to the parish cemeteries. In later centuries substantial numbers of townsmen were to have wills redacted in their country homes, and these documents expressed abiding affection for the beloved parish. The parish district was more than a new administrative unit; it was the focus of pious sensibility and civic concern.[8]

Religious reformers of the eleventh century preached against the lay proprietary system, urging the restitution of property and tithes to the parish church. Struggles to free the Church from secular dominion were bitter, protracted, and often indecisive. In Tuscany, however, the reformers' victories were dramatic. Feudatories in the Lucca and Pistoia regions were finally to relinquish rights over baptismal churches, monasteries, and chapels. Again we notice that small landholders partici-

pated in the movement for religious reform, restoring tithes and properties to the parish, particularly in the Arezzo region. By the end of the
century, the lay ownership of churches had dwindled, becoming merely
a right of patronage, with a lay patron presenting a priest to the bishop
for appointment. Old patterns did survive among nobles of the Luccan
contado: for several generations they continued to collect tithes and
exercise prerogatives attending an advowson. But the trend was toward
the loss of noble families' rights over rural churches as episcopal and
communal authority was asserted. By the twelfth century parochial institutions were assuming complex and variegated structures as the task of
caring for a burgeoning population, now being linked by a vast network of roads, became more demanding.[9]

Communal assemblies were charged with administering parish properties and caring for those instruments of cult necessary for the church
service. Popular festivities on holy days were community enterprises, as
was the enforcement of laws against heretics and other subverters of the
true faith. Soon city officials were to intervene in parish matters to im-
plement regulations against blasphemers and those bent on disrupting
religious life. By the thirteenth century relations between city and rural
parish had become more exacting: the military organization of the
Florentine *contado* was founded on the rural parish as the administrative unit. Migration from countryside to city was causing the urban
population to soar. The rural-urban ratio was shifting throughout Tuscany and, according to evidence from the Prato and San Gimignano
districts, this area may have been the most highly urbanized in all of
western Europe. Market towns, such as Greve and Figline, were founded
and the new Florentine suburb of the Oltrarno established. At the beginning of the twelfth century the population of Florence was twenty-
five to thirty thousand; estimates for the end of the century indicate an
increase of about 100 percent. Within a century it almost doubled
again. In 1172 the commune started constructing a new circle of walls
to protect its burgeoning population: the enclosed area was approximately two hundred acres, more than twice as large as the primitive
Roman city. In 1284 another circle was projected to be completed half
a century later: the enclosed area was almost sixteen hundred acres.
The growth of nearby Pisa, though not as spectacular, represented a
400-percent increase in the enclosed area from 1182 to the end of the
thirteenth century. In such towns as Borgo San Donnino, Orvieto, and
Poggibonsi, the influx brought to the fore a great variety of tradesmen
and artisans, whose presence demonstrates the extent of specialization
and diversification of economic life. In the Florentine *matricula* of
minor guilds almost 50 percent of the smiths, butchers, tailors, and

lesser tradesmen lived in the surrounding market towns and fortified villages. They were the *populares*, referred to in documents of the period as "weak and impotent and common men" and who were so frequently to petition governments for protection, seeking security in the guild and religious confraternity.[10]

II

A new esteem for the pastoral obligation of clergy was much in evidence in the writings of religious reformers and in the biographies of Italian saints in the eleventh and twelfth centuries. Salvation of society was no longer entrusted so generally to the prayers and spiritual exercises of monks. We have few documents pertaining to the religious activities of priests and laity during earlier times, but by the eleventh and twelfth centuries the spiritual efforts of priests and lay folk were being carefully chronicled. Bequests and donations demonstrate a keen awareness of new spiritual possibilities and obligations. Benefactors called for the prayers of all Christians and made offerings for the redemption of all Christian souls: sentiments of mutuality and interdependency were coupled with a heightened sense of religious activism. We can observe something of the dimension of change by comparing the messages of two saints so revered by the Tuscans. In the eleventh century Romualdo had appealed to professionals to build the Church; he exalted the contemplative life to the point of deprecating manual labor. Two centuries later Francis of Assisi was to instruct all Christians that it was their first and most solemn duty to rebuild churches but that the construction was to be done with their own hands, not through gifts to a wealthy monastery.[11]

In Tuscany grants were ordinarily being made in favor of regular canons, whose renunciation of personal property and embracing of the common life (*vita comune*) evoked a deep response from benefactors of the late eleventh and early twelfth centuries. They were eager to support those communities of monks and clergy willing to follow the model of the apostolic life. Early in his career Romualdo had persuaded parish clergy to repudiate simony and cease living according to the customs of laity; instead they were to obey the prior and live in a community. In 1025 canonical life was established in a rural parish of Lucca, and soon laity were giving private church property to priests, provided that they followed the common life—"dwelling in chastity in houses close to the church." In Milan the reformer Arialdo received a gift of a private church, which he then organized as a semimonastic community, with clergy entering a life of individual poverty in imitation of Christ and His Apostles. These communities had an irresistible appeal to laity; townspeople and countryfolk flocked to a church "where they could hear God's word with free minds and partake of the sacraments." Indeed, contemporary accounts suggest that this democratization of the spiritualities proved vitally attractive to laity. Just before his election as pope, Bishop Gherardo of Florence, who introduced the common life into many Tuscan parish churches, approved reforms by cathedral canons eager to profess the common life *ad instar primitivae ecclesiae*.[12]

The supernatural was becoming less resistant to immediate social and personal concerns. In an earlier time, when narrating the life of a saint, the writer was wont to emphasize the martyrdom of his spiritual hero, paralleling it with that of the Savior; now it was the entire life of the saint lived in imitation of Christ that was to be the occasion for inspiring the faithful. Voluntary poverty was seen by many as essential to the exercise of a spiritually valid pastoral role. The need to balance moral claims against the fulfillment of religious obligations produced tension: on the one hand the need remained to protect the clergy from temptation; on the other the expansion of pastoral duties and parish life tended to isolate the priest from his fellows. The resolution was to combine an active ministry and the common life. The practice of asceticism and the exercise of charity came to be hallmarks of the holy man; even his miraculous powers were to be subordinate to them. Reformers challenged the idea of the efficacy of ritual alone or the vicarious offering of worship; the mechanical operation of grace emanating within rigidly prescribed channels was also repudiated. Damiani had little appreciation for liturgical splendor, criticizing "the unnecessary sounding of bells, the protracted chanting of hymns, and the conspicuous use of ornament." Contemptuous of churchmen who devoted themselves to the construction and adornment of monasteries, he told of a certain abbot who was seen in a vision burning in hell and sentenced to setting up scaffolding to eternity for his immoderate tastes. Indeed, the tendency was for the Church to define the cult of sacred images less in terms of worship than of veneration. Personal responsibility was being accented, and it heightened the understanding of the lure of temptation.[13]

The Last Judgment remained a compelling concern for the faithful but was losing something of its "anguished imminence." The supernatural was less remote and opaque and judgment not exclusively perceived as a day of punishment: now it carried a prospect of reward. The wrath of God was not so certain, and confidence in His great mercy (*magna misericordia*) was on the increase. Expectations of divine justice and forgiveness mounted, whereas descriptions of hell fire and brimstone were less frequent. Christ was portrayed as intercessor and judge, with his redemptive power lent new prominence. The possibility of being counted among the saved on Judgment Day was enhanced, as was individuals' spiritual capacity to merit eternal life. Grace was more often described as acquired rather than instantaneous, as in the earlier document. In the eleventh and twelfth centuries the emphasis was upon what the individual could accomplish, with the admonition that one should not depart from this world without performing good works (*sine aliquo boni operis*). A more vivid sense of interiority was expressed by donor and testator, who no longer felt so oppressed by the weight of sin (*pondera peccatis*). The most terrifying descriptions of hell fire were admonitory, summoning the transgressor to repent. For the first time in the history of Italian art we observe the Six Works of Mercy connected with the portrayal of the Last Judgment, by the sculptor Benedetto Antelami at Parma in the late twelfth century.[14]

The concentration on God's mercy and love was accompanied by concern for one's progeny; the needs of the family were a matter of greater preoccupation and planning. Less ancestral and restrospective than earlier ones, the twelfth-century document revealed more confidence in the future. In its main outlines the future was likely to resemble the past; therefore, sentiments of historical continuity were fortified. The wider use of the will among middling folk, as well as among the affluent and well born, was becoming a telling feature of thirteenth-century social life. Not only did an elite have elaborate norms for succession, which were to be authenticated by a public act, but middling people were also conforming to these standards and procedures. A more individualized conception of wealth allowed donor and testator greater freedom; further, they were to look to their immediate kin for spiritual intercession in that most germane of all concerns, salvation of the soul. Affective ties were more durable, and the idea of solidarity was less prone to be expressed in concrete forms, such as the *mercede*. The doctrine of purgatory was being formulated and the living exhorted to work for the spiritual well-being of the dead. Testators entrusted preservation of their earthly memories to kinfolk, making the basic assumption that ties of affection would endure and human volition prevail. The sense that human arrangements were lasting and temporal institutions effective was gaining currency. Piety was becoming more personal and individualized as larger sums were bequeathed for private masses, altars, and the construction of chapels.[15]

Before 1000, pious benefactors were more likely to enter into arrangements with a bishop or abbot for donations to be distributed posthumously. After this date gifts continued to be made on the deathbed, but such gifts were exceptional. More commonplace were donations made during the lifetime of a benefactor for the salvation of his soul (*pro remedio animae*). Donors and testators were more spiritually active, tending to view salvation as a reward for charitable deeds performed during one's time on earth. Social concerns were expressed with immediacy. Here the statistics on the founding of hospitals again prove illuminating: in the Florentine *contado* the increase in the number of hospitals from the eleventh through the twelfth century was 400 percent; by the fourteenth century it is possible to identify 122 hospitals for rural Tuscany and to fix their locations. Several others are known, but their geographic whereabouts cannot be precisely determined. Many of them were small, the result of gifts from middling people, converting their houses into hospices for shelter of the poor and ill; indeed, what is striking are the numerous small bequests of beds, sheets, and foodstuffs for the aged and infirm. By the early thirteenth century personal involvement in these good works was regularly being undertaken by a legion of pious men and women from all strata of society. The influential Franciscans identified with the poor and afflicted; compassion flowed from direct personal contact with victims of misfortune. Therefore it was thought that alms should not be dispensed from a position of superiority.[16]

III

The possibility of living an authentic Christian life while remaining in the world was slowly, haltingly, but certainly gaining force. For many lay folk the question of whether a "life pleasing in the sight of God" could truly be pursued beyond the world of religious orders, without pitting oneself against Mother Church and hierarchy, had become ever more pressing. At Vallombrosa, sometime between 1039 and 1051, Giovanni Gualberto introduced a special type of lay brother or monk—the *conversi*. (They were later to appear at Hirsau, in Germany, in 1077.) *Conversi* worked for the rest of the community, leaving the monks free for a life of eremitic contemplation. They took the same vows as did monks except for pledging silence when marketing for the convent or toiling in the great world. Soon the term was being applied to pious lay folk, unlettered and living outside sacred orders. Many were people of modest origins who seem to have compensated for their inability to read and meditate upon the word of Christ by submitting to harsh mortification of the flesh and the rudest penance.[17]

The formation of fellowships, or cult associations centering upon communal drinking or sacrificial rituals, went back into prehistory and was much in evidence in the tribal societies of early medieval Europe. During the eighth and ninth centuries these fraternities did not change character when grouped under the patronage of a Carolingian noble or Christian saint. Assistance during such emergencies as fires and sea disasters in the coastal provinces was a matter of mutual concern. But these associations were suspect and, during the Carolingian period, were denounced by leading churchmen; magnates were encouraged to suppress them. In turn, oath guilds were formed for protection in those areas where nobles were particularly lawless and violent. Meanwhile, complaints were directed against cultic associations assembling at the time of the new moon to make special incantations; indeed, these reunions were considered sacrilegious—evidence of pagan fallout—and Charlemagne was prevailed upon to prohibit their assemblage. Confraternities for the care and maintenance of aged and infirm clergy were an expression of yet another impulse. Early documents indicate that at Arezzo the fraternity of the parish of Sta. Maria in Gradis was composed of these professionals. By the twelfth century, however, cultic and religious sodalities were changing dramatically. Neither cultic nor professional impulses were to retain their preeminence: laity were being received "in ordine fraternitas," and the social element of the brotherhood was much enhanced. Those laity joining the fraternity were expected to achieve "reconciliation with their neighbors and make restitution of ill-got gains to others." These two provisos were quintessential to the Italian experience.[18]

At San Appiano in the Val d'Elsa of Tuscany, lay folk constituted themselves as an order (*ordo*), living in strict imitation of an apostolic community. The dignity of laic life was intertwined with the apostolic ideal; this ideal readily assumed a social or communital dimension. Such influential laic movements as the Arnoldists, the Humiliati, and the Poor Men of Lombardy exalted the common life and did not abjure manual labor. The French Waldensians, the forebears of the Poor Men of Lombardy, interpreted the vow of absolute poverty so strictly that they refused manual labor, practicing mendicancy instead. Their Italian confreres, who were soon to split from them, formed workers' associations (*congregationes laborantium*), retained property, and upheld such institutions as marriage and the family. Catharism was also to develop differently south of the Alps: the dualism that accorded the devil a more prominent place than God in the theology of French Cathars was considerably mitigated by their Italian brothers. The latter also substantially muted the world-renouncing commitment to poverty as well as the severe strictures against monetary gain.[19]

In the eleventh and twelfth centuries the idea that laity, particularly nonnoble, might achieve a high level of perfection was popularized by such groups as the Patarines of Milan and Florence. These reformers challenged an ideology rather generally subscribed to in the past in which Christian society was divided into orders and hierarchies. With the Patarines individual merit and the moral quality of the believer's life assumed unprecedented relevance. Clergy zealous for political reform allied with *il popolo* in a program of refusal to participate in holy offices celebrated by unworthy priests. Pious lay folk were emerging from a subaltern and passive position to one of active participation in church reform. This movement was encouraged by the pastoral activity of clergy and itinerant preachers who proclaimed that God was active among the people. The surge of popular involvement by laity from all classes in the work of church renewal caused misgivings even among clerics sympathetic to the program of reform. Beyond the grave questions of challenging the efficacy of sacraments administered by the unworthy priest and casting into doubt his holy office, there remained the clerics' deep-seated prejudice against lay people in general and merchants in particular.

Bonizone, bishop of Sutri, wrote of the struggles of *il popolo* in his natal city of Cremona uniting in communal organization to side with reforming clergy to expel simoniac and concubinary priests. Concerned with the spiritual plight of laity, he composed a practical manual (*Liber de vita christiana*, 1090–95) in which he offered extensive information on modes and norms required for an authentic Christian life. His loyalties were clearly to a military nobility, to whom he remained entirely deferential. Peasants were good because their lives subjected them less to temptation and sin. They were warned to maintain faith with their lord and not to steal from him. They were to pay the *decima* and first fruits to the Church of God. Artisans were required to work diligently and, above all, to give alms and be generous to the poor. As to merchants, it was not by accident that the Holy Father had prohibited "mercature" to whoever undertook public penance. The spiritual risks of trade were infinite; albeit Bonizone grudgingly conceded that the activity might be useful to the world. Merchants were admonished to give alms and build hospitals and churches. The idea of hierarchy was axiomatic for Bonizone; the only clergy he would punish or restrain were those lacking in "true Christian" commitment or showing disobedience to the pope. In his view of society, lay folk played a passive, modest, almost peripheral role; they were able to do little to enhance prospects for salvation beyond the time-honored acts of charity and obedience. But he did emphasize the preaching duty of the bishop and priest, arguing that they must adapt their sermons to varied audiences; in this he followed the eleventh-century trend toward highlighting the pastoral function. However strong the urging was, though, sermons of the period tended to be schematic elaborations of patristic and postpatristic texts; only gradually were they to develop into a textured and innovative genre.[20]

In the next generation the Camaldolese monk Gratian assumed a similar stance. The great canonist also acknowledged the importance of pastoral discourse, yet he sharpened the dichotomy between clergy and laity. These were two separate categories of Christians (*duo sunt genera christianorum*). This dualism was to inspire leading theologians of the twelfth century, who, in increasing numbers, took a similar view. Gratian, however, displayed a deep historical appreciation of the threat laity posed to ecclesiastical hierarchy. In preceding generations Gregorians had mixed feelings about the participation of laity in the work of church reform. Eager for laic support in extirpating corrupt religious practices, clergy stood as staunch opponents of laic claims for spiritual autonomy and competence in matters of church government. But the Camaldolese monk did more than underscore the political incompetence of laity. Only in a single tract, *De matrimonio*, did he consider their spiritual prerogatives. His is one of the first juridical texts to define the status of laity: it was permitted to them to have wives and to "till the soil, to adjudicate among men, to pursue their own affairs." Unlike clergy, laity could possess "worldly goods for use only." They were to pay tithes and deposit their offerings on the altar of the church; if they followed these practices, they might be saved, provided that they shunned vice and pursued the path of Christian charity. Gratian distrusted the initiative of simple believers and would scale down the influence of hermits and lay preachers. In the twelfth century, when hermits who preached without ecclesiastical license were challenged, they claimed the right by virtue of mortification of the flesh. Gratian was hostile to such pretensions, opining that when laity were in the presence of clergy, they should not be permitted to deliver a sermon unless at the latter's request. True, holy men preaching the gospel had performed wondrous deeds while following in the footsteps of Christ; indeed, miracles were being reported that, some said, rivalled those of Biblical times. Gratian agreed that these marvelous acts ought to be admired, but he thought that they could not be presented as examples to guide human actions. He sought to limit the exemplary power of the life of Christ and, in so doing, was striking at the heart of the evangelism of his time. He saw the juridical church as distinct from evangelical experience; the legitimacy of the Church was not to be rooted in the history of the life of Christ or even in His example but rather in the history of salvation. In considering the question of whether laity could bring accusations against clergy, Gratian cited Christ, who, when suffering insult and persecution, said, "If you speak evil of me, give me evidence. Who among you has accused me of having sinned?" This quotation appears to indicate that laity could accuse prelates, yet Gratian goes on to argue just the opposite: Christ, in His humility, provides us with an example of perfection, not a principle of action.[21]

IV

Biographers of itinerant preachers of the eleventh and twelfth centuries, reluctant to offer miracles as testimony to the sanctity of their subjects, depicted the holy man as traveling barefoot and in tatters through towns and villages to preach the word of God. Carrying the message of the Gospels to the poor and downtrodden, the itinerant preacher, however, was imitating the life of the Savior. His ministry was devoted to tending the sick, bathing the leper, and consoling the bereaved and desperate, but his greatest spiritual achievement was reviving the dead souls of those who had sinned grievously and were brought back to life to be united unto God. These were not cadavers raised from the dead but erring Christians recalled to spiritual life. The Christ being imitated was the historical Jesus—that poor, discredited figure standing at the center of Christian evangelism. Unlike Gratian, these itinerant preachers sought the historical Jesus and preached the exemplary value of His life. History appeared to provide support for the pious aspirations of a laity less encadred, more mobile and risk taking. Already in the early eleventh century, in one of the first recorded instances of popular heresy of this period, the followers of a certain Italian, Gundolfo, upon being examined by the bishop of Cambrai (1024–25) as to their doctrine, discipline, and way of life, replied to the question "How do you reconcile your belief in the Gospels with preaching against them?" as follows:

> Nobody who is prepared to examine with care the teaching and rule which we have learned from our master will think that they contravene either the precepts of the Gospels or those of the apostles: This is its tenor: to abandon the world; to restrain the appetites of the flesh, to earn our food by the labour of our own hands, to do injury to nobody, to extend charity to everybody of our own faith: If these rules are followed baptism is unnecessary; if they are not it will not lead to salvation. This is the height of righteousness, to which there is nothing that baptism can add if every rule of the Gospels and apostles is observed in this way. If anyone says that baptism is a sacrament we would deny it on three grounds: first, that the evil life of the

minister cannot be the vehicle for the salvation of him who is baptised; second, that the vices which are renounced at the font may be resumed later in life; third, that the child who neither wills it nor concurs with it knows nothing of the faith and is ignorant of his need for salvation, does not beg for rebirth in any sense, and can make no confession of faith: clearly he has neither free will nor faith, and cannot confess it.[22]

These were men who regarded themselves as solely responsible for their salvation; furthermore, they denied the need for the priest to serve as intermediary between man and God, affirming the voluntary character of spiritual regeneration. Gundolfo's teachings, as understood by his disciples, were an exact and clear formulation of the ideals of evangelical Christianity. Just a few years later the archbishop of Milan, Ariberto, while at Turin on a visitation of his suffragan dioceses, received word that "a new heresy had recently been established in the castle above a place called Monforte." One of the heretics, an educated man named Gherardo, was summoned to expound on his views before the archbishop. At the base of his religious conviction was a commitment to chastity and the common ownership of goods. Refusing to eat meat and engaging in continuous prayer, these heretics conformed quite closely to the ideas and practices of the voluntary religious communities being founded throughout Italy during the eleventh century. Indeed, under more orthodox inspiration, this same impulse was to inspire the religious orders at Camaldoli, Fruttuaria, Fonte Avellana, Pomposa, and Vallombrosa.[23]

The first chronicler to discuss the earliest appearance of popular heresy in the West during this period was the very gifted Adhermar of Chabannes, who, after making the usual references to Manichaeanism—traditional since the time of Augustine for designating those who led the faithful astray—proceeded to state, "They did not eat meat, as though they were monks, and pretended to be celibate, but among themselves they enjoyed every indulgence." Throughout the eleventh century we see conspicuous manifestations of popular religious feelings similar to those described by the chronicler in the cities of Brescia, Cremona, Milan, and Piacenza and throughout Tuscany, especially in Florence. The evangelical, pauperistic, laic base of these movements, with their appeal to Scripture, provided momentum for reform. At mid-eleventh century such spiritual leaders as Arialdo of Milan summoned laity to the holy enterprise of cleansing the church after failing to persuade clergy to assume this sacred task. Giovanni Gualberto's message, delivered on " a day on which he was certain there would be great crowds," was so eloquent that for the first time nobles and commoners were galvanized into a politically self-conscious unit, *il popolo fiorentino*. It was under the aegis of reformers that the civic ethos first became programmatic.[24]

Even in the time of Gualberto the risk of popular uprisings against the church hierarchy was apparent. Such reformers as Damiani remained fearful of the impact of direct appeals to agitated segments of the community and took the Vallombrosans to task for just such rabble rousing. However, Damiani and others were not consistent in continuing to support the revolutionary Patarines in Milan and Florence. Between 1050 and 1100 the need for reform took precedence, and Gregorians tended to work in tandem with popular urban movements to restructure religious life. Society was regarded as a field of battle on which the disciples of Christ were to join forces in a holy contest against evil. After 1100, however, the threat of popular participation led to a radical clericalization of Christian life: reformers exalted the role of priest while desacralizing secular authority. The tension was becoming acute between popular evangelical movements and a clergy determined to make the sacred their exclusive domain. Emblematic of this change was the fact that at the close of the eleventh century, communion in both kinds was discontinued. Only clerical and monastic vocations were perceived as meriting consecration. The interior space of the church was reorganized in the twelfth century: vast barriers of stone ornamented with sculpture were erected, isolating the clergy, grouped in the choir, from the faithful, assembled in the nave.[25]

But significant inroads had been made. Laity were no longer being portrayed in religious iconography as a passive presence: now they were depicted performing works of piety and charity. No longer was fighting for the true faith regarded as being of little spiritual value. Warriors were given an opportunity to ensure their own salvation without renouncing their aristocratic military vocation. In an earlier time the call to join "the militia of Christ" meant enlisting as soldiers in the spiritual warfare of monastic life. In the cloister "knights of Christ" carried the sacred charge of doing battle against the temptations of the devil. During the Carolingian period, when Jonas of Orleans wrote his *Mirror of the Laity*, nothing was mentioned about the practical morality of warriors. In dealing with the military ethic, Hincmar of Rheims had commented only on the crimes and predations of soldiers. Raterio, bishop of Verona, did discuss the obligations of the several orders of tenth-century society, beginning with warriors, but, like the others, he was to dwell upon the negative side of soldiering: the warrior's principal duties involved the prevention of such crimes as murder and robbery, especially the plunder of church property. Atto of Vercelli contended that warriors should obey the minimal standards of fidelity to king and obedience to church law. Only with the eleventh century do we notice the onset of the ecclesiastical elaboration of the role of knight. The first moves were halting, timid, and even hostile. The chief proponent of reform in church government, Cardinal Humbert of Silva Candida, had every reason to appeal to the warrior for support in the battle for church reform. He acknowledged that there were laymen who held "the right belief" and defended "the church with words and temporal power in a conflict with heretics, but who, for the rest, do not manifest in their works the faith they defend. . . ." He was to reproach these individuals, proclaiming, "their souls are dead." Damiani, of course, was inconsistent, rejecting "an ecclesiastical right of resistance by the lower elements of society," yet he would intervene on the side of the Patarines; this indeed was a turning point. As we have seen, the knight Erlembaldo, leader of the Milanese Patarines and erstwhile supporter of the Gregorians, had been persuaded not to enter a monastery. Instead, he was to lead "the knights of Christ" behind the banner of St. Peter to victory over the simoniac and concubinary clergy. Martyred in the service of the true Church, Erlembaldo was the first Italian lay figure to be canonized.[26]

Writing in about 1070, Erlembaldo's contemporary the chronicler Arnolfo regarded the bestowal of St. Peter's banner on a lay person as sacrilegious. The chronicler's suspicion that the pope's action was a portent of new attitudes on the part of the Church was not far from the mark. Arnolfo was most anxious about the intervention of inexperienced laity in religious matters: he was scandalized by the presumption that St. Peter had yet another banner different from that given him by Christ. This was nothing short of preaching a new gospel. But after Erlembaldo suffered a martyr's death in 1076, miracles began to occur around his grave. He and another lay champion of reform, the Roman prefect Cencius, soon became cult figures. The role of *milites Christi* was sacralized and the use of arms "in defense of righteousness and on the advice of pious bishops" granted ecclesiastical sanction. The rule that penitents could not bear arms was relaxed, and soon crusading was being linked to the penitential act: since adversity suffered by crusaders was from the hand of God, they were as certain of salvation as were the martyrs of the Church in days of old. Popularization of the very laic idea of pilgrimage was a vivid feature of eleventh-century European life. The experience was no longer perceived as exile but as a quest for spiritual enrichment and adventure. Crusades and pilgrimages were undertaken "in place of penance" (*loco penitentiae*) and were proving most attractive to restless laity of the late eleventh and early twelfth centuries. The first crusade was to make its dramatic appeal to knights rather than to the crown heads of Europe.

Despite the substantial enlargement of opportunities for the expression of lay religious sentiment, Christianity was not realizable in its entirety by men and women engaged in the work of the secular world. The traditional tripartite division of society into clerics, knights, and peasants was almost sacrosanct. But this division of society into orders, temporal as well as ecclesiastical, in accordance with divine plan furnished neither religious nor sociological identity to important segments of the European population. City dwellers in general and merchants and bankers in particular could find little favor in the sight of God. But the list could be extended to artisans, professionals, women, and even nobility, whose spiritual aspirations were still not satisfied by their newly acquired status; there was a large clientele for whom this rigid tripartite scheme had limited appeal.[27]

Ivo of Chartres was a moderate among twelfth-century canonists, understanding clearly the archaism of a doctrine of the orders relegating the largest segment of laity to inferior status. Exceptional among latter-day Gregorian reformers, he acknowledged the validity of the spiritual aspirations of lay folk for religious dignity. He was respectful of the claims for autonomy in certain spheres of activity by the Levites of his time, who, like their Biblical forebears, tended the Temple of the Lord. He was the first prominent writer in five centuries to use the word *humanitas* in the classical sense. For almost half a millennium the term had been used pejoratively to signify the depths of human frailty and man's proclivity for sin. Ivo returned to the ancient meaning of philanthropy and kindness so that the word *humanus* again bore a positive connotation. Of course this delight in humanity was theologically oriented, with the grandeur of man depending upon the fulfillment of his divine vocation. If his calling was sacred, then the moral possibilities open to humankind were much amplified. Certainly, few cultivated writers of the twelfth century took a more generous and open view of human potential than did Ivo. He belonged to a school of clerical scholars teaching at Chartres who stressed the fact that man was created in the image and likeness of God. The emphasis of this school on human spiritual worth and achievement, though not novel in particulars, did represent the first sustained and programmatic effort to revise a radically pessimistic earlier view highlighting man's fall from spiritual dignity through the original sin committed by our ancestor Adam. The path of salvation had been illuminated exclusively by monastic ideals and the stern injunction to disvalue the possibility of achieving a meaningful spiritual life in the secular world.[28]

Ivo discussed matters seldom considered by canonists before the thirteenth century. He understood very well new forms of associative life and economic activity so vital to the urban scene. He observed that merchants did not operate exclusively as individuals; perhaps he was a century ahead of the legal discussions of his time in viewing the partnerships of merchants as a legitimate type of contract. Although the *societas* formed for profit did not carry high spiritual risk in Ivo's opinion, there were bounds to the confidence he was willing to extend to those venturing into this new society. His letters reveal anxieties provoked not so much by the base proclivities of merchants as by other menacing developments. It was not commerce and other laic involvements with the secular world that bothered him, for Ivo was not unsympathetic with much contemporary change. What he feared were the popular religious movements of his day, with their itinerant preachers and holy men, who disturbed the consciences of weak-willed men and women. So dangerous did he consider these wandering hermits and preachers that he believed only a "few solitaries" would be required to subvert the authority of Holy Mother Church. These extremists, with their probing into matters of faith and polemical disquisitions on spiritual questions, were sure to undermine the trust of simple and unlettered laity in the ministry of the Church. Comprehending little of the word of Christ and without a "crumb of intelligence," these sowers of discord preached pauperistic sermons vituperating against a hieratic church possessing enormous wealth. In the hearts of their listeners they aroused Utopian visions of apostolic times.[29]

Ivo and the school at Chartres recognized the potential of the laic order for achieving spiritual ends. The recovery of the classical meaning of the concept of *humanitas* gave evidence of a strengthening of the individual's ability to exhibit concern for the well-being of his fellows. Despite the emphasis on man's capacity for charity and compassion, a deep and abiding perception of his misery and weakness darkened the prospects for salvation. If indeed man was created in the image of God, still only the most tentative and rudimentary relationship could be discerned between this unique aspect of his nature and his fallen condition in the secular world. Ivo regarded the preachings of hermits and itinerants as kindling in men ideas threatening to the purity of faith and subversive to the structure of ecclesiastical institutions. We observe contradictory impulses at work: empathy for the religious aspirations of laity and sensitivity to their quest for dignity competing with recognition of the spiritual risks incurred in this tempestuous world. A desire to respect the efforts of the *ordo laicorum* in the divine economy of salvation was matched by an awareness of its susceptibility to the preachings of false prophets disseminating apostolic dreams and pauperistic ideals.[30]

Attacks against monasticism by the hermit Reginald evoked a polemical response from Ivo. The hermit sought to demonstrate his sanctity by rejecting even the stabilized poverty of the Benedictine house: "You know as well as I that cenobitic cloisters rarely or never include this standard of perfection . . . because they exclude as much as possible the poverty that Christ the pauper preached." This hermit, in conjunction with other itinerants, ignored the distinction between clergy and laity, going beyond the aims of the Gregorians. The role of laity had expanded considerably during the Gregorian era, with the spiritual status of the warrior elevated and lay folk enlisted in the work of reform. The same holy spirit inspiring the reform of the regular canons was now perceived to be at work among laity, whose communal life was modeled on the "distinguished pattern of the primitive church." Urban II sought to protect "an innumerable multitude of men and women including the unmarried and married" who were living the common life and being agitated against and mistreated. The canons were receiving these obedient laymen into the common life according to the customs of their communities. Ivo, like Urban II, drew inspiration from the reform of the canons: both laity and clergy would find virtue and spiritual strength in observant and settled communities. Moreover, reform should be directed toward subduing clerical avarice. Not only did the more radical proposals ignore the distinction between laity and clergy, but they would jettison an economic system. In responding to Reginald, Ivo took the Benedictine point of view, castigating all who would sponsor the eremitic life for the sin of spiritual pride. Lacking opportunities for performing acts of fraternal charity and benefiting from brotherly reprimands, the solitary hermit was all too prone to this sin.[31]

V

Attempts to limit the exemplary value of the life of Christ and distinguish a hieratic and juridical church from a Utopian reconstruction of the primitive church became increasingly difficult over the course of the twelfth century. Popular attention was focused on the historicity of the message of the Savior, and the idea of the imitation of Christ by laity and clergy alike worked to undermine the claims of a bureaucratized and legalistic church. The exemplary nature of the Redeemer was enthusiastically endorsed by the evangelism of popular religious movements, and even in learned monastic circles these views were finding new support. Interpretations of the incarnation were being revised, and,

as we have noted, St. Anselm rejected the view that its significance
rested in satisfying the claims of the devil. The teachings and example
of the life of Jesus demonstrated beyond question God's love for
mankind. The power of forgiveness was no longer presented as an
affront to justice. The idea of indulgence was beginning to express the
rich, untapped resources within the grasp of ordinary men and women.
Anselm captured the optimism and confidence of those times.[32]

The concept of Christ as ransom for the redemption of sinful humanity from thralldom to the devil was distanced, of course, from both
the letter and the spirit of the New Testament. However, it had not
been alien to a social world secured by tangible bonds nor to a mentality
committed to emphasizing the materiality of quotidian relationships.
Leading clerics, from Anselm to St. Bernard of Clairvaux, were to take
a more optimistic and liberating perspective. However generous Anselm's views, his language remained close to the archaic world of the
gift. For him it was certain that God loved a cheerful giver. He was
to compare man to a pearl that had been struck from God's hand by a
blow from Satan and fallen into the mud of sin. God would retrieve it
and cleanse it before storing it securely in the treasure house of His
heaven. The death of Christ was not itself payment of a debt but a gift:
"Reason has also taught us that the gift which He presents to God,
freely, not from debt, ought to be something greater than anything in
the possession of God." When Anselm countered the older view of
atonement, he opted for an understanding of God's justice highlighting
His mercy. Although this interpretation was distanced from the strict
justice implicit in the contemporary social code, still Anselm spoke
from a conservative monastic and feudal perspective. His imagery was
derived from a social order founded on subordination, obedience, and
complete submission:

> It was certainly proper that that atonement which Christ made should
> benefit not only those who lived at that time but also others. For, sup-
> pose there were a king against whom all the people of his provinces had
> rebelled, with but a single exception for those belonging to their race,
> and that all the rest were irretrievably under condemnation. And sup-
> pose that he who alone is blameless had so great favor with the king,
> and so deep love for us, as to be both able and willing to save all
> those who trusted in his guidance; and this because of a certain very
> pleasing service which he was about to do for the king, according to
> his desire; and, inasmuch as those who are to be pardoned cannot all
> assemble upon that day, the king grants, on account of the greatness
> of the service performed, that whoever, either before or after the day
> appointed, acknowledged that he wished to obtain pardon by the work
> that day accomplished, and to subscribe to the condition there laid

down, should be freed from all past guilt; and, if they sinned after this pardon, and yet wished to render atonement and to be set right again by the efficacy of this plan, they should again be pardoned, only provided that no one enter his mansion until this thing be accomplished by which his sins are removed. In like manner, since all who are to be saved cannot be present at the sacrifice of Cheiar, yet such virtue is there in his death that its power is extended even to those far remote in place or time.[33]

Although Anselm held the most advanced views on questions of language and theology, contributing mightily to the spiritual optimism of his times, he anxiously guarded God's honor against all violations. In conversation he was to maintain that God is like a great lord and the devil like his most bitter foe. The rules applying to God and Satan derived from the world of feudal obligation. What constituted sin was saying, doing, thinking, or even imagining anything not in perfect conformity with the will of God. Anselm was uncomfortable with the forces of change, both intellectual and social. His epistemological radicalism does not necessarily suggest that he was at ease in a world of controversy and transition. He was drawn into disputes and a defense of orthodoxy my Pope Urban II, and his later treatises, though reaching a far greater audience, lost much of that brilliant play of mind demonstrated in such early writings as the *Monologium* and the *Proslogium*.[34]

The canonist Anselm of Lucca used language similar to that of a pseudo-Augustinian canon when discussing the question of tithes: "For the Lord God demands not reward but honor." Gregory VII was to write that he despised money paid to the Church "without honor." Bitterly did he decry the fact that so few were willing to shed their blood in resisting the godless: "Just think of how many knights die for their lords for the sake of vile lucre. But what do we do or endure for the highest King?" The evils of feudal society were perceived as perverse, but this in no way caused the code of honor to lose its force. Moral strictures launched against society by such eloquent reformers as St. Bernard did not strike at the fundamentals of commercial exchange or the institutional structures of society. In reproaching the clergy and papacy, he expressed moral concerns, with invective directed toward avarice and pride rather than the settled world of religious community.

The progress envisioned by the reformers had limits. Most of the writings of the eleventh and twelfth centuries on the rejection of worldly values detailed the struggle against simony. Those tainted by this sin were prisoners of the flesh and the devil. Like Simon Magus (Acts 8:9–25), who went to Peter and offered him a sum of money in return for the gift of the Holy Ghost, these sinners were attempting

to acquire through gifts what in truth could be gained only as a consequence of a free act. This critique of wealth challenged the moral legitimacy of gift and countergift as a structural base for spiritual life.
Reform monasticism at Vallombrosa and Camaldoli required not only
that the brothers be poor but that the community itself be deprived of
wealth. Monastic life as a quintessentially communal experience was
challenged in favor of cultivation of the individual soul through prayer
and contemplation. Holy men struggled not only to practice sexual continence but to shatter "the bonds of bodily desire." Monastic communities were to be secured not so much through discipline, or even vows,
as by "sacred cords of charity" and "true spiritual friendship." The
pursuit of the holy was through the path of personal perfection, and it
permitted the individual to move beyond the narrow ties of an archaic
society. The sanctity of the holy man was confirmed through his renunciation of gifts, feuds, clan ties, and even the stability of traditional
Benedictine monasticism. Often he accepted the precarious status of an
itinerant or even, like the outlaw, wore the head of a wolf, but the
ultimate effect of his actions was to lead to the reform of cenobitic
monasticism. Although he dramatized ways in which the spiritually
qualified could renounce familiar networks of relationships to explore
new forms of social space, the result of his acts was not the creation of
legions of solitary ascetics. Great reformers of the early eleventh century, inspired by the first wave of eremitic idealism to strike western
Europe since antiquity, were to become, sometimes inadvertently, found-
ers of monastic communities. The highest ideals of the reform movement of the latter half of that century involved the implementation of
the common life for regular canons, and the consequences of this program brought increased stabilization. Yet, this equilibrium was not to
endure. Segments of the populace animated by evangelical visions and
searching for spiritual perfection were to disvalue this hard-earned
stability.[35]

VI

Within a generation after the death of Anselm of Aosta, theories of
redemption and atonement broke out of the feudal monastic matrix:
Christ had not come into the world to establish a just order broken by
sin, nor was He the ransom paid to Lucifer to placate his wrath against
humanity; instead, He was a man-God come into the world to demonstrate the power of love. His passion and death were no longer so likely
to be seen as blood sacrifices necessary because mankind had violated
the pact with God, but they were understood as the realization of His

love and were to be taken as a model for those aspiring to reach the glorious ecstasy of self-sacrifice. Again the power of emotion, moral autonomy, and individual responsibility were asserted in the face of traditional and narrow sensibilities. This more confident view was an endorsement of the force of love as opposed to the older, more punishing vision of redemption.[36]

As the life of Christ assumed greater authority, imitation of the primitive church became a call to collective action rather than a theme for solitary meditation. The Church as a juridical organism stood as an obstacle in the path of restoring the *vita apostolica*. The evangelical message challenged the legal justification of a church's holding vast patrimony. The first heretics in the West, about 1000 at both Arras and Monforte, held comparable views. As we have noted, they sought to imitate the Apostles, desiring to hold all goods in common. Spiritual devotion was to center upon prayer and the reading of Scripture. Rejecting sacraments mechanically administered, they repudiated ecclesiastical structure; emphasis was on the voluntary character of spiritual regeneration. The spokesman for the heretics of Monforte appealed to the peasants of the region who had grievances against the archbishop of Milan and oppressive landlords. The chronicler informs us that when the heretics were transported to Milan, they seized this opportunity to make converts to their faith and "behaved as though they were good priests, and daily spread false teachings wrenched from the Scriptures among the peasants who came to the town to see them." At mid-eleventh century Arialdo, son of a small, landed proprietor and deacon in the *contado* of Milan, directed his first appeal for reform of the Church to clergy of rural parishes. When this attempt failed, he commenced delivering sermons to rustics of the area. Once inside the city of Milan, he extended his call for renewal of the Church to include the many who had been denied dignity and status within the Ambrosian church for so long. Illiterate as well as literate, peasant as well as landlord, and of course urban artisans and workers, all came to appreciate that the teachings of Arialdo were "both true and useful."[37]

The Patarines elevated the status of laity, who then became active participants in movements to reorganize the Church. In Florence, Vallombrosans were militant in their commitment to engage the masses in the struggle for reform. Energetic involvement by laity went far beyond the passive role prescribed by Roman councils of abstention from services conducted by simoniac and concubinary clergy. The Patarines did not aim to put in place a hierarchy based on merit, yet just such a prospect was present in the popular conscience. However, at the same time, overzealous clergy were subject to ecclesiastical censure; revolutionary appeals to laity contradicted the exemplary and prophetic functions traditionally ascribed to venerated monks and hermits. Seditious clerics were reproved because they were willing to debate any issue in public— even calling into question the sanctity of popes Leo and Gregory the Great. Under the leadership of the Patarines the populace of Milan and Florence became enraged against the hieratic church, even to the point of sitting in judgment on errant clergy. That the monastery was no longer an island of peace and prayer was sorely lamented; reforming monks were accused of being locusts intent on devouring the green pastures of the Church, and the prediction was made that they would be drowned like the Egyptians in the Red Sea. By the end of the eleventh century the Patarines were perceived as latter-day Donatists, who were instructing faithful and simple folk to reject the sacramental offering of a priest in sin. Vallombrosans, who led the battles for reform, preaching so effectively in the cities, were now forced by Rome to remain in the cloister and to obey church hierarchy irrespective of merit. Itinerant preaching, which had received such encouragement in the time of Gregory VII, was now regarded as dangerous and subversive. Church councils acted to protect instruments of cult, setting up norms and prohibitions against laic associative life.[38]

Bitter polemics had been directed against wealth, with pauperistic choice and renunciation of the world judged essential to all who would exercise a spiritually valid pastoral role. However, during the Gregorian period the choice of poverty was not institutional but personal. Reformers sought to recover church property (*res ecclesiae*) and ensure ecclesiastical liberty (*libertas ecclesiae*). Wealth and land belonging to the Church were inalienable and an integral part of "the body of Christ" (*corpus Christi*). Change was to be sponsored within the framework of a social order in which territorial stability and hieratic organization were the primary coordinates. The dilemma of a judicial church maintaining its structure in the face of movements and sensibilities nourished by evangelical aspirations was generating serious tensions: could the authority of the Church be grounded in the history of salvation, or was its legitimacy to be based exclusively on the example and life of Christ? Already in the Italian towns of the late eleventh century the call was for a return to the evangelical church. The invective was fierce against the acceptance of gifts in return for spiritual benefits. Even among the most orthodox reformers contradictions were apparent between their ambition to conquer and govern the secular world on the one hand and to disparage and renounce it on the other. Lack of feeling for the exigencies of secular power was matched by disbelief in the possibility of realizing any substantial part of the Christian message

through the agencies and instrumentalities of this world. The fundamental incompatibility of the message of Christ with the general direction taken by society undermined traditional notions of politics. The
new monasticism had insisted upon contradictions, dilemmas, and radical action: it was Christ or the world. Little effort was expended on
reconciling tragic discrepancies between the teachings of the Gospel
and the historical development of society.[39]

VII

Eleventh-century religious ferment centered upon simony and severing literal ties between church and society. The archaic culture of gift
and countergift and the materiality of systems of exchange, both economic and spiritual, came under scrutiny. Political rhetoric grew more
strident and extravagant as attacks by clerics against rulers and secular
institutions were being elaborated in fiery detail. The scaling down of
imperial prerogatives was part of a process of desacralization of the
political order begun at mid-eleventh century. Attempts to strip rulers
of their sanctity were matched by efforts on the part of secular spokesmen to force the papacy out of politics. Reformers eager to divest the
emperor of supernatural power were inadvertently contributing to the
recognition of the autonomy of the temporal sphere. Religious culture
was becoming more technical and complex, losing its capacity to formulate issues posed by societal development. The role of the Church as a
decisive presence in history was most problematic. In 1111, when Pope
Pascal II, who had been a Camaldolese monk, made the proposal to
Henry V that the Church give up the regalia and live on its offerings
and tithes (Convention of Sutri), he was attempting to realize the vision of a spiritual church (*ecclesia spiritualis*). The emperor accepted
the generous terms with one significant reservation: that this "trans-
mutatio" be corroborated "by the opinion and the accord of all the
Church"; he knew well that this would not happen. Of course, history
was to prove his skepticism well founded. The opposition between empire and church had generated such an extreme tension that release was
possible only through the projection of Utopian visions of apostolic
poverty. The political alternatives of compromise between *regnum* and
sacerdotium or the continuation of terrible wars lent little reassurance
to those in search of a Christian presence in the world.[40]

Twelfth-century holy men, such as Arnold of Brescia, demonstrated
a resolute commitment to apostolic ideals and ascetic practices. Like his
forebears of the preceding century, Arnold strived for victory over the
carnal self by leading a life of poverty and chastity. His most implacable

enemies—and there were many—freely admitted that his personal life was pure and blameless. Wandering over vast regions of Italy, France, and Switzerland, he demonstrated a talent for moving beyond the world of orders, pledges, and vows. John of Salisbury tells us that when he taught *divinas letteras* to poor scholars in Paris, they "begged from door-to-door to maintain themselves." Arnold attacked the bishops for their avarice and pride, for they "professed to build the Church of God on blood." His pursuit of holiness was preliminary to his radical involvement in the religious and civic conflicts of his age. Though his Brescian origins are obscure, he probably was a minor noble and prior of a community of regular canons in his natal city. From the first he "mortified his flesh with fasting and coarse raiment" and made fervent appeals to laity for church reform. So successful was he at Brescia that the citizens were able to prevent the "corrupt" bishop, who had momentarily absented himself, from reentering the town. In preaching to laity Arnold "said things that were entirely consistent with the law accepted by the Christian people but not with the life they led." His denunciation of the vanities of the world and his deeds of spiritual valor were in fact familiar ingredients in the lives of holy men. His espousal of apostolic poverty caused his life to be reckoned "sweet as honey." But unlike his forebears, he had the ability to translate these holy impulses into political alternatives.[41]

This austere preacher against earthly blandishments understood quite well the contradiction between the world of apostolic poverty, before the Church was burdened with great wealth, and the present corrupt times. His response was one of immediacy in which he proved attentive to the drama of everyday life and the political ambitions of his contemporaries:

> Whilst dwelling in Rome under pretext of penance he won the city to his side, and preaching all the more freely because the lord pope was occupied in Gaul he built up a faction known as the heretical sect of the Lombards. He had disciples who imitated his austerities and won favour with the populace through outward decency and austerity of life, but found their chief supporters amongst pious women. He himself was frequently heard on the Capitol and in public gatherings. He had already publicly denounced the cardinals, saying that their college, by its pride, avarice, hypocrisy and manifold shame was not the Church of God, but a place of business and den of thieves, which took the place of the scribes and Pharisees amongst Christian peoples. The pope himself was not what he professed to be—an apostolic man and shepherd of souls—but a man of blood who maintained his authority by fire and sword, a tormentor of churches and oppressor of the innocent, who did nothing in the world save gratify his lust

and empty other men's coffers to fill his own. He was, he said, so far from apostolic that he imitated neither the life nor the doctrine of the apostles, wherefore neither obedience nor reverence was due to him: and in any case, no man could be admitted who wished to impose a yoke of servitude on Rome, the seat of empire, fountain of liberty and mistress of the world.[42]

Arnold had had a stormy career as critic of church hierarchy in his native Brescia. Exiled from Italy on this account by the pope shortly after the Lateran Council of 1139, he went to France, where he championed the cause of Peter Abelard, with whom he may have studied as a young man. When Abelard was condemned at the Council of Sens, Arnold journeyed to Paris to teach "the Scriptures to scholars at the Church of St. Hilary where Peter [Abelard] had lodged." Perhaps he and his impoverished students shared with the French philosopher a moral and evangelical view of Christianity; this outlook, based on those practices authenticated by the life of Christ, in turn may have threatened any clerical or aristocratic monopoly of religious truth. Incurring the enmity of the powerful St. Bernard of Clairvaux, Arnold again fled into exile; this time he entered Switzerland, betaking himself to the strife-torn diocese of Constance. A bitter contest for church reform was in progress in the city of Zurich, and Arnold joined the battle. Apparently, he encouraged the intervention of the strongest and best-armed citizens (*potentes et milites*) in the religious struggles for the purpose of enforcing poverty on ecclesiastical hierarchy: again his fate was banishment. His stormy career continued until a reconciliation was effected between the fugitive and the new pope Eugenius III at Viterbo, probably in 1146. The pope was a moderate who had dealt with communities of regular canons espousing pauperistic ideals against the bishop of Milan. His resolution of such tense problems was influenced by his recognition of the Church's need for good preaching; he was not eager to alienate talented clerics. In 1147 Arnold, with papal permission and after taking a vow of public silence, entered the city of Rome as a penitent. The city had been in revolt since the early 1140s: a commune had been sworn to, and in 1144 the *renovatio* of the Roman senate took place. The office of prefect, controlled by the pontiff, was abolished, and in its stead a leader of the government (*patricius*) was appointed by the senate. This revolution did not aim for control of the papal throne, as in past insurrections, but, animated by dreams of ancient Roman glory, sought to realize political autonomy. St. Bernard called the Romans vulgar and filthy, noting that they had learned to boast of their lost grandeur but that in fact they were capable of only trivial undertakings.

Hollow or not, pride in Rome's pagan legacy was at the base of the best and most popular cultural endeavors of the day. Immediately after the pope departed from Italy for France, Arnold broke his vow of silence, appealing to the Roman populace and then to the emperor. The ascetic preacher believed that in order to preserve the spiritual authority of the Church, it would be necessary to curtail its temporal power: the Romans must save the Church from its own corruption. The Holy Spirit worked in historical time through earthly agencies to purge Mother Church of all vice. Wenzel, a supporter of Arnold, perhaps from his days in the diocese of Constance, may have joined him at Rome out of sympathy for his cause. The learned Wenzel wrote to Frederick Barbarosa on the eve of his election as king of the Romans (9 March 1152) exhorting him to recall the ancient political and juridical traditions of early Rome and to impose strict limits on clergy. Knowledgeable about the law, Wenzel denied the authenticity of the Donation of Constantine, presenting numerous citations from the Gospels and church fathers to support the enforcement of pauperistic choice on the Church by the king of the Romans.[43]

VIII

St. Bernard saw Arnold as an overproud reformer, dangerous because of his austere life and powers of persuasion; Arnold influenced simple, unlettered men and women sorely in need of guidance from the Church. John of Salisbury, writing shortly after events in Rome (1164), established the *cursus honorum* of Arnold's preaching from the initial formation of small groups to the spread of his reputation throughout the Eternal City. From ascetic reformer, intent on converting citizenry to the apostolic life, he moved into the arena of politics. His major crime was that he sowed sedition among the populace. Addressing them on the Campidoglio, he was to speak ever more directly, articulating his revolutionary message most clearly (*iam palam*). The chronicler and uncle of the German emperor, Otto, bishop of Freising, portrayed Arnold as "a disparager of the clergy and of bishops, a persecutor of monks, *a flatterer only of the laity*. For he used to say that neither clerics that owned property, nor bishops that had regalia, nor monks with possessions could in any wise be saved. All these things belong to the prince, and should be bestowed of his beneficence for the use of laity only."[44]

Otto, like many other well-informed observers of the Italian civic scene, found that "virtually the entire land is divided among cities" and "scarcely any noble or great man can be found in all the surrounding territory who does not acknowledge the authority of his city." The chronicler then argued that the wealth of the Italian cities fed their appetite for autonomy and liberty: "They are governed by the will of consuls rather than rulers." The social consequences of communal politics were formidable: "In order that they may not lack the means of subduing their neighbors, they do not disdain to give the girdle of knighthood or the grades of distinction to young men of inferior station [*juvenes inferioris conditionis*] and even workers from the lowest mechanical crafts [*opifices mechanicarum artium*] whom other people bar like the plague from the more respected and notable pursuits." Other foreign commentators called the attention of their readers to town education in Italy, "where all youths are sent to sweat in school," comparing the advanced state of lay education in those cities with that in Germany, where "people deem it useless or base to instruct anyone unless he is a clerk." The continuator of Otto's chronicle was astonished at the skill and delight of Italian townsmen in oratory and public debate. The cities were to become centers for the study of that most public of all arts, rhetoric. In Florence at mid-twelfth century we have an anonymous handbook (*dictamen*) containing a model of a letter suggesting the most effective modes of persuading a community to raise a contingent of knights and foot soldiers. Over the next years manuals for the instruction of citizen-magistrates and handbooks providing model orations for communal councilors were to be a prominent literary genre. The study of rhetoric in the twelfth and early thirteenth centuries in Italian cities was now an intrinsic part of public life.[45]

Communal movements for religious reform can be traced back to the eleventh century; religious symbolism, of course, was regularly being invoked to achieve the spiritual pacification of warring parties in the Italian towns. As early as the eleventh century, the veneration of the Holy Cross at Lucca was connected with promoting civic harmony. In this same period communes inaugurated the use of a special cart for bearing their standards into battle. The earliest documented appearance of the *carroccio* was at Milan in 1037, when Archbishop Ariberto had constructed "a high wooden pole like the mast of a ship which was fixed to a strong wagon; at the top was a gilded apple and from this descended two ribbons of dazzling white cloth, and in the center a holy cross was painted with our Saviour portrayed, His arms extended." Soon this practice became widespread, and the elite troops of Parma, Bologna, and Florence fought under the religious banner. Sacred imagery became more elaborate as the *carroccio* took first place in civic ceremony. Patron saints of the towns became more active and dynamic; no longer were they perceived as defensive and apotropaic figures. Meanwhile, religious dissent led more often to political insurrection. Clearly, the citizenry of Italian towns were active in religious causes, and these causes, in turn, were assuming a great civic and public dimension.[46]

Spiritual leaders in the late tenth and early eleventh centuries had portrayed church and society as weighed down by sins of such magnitude that it would hardly be possible to revitalize Christianity by resorting to contemporary values and agencies. Society was perceived as distanced from the norms of a sacred past, and surely the observation was far from naive. The Italian cities, with their heightened social mobility, new wealth, far-flung trade, and elaborate credit operations, stood as a tangible reminder of the disparity between an archaic society and the world brought into being by a commercial revolution. It was not easy, either, to furnish a rationale for an urban society where wealth was acquired through charging interest rather than as a reward for faithful service and virtuous deeds. The literature of the eleventh century was obsessed with the theme of avarice, projecting the view that it was this vice above all others that differentiated the sordid present from the purity of an Arcadian past. Only with the eleventh century do we find the theme of the restoration of the primitive Church achieving currency; seldom was it referred to in the literature of the tenth century.

If the takeoff was distancing townsmen from Christian imperatives and the noble values of an archaic society, their newly acquired wealth and status were conferring exceptional dignity on their persons and enduring value on their secular achievements. Further, this laity had become active participants in the great religious and political struggles of the Gregorian age. In many regions of Italy ecclesiastical art demonstrated an aptitude for bringing the spiritualities closer to everyday life. Saints were now depicted in frescoes as having a "special appeal for the populace at large since they gave timely help in the hour of peril." At Milan and Florence we observe the intensity with which the populace struggled to bring the teachings of Christ close to daily experience. The effort to allow the truth of the Gospel to permeate the social and political structure of the community was gaining strength over the twelfth century. At the time of the Gregorian reforms appeals to *ecclesia primitive* were made to further monastic and canonical changes; the ideal of the common life was sought as either a basis for the office of preacher or an end in itself. By the twelfth century, however, the evangelical vision, no longer exclusively a monastic ideal, was inspiring the quest for the "right order" in politics as well as in personal life.[47]

A laity whose activities distanced them from the values of apostolic times and who yet remained conscious of their spiritual dignity and the worth of secular achievement occupied a paradoxical position. Arnold of Brescia, "a priest by office, a canon regular by profession, and one who had mortified his flesh with fasting and coarse raiment," had entered Rome as a penitent eager to perform fasts, vigils, and prayers. It was this ascetic's quest for evangelical perfection, rather than proclamations of theological doctrine, that galvanized his supporters into action. The call for repentance was linked with a summons to battle for the rejuvenation of contemporary institutions. The apostolic spirit was to work through earthly agencies:

> He set forth the examples of the ancient Romans, who by virtue of the ripened judgment of the senate and the disciplined integrity of the valiant spirit of youth made the whole world their own. Wherefore he advocated that the Capitol should be rebuilt, the senatorial dignity restored, and the equestrian order reinstituted. Nothing in the administration of the City was the concern of the Roman pontiff; the ecclesiastical courts should be enough for him. Moreover, the menace of this baneful doctrine began to grow so strong that not only were the houses and splendid palaces of Roman nobles and cardinals being destroyed, but even the reverend persons of some of the cardinals were shamefully treated by the infuriated populace, and several were wounded. Although he incessantly and irreverently perpetrated these things and others like them for many days (that is, from the death of Celestine until this time) and despised the judgment of the pastors, justly and canonically pronounced against him, as though in his opinion they were void of all authority, at last he fell into the hands of certain men and was taken captive within the limits of Tuscany. He was held for trial by the prince and finally was brought to the pyre by the prefect of the City. After his corpse had been reduced to ashes in the fire, it was scattered on the Tiber lest his body be held in veneration by the mad populace.[48]

From the eleventh century on, the quest for spiritual perfection pervaded the civic and religious life of the towns in north and central Italy. At first it was associated with church reform and its possibilities limited to monk and priest. By the twelfth century, however, its potential extended to laity seeking to live an authentic Christian life while still honoring their terrestrial obligations. Such a laity, beneficiaries of new wealth and enhanced status, had become increasingly confident and detached from a feudal society with its archaic economy. Yet, withal, townsmen continued to be apprehensive about the very changes that had yielded such progress. Otto of Freising was candid in his melancholy: "I do not really know whether the current prosperous condition of the church is more pleasing to God than its earlier humility. The earlier condition was perhaps better, but the present more agreeable." Townspeople were attracted in greater numbers to the idea that poverty was the only legitimate condition of the Church in this world. For the spiritually minded, poverty represented liberation from the temporal security of a tribal world as well as rejection of the vanity and cupidity of the domain of the new. The very advances of economy and society in the eleventh and twelfth centuries not only instilled confidence in Italian townsmen but were a source of spiritual preoccupation. Greater faith in the power of temporal agencies working toward a renewal of society was rivalled by a heightened sensitivity to the distress of sinners and the evils of competition. An improvement in the status of laity and a strengthening of structures of government were undeniable, but so, too, was a democratization of the quest for evangelical perfection, in which penance and the penitential achieved exceptional urgency.[49]

Faith in the dignity of the individual and the worth of laic culture was then sustained by a paradoxical spirituality: concern for the world was exhibited in programs whose first steps involved renunciation and penance. Those most sensitive to the imperatives of charity were exhorted to share the joys and sufferings of Christ. His passion was no longer remote to laity; the discovery of the apostolic life of the early Church was depriving monasticism of its traditional primacy. The penitential life was extended far beyond the bounds of religious orders into the world of the everyday. Flagellation, once the preserve of heroic ascetics, was soon to become a popular ritual. Laity were continually reminded of their sinfulness, but this reminder led not to self-abasement and meaningless mortification of the flesh but to programs of self-renewal and collective regeneration. Evangelical principles supported a break with an ancient realm in which the gift, the benefice, the oath, and even the feudal glamor of liturgy were to be renounced in favor of fraternal ties and more abstract bonds of association. Manual labor was to be valued more than lavish display or liturgical pomp. As the norms of society became more impartial and judicial, the need for collective ideals heightened; a belief in the power of love, charity, and brotherhood found new forms in the guild, the confraternity, the festival, and philanthropic enterprise.

In the eleventh century the quest for evangelical perfection produced moral dissent, by the twelfth century it was assuming revolutionary immediacy, and by the thirteenth century it was being vividly projected as a base for the construction of community. The holy man was to celebrate the spiritual and material benefits accruing to townsmen through realization of a total fraternization. These gifted improvisers, addicted to the spontaneous, conferred luster on the grace of God by formulating terrestrial visions of loving solidarity. These fraternal ties, with their lively sense of equality, were to replace the mechanical and literal bonds of an ancient regime. The holy man dramatized social responsibility by tending to the urban poor and ill: no longer was he so closely associated with the relic, nor was he so likely to be perceived as an icon. Instead he had become an active spiritual force in the community, and society would be sanctioned from within. In the eleventh century the *vita apostolica* was the preserve of monks living in common and possessing no property of their own. A hundred years later this *vita* united the itinerant preacher with the poor. In the older Benedictine community the monastery was a place of sanctification. *Caritas* was to be realized fully among its members, and thus would the celestial Jerusalem be anticipated. The monastery was inserted in a world of wealth and feudal obligation; now the limits of community were extended, and the sense of fraternity came to encompass laity. Finally, those living in orders were more willing to embrace risk and insecurity.[50]

IX

An appreciation for the complex texture of change in the twelfth century was eloquently voiced by Gerhoh of Reichersberg, a fellow regular canon of Arnold of Brescia. Deeply deploring Arnold's execution, he blamed the Roman clergy for not having impeded this dastardly act: they had forgotten their Lord Jesus Christ, who was so gentle and humble of heart. Gerhoh knew well that Christian society was at the crossroads, and he was sympathetic to the spiritual aspirations of laity: "Judges, knights, tax collectors, merchants, and peasants [who] follow the apostolic rule. . . . Whether rich or poor, noble or serf, merchant or peasant, all who are committed to the Christian faith reject everything inimical to this name and embrace everything conformable to it. Every order and absolutely every profession, in the Catholic faith and according to apostolic teaching, has a rule adapted to its character; and under this rule it is possible by striving properly to achieve the crown of glory."[51]

Himself a moderate in matters of church reform, Gerhoh still saw Christian value in the apostolic way for laity from every walk of life. Such lay folk, however, lived in a society soon to undergo terrible trials. Indeed, this was the age of the Fourth Night Watch and had been initiated by the Gregorian reforms. These tempests had already transpired, and the fourth was raging fiercely: the first was the age of the martyrs, the second that of heresies, and the third the corruption of morals begun with the Donation of Constantine. The present age, inaugurated by the bitter controversies between pope and emperor, was the age of avarice, and the forces of the Antichrist ravaged the world as a consequence of the immediate dislocation of all forms of social life. Gerhoh's eschatology turned from the problem of exploring the world at the end of time to researches into the forms that evil would assume when manifesting itself in history. He projected a vision of the Antichrist's having deep social roots. Two of the great sins of his century were, of course, simony and concubinage. Prelates sought to increase their wealth and to distribute it among the knights, forgetting that Christ had entrusted them with riches in order to minister to the poor. Avarice and corruption tempted the best in all social orders, and the risks of spiritual life were increased for laity in almost direct proportion to its opportunities. Hostile to the feudalization of the Church, yet he understood her dilemma: without wealth she would not be free to minister to the poor. Sympathetic to the spiritual aspirations of laity, yet he confronted them with negative and malevolent forces rooted in the history of the times.[52]

The decline of eschatological tensions in twelfth-century monastic spirituality appears related to the higher evaluation accorded terrestrial experience. The attention devoted to the reform of contemporary society diminished the preoccupation with those distant events of the final days before the advent of the Last Judgment. Late in the century Joachim, abbot of the Cistercian monastery of Curazzo in Calabria and founder of the new monastic order of Fiore, took up the Augustinian concept of providence, endowing it with exceptional precision. Through intricate calculations he fixed the character and duration of the ages of history. When he meditated on the correspondence of each of the three historical periods to a figure of the Trinity, his speculations achieved the status of a philosophy. The social dimension of his thought was evidenced in his elaborate attempts to prove that the associative life of man was itself subject to successive interventions of the divine. These epiphanies, intelligible and occurring in sequence, interacted with dominant forms of social organization to alter human relationships dramatically. The present was a time of heretical preaching, and the Patarines —Joachim's generic term for all heretics—were the beast of the Apocalypse "rising from earth." Signs of divine wrath were visible everywhere: discord severed the bonds of community, setting neighbor against neighbor and brother against brother.[53]

4

Toward Acceptance of the Problematic and Ambiguous

ARNOLD OF BRESCIA had come to Rome as a penitent, inspiring his followers to seek the apostolic life. He had called for a renewal of self and society, presenting a vision of secular life free from irreconcilable and tragic contradiction. By divesting the Church of wealth and worldly power, one would recover a lost innocence. Pauperistic and penitential impulses had been part of the fabric of political and religious life in north and central Italy since the early eleventh century. The charismatic German emperor Otto III had spiritual ties with Romualdo and Nilo; the monarch's heart was heavy with guilt, for he believed himself to be the perpetrator of heinous crimes. His confession to Romualdo and his visit to St. Nilo only deepened his spiritual anguish. What commenced as a private affliction of a penitent sinner was now extended to encompass universal aspirations for the renewal of the True Faith. His life became a religious odyssey as he assumed spiritual responsibility for the Christian republic. His grandiose schemes for elevating the empire into a realm of pure spirituality captured the imaginations of leading churchmen in eleventh-century Italy. Penitential sentiment was at the heart of so many of the religious projects of the day; the pilgrimage, a laic religious practice, was, of course, penitential in inspiration and was achieving immense popularity. Crusading was also penitential, and descriptions of the crusades, with their massacres, conquests, and booty, were couched in traditional terms of exile, renunciation, and flight from the world. Such a penitential perspective bore little resemblance to the events themselves but was consonant with the subjective mode in which the events were experienced. Care and concern for the world was frequently expressed in ideologies and movements that, at the level of theory, involved the principle of renunciation.[1]

An older regimen of fixed and prolonged penance explicitly codified in the penitentials was being replaced by a new program of redemptions. Tariffs and penalties, literally understood, were slowly receding before the onset of a voluntaristic system. The individual was expected to be responsible for his own transgressions; penance was to be undertaken directly by the sinner and was not to be assigned to a third party. Long and wrenching penalties gave way to more manageable punishments. In the penitential process the quintessential element was displaced from the act of expiation to the moment of confession. Soon the sacrament of penance would be designated under "confession." Recognition of the sin as an offense against God was more important than satisfaction of the penalty.[2]

I

In the eleventh century the term employed to signify the ideal of perfection for laity was *poenitentia*, a term whose usage was very different from that familiar to spiritual leaders of a former time, such as Gregory the Great and St. Colombano. We have already observed that when laity acquired spiritual dignity, the road to an authentic Christian life was opened to those from *ordo bonorum coniugatorum*. Soon they were to become "brothers and sisters who do penance." Zeal for the evangelical life was quickening, and the spiritualities were becoming accessible to a laity eager to engage in voluntary penance. By the close of the twelfth century taking vows of perpetual continence was no longer obligatory; many of the "laicus ordinis fratrum de poenitentia" probably continued to have conjugal relations, observing continence only during times of fasting and on holy days. The question devout laity put before the companions of St. Francis was both central and vexing: we have wives we are unable to leave; can you teach us, then, what road we can take to salvation? According to the *anonimo* of Perugia, the audience for early Franciscan preachers was dumbstruck when hearing of the spiritual possibilities open to married laity. So stunned were they by these pronouncements that they requested that the consoling message be repeated several times.[3]

In Tommaso da Celano's *Vita prima*, written in 1228, only two years after the death of Francis, the biographer portrayed the saint as warmly endorsing the idea that laity could remain in this world honoring their marriage vows and doing the world's work yet follow the penitential life. As we have noted, groups of penitents had been living either singly or in family communities well before the time of Francis, and the Franciscan rule for the Third Order was an adaptation of earlier provisions governing confraternal life. The saint and his companions certainly did not originate the idea, but they did much to popularize it—even to launch it among lay folk. Francis was the leading figure in advancing the belief that it was truly possible for brothers and sisters outside monastic orders to lead a penitential life. The Dominicans were to look to the Franciscan Brothers and Sisters of Penance as a model for their penitential fraternities. Francis, expanding the conception of the religious life, offered an elementary proposal for a coherent Christianity for all of society—that is, for all those outside the canonically constituted structure. Such a program did indeed complete the circle: laity were now endowed with sufficient spiritual worth that they could lead a life pleasing in the sight of God outside the world of hierarchy, vows, and orders. The holy man had invested laic life with a religious value that would permit laity to step outside the world of literal and concrete ties with an assurance that they would not fall out of being or succumb to omnipotent, malevolent forces.[4]

Those voluntarily assuming the penitential life, as we have seen, were designated "conversi" and "conversae." In earlier times the expectation tended to be that penitents would make a radical break with the everyday world. The great interest demonstrated in penance by such writers as the Venerable Bede, Jonas of Orleans, and the Pseudo-Augustine was strongly inspired by monastic custom, with trivial faults called to account. Germanic laws (*leges barbarorum*) were influential, of course, in establishing scales for damages in penitential books. Intended for the guidance of confessors, these tracts were for the most part juridical and legal in their approach to sin. The penalties differed according to the status of the transgressor and were codified mechanistically. Penance tended to be public, and it was only with the arrival of the twelfth century that this practice became the exception. Stern renunciations of former times were gradually replaced by less literal, more individualized penalties. Gratian's discussion of "solemn penance" (*poenitentia solemnis*) at mid-twelfth century lent weight to the requirement of private penance for private sins. In this he was continuing the researches of such eminent figures as Anselm of Lucca and others who were transforming the idea of the penitential. In the twelfth and thirteenth centuries, discussions of the sacramental effects of penance were rich and textured; its objectives were shifting from reconciliation with the Church to reconciliation with God. In Tuscany harsh public penance continued but was exceptional and meted out only for public crimes. Again we observe the transformation of practices once materially understood and concretely realized into more abstract and psychologically oriented forms of behavior. Inner repentance gained authority; the celebration of Mary Magdalen became increasingly popular in Tuscany, as did the desire to assimilate the expiatory and salvational experiences of Christ. Penance was being converted into sentiment and feeling; in turn these emotions were being extended to encompass the wider society.[5]

Confraternities in Tuscany commenced to proscribe lewdness, gambling, abusive language, and, above all, the practice of usury. The term *conversio* conveyed the idea of the restitution of ill-got gains and the payment of all just debts. We have already noted that religious brotherhoods were, in the first instance, cultic associations or professional societies; they assumed the role of a beneficent sodality, often managing hospitals. These philanthropic services increased in the thirteenth century as the notion of mutual aid in imitation of Christ grew more compelling. Brothers visited the sick, cared for their families, prayed, and sang psalms in memory of the departed in a quest for religious perfection. Most telling was the assumption of collective responsibility by confraternities, which now acted as guarantors, going surety for debtors and those in trouble with the law. As has been mentioned, penance, the sacrament of reconciliation, formerly had as its principal objective the restoration of damaged relations between the sinner and the Church. Scholastics of the twelfth and thirteenth centuries saw this sacrament as restoring the sinner to God. In the Italian cities, however, this reparation had acquired an ineradicable social dimension. Confraternities were becoming deeply implicated in the repair of tense relations between neighbors and the resolution of bitter conflicts between politically antagonistic factions. By the thirteenth century these laic societies were assuming political and even paramilitary functions in the community. The civic character of the confraternity was evident in the system of voting and representation, which duplicated the procedures of communal government. Conversely, the spiritual derivation of secular government was apparent likewise. The chronicler Giovanni Villani tells us that the head magistrates of the Florentine republic assumed the name "prior" because they were "the first, chosen over the others; and it is taken from the Holy Gospel, where Christ says to His disciples, 'Vos estis priores.' "[6]

II

Increasingly over the thirteenth century expiation of sin was understood as a dramatic imperative and one that concerned all of Christendom. The perspective was eschatological, involving, as it did, the spiritual destiny of the collectivity. Expiation was frequently seen as a general problem concerning citizenry living in a society convulsed by factionalism, competition, and civic violence. The sensation of an imminent transformation of values fueled the anxieties and hopes of the crowd. The prophesies of Joachim of Fiore were widely disseminated and laicized. His ideals penetrated the world; a monastic order of five oratories would be founded, each of a different degree of severity. Included would be the oratory of the married laity (*conjugati*), living the common life with family and having intercourse for the purpose of procreating children rather than from libidinousness. The Calabrian abbot believed that the agencies required "to bring the church through the transition period must be human, albeit divinely commissioned and inspired." The transition from "the time of troubles" to "the age of the holy spirit" would be accomplished in historical time. Moreover, leadership would devolve upon "new spiritual men," who, in Joachim's vision, surely resembled those groups desiring to "express their commitment in terms of service within the secular order."[7]

In the thirteenth century confraternities and flagellant societies were multiplying. Further, they were becoming active participants in the ideological struggles convulsing communal society. Leading confraternities assumed paramilitary functions in prosecuting heretics. Enlisting behind the papal banner, they fought for the cause of Guelfism. In January of 1246, during the war with Frederick II, when the city of Florence was ruled by Ghibellines, the pope exhorted the penitential brotherhoods of the city to work assiduously for peace and unity within the community. Of course this implied that a pacified town would be restored to obedience to Holy Mother Church. Confraternities carried standards, wore the cross, and enjoyed the honors of knighthood as they fought at the side of the Tuscan inquisitor. Companies associated with Peter Martyr (Pietro da Verona) fought against Ghibelline miscreants in the streets of Florence and its *contado*. Heretical Cathars of Florence sided with the messianic personage of the Holy Roman Emperor in the civil wars of those turbulent years.[8]

Popular religious movements over the thirteenth century took on a public character and were animated by collective purposes. The great penitential movement of 1260, originating in Umbria and then making its way north into Tuscany, Lombardy, and Liguria, aimed to transform a civic world rent by fratricidal factionalism into a domain of peace and concord. The flagellants, who marched through city and countryside free from ecclesiastical authority, dramatized millennial aspirations for the onset of an age of fraternity and love when neighbors would forgive each other their debts and trespasses, when usurers would make restitution of ill-got gains, when women of disrepute

would vow chastity, and when all would exchange the olive branch and
kiss of peace. This public expression of social hope in many respects replicated the Great Alleluia of 1233, witnessed by Franciscan chronicler
Salimbene. He well remembered how, as a boy in his native Parma, he
had marveled at the reconciliations between sinful and factious citizens
who, in the name of charity and love, acted to reconstitute the fragile
bonds of community. The Franciscan described the populace as becoming "drunk with heavenly joy":

> This Alleluia, which lasted for an entire season, was a time of peace
> and quiet during which all weapons were put aside; a time of merri-
> ment and happiness, of joy and exultation, of praise and rejoicing.
> And men chanted hymns in praise of God; kind and simple town and
> country people, young men and women, old and young with but a
> single will. This devotion was celebrated in all the cities of Italy; and
> people came from villages to the town with great banners in droves;
> men and women, lads and maidens assembling together to hear the
> preaching and praise the Lord. . . . And men held stations in the
> churches and squares, and raised up their hands to the Lord to praise
> and bless Him unto eternity; and they would not desist from praising
> the Lord, so inebriated were they with His love; and blessed was he
> who did most to praise the Lord. No anger was among them, no
> trouble nor hatred, but all was done in peace and kindness; for they
> had drunk of the wine of God's sweet spirit, of which if a man drink,
> things of the flesh have no more savor for him.[9]

Expressions of collective sentiment by spiritually minded laity are recorded and explicated as far back as the eleventh century. Gerardo of
Monforte had explained to the archbishop of Milan, "We hold all our
possessions in common with all men." Restitution of the fruits of avarice was an essential step on the road to *conversion*; renunciation of
wealth was yet another. Vows of voluntary poverty and identification
with *pauperes* implied empathy for the powerless, who were not always
marked by extreme poverty. God was bringing forth "new spiritual
men," who were destined to destroy avarice by embracing voluntary
mendicancy. These generalized and universal goals could be furthered
by action taken by men and women continuing to honor commitments
within the secular order. By the late twelfth and thirteenth centuries
laic confraternities exhibited greater autonomy, and in part this change
was a consequence of their corporate involvement in communal society.
Educated in political and guild life, the brothers elected their own leaders and administered their own properties. The congregation of St.
Dominic, founded at Bologna shortly after his canonization and whose
statutes are known from a letter of confirmation by the master general

of the order (1244), was open to all except those known to be or sus-
pected of being in error on matters of faith. Rectors were to be selected
from each of the four quarters of the city, as were the rulers of the
commune. An identical provision was made in a rule written by the
Dominican Pinamonte Brembate for the Misericordia of Bergamo. This
lay confraternity was established in 1265 by the Dominicans and Franciscans. In Florence a penitential confraternity owned and managed all
benefactions conferred on the Dominicans; these administrators were
leading citizens, and their role was like that of the "spiritual friends"
of the Franciscans. Clerics were often relegated to the role of chaplain
and charged with performing the sacramental ministry. They escaped
the confines of clerical governance without attaching themselves to a
church or patron saint. Soon they were to be drawn to the new mendicant orders of the Dominicans and Franciscans and move outside the
routine of parish religious life to participate in civic and penitential
movements of the day. The laity were now deeply involved in the history of church and society.[10]

III

Flagellation had long existed in the Church as a means of punishment. Its punitive role is well documented, and it was employed within
the monastic context to subdue obdurate sinners. There also was voluntary penance, whose origins could be traced back to the early desert
fathers. However, flagellation did not become a "widespread monastic
practice" until the eleventh century, and then its first great proponent,
as we have noted, was Peter Damiani. He encouraged the practice not
only for hermits and monks but also for laity. We know his zeal did
not always gain acceptance, as we can observe from his letters to the
Florentine clergy. Damiani was in no way deterred from *de laude fla-
gellorum*, affirming that it was soon to be taken up by men and even
women of noble birth. Nowhere did this practice find greater acceptance
than in the urban centers of Italy. What was noticed most readily by
contemporaries was that the flagellant movement of 1260 was a product
of lay initiative. Chroniclers marveled at its spontaneity and lack of
papal direction; the Church was a diminished factor in activating community consciousness.[11]

Flagellants disciplined themselves not only to gain individual merit
but to assist humankind in overcoming its sins. The primary civic function of the confraternities was to reduce the distance between classes
and bring peace to the community. The desire was to have Christianity
serve as a more decisive presence in society; religious feeling was not

resolved so exclusively in terms of individual morality. Religious sensibilities were less likely to be satisfied by interior or personal renewal and more prone to be realized in abstract and extended schemes for the regeneration of collective life. The call was for the reform of society and church, and the sins featured were those against community: public violence, insensitivity to the sufferings of others, heresy, gambling, usury, economic exploitation, and sexual vices. The flagellants sought to extend the blessings of peace from one region to another, reconciling internal dissension and sometimes even releasing prisoners to a forgiving community. The call was for public repentance for the purpose of purifying society. The remedies were global and the message directed toward an entire city. In Perugia all work was to be suspended for fifteen days so that the spiritual benefits of the penitential devotion could be realized collectively. The notion of personal spiritual regeneration was translated into civic and operational terms. The movement included citizens from all orders:

> Such was the fear of God engendered in them that nobles as well as the low-born, old men and young, children of only five years, processed through the squares of the city stripped to the waist. Covered in shame . . . they marched two by two each one carrying a whip with which they continually beat themselves on their shoulders until the blood began to flow, uttering groans and shrill lamentations. . . .[12]

The public dimension of religion was nourished by confidence that collective goals were clearly in prospect. Conversion of the individual was being translated into *metanoia* of community. Flagellation led to spiritual rebirth of the individual, and this in turn would produce expiation of the sins of Christendom. In Asti the movement for collective repentance was encouraged by penitents exhorting crowds to "do penance because the Kingdom of Heaven is nigh." A Joachite influence was discernible in pronouncements that the age of the Holy Spirit was imminent. Hermits, inspired by Biblical accounts of the prophet Jonah, fueled enthusiasm for a spiritual renewal of society in which the discord of the present would soon give way to social harmony. It was the lay penitent Raniero Fasani who brought the Perugians to an appreciation of the need to expiate the sins of humanity and participate in the passion of Christ by scourging themselves publicly. Yet, from Perugia to Asti, public processions were orderly and sermons orthodox. Unlike the north of Europe, penitential movements in Italian towns did not provoke social disturbances or fuel exaggerated millenarian expectations. Indeed, the opposite was true, albeit for only a brief time: classes and orders were brought together in a celebration of civic and spiritual concord. The principal result of the penitential movement of 1260 in the Italian towns was an increase in the number of religious confraternities. The effect was to strengthen the bonds of associative life rather than disrupt them.[13]

IV

The lauds were paraliturgical hymns in which the Virgin was repeatedly saluted by her admirers. These hymns of praise were to become a most prominent feature of the new vernacular culture and a popular mode for voicing intense religious sentiment. By the early thirteenth century any lyrical religious poem in the vernacular was designated a laud. The literary development of this genre was concentrated in Umbria and Tuscany, where Perugia, Siena, and Florence took the lead. The sufferings of Christ and the dolor of the Virgin were evoked with intense pathos in this widely popular art form. The significance of the laud was not, however, in its individual inspiration but in its collective character. The company of the *laudesi*, who sang each evening at the Dominican Church of Santa Maria Novella at Florence, may well have been the progenitors of this type of choral society. At mid-thirteenth century we also find the Confraternity of the Virgin in Siena performing its melodious celebration of the sufferings of Christ and Mary as a central theme of communal spiritual life.[14]

The thirteenth century in Tuscany witnessed the peaking of collective sentiment. The most prominent religious edifices in the towns were, of course, the baptisteries, and Pisa and Florence provided truly elegant examples. Baptisteries were those sacred places in the city-state for performing that sacrament which brought the child into the Christian community. Here, also, vendettas were renounced and enemies reconciled, debtors and prisoners liberated, and the banished restored to the community. At Eastertide collective baptismal rituals were performed, and citizens exchanged the kiss of peace under the olive branch. The baptistery of Florence was the locale for the greatest single artistic enterprise of the thirteenth century, the mosaics of the Last Judgment. At Pisa the most revolutionary of all thirteenth-century Tuscan artistic creations, the pulpit of Nicola Pisano, was located in its baptistery. Perhaps these two commanding works of art can be regarded as emblematic of tensions implicit in thirteenth-century communal spiritual life. The mosaics of the Florentine baptistery present a hieratic vision of the Last Judgment with the terrors of hell altogether explicit. Clearly, this monumental projection was a clarion call to repentance. Pisano's sculpted pulpit used classical forms and motifs to invest the individual with exceptional spiritual dignity and worth. Despite its many restorations one can perceive that the Last Judgment in the Florentine baptistery has an immediacy and expressiveness not to be found in the twelfth-century mosaics at Torcello. The color scheme is more varied, and the figures in hell twist and turn, gazing at each other and the viewer. There is a narrative underlying the thematic progress that establishes a more subtle continuity. Hell is being transformed from a symbolic reminder into a dramatic narrative. Although the figures are flat and elongated, the hieratic impulse is countered by a series of anecdotes to which the viewer must respond. The message of the Last Judgment is directed toward contemporaries. Pisano, in his Last Judgments at Pisa and Siena, researched a new perspective system, creating deeper spaces for figures of exceptional spiritual dignity. His hells admit bishops, monks, and even a royal personage. Indeed, in his disordered narrative we have types for specific sins included among the damned. The assimilation of antique conventions was allowing sculptors and painters to represent the spontaneity of the human spirit, thus lending poignancy and pathos to this final act in the Christian drama. If we turn from Nicola Pisano to his son Giovanni and examine the Last Judgment panels of his sculptured pulpits at Pistoia, and Pisa, we observe that the damned are caught in a guilt-ridden frenzy and cornered in hell under the eye of a sadistic and gleeful Satan. Giovanni expresses the psychological anguish of those who had rejected Christ's sacrifice and its blessed consequences for humankind. Even the Apostles renounce their customary neutral stance and are seized by pity for the damned.[15]

We can readily note a variety of seemingly contradictory stances expressed in the religious writings of the day. Here, too, we find replicated the many paradoxes characteristic of painting and sculpture. Claims for the dignity and worth of the laic condition were very likely to carry frequent exhortations to repent. So widespread was the expression of this apparent antithesis and so immediate its representation that one can only suspect that it was sharpened by structural contradictions in the communal society of the thirteenth century. We notice a heightened concern for the collective regeneration of society and the Church, yet clergy and secular rulers stand accused of a battery of transgressions. The crimes of church and communal governments were certain to bring down the wrath of God. At the very moment when laity had achieved substantial dignity in the sight of God, their proclivity for evil was being dramatically highlighted. When their accomplishments were commended most extravagantly, they were regarded as suffering under the greatest burden of collective guilt. Church and clergy were the beneficiaries of extraordinary spiritual authority, but they, too, were seen as easy targets for the forces of evil.[16]

V

Nonconformist lay groups, such as the Humiliati (Humble Ones), the Arnoldists, the Waldensians, and the Patarines, dedicated themselves to a way of life based on the study of Scripture, voluntary poverty, mendicancy, manual labor, and preaching. A contemporary observer concluded that the majority of the Humiliati were literate, and another said of these pious lay folk in general: "All men and women, small and great, night and day learn and teach . . . whoever is a disciple for ten days seeks out another to teach." At first these laity tended not to regard their movement as an alternative to established institutions; their concern was not to convert people to another creed but to a different way of life. The great Dominican preacher Humbert of Romans at mid-thirteenth century characterized the Humiliati thus: "These people live by the work of their own hands after the manner of the primitive church." In their pastoral and evangelical teachings they were supportive of the dignity of the laic condition and confident about the possibilities of redemption for Christians outside the bounds of organized religious life. Once again, however, the direction of social and economic change proved threatening to their commitment of the sacral values of apostolic life. Living in small groups and communities, they associated themselves with those holding little power; the Humiliati made their livelihood through the manufacture of coarse cloth. However, they did not form any coherent vision of society itself, preferring instead to reject the logic of the world. A contemporary account of one of these groups describes it as follows:

> At that time [1178–79] there were certain inhabitants of Lombard towns who lived at home with their families, chose a peculiar form of religious life, refrained from lies, oaths, and law suits, were satisfied with plain clothing, and presented themselves as upholding the Catholic faith. They approached the pope and besought him to confirm their way of life. This the pope granted them, provided that they did all things humbly and decently, but he expressly forbade them to hold private meetings or to presume to preach in public. But spurning the apostolic command, they became disobedient, for which they suffered excommunication. They called themselves Humiliati, because

they did not use colored cloth for clothing but restricted themselves to plain dress.[17]

Within a generation these Humiliati had been restored to Mother Church and their three orders approved by Innocent III. Making a distinction between preaching doctrine and giving witness in matters of faith and morals, the pope took the dramatic step of also sanctioning lay preaching by the "humble ones." When Jacques de Vitry, cardinal and celebrated preacher (ca. 1180–1240), stopped at Milan on his travels to Rome and the Holy Land, he called the city "the womb of heretics" and felt compelled to remain there for some days in order to preach the True Gospel:

> One can scarcely find anyone in the whole city who resists the heretics except for certain holy men and religious women who are called Patarines [that is, heretics] by malicious and secular men, but who are called Humiliati by the pope from whom they have received the right to preach to fight the heretics, and who has confirmed their order. These are they who, leaving all for Christ and assembling in diverse places, live from their own manual labour, frequently preaching the word of God. . . . And so greatly has this order multiplied in the diocese of Milan that they have founded one hundred and fifty conventual congregations, men in some and women in others, not counting those who remain in their own homes.[18]

Peter Waldo, a wealthy merchant, was from the city of Lyons. Though Lyons was much smaller than Milan, this French town bore a marked resemblance to the greater metropolis. At the crossroads of two rivers, this bustling center accommodated pilgrims and merchants passing over the Alps. The economy relied on cloth making, commerce, and money lending. There were years of famine during the 1170s, and Waldo regularly distributed food to the less fortunate, reminding all that "no servant can be a slave to two masters; you cannot serve God and mammon" (Matt. 6:24). He was inspired to sell all that he owned and give the proceeds to the poor after hearing a street minstrel sing the legend of that most laic of all saints, Alexis, who renounced family and fortune to follow the authentic Christian life of a mendicant. Waldo addressed the crowds himself, saying:

> Citizens and friends I have not become mad as you believe, but I am revenging myself over these my enemies that have made me a slave to the point that I was always more solicitous of money than of God and I was a servant more of the creature than of the creator. I know that many criticize me because I have done it openly. But I did it both for myself and for you: for myself so that those who henceforth see

me in possession of money can declare me insane; but in part also for you, so that you may learn to place your hope in God and not to trust in riches.

This was no condemnation of riches per se; rather, it was a pronouncement of the stark alternative—either the world or God. Nor could Waldo's message be readily converted into a set of social or legal principles. His was a message that each listener was to follow in light of the truth of the Apostles' lives and according to his own capacities.[19]

The Cathars differed from other sects in that they boldly confronted the tragic contradiction between the purity of the apostolic life and the direction taken by a burgeoning and competitive urban society. They attacked orthodox Christianity, seeking not to reform it by returning it to its beginnings in the early Church but to displace it. Making a sharp distinction between a pure elite of *perfecti* and the mass of believers (*credentes*), they sought to resolve the contradiction by having the former embrace a regimen very like that of the most ascetic monks of the early Middle Ages. They were indeed "spiritual proxies" for the masses, who might continue their indulgent lives. These *perfecti* were preoccupied with the problem of evil and therefore harsh in their renunciation of sins of the flesh. Committed to celibacy and refusing to kill animals or eat meat, their doctrinal propositions appeared to be most difficult to translate into practical terms. Fierce in their opposition to Catholic hierarchy, they condemned even monks and canons regular for possessing property in common. They alone were the true poor of Christ, living like the Apostles—not lovers of the world, as were clergy. To contemporaries they were perceived as foes of all forms of social organization, condemning, as they did, all wars, cruel punishment, the sacrament of marriage, and the idea of purgatory. They would even disrupt links between the living and the dead. Many disorders were attributed to Cathars because it was believed that they were not restrained from reckless words and vile deeds through fear of hell.[20]

The Cathars preached a strict dualism between the forces of light and those of evil, emphasizing the disjunction between the direction of quotidian social and economic life on the one hand and the pristine truth of the apostolic life on the other. Yet, as we have seen, in Italy they did modify their strict dualism: God occupied an elevated position, and therefore the forces of good were more likely to triumph over the hosts of Satan. The principle of evil was not so resolutely featured by Cathars of the Italian towns, and they were not so sweeping in their condemnation of weath. Other sects, such as the Poor Men of Lombardy, differed from their confreres in the north of Europe. Outside Italy the tendency was to interpret the vow of poverty so strictly as to even refuse to perform manual labor; not so with this north Italian sect. From these religious movements new forms of civic engagement and associative life were surfacing. Confidence that ordinary individuals could band together in groups based on common property, preaching of the word, reading of Scripture, manual labor, and that most abstract of all ideals, the imitation of Christ, was pervading the social sensibilities of all classes. The lay brother Bonvesin de la Riva, writing in 1288, apprises us that at Milan "there are fully 220 houses (not convents but small buildings similar to private homes) of the second order (quasiregulars) of the Humiliati of both sexes in our city and *contado* in which are a copious number of individuals leading the religious life by laboring with their own hands. . . ." This count does not include members of the third orders of the Humiliati and of the Franciscans and Dominicans. Presumably, if the tertiaries were included, the figure would be increased severalfold. Earlier in the century (1216) Jacques de Vitry had fixed the number in the diocese in Milan at 150.[21]

In considering the modifications of the teachings of the Cathars and other sects, we can appreciate the extent to which they were responsive to the advanced social dimensions of urban life in north and central Italy. From the eleventh century, spiritual leaders had exhibited dual concerns: on the one hand they celebrated those heroic and ascetic values characteristic of monastic idealism, and on the other they displayed a deep commitment to pastoral obligations and heightened sympathy for the spiritual aspirations of laity. We can observe something of the distance traversed between the early eleventh century and the late twelfth century. When Damiani reported on the preachings of his hero Romualdo in the Orvieto region (ca. 1012), he described the founder of the Camaldolese monks as speaking "as if he desired to convert the entire world into a hermitage and to associate a multitude of people under the monastic order. And indeed he stole many from the world whom he scattered among numerous holy settlements." Joachim of Fiore, writing almost two centuries later, gave evidence of the extent to which the monastic ideal had penetrated the secular world. He posited a monastic order composed of five oratories, each differing in the degree of severity. Included among them was the oratory of *conjugati* (married laity), "living the common life with their sons and daughters and using their women for procreation of children rather than libidinousness." New concepts of spiritual community were popularized whereby men and women were bound together not by wealth but by vows of voluntary poverty; this notion was extended to encompass an entire communal society. Fasani, who is alleged to have initiated the penitential movement of 1260, was visited in a dream by the saintly hermit Bevignate, who induced him to persuade the citizens of Perugia to recognize their own sinfulness and desist from the crimes of avidity, usury, luxury, and display. The idea of townsmen tied together by the holy cords of charity and love was the exact antithesis of an archaic tribal culture of gift and countergift, of the bestowal of honors and jurisdictional privileges. Voluntary poverty was the exact opposite of that display of opulence and magnanimity creating the image of self-sufficiency and power so important in an earlier time to fend off disorder and forestall chaos. Evangelized by holy men eager to promote ideas of association and community based on *caritas* and love, the populace commenced to entertain visions light-years away from those of an archaic society, with its lavish display, gift, entourage, and public pomp.[22]

Joachite teachings were emblematic of those spiritual promptings encouraging people to believe that it would soon be possible to live beyond the bounds of coercion and law in the free zone of spontaneity and love. The will to believe that personal bonds and material ties could give way to more abstract and spiritualized relationships had become a cultural imperative shaping the social psychology of townspeople in early thirteenth-century Italy. Holy men were bent on proving that individuals could release themselves from the world of clan, vendetta, and the blood oath yet not be swept away in the chaos sure to follow. An exploration of new forms of social space charted out residual forms of being and supportive networks for those renouncing narrow clan obligations. In the towns, where the confidence in abstract ties and new associative forms was most evident, projections of Edenic and Utopian visions were highly visible. Here, too, attacks against avarice led to the espousal of ideals of voluntary poverty. Not only had an archaic culture, with its notions of wealth as a reward for virtue, experienced its greatest stresses, but polemics against ecclesiastical riches intensified; further, they were becoming laic and vernacular in inspiration rather than clerical and Latin. The idea of the holy involved repudiation of the material and ostentatious, rejection of the direction assumed by contemporary society, elevation of the quest for the spiritual innocence of apostolic times, and, finally, secular agitation for divesting the Church of its wealth, thereby restoring it to that pristine state before the corrupting gift of Constantine.[23]

This rigorism, asceticism, and rejection of contemporary social values did not lead, as in an earlier era, to deprecation of the power of the sacred in ordinary life. Indeed, the opposite was true: the highest premium was placed on the incidence of the holy in the realm of everyday life. For example, in the city of Florence, at the moment when penitential and ascetic ideals were widely embraced by the nobility and a professional and business class, we note the beginnings of that thorough exploration of the spiritual possibilities implicit in daily experience. This patient and objective investigation was at the very center of the artistic revolution that was to culminate in the paintings of Giotto and his followers. Holiness, which had once found its highest expression in unusual acts remote from ordinary life, conveyed the impression that the sacred was distant and unobtainable. Individuals were required to break decisively with the round of quotidian life since professional and family activities were viewed as contributing little to spiritualization of the world. The perspective taken on most laic activities was dominated by centuries of monastic culture. The evangelical life tended to be identified with monk and priest; grave doubts were voiced as to the religious possibilities open to men and women living beyond the boundaries of hierarchy and vows: "As the light differs from the darkness so does the order of clergy differ from laity." Such pessimistic judgments were being challenged as new spiritual possibilities were discerned; the holy seemed more likely to be discovered in the round of commonplace activities as the distance between the sacred and ordinary narrowed. Again, cultural developments in Florence allow us to perceive how the lives of Christ and the Apostles were being located by artists in a time and space little different from that experienced by ordinary mortals performing humble tasks.[24]

Such groups as the Waldensians, Arnoldists, and Speronists bitterly attacked the Church, contending that the sins of clergy were undermining her spiritual authority. These sects, along with the Cathars, maintained that salvation was the reward for inner purity. Endorsing the spiritual claims of laity, they contended that an authentic religious life could indeed be realized beyond the bounds of the Rule. The Humiliati, numerous in Florence as well as Milan, pursued the common life, aspiring to realize true Christian humility. The programmatic appeal of popular religious movements (heretical and orthodox) was readily located by contemporary commentators, sympathetic as well as hostile, in the religious commitment of groups to the ideal that an ascetic life directed toward evangelical perfection did not require the renunciation of family and community bonds. In fact, lay asceticism heightened sympathy for the needs of community, the power of love, and the burden of suffering. The proliferation of evangelical and heterodox sects, so much a feature of the twelfth- and thirteenth-century urban scene, united men of different social origins and status. It was no accident that this was the era of maximum urban growth, not to be rivaled until the industrial revolution of modern times.[25]

VI

The religious figure best epitomizing the opportunities and risks of a rejuvenated lay piety was, of course, St. Francis. In his life we can observe the contradiction between a deep penitential commitment on the one hand and an extravagant appreciation of the claims of the ordinary on the other. His ecstatic dedication to renunciation and asceticism led to the choice of Christ and evangelical life, with its many paradoxes. When describing his conversion, the first act of which Francis spoke was his service to the lepers:

> This is how God inspired me, Brother Francis, to embark upon a life of penance. When I was in sin, the sight of lepers nauseated me beyond measure; but then God himself led me into their company, and I had pity on them. When I had once become acquainted with them, what had previously nauseated me became a source of spiritual and physical consolation for me. After that I did not wait long before leaving the world.[26]

This voluntary penance bore the mark of exquisite social concern; it was not merely a deed of expiation or charity. The sweetness of living among the most marginal element of society, whose illness was generally regarded as punishment for sin, led Francis to the staggering discovery of the meaning of the crucified Christ. His espousal of voluntary poverty was likewise no exercise in spiritual humility or perfection, nor was it an act taken to gain merit; rather, it was an expression of ultimate fraternity and solidarity with the vile, the despised, the poor, and the weak. One must share suffering, and the greatest sin is to lack feeling for one's fellow creatures. Fraternal love was found beyond the boundaries of *good sense* and *reason*. Francis sought to realize a new type of Christian presence in the world—a new mode of being.[27]

The mystery of Christ was incarnated in daily life through acts of fraternal love. The Eucharist celebrated the real presence of Christ among men, and its meaning went beyond the exemplary and moral toward a new state of being: "And God said to me that he wanted me to be *unus novellus pazzus in mundo*." Contradiction led to empathy for the plight of one's fellow creatures. Paradox was not expressed in a view of history affirming hieratical disjunction between a corrupt present and an Edenic past. The individual was not summoned to repudiate a contemporary church fallen into corruption after the pope had taken temporal property from Constantine. Like many of his spiritual forebears, Francis spoke of the contradiction between the logic of the world and the message of Christ. Like them he rejected the values of contemporary society, but he converted contradiction and paradox into sentiment and a mode of being. He encouraged a view of nonmonastic penitential life in which laity living outside the world of vows, orders, and hierarchy could pursue evangelical perfection and find favor in the sight of God. This felicitous state of being could be achieved without pitting oneself against the Church or abandoning its sacred confines, for was it not the first duty of the Christian to build the Church with his own hands? New forms of piety, not only doctrinal but liturgical, were created distinct from those of clergy. The evangelical was rendered contemporary through a mimetic representation of the Christian legend. The crèche, devotion to the Virgin, and the suffering Christ domesticated the spiritualities. So accessible were these spiritualities that they confirmed the religious dignity of laic audiences to whom they were directed. In the early fourteenth century a French cardinal visited Assisi to give a sermon at the Portuincula on the Good Samaritan. Upon arrival he found himself recollecting his childhood experience of first viewing the parables, or histories of the lives of the Apostles, on the walls of a church. As a boy he had not understood the significance of the images, which mixed laity and clergy. A young layman, standing beside him, remarked that these frescoes, bringing together lay people and clergy, were a proper exposition of the history of the Evangelists. It must be that these histories were painted during the times of the blessed Francis.[28]

Francis was a very laic saint, and among his early disciples only one was a priest. The first individual since Christ to receive the stigmata from God, he was only a deacon in Mother Church, yet so exalted was his spiritual worth that he was soon to be portrayed in a fresco as a witness to the Crucifixion. That his life was depicted in twenty-four scenes in the frescoes of the upper church at Assisi was a stunning visual tribute to the sanctity of the ordinary. The life and legends of Francis domesticated the holy—even tamed the dreadful. He met poverty with the same happy spontaneity as did a woman running to greet her knight. His courtship of and marriage to Dame Poverty was an extravagant instance of the saint's acting in a commonplace way to illuminate the horrible darkness lurking just outside the well-lit compound of life's routines. To take as a spouse that most frightening of all creatures and to do it with such gallantry was to fill the abyss with the breath of loving tenderness. Francis internalized the heroic and made the epic deed of chivalric literature the stuff of everyday spiritual life. Desirous that all men and women live in harmony, he worked to cast out the demons of discord from the commune so that love and peace would fill the hearts of the great citizens and their poor confreres. With all his refined social concern and appreciation for courtesy and etiquette, he was at heart a man of penance. He and his followers were to call themselves "viri poenitentis" and were to exhort the crowds to:

> Do penance, make fruits worthy of penance, for know that you will die. Give, and it will be given unto you. Forgive, and it will be forgiven unto you. And if you will not have forgiven men their sins, the Lord will not forgive you your sins. Confess all your sins. Blessed are those who die in penance, for they will be in the kingdom of heaven. Woe to those who do not die in penance, for they will be the sons of the Devil, whose works they do, and will go into eternal fire. Beware and abstain from all evil and persevere up to the end in good.[29]

Even after Francis and the brothers received permission from Innocent III to preach, these early disciples (*viri poenitentis*) preferred to stay in the Sabine mountains, forgetting the world and leading an ascetic life like the desert hermits of old. On the earliest mission northward the saint dispatched his first convert, Bernardo di Quintavalle, the merchant of Assisi who had renounced his riches to do lonely penance. He desired above all to reject the world, dwell in solitude, and seek the salvation of his own soul. But it was that "Venerable Bernardo," the one who Dante tells us "first threw off his shoes and ran," whom Francis sent to Florence to preach the gospel. More than any other brother Bernardo desired to be separated from earthly concerns: "And twenty or thirty days at a time he wandered by himself on the highest mountain tops and contemplated the things that are above." In the company of another early disciple, perhaps brother Giles, Bernardo arrived in the Arno city. Francis's imitation of Christ was so literal that he sent his followers out in pairs, as had his master. In Florence, according to an early chronicle of the life of the saint, the two brothers received a cold reception. Vainly did they seek a night's lodging, and when a woman agreed to allow them to sleep in a woodshed outside the house, her husband returned and wanted to deny them even this modest hospitality. She pacified him by saying, "They can steal nothing but a little firewood down there," and with that he gave permission. However, he would not allow her to lend them cover for protection against the cold of winter. The presentation of all this detail by the chronicler only highlights the stunning triumph of Franciscanism in the most commercially advanced of all the cities of central Italy. The following morning, when Bernardo and his companion went to church, a certain Guido, a pious Florentine accustomed to giving charity to beggars, offered alms to the brothers. When Bernardo refused, Guido was astonished, asking, "Are you not paupers like the others, that you will take nothing?" Bernardo replied, "Certainly we are paupers, but poverty is no burden to us, for in our case it is voluntary, and it is in obedience to the will of God that we are poor."[30]

Contemporaries testified that when St. Francis preached, he scorned academic methods and rules; his inspiration came from the heart. He preached not *per modum praedicandi* but *per modum concionandi*. The first mode developed a Biblical theme according to definite rules, whereas the second utilized rhetorical techniques habitual to those addressing citizen assemblies. In the commune matters were discussed in the assembly with *il popolo* responding, "Fiat, Fiat!" or with a resounding "Non, Non!" Like the popular orator, Francis spoke simply and directly to his audience, exhorting them to virtue. Frequently, the substance of his discourse stressed the abolition of enmity and the need for peace among his neighbors. Tommaso, archdeacon of Spalato, wrote:

> In that year [1222], I was residing in the Studium of Bologna; on the feast of the Assumption, I saw St. Francis preach in the public square in front of the public palace. Almost the entire city had assembled there. The theme of his sermon was: "Angels, men, and demons." He spoke so well and with such sterling clarity on these three classes of spiritual and rational beings that the way in which this untutored man developed his subject aroused even among the scholars in the audience an admiration that knew no bounds. Yet, his discourses did not belong to the great genre of sacred eloquence: rather they were harangues. In reality, throughout his discourse he spoke of the duty of putting an end to hatreds and of arranging a new treaty of peace.
>
> He was wearing a ragged habit; his whole person seemed insignificant; he did not have an attractive face. But God conferred so much power on his words that they brought back peace in many a seignorial family torn apart until then by old, cruel, and furious hatreds even to the point of assassinations. The people showed him as much respect as they did devotion; men and women flocked to him; it was a question of who would at least touch the fringe of his clothing or who would tear off a piece of his poor habit.[31]

Francis's concern was with an active transformation of the present rather than a contemplative expectancy of the future. His own conversion had been an entirely personal and individual experience: his aim was for individual salvation, and his vision of Christian life focused on daily practices. Morality was less Biblical and ecclesiastical and more individual. To save one's soul one must not withdraw from human fellowship or break from the rhythm of everyday life. What he emphasized was the humanity of God and the humanity of Christ. Accent was placed on economic spontaneity, private feelings, and the most elementary textures of emotional relationships, particularly when rooted in the precepts of love. Charity and love replaced the rule of coercion. Human solidarity and fraternity could be realized if men would gaily sever the ties binding their Christianity. *Il Poverello* would preach that happiness was not synonymous with riches and that property was no source of joy among men. He would convert the chilling fear of pauperism into a blazing love affair with Lady Poverty: "For what else are the servants of God than His singers whose duty it is to lift up the hearts of men and move them to spiritual joy."[32]

Francis was a preacher of joy, but he was also John the Baptist summoning all sinners to repent: were not the wages of sin eternal hell fire? There was nothing sentimental in a saint who, when his audience would not listen to his words, preached instead to the birds who ate cadavers in the cemetery; this scene was reminiscent of Apocalypse 19:17–18. He threatened men with the judgment of God, and his speech was like a sword piercing the heart. Yet withal he remained genial, projecting a new model of sanctity—the troubadour of God. Anxious that his religious confraternity not become another monastic order with a detailed rule like that of the Benedictines, with its twenty-three chapters regulating each detail of the monk's daily life, he prized spontaneity and would live "secundum formam sancti evangellii": "And the Lord told me that He wished me to be a new fool in the world and that He did not want to lead us by any other way than by that of wisdom, for by your learning and your wisdom God will confound you."[33]

Going beyond the penitential role, Francis heralded the possibility of Christian perfection for laity: "Also you can be members of a living church, also you can be saints." Embracing the penitential life did not lessen social concern, and indeed it was no barrier against involvement with the despised, the poor, the sick, the lepers, and the beggars and robbers by the road. The evangelical choice lay outside every criterion of good sense, beyond the norms of traditional society. The mystery of Christ celebrated in the Eucharistic sacrifice was incarnated in quotidian life through fraternal love. One could therefore leave the world of kin, clan, party, property, wealth, and status, yet find community. Did not such a renunciation of wealth and power lighten the human heart, filling it with cheer and love? Moreover, this drastic rejection of riches and power led to self-criticism, not conflict with Mother Church. The accent was on the individual and that spiritual joy emanating from purity of heart, not on reform of institutions. From a world in which security was literal and concrete we pass to one in which it was to be converted into spirit and sentiment. Francis found security in that which made men most anxious. He subscribed to the logic of the carnival, where poverty was riches and perfect happiness consisted of being despised.

This was surely the popularization of a mode of being generally reserved for privileged moments and exceptional times on the religious calendar. The carnival atmosphere of reversals and geniality allowed the dissipation of tensions between the teachings of the Apostles and the ways of the world. Contradictions were perceived as only apparent and not real: in sermons of the *novellus pazzus* poverty was riches and vilification happiness. Overturning commonly accepted values was proof of Christian vision, but, as we have observed, such reversals offered no provocation to the Church or its hierarchy.[34]

The fiction was that the logic of the carnival was no fiction. It was possible to care intensely for the world, live in it joyfully, yet embrace the ascetic and penitential life. Scorn and pity for material wealth and earthly success, together with the call to repent, led not to negation and rejection but to heightened appreciation of a world where love, marriage, chivalric idealism, human suffering, and joy were tenderly endorsed.

The disconcerting model for Francis's life was voluntary material hardship combined with spiritual serenity. Because he had discovered such interior riches, he understood that the goods of the world served not at all. It was sufficient to possess all spiritually and internally. Voluntary poverty meant suffering and reliving the passion of Christ. One found neither pleasure nor enjoyment in it, but this was no masochism, for life had positive value. Perhaps it would be too much of a leap in the direction of a poetic sociology to suggest that Francis's vision encouraged his contemporaries on the road toward "this worldly asceticism." Max Weber's oft-cited phrase vulgarizes, while at the same time illuminating, the Umbrian saint's teachings. Certainly Francis conferred an exceptional dignity on the existential situation of laity, and, by making the penitential a prerequisite of social concern, he encouraged ascetic laity to involve themselves spiritually in the life of the community. One cannot measure the extent to which this saint, who distrusted the world of orders and regulation, preferring instead the free and spontaneous, succeeded in releasing energies locked in fear and dread: by severing material cords, which provided security according to the logic of the world, Francis sought to transform social reality. Perhaps it is fit that we seek to illuminate a problem of poetic sociology by quoting the sublime verse of canto XI of Dante's *Paradiso,* where St. Thomas Aquinas narrates the wondrous love of Francis for Lady Poverty:

> He'd not long risen when the earth was stirred
>   By touches of invigorating power
> From his great strength, as boldly he incurred,

Yet young, his father's stern displeasure for
   A Lady's sake, to whom, as unto death,
   No man is eager to unbar the door;

And unto her he pledged his wedded faith
   In spiritual court and *coram patre* too,
   And loved her more each day that he drew breath.

She, of her first Spouse widowed, had lived through,
   Obscure and scorned, twelve centuries, or near,
   With never a lover, till he came to woo.

Nought it availed that she so constant was,
   And so courageous, that when Mary stayed
   Below, she leapt with Christ upon the cross.[35]

Florence was perhaps the first of the towns to be visited by the companions of Francis. And, if the initial reception was grudging, this situation was to be corrected generously in the very near future. In his
great missionary year (1211–12) Francis entered Tuscany after pacify-
ing the feud-ridden Perugia. It was alleged that when arriving in Florence, he was joined by the eminent jurist Giovanni Parenti, later to
become general of the Franciscans (1227–32). Legend has it that Parenti, while walking, overheard a swineherd shout as he drove his
charges into the pen: "Hurry up into the sty, pigs, as lawyers hurry into
hell!" Dante begins canto XI, devoted to St. Francis, with the lines "O
imbecile ambition of mortality!" and quickly singles out those "chasing
juridical or aphoristical/Successes. . . ." Indeed, Francis did "unbar the
door" to many a Florentine lawyer, notary, physician, and banker desirous of the penitential life.[36]

The Arno city, long the center of lay piety, where men of the professions and merchants had embraced the penitential life as *conversi*, was
now experiencing profound changes. Precisely during the early years of
the Franciscans and Dominicans, the wills and pious benefactions of
affluent and high-status Florentines display a growing awareness of the
specific nature of sin—for example, usury—while revealing a heightened concern for collective, even global, remedies for its remission.
Further, the search for expiation was becoming more immediate and
less vicarious. In earlier times monks and priests performed the rituals
for spiritual reparation; now the likelihood increased that laity itself
would participate directly in acts of expiation. By the thirteenth century
the number of eminent Florentines directly involved in the penitential
life and its demanding round of pious acts and ascetic practices was on
the rise. Moreover, pious bequests demonstrated greater empathy and
concern for the suffering of others. It is significant that at this time

concern tended to be generalized to include large segments of the downtrodden population of the city. Possibly at no other time in the annals
of the city was the balance more exact between individual needs for
salvation and the collective requirements of communal society. Wills
and benefactions were strikingly less egoistic during the thirteenth and
fourteenth centuries than they were to be later. Franciscans and Dominicans gave support to the balancing of individual spiritual concerns on
the one side with a more ample appreciation for the global social problems of community on the other.[37]

To focus on Franciscanism is to observe the crystalization of a greater
confidence in the ability of laity to move beyond the world of clan obligation, honor, and display of wealth. Spirituality prompted risk taking
as the individual was challenged to step outside the familiar world. To
the contemporaries and near-contemporaries of Francis, conversion
brought gaiety and that joy of release of which Dante speaks when portraying the saint's early disciples as throwing off their shoes and "running to so great peace." Lady Poverty brought wealth undreamed of as
she rose, phoenixlike, from the ashes of a gift culture in that most commercial of all regions of medieval Europe. As we have observed, the
brothers and sisters of penance were drawn from the top echelons of
Florentine business and professional life. Renouncing customary roles—
at least in theory—they could remain in the world yet realize the joy
of evangelical life. The prophetic tradition placed special emphasis on
the fact that new "spiritual men" would soon be found in increasing
numbers to serve as intermediaries between the life of contemplation
and the active world. They were destined to lead the Church and Christian society through the tribulations of the present into an age of peace
and beatitude. Particularly telling was the imagery used to describe
these *viri spirituales*, whose evangelical preachings and conversation
were as seemingly light and spiritual as the clouds. It was as if such
prophets as Joachim of Fiore were invoking a language of weightless-
ness in order to describe the exhilarating experience of being released
from literal bonds and the constraints of narrow, inner rituals.[38]

VII

Florence was a center of the religious ferment of the thirteenth century. However, unlike the times of the Investiture controversy, these latter-day movements tended to focus on the religious needs of laity. The
twelfth century had witnessed a harsh reaction to the spiritual claims of
laity by the ecclesiastical hierarchy. The temporal power and authority
of the Church operated to elevate the role of priest, separating him

from the congregation of the faithful; the price was to be a widening of the breach between laity and hierarchy. Certainly the Church was strengthened, but the religious aspirations of laity, inflamed by the preaching of reformers, remained unfulfilled and even frustrated. Masses of townspeople were involved in heated contests to reduce the discrepancy between the wealth of the Church and the by-now-so-popular ideal of apostolic poverty. As we have already observed, at the time of Arnold of Brescia in the conversation between John of Salisbury and Pope Hadrian IV when the question of evangelical poverty was raised, the pope responded that it was impossible to rule Rome without gifts: the city was dependent upon the largesse of the Holy Father and the gold of the pilgrims. Against this practical counsel, Arnold and numerous other charismatic leaders did battle, exalting evangelical pauperism. The Arnoldists, like the Patarines, struggled against concubinary and simoniac clergy. They also fought against the encadrement of the Church in a feudal world of gifts, honors, and lavish display, challenging the notion that this ostentation was a legitimate means of creating islands of security in a sea of chaos. Fervent preaching against the temporalities of the Church led to the proposition that by dismantling it one could restore it as a paleo-Christian community. The Cathars, of course, went much further, establishing a church with a hierarchy, sacraments, and a theology paralleling the orthodox institution but without its commitment to wealth and pomp. So little were they persuaded by the prospect of reform and so obsessive was their concern with evil that they were finally to abandon carnal Mother Church entirely.[39]

In Tuscany in the early thirteenth century these sects continued to gain popular support. The involvement of laity in spiritual matters had extended their familiarity with the sources of Christian faith. Knowledge of Scripture, attendance at sermons, and increased literacy made their Christian culture more secure. In turn, this change had led to a heightened sense of laic confidence and responsibility in religious matters. A vivacious literature of anticlericalism, laic in perspective rather than ecclesiastical, was to flourish. Areas of mutuality and social concern were strengthened and lent durable form, with laity establishing "congregationes laborantium" on the model of the artisan corporation. The role of laity in the Christian community was evidenced by their extensive participation in heretical movements as well as in the compaigns against heretics. Third Order groups and confraternities came to include large numbers of lesser tradesmen and artisans, who were then introduced to strict religious discipline.[40]

Differences between popular movements of the thirteenth century and those of earlier ages were gradually becoming apparent. In the diatribes against Arnold of Brescia, such commanding figures as St. Bernard of Clairvaux spoke as members of a monastic elite responsible for the spiritual destiny of the Church. Bernard was convinced that the people required strict religious guidance, for many were rustics, illiterate, base, and credulous. Itinerant preachers were a spiritual menace: "These are they who take to themselves the appearances of Godliness but deny the power thereof, and mix profane novelties of speech and meaning with heavenly words, like poison with honey. Avoid them like poison, and know that under the guise of sheep they are ravening wolves." In a sermon of 1144 St. Bernard attacked "fox-like" heretics in general as perpetrators of spiritual disruption among weak-willed lay folk: "Women, leaving their husbands, and also men, rejecting their wives, are crowding around those people [heretics]. Monks and priests, young and old, are leaving their congregations and churches, and are regularly found among them in the company of weavers of both sexes. Is that not grievous damage? Is that not the work of foxes?" Needless to say, Bernard was highly suspicious of the heretics' claim that they could remain chaste in mixed company: "To be always in the company of a woman, and not to have intercourse with her, is this not more than to raise the dead? You cannot do the lesser of these, so why should I believe that you can do the greater? Daily you sit beside a maiden at table, your bed is next to hers in the sleeping room, your eyes meet hers when conversing, your hands touch when working, and you still wish to be thought chaste?"[41] Repeatedly Bernard affirmed, "These people [lay folk] are truly crude and rustic, unlettered and entirely lacking in fighting qualities; indeed they are foxes and rather puny ones at that." Bernard's stance was distanced, and his sympathies for a warrior nobility were clear. His interests were more with the spiritual reform of the orders of knighthood than with the spiritual plight of *conversi*. His hatred of heresy was mightier than his empathy for the collective anguish of a pious laity. Rigidly puritanical and fascinated by exaggerated asceticism yet involved in the major political controversies of the times, he shunned contact with the swirl of social development.

A hundred years later Humbert of Romans, fifth master general of the Dominicans (1254–63), composed his influential preacher's manual *De eruditione praedicatorum* animated by the desire to satisfy the spiritual needs of laity. The Dominicans were vitally occupied with preaching and saving souls: ". . . in this," boasted Humbert, "it excels all other orders since these others were founded for the salvation of their members alone." He was very willing to go beyond traditional distinctions between clergy and laity, emphasizing the prospects open to the latter for working toward personal salvation. In Florence, where the first substantial collection of vernacular sermons is preserved, eminent Dominicans took up this modern method of preaching, with its goal of involving laity in the supreme task of spiritual striving for personal salvation. Humbert was a clear-headed observer, knowledgeable about the intricacies of the Italian social scene; he was particularly attentive to the force of lay piety and the role of the preacher. He reminded his listeners that the Son of God had spoken thus: "Let us go into the neighboring villages and towns, that I may preach, for this is why I have come" (Mark 1:30). Especially mindful that laity did not comprehend the words recited in the Divine Office, Humbert was to emphasize the value of instruction by preachers. The supreme manifestation of lay piety was the religious confraternity, and he noted that these sodalities existed in many nations but that nowhere were they more splendid and prolific than in Italy.

The popularity of the confraternity and the "modern" vernacular sermon indicate the primacy lay religious needs assumed in this century. Indeed, religious leaders were becoming increasingly aware of the spiritual claims of laity. The pulpit of the Lombard church was to be much enlarged during this epoch. Jacques de Vitry (1170–1240), one of the earliest enthusiasts for the Franciscans, was sometimes extreme, but the following statement suggests a dimension of the cultural change: "Not only those who renounce the world and go into religion are *regulares*, but so are all the faithful of Christ who serve the Lord under the Gospel's rule and live by the orders of the single greatest Abbot or Father of all." In a sermon composed for delivery to guildsmen and artisans, this influential preacher was to liken the division of grace into the various spiritual gifts to the several gradations in the mysteries of the crafts and mechanical arts.[42]

VIII

In the eleventh century reformers sought to purify the Church and its clergy, whereas in the next century their objective was spiritual regeneration through ecclesiastical pauperism. In the thirteenth century many continued to entertain these ambitions, but another imperative was surfacing. Earlier struggles had been directed toward releasing the Church from its ties to an archaic society of gaudy display and concrete obligation. Subsequently, the purpose had been to divest the carnal Church of its wealth so that it could recapture the purity of apostolic times. The new challenge still housed many of the same impulses, even featuring them in radicalized form, but, as we have observed, the po-

lemic against wealth was more laic and vernacular in inspiration than
clerical and Latin. Ideals of charity and abnegation, explicitly or implic-
itly, condemned the fiscal and curial Church. The idea of the holy
repudiated the material and ostentatious. Yet these challenges, at first
glance so severe and ascetic, were proffered in a very different context.
As we shall notice, in the thirteenth and early fourteenth centuries
preaching and vernacular tracts were filled with diatribes against wealth
and avarice, but these writings were generally an invitation to restraint,
resignation, and social peace. Seldom did they aim to undermine the
order of society, thereby diminishing the sense of community.[43]

Eleventh-century spiritual leaders had expressed dual concerns: on
the one hand they celebrated those heroic and ascetic ideals characteristic
of monasticism, and on the other they exhibited a deep commitment to
pastoral obligations and a growing empathy for the spiritual ambitions
of laity. New concepts of community were popularized whereby men
and women were bound together not by wealth but through the vows
of voluntary poverty. This ideal was the antithesis of an archaic tribal
culture, with its lavish displays, public honors, and gift and countergift.
Rigoristic and ascetic laity formed small, self-contained communities,
renouncing pomp and riches and living, as it were, in sacred space. In
the thirteenth and early fourteenth centuries similar denunciations of
wealth and ostentation were to have somewhat different social consequences: they were to be translated into legal programs and elaborate
codes of personal conduct. Legislation would be enacted restraining
profits, limiting prices, curtailing interest rates, prohibiting "manifest"
usury, and restricting that broad range of behavior defined under the
rubric of conspicuous consumption. Florence was to be in the avant-
garde of European cities in the enactment and enforcement of detailed
sumptuary legislation encompassing an array of items of dress and
adornment as well as ceremonial occasions from weddings to funerals.
Merchant diaries, memorials, and letters were almost unanimous in
praising the virtue of moderation. Merchants won their reputations
through fiscal reliability rather than public display.[44]

The tendency of laity to achieve greater autonomy in political and
social life was evidenced in the transformation of the thirteenth-century
commune. A lively sense of participation in public affairs was strengthening citizen life. In religious life we perceive that such fundamental
laic institutions as the confraternity were also attaining self-sufficiency.
Priests performing sacred rituals in the domicile of the confraternity
were regarded as first among equals and even inscribed among the
membership. Priors of the confraternities were elected democratically,
and daily business was transacted very much like in an artisan corpora-

tion. In the contemporary arts the confraternity was represented as a corporate body headed by a celestial captain, the patron saint. Members were portrayed as soldiers sworn to do battle for his holy cause. Flagellant societies were depicted as associations of laity assembling under the mantle of the Virgin. Under the influence of Franciscans and Dominicans ordinary people were considered spiritually worthy to identify with the incarnate Christ and His sufferings on earth.[45]

The liturgical religiosity of monastic communities had emphasized the importance of flagellation. Above all it was regarded as an act of love expressing the solidarity of Christians in an enclosed community. As has been noted, Peter Damiani was the first protagonist of voluntary flagellation to extend this form of penance to laity. His efforts were greeted with opposition from Florentine clergy and monks. By the thirteenth century, however, this form of voluntary penance had become especially prominent in Tuscany, Umbria, and Lombardy. From the wills of Florentines we can surmise that embracing the penitential life was itself a sign of conversion; moreover, large numbers of laity having this conversion experience were yet able to remain in the everyday world. As we have seen, the experience of *metanoia* in earlier times implied renunciation of worldly ties and entry into a religious order. Furthermore, the expiation resulting from mortification of the flesh served to restore individuals to society at large. Laity were now assuming increased responsibility for the spiritual well-being of their communities, and the Church was losing some of its importance as a mechanism for activating community consciousness. We have already noted that contemporaries of the Great Flagellation of 1260 made pointed comments about its lay initiative. Chroniclers had marveled at its spontaneity and organization free of papal direction. A grand purpose of this mass movement, like the Great Hallelujah of 1233, was nothing less than a spiritual regeneration of society, to be achieved through a universal pardon and the restitution of ill-got gains. Exploitation of the poor by the rich was to be terminated; exiles were permitted to return and enemies reconciled. Conflict between the orders was to cease and the reign of peace, love, and amity inaugurated. Of course it would be necessary for penitents to undergo harsh and voluntary punishment in order to end their own spiritual alienation from the community. At the same time these flagellants, by participating in the expiatory sufferings of the Savior and mystically sharing in His passion, would take unto themselves the sins of society: in this way would an angry God be propitiated.[46]

Confraternities and penitential companies played a dramatic role in the public life of urban communities in north and central Italy: they performed crucial civil tasks, such as reconciling enemies and conducting diplomatic negotiations between rival factions and warring cities; most important, they sought to establish concord among the various social orders. Indeed, the most enduring consequence of the flagellant movement of 1260 was the founding of numerous lay confraternities dedicated to voluntary penance. Increasingly, these penitents, or *battuti*, were called upon to serve as peace makers: by undergoing public flagellation they had demonstrated their transcendence over worldly interests. In the factional controversies of the thirteenth century, Ghibelline exiles, when restored to citizenship in Guelf cities, wore the garb of *battuti*, thus publicly demonstrating spiritual concerns rather than political ambition. The work of pacification was frequently entrusted to penitents, whose asceticism and mortification of the flesh elevated them above the harsh world of competition, avarice, and advantage. In the cities and countryside of north and central Italy confraternities worked at the neighborhood level to settle disputes, avert vendettas, manage hospitals, and dispense alms to the poor and ill. At the global level they constituted themselves as a militia, rallying behind the banner of Christ to rout heretics from the community.[47]

Civic and social preoccupations called for novel religious solutions. Traditional landmarks were being effaced: ideological divisions and bitter factional disputes made exile and banishment an everyday occurrence. Confiscation of the properties of heretics, Ghibellines, and Guelfs transpired in a seesaw world of politics in which propapal forces were displaced by proimperial supporters on one day, only to have the situation reversed on the next. Those outlawed during civil wars could hope to be restored only through miracles performed by new saints or the intervention of holy men. At this time we see the rise of just such spiritual personages, capable of reducing the most factious population to peace and concord. The need for collective and communal salvation was increasingly felt as a dramatic and compelling social imperative. The idea of reform and renewal was expanding to include the entire population of towns. Preparation for this transformation was not to be achieved by ritual or martyrdom alone but through a series of expiatory acts intended to strengthen social solidarity.[48]

Reformers of the eleventh century regarded poverty as an evangelical act in imitation of Christ; it stood as a special component of the spiritual life and a sign of moral conversion (*conversio morum*). Poverty ranked second to the highest of virtues—chastity. The salvational character of the sacraments was firmly endorsed by such groups as the Patarines: for them poverty was also secondary. The priest was expected to imitate Christ, but this *imitatio* was not centered exclusively on the Lord's poverty. Spirituality was anchored in humility, and the priest was expected to live within an institutional cadre; his religious life found highest expression in a community of canons regular. The aim of reformers was to take the Church beyond the bounds of a gift culture, freeing it from dependence on the material world, its power, and its riches. Battling against the prevalent view that wealth alone created solidarity among men, these reformers sought to project a network of more abstract ties. They did not argue, however, that true solidarity among peoples could be based on the idea of poverty. Such arguments achieved popular appeal only in the thirteenth century.[49]

The imperatives of collective life were increasing their hold upon city dwellers in north and central Italy. As we have indicated, the popular religious movements of the first part of the thirteenth century had as a principal objective a reduction of conflict between the orders of society. A leading purpose, then, was to reduce the distance between social classes. Popular preachers moved their audiences of rich and poor, old and young, noble and commoner to exchange the kiss of peace, to extend pardon, and to make restitution of ill-got gains. As already noted, confraternities and flagellant societies drew their memberships from every social class and were increasing exponentially. These sodalities projected in microcosm the compelling illusion of a classless society. In thirteenth-century Florence, and indeed elsewhere, these religious companies were characterized by a keen sense of mutuality; the responsibility of one member for the other and all for the collectivity may well have reached its highest point in the late thirteenth and early fourteenth centuries. Perhaps never again was there to be so exact a blend of individual and collective interests. Further, these associations had their most ample civic commitments at this time and were therefore more public in character than they ever were to be again. Like the numerous Florentine guilds of the late thirteenth and early fourteenth centuries, these religious associations participated vigorously in political and ideological contests of the day.[50]

IX

The belief that society's problems were susceptible to a general solution was encouraged by the prosperity and demographic growth of such expanding centers of international trade as Florence. As we have seen, the growth of the Arno city was spectacular: in the thirteenth century it encompassed a geographic area three times that of Roman antiquity. A new circle of walls, bridges, piazzas, churches, and hospitals were created by a new commercial, banking, and manufacturing elite. By 1182 the Guild of the Merchants was functioning according to the model of a

Society of Knights. Shortly thereafter, guilds of bankers, wool manu-
facturers, and silk merchants were formed. A sizable part of the population was now able to participate energetically in this booming world
of economic growth. Newly arrived to wealth and power, these bankers,
merchants, industrial entrepreneurs, well-to-do artisans, tradesmen, and
professionals demonstrated a heady blend of confident assertiveness
with a clear recognition of man's radical insufficiency in the sight of
God. Again we note that marked contradiction, heightened by experience in the Italian towns, between man's claim for dignity and his appreciation of human frailty. In their last wills and pious benefactions
we can observe a complex mix of ascetic renunciation and profound
social concern coupled with a sturdy regard for personal immortality.
These documents disclose an awareness of certain structural contradictions: although spectacular commercial advances were being made, the
harsh norms of a traditional world persisted. Wretched poverty existed
cheek by jowl with gaudy luxury.[51]

The citizens of Florence, from the poet Dante to the chronicler Giovanni Villani, were troubled by these polarities. As we have observed,
the commune, with its detailed legislation against extravagances in
feasting at weddings, funerals, and christenings, was in the vanguard
of European cities. Dress and dowries became targets of philippics as
well as sumptuary laws. Statutes were enacted regulating the value of
betrothal gifts and wedding portions. As late as the 1340s the government was conducting an extensive canvass of items of apparel in
violation of public law. Indeed, the very engine of communal life was
impelled by the urge to elaborate collective norms. The effects were felt
in many areas of associative life, with prohibitions against cartels and
monopolistic practices. The motives for these enactments were explicit:
"fear of God" or "giving grave offense to the Most High." Clearly, the
regulation of interest rates, profits, and the cost of necessities fell far
short of the lofty goals. In addition, secular trends operated to raise demand as the population increased dramatically. The oversupply of workers and peasants reduced wages and made leases unfavorable to tenants.
All evidence indicates that as merchant profits grew, the living conditions of the "thin people" (*il popolo minuto*) deteriorated. Overpopu-
lation made labor cheap and grain dear.[52]

Of course, those with great wealth—the beneficiaries of the prosperity of the twelfth and thirteenth centuries—did not gain exemption
from the harsh norms of a preindustrial society, with its high mortality
rates, widespread disease, and chronic discomfort. Quotidian life was
precarious also for those only recently come to wealth; the very economic forces compelling *novi cives* to the top were likely to bring them

down. Bankruptcies were an all-too-familiar feature of the commercial landscape. Anxiety about money and power had become programmatic and would soon spawn an abundant literature of vernacular timorousness; Florentine burghers were to be the stalwarts of this new prose form. Despite self-doubt, the achievements of the "fat people" (*popolani grassi*) were real enough, though they did have every reason to be anxious. Florentine wills and pious donations represented a heroic effort to acknowledge these tensions, honor them, and, in so doing, alleviate them. Large numbers of well-to-do laity bestowed their wealth on new charitable institutions, founded in record numbers during those days. Donations served a variety of ends: first, expiation for the benefactor; second, satisfaction of some generalized communital need; and, finally, specific ego claims of the testator and donor. Interestingly enough, the last benefit was less important at that time when compared with other considerations. Bequests were more impersonal than were the wills and donations of the late fourteenth and fifteenth centuries. A greater equilibrium existed between the strains and preoccupations of everyday life on the one hand and salvation of the soul on the other. In turn, this equilibrium was realized in the balance between claims of the ego of donor or testator and the values of community. As compared with testaments of a later period, those of the thirteenth and early fourteenth centuries contained fewer provisions for the mass, candles, commemorative meals, elaborate rituals, lavish funerals, and costly monuments. The maximum effort was directed toward reducing the dysfunction between redemption and sociability.[53]

Global solutions to poverty led to generalized bequests to "Christ's poor." Prophetic announcements that God would soon bring forward a race of men dedicated to voluntary mendicancy, sure to eradicate avarice, gained popularity. Aspirations for the recovery of solidarity and fraternity led to a multiplication of millennial and Utopian schemes. Political and religious ideologies were being directed toward the spiritual rejuvenation of society. The restoration of the primitive Church was certain to inaugurate an age of universal brotherhood, charity, and love. Eden was assuming a markedly social character. The Golden Age would occur in historical time, and one could prepare for it by changing society rather than by seeking martyrdom or performing ritual gestures. Grand schemes were promoted for reducing societal malfunction. The idea of reform, once the preserve of monastic institutions and the priesthood, was moving into the secular world. Those most eager to initiate the reign of charity and love made restitution of ill-got gains and joined the ranks of the penitents. Indeed, in Florence over the course of the thirteenth and early fourteenth centuries the members of confraternities came to regard penance as a way of life no longer distinct from the world of everyday concerns. The idea of penance was being diffused through the preachings of Dominicans and Franciscans; fear of divine punishment stimulated the good sense of merchants and artisans to contribute to the city's poor. This charitable impulse was inspired by what the philosopher and psychologist William James might well have described as "the sentiment of rationality." The language preachers used to diagnose sin was harsh and polemical, but the remedies they proposed were becoming increasingly measured and practical. Now greater attention was being focused on the circumstances and problems of laity.[54]

X

In Florence, Arezzo, Orvieto, Prato, and other central Italian towns, religious dissidents, such as the Cathars, had recruited from all classes, but especially merchants and artisans. Florence was at first a missionary base, then the seat for the heretic bishopric, and finally the center for all Tuscany. The Cathars held the strong conviction that original sin would exclude them from salvation and that initiation into the spiritual community called for a radical conversion from a life of sensuality and materialism. Extremely ascetic and influenced deeply by monastic ideas and aversions, the Cathars dwelled upon the problem of the stain of evil. After receiving *consolomentum*, or the laying on of hands (the central sacrament), one was counted among the elect and required to live a life unblemished by carnal sin. Such purity necessitated extreme renunciation of the flesh and things of the material world. The appeal of this ascetic doctrine was most widespread in southern France and Italy, where socioeconomic change and urbanization had proceeded so rapidly. In north and central Italy, the intellectual interest in Catharism was more speculative than in Languedoc; also, there appears to have been little or no peasant involvement. Logically enough, it was precisely in these regions that men and women of the later Middle Ages felt themselves most distanced from the pristine truths of early Christianity. As we have noted, such sects as the Cathars accentuated the radical separation between the primitive Church and the direction of contemporary urban life. In the eleventh and early twelfth centuries dissident and penitential movements appear to have originated in the countryside, but by the second half of the twelfth century they had their firm base and constituency in the cities of south France and Italy. The Cathars made a wide appeal to the urban populace with their call for renunciation and sacrifice.[55]

The more extreme the sect, the more limited the opportunity for salvation; the more radical the doctrine, the more essential would be the gift of the Holy Spirit. Yet, with all the discourse on asceticism and renunciation, these sects bestowed an unaccustomed worth upon laity. It is true that the more radical the penitential group, the more preoccupied they were with the susceptibility of human flesh to sin, but they also lent ample endorsement to the aspirations of laity for Christian perfection. Though confronted with a rigorism deeply pessimistic about the deadly consequences of compromise with evil, these sects continued to sanction laic prospects for an authentic Christian life. Of course, there were middling groups, such as the Humiliati, Poor Lombards, Arnoldists, Beguines, and Beghards, who did not take so strict a view of the human proclivity for sin, but they, too, desired to seal off their membership from the pernicious influences of a commercial society. They perceived spiritual risk and impurity as so threatening that it would be necessary to imitate—literally—the lives of the Apostles. Further, they followed a program that rejected contemporary economic values: they would own land in common, work together communally, follow humble occupations, despise wealth, refuse to bear arms or take oaths, and even disdain to pay tithes. Severe in their condemnation of social evils, these sects sought to cordon off their membership from contamination. Yet, within these communities there was a wide range of options, each lending dignity to the laic condition. The rejection of spiritual dependency on priests as mediators heightened the sense of individual responsibility. The reading and teaching of Scripture allowed reinforcement of a piety rooted in everyday concerns. Again we observe that the spiritual life could be lived outside the world of vows, hierarchy, and religious orders. Communities could be united through love and charity instead of riches and display. However, these groups, bound by religious sentiment, found it necessary to segregate themselves from the greater society.[56]

Earlier challenges to a religion with a focus on material success and wealth represented a heightened consciousness of the deficiencies of an archaic and gift culture. The desire to move beyond mechanical solidarity toward more abstract forms of associative life found ample expression in the lives of holy men. In the late twelfth and early thirteenth centuries it led to strict ideas of penance and the formation of small groups of spiritually minded laity anxious to avoid contamination from the greater society. The tendency toward rigorism and asceticism was the mark of religious sects and lay confraternities. In the thirteenth century, however, the notion of abandoning the world, even at moments of collective terror, was exceptional. Popular prophecy was converting fear of the Last Judgment into programs of communal action for the expiation of society. The world, though full of occasions for sin and opportunities for damnation, was not drained of authenticity. Religion and piety were beginning to be regarded as irreducible elements in the daily lives of lay folk. Spirituality was moving in the direction of rejecting the certainties of an older world, positing instead a much more problematic view of human existence and social life. The cities of north and central Italy were, of course, the locale for the most dramatic economic and social changes to be experienced in the later medieval world. Emerging communal societies were characterized by interdependence and specialization. Mutuality and a highly articulated social structure made for collective norms. Life at each level—from that of day laborer to guild master to entrepreneur—was acquiring a higher degree of organization and in turn being subjected to greater controls. The direction of social change was clearly from mechanical to organic solidarity. Such a trend can be observed elsewhere in Europe, of course, but nowhere was it more intense than in the cities of north and central Italy.[57]

Laity were now encouraged to step beyond the world of sects and small groups in order to enter the greater society. Surely the spiritual dangers were acute. Earlier solutions to these risks had involved the internalization of monastic models of asceticism designed to avoid contamination. The teachings of the sects indicate an obsessive preoccupation with evil and the risk of sin. Fear of corruption led to the democratization of ideals of voluntary poverty; fear of the sins of the flesh and transgressions by the community led to the popularization of voluntary flagellation. In the late twelfth and early thirteenth centuries we perceive the vitality of spiritual impulses as they operated to transcend the limits of a world of mechanical solidarities. For St. Francis the insignia of salvation were courtliness, kindness, and neighborliness: a spiritual premium was placed on sociability and conviviality. For the sects, however, the risks of contamination were so great that new boundaries and limits were quickly drawn. A consciousness of breaking the bounds was matched by a dramatic appreciation of the spiritual dangers confronting laity.[58]

Previously, faith had been expressed in exterior forms; concern was focused on the miraculous rather than the supernatural. Ritual was detailed and repetitive; the liturgy multiplied precautions and immediate remedies. The life of the Christian was inserted within a system of stringent obligations. With minute exactitude religion explicated spiritual exercises; indeed, the liturgy tended to become a branch of the law. The hierarchy of spiritual values evidenced a stark materialism. Sermons of ninth-century Italy express very well the power of literal bonds. The believer was under the *mundium* of the *Dominus* and commended himself to God with all reverence. The believer's *servitia* and *obsequia* were exchanged for *nutritio*, *tuitio*, and *protectio*. Once these practices, so appropriate to an archaic society, were challenged and ritual no longer perceived so single-mindedly as a magic lamp to be rubbed to gain unlimited health, strength, riches, and power, new sensibilities were seen to be valid. Laity had been liberated from many of the traditional ties; moreover, the possibilities for redemption and salvation had increased markedly, but so, too, had the preoccupation with spiritual perils and prospects for damnation. Commanding figures, such as Innocent III, assessed the weight of sin as so heavy and the human condition so dolorous that the Christian stood in dire need of the spiritual intervention of the priest. Resolution of the dilemma, according to Innocent, was possible if greater faith was rendered to church hierarchy. The Cathars maintained a strict dualism, rejecting the mass because it utilized vile matter. The Waldensians, Humiliati, and other sects celebrated lay piety, but only within the confines of communities dedicated to ascetic and pauperistic ideals. Each of these groups repudiated an older world of legalism and hierarchy, encouraging their members to revile ecclesiastical authority and monastic encadrement. They were resolved to lead their adherents away from dependence on riches, vows, oaths, and pledges. Once freed, however, their members were expected to refuse to compromise with the greater society or its instruments of power. Only by remaining powerless would their religious rites prove efficacious and protect them from contamination.[59]

XI

One can suggest that, at least for Florence, the victory finally belonged to St. Francis and not the Cathars. Exuberantly, the saint rolled naked in the mud and filth; not only did he wed Dame Poverty, but he welcomed Sister Death. For him sickness was a blessing and a sign of God's love for man. Francis was to dwell on the passion of Christ, for Our Lord was no stranger to the sufferings of the human condition. The life of St. Francis illuminated a basic mystery, and in this mystery was dramatized the darker side of experience. Further, his life conveyed a perception of reality characterized by paradox and contradiction. Pain and death were now seen as an integral part of nature and therefore to be embraced rather than eradicated or transcended. Illness, once regarded as punishment for sin by an irate God, was now identified with the earthly torments of Christ. The dead Christs represented on crucifixes in Umbria and Tuscany were among the earliest examples of this

subject matter to appear in the art of the West. Francis would relive
the passion of Christ; the model for his life was the crucified Christ.
Poverty was suffering but was not to be fled from or shunned; instead it
was to be accepted as an ineradicable dimension of life.[60]

Indeed, the perspective offered on such fundamental experiences as
love, suffering, and death displayed a greater sensitivity toward the laic
condition. The projection of a more problematic and ambiguous view
seemed an endorsement of a version of reality wherein no set of rituals,
formulas, renunciations, or vows would spare the individual from trials
of the flesh. Truly, had not our Lord Jesus Christ been subject to these
same tribulations? The Cathars, Waldensians, Patarines, Humiliati, and
the rest had confronted the problem of death and evil in ways owing
much to the world of the monastery: one could avoid contamination by
ascetic practice and ritual. With the Cathars penance was imposed for
not adhering to "fussy" rites; moral and dietary indiscretions were
equated. Theirs was an obsessive literalism in which evil was perceived
as a "soiling" rather than an act of will. The new stance offered by the
mendicants amply acknowledged that no ritual or dramatic renunciation
could banish illness, forestall death, or secure riches. The human condition was accepted with all its sorrows. A vision wherein illness, suffering, and poverty were part of the texture of everyday life was closer to
the experience of a society whose membership was no longer encadred
and therefore more vulnerable. Social mobility, specialization, credit,
and technology were weakening literal bonds and mechanical solidarities.[61]

Earlier we observed such great religious figures as Nilo di Rosanno,
Romualdo, Damiani, and Giovanni Gualberto attempting to resolve
their religious disquiet in heroic style. Rigoristic and contemplative,
these spiritual masters made radical demands, calling for harsh sacrifice
and strenuous action. The Cathars, Waldensians, Patarines, and Humiliati, among other sects, also preached an evangelism requiring costly
choices. The consequences of these renunciations for church and society
would be nothing short of total spiritual regeneration. The defeat of
these grand and heroic schemes, at least for Florence, was to have a
significant impact. Although the sects elevated the dignity and worth
of each believer and vigorously challenged the world of hierarchy and
vows, they did not endorse a vision of reality indeterminate or problematic. For them an ultimate solution was in the offing—Utopian, millenarian, or rigoristic. Aspiring to lead their followers from a world of
narrow loyalties and self-interest back into a lost Eden, the sects were
reluctant to tolerate definitions of reality predicated on ineradicable am-

biguities. For them the vicissitudes of daily life might have to be endured in the short run, but the overarching problems facing humanity were susceptible to a single solution. The restoration of the primitive Church, the rule of fraternity, voluntary pauperism—these were but a few of the epic remedies advocated so fervently. Having launched a crushing challenge to a world of riches, hierarchy, and ascribed status, yet they withdrew into the security of small communities dedicated to voluntary poverty and penance. Reluctant to confer an irreducible quality on laic experience or to sanction the durability of social arrangements, they continued to live in expectation of radical historical changes, heralding the coming of a new Jerusalem. Their call was for social rejuvenation; meanwhile, they remained cordoned off from the ills of society.[62]

To project a social space of greater fixity and texture, it would be necessary to endow quotidian sentiments and emotions with new dignity. Though it was certain that laic feelings and experiences were radically insufficient in the sight of God, they must be deemed worthy of careful analysis and patient description. There would be lyrical moments when the ordinary was mystically transformed and the commonplace alchemized into pure spirituality. The subjective and interior would gain exceptional prominence, with compassion the talisman of true piety. This and much else were the particulars of a generalized perspective from which crucial intervals in the life of the individual were lent existential meaning. One might conduct a protracted meditation on death, love, or human destiny and then abruptly arrive at that most traditional of all conclusions, that all is vanity. The critical significance of the exploration, however, was in not the answer but the perspective itself. No easy strategy was adopted to discredit the laic vantage point: the experience was regarded as an undeniable fact, no matter what conclusions might be reached. Similarly, it was sure that social arrangements were fragile and insubstantial in the sight of God, but they could not be undone or dismissed even for this glorious reason. The certainty of laic involvement in worldly and social concerns was not to be legitimized from the perspective of eternity but accepted existentially. The universe of trade and exchange was growing increasingly complex; no longer was it possible to distinguish exactly between licit and illicit business transactions. Even the most subtle canonists and jurists were unsure of the moral legitimacy of credit dealings. As the ethics of the exchange system grew more ambiguous, religion became more responsive to the problematic in human negotiations. The salvation of the usurer's soul was now a matter of overwhelming spiritual concern. For the first time the region of purgatory was charted and mechanisms identified for allowing lay folk to make a felicitous transit.[63]

Acceptance of the lay predicament, with its burdens and possibilities, was acquiring literary cachet. Even among those seeking to persuade men to disavow terrestrial commitments it would be necessary to assume a rhetorical stance giving full recognition to the laic condition. Indeed, in Florence during the thirteenth century a leading genre was to be the prose and poetry of consolation. Here was revealed the extent to which writers, convinced of the vanity of human desires, would yet lavish sympathy on the spiritual plight of laity. The anxieties and triumphs, pitfalls, and accomplishments of secular life were acquiring their first sustained, dramatic vernacular representation in the literature of the towns in north and central Italy. The enemy of human happiness and stability was more often found by literati to be death and the caducity of the flesh than man's inadequacy in the face of God's commandments. Even those writers most eager to discredit the durability of human arrangements were required to explicate, with minute precision, the phenomenological reality of ordinary lives. Iacopone da Todi, Umbrian noble and man of legal affairs, after suffering the loss of his beloved wife in a horrendous accident, became a Franciscan lay brother. His anguished sense of conflict between earthly reality and spiritual ideals found expression in the creation of evocative poetry rivaling that of Villon. No amount of mystical rapture could negate earthly suffering, nor could the travails of life be elevated through metaphysical speculation. The call to penance readily acknowledged the obdurate and intractable features of secular experience. The paradox was that as laic sentiments and emotions gained force, thus ceasing to be undervalued, the fear of death and loss was to receive its most vivid and popular representation.[64]

A willingness to reward the subjective and social experience of laity with a religious and intellectual seriousness was the capstone of the emerging culture. This seriousness was evident even in the numerous literary instances where earthly duties were ultimately dismissed as vain and useless. It is unnecessary to match these dismissals with the many examples of warm, even passionate, endorsements for the round of laic, civil, and social obligations. The new starting point was coming to be defined by its vernacular, quotidian, and even commonplace point of view. To pursue this theme, however, requires that we gaze beyond this vernacular zone. If social experience was achieving greater fixity and social arrangements regarded as being more durable, then the millennial, the messianic, the Utopian, and the rigoristic should have been undergoing significant mutation. Clearly, they continued to exert a fatal fascination, but part of their attraction was being converted from popular movements for the grandiose reform of church and society into sentiment, ideology, and political philosophy.[65]

The thirteenth and early fourteenth centuries were to be the locale for a heightened trust in the power of abstraction. This confidence, general throughout Europe, was especially prominent among Florentine writers, from Brunetto Latini to Dante. The accent was on the "companionable" nature of man and his talent for sociability. This trust was matched by a firm conviction that the thirst for understanding was certainly the most glorious feature of the human condition. This belief spurred these writers to undertake the monumental task of popularizing scientific and ethical theories of the classical and medieval world. Dante's *Convivio* stood as a solemn tribute to the art of making the world of high culture accessible to his fellow townsmen. The popularization of Aristotelian conceptions of the ethical and political life led to the conviction that it would be indeed possible to govern states according to the rules of a science. The classical notion of the positive origins of the state refuted the Augustinian idea that governments were punishment for sin; instead, they were viewed as having natural origins in the desire of men for community. The associative life was perceived as being quintessential to the realization of man's nature. No longer was it possible to recount the history of the city of Florence by narrating the machinations of great clans; now it would be necessary to describe the world of guild association and, ultimately, that greatest of abstractions —the Florentine state![66]

From the earliest vernacular poetry to Dante's *Vita nuova*, religion and philosophy served as instruments to value a culture prizing the soul of man as manifest in thought and emotion. A critique of stoicism gained strength: from the first serious poem of Arrigo da Settimello, *Elegia de diversitate fortunae* (1193), to the writings of the humanists in Petrarch's generation, a critical reflection on stoic and ascetic doctrines was a major intellectual preoccupation. Leading Florentine writers debated the idea that Roman culture was great because it was schooled in stoic philosophy. Ideals of heroism founded on a denial of man's emotionality or the notion that immortality could be gained through repression were vigorously challenged. Literary strategies were developed by writers from Guittone d'Arezzo to Boccaccio for dramatizing the psychology of a middling zone between monastic asceticism and renunciation on the one hand and aristocratic excess and playfulness on the other. The effort to give subjective states a visual and literary objectivity was in itself a reversal of that stance described above. Instead of making material bonds tangible and palpable, the resources of culture were turned to charting psychological and spiritual ties.[67]

The direction of Tuscan literature was toward a passionate affirmation of lay moralism. Even when amorous doctrines and emotive bonds were repudiated, it was not for some rigid antiascetic reason but from the experience of a man of the world. Guido Cavalcanti and other poets catalogued and classified the laic sensibility in order to elevate it to a poetic science. Providing metaphysical theories for understanding the power of emotion necessitated borrowing from scholastic science and the revered mystics. At its most extreme this effort led to a quest for an autonomous terrain on which it would be possible to chart laic sentiment. A new concreteness was lent to the movement of the heart, the emotions, the spirit, and the soul. The effort to endow interior events with literary objectivity was yet another aspect of the vernacular quest to make manifest the force of spiritual affinities. Literature and art, then, rendered interior fantasies palpable. The most fundamental of all changes, however, concerned the nature of language itself: Florentine literati undertook a series of forays into the mechanics and expressive possibilities of the *volgare* as they strived to advance the vernacular into a linguistic position allowing it to achieve expressive powers hitherto unimagined. Students of language set out to elevate the vernacular rhetorically and syntactically to rival classical Latin. Nowhere is this phenomenon more evident than in the numerous translations of classical texts into Tuscan dialect. Fine translators, such as the Florentine judge Bono Giamboni, a contemporary of both Latini and Dante, demonstrated the potential of the vernacular for explicating the world of laic sentiment and emotion.[68]

Science, logic, and philosophy found popular expression in the Arno city as literary efforts were mounted to systematize culture according to an organic plan. The ordering and encylopedic impulses of the grand theological *summae* were primary influences in forming the philosophical base for the study of language. Logic and metaphysics treated the disjunction between speech and thought; further, they provided a structure for the grand vernacular compendia of natural science, philosophy, psychology, cosmology, history, and geography. The finest talents in Florence, over the three generations from Latini to Dante to Boccaccio, labored to present popular, systematized accounts of philosophical and scientific problems for a wide audience of literate townsmen. Moreover, thirteenth-century vernacular writers were themselves deeply implicated in political struggles and civic culture. The mark of this involvement was most apparent in the trajectory of the development of rhetorical studies. A style less artificial and decorous was created, prizing order, clarity, proportion, and harmony. In an earlier age Tuscan rhetoricians had belittled the public forum; with Latini, however, it became a part of civil science. Truly, it was the greater part because those who knew its rules and strategies could "move the council and bring peace and benevolence." The power of rhetoric to create peace caused Tuscan writers to relate it to philosophy; its nobility and loftiness were amply demonstrated by its utility in instructing citizens on the art of government. This view was far removed from an earlier theory that persuasion had been invented by Lucifer when convincing the angels to follow him against the Lord. The other celebrated instance was Lucifer's successful appeal to Adam and Eve to eat the forbidden fruit. The new rhetoric posited a very different view: it was rhetoric, coupled with wisdom, that first brought man out of his bestial and marauding world. In primitive times it was surely the war of everyone against everyone. Wise and eloquent men made people aware of their capacity to accomplish great things: know God, understand their neighbors, and maintain the sacred peace. Through speech humans became aware of their ability for the good.[69]

XII

The heightened popular trust in such abstractions as culture, philosophy, logic, and the emotive force of love was in itself a tribute to the enhanced possibilities and risks of associative life. When humans were bound together by strict ties and literal bonds, culture tended to validate the materiality of quotidian life. This phenomenon was not explicable, as has been recently suggested, in terms of a Piagetesque child psychology. There was nothing childish about this culture: instead, it housed sophisticated and ingenious intellects seeking to appreciate and understand the possibilities of concrete logic and even transcend them. The perils and dangers of stepping outside the bounds of literal ties caused this type of logic to be prized even by those challenging its stern demands. With the eleventh- and twelfth-century takeoff we observed a gradual loosening of strict bonds and the relaxation of narrow allegiances. We can discern a measure of this expanded trust in the decline of interest rates and the rise of deposit and transfer banking. A *collaborative* attitude between borrower and lender was becoming pervasive in the cities of north and central Italy.[70]

As the confidence in abstract economic and social arrangements grew, so, too, did the trust in dialectic. One could argue that the shift from archaic and tribal organization to a commercial and communal society conforms to certain of Lévi-Strauss's mappings of change. In characterizing the primitive, Lévi-Strauss argues that concrete logic, while manipulating and shifting discrete elements of nature and experience, did not reduce them to the "economy" of a single code. Moreover, primitives harbored totalitarian ambitions: if you cannot explain everything, you have explained nothing. If we make the analogy between early medieval and primitive, then we can venture certain propositions: intellectual interest and objectivity were expressed in both cultures by a concern—almost a reverence—for the discrete at the everyday level. This particularizing was coupled with the totalitarian ambition to explain everything. What emerged in the eleventh and twelfth centuries was a change of mentality: on the level of the quotidian the force of abstraction came into play with a mounting trust in new forms of associative life. At grander heights of intellectualization and objectivity, the drive was no longer so markedly in the direction of all or nothing; rather, the impulse was toward breaking problems down, reducing the number of discrete elements, and then self-consciously systematizing. It was as if the new society could now tolerate the separation between mind and matter, thought and experience, and word and thing. The nexus was problematic and the product of human mental activity. The tools, of course, were reason and dialectic. A new ordering was therefore possible, allowing a greater mastery of nature. In turn, this ordering led to a very different valuation of nature and emotion. At all costs the archaic culture maintained the illusion that nature could be controlled: either it could be understood entirely or not at all. So, too, strict and material ties projected the illusion of God's concern for humankind. Similarly, social arrangements were rendered durable by gift, oath, and display. The new science and economy were released from the quest for absolute security in order to pursue a very different kind of mastery.[71]

NOTES

1. M. Becker, *Florence in Transition* (Baltimore, 1968), II, pp. 151–200.

2. Biblioteca Nazionale in Firenze, Magliabechiano XXV, 43, cc. 101 ff.

3. I wish to thank my colleague Sylvia Thrupp and friend Richard Goldthwaite for their suggestions and ideas on the complex topic of offsetting and credit.

4. On the strength of Germanic traditions in the family life of north and central Italy, see J. Heers, *Le clan familial au Moyen Âge* (Paris, 1974), pp. 27 ff. For materials on the jus Langobardorum and its persistence in Tuscany, see L. Chiapelli, "L'età longobarda e Pistoia," *Archivio Storico Italiano*, LXXIX (1921), 228–338.

5. For a comprehensive discussion of changes in the conception of the dowry as it was converted from gift to credit, see P. Cammarosano, "Aspetti delle strutture familiari nelle città dell'Italia comunali," *Studi Medievali*, 3rd ser., XVI (1975), 417–535.

6. The importance of fidelity is suggested in the legend recorded by the chronicler Erchemperto and the Anonimo Salernitano. When Paul the Deacon was summoned to judgment before Charlemagne and his nobles on an accusation of having plotted against the emperor, Paul did not seek to exculpate himself or beg for mercy but replied with simple dignity that he had always been faithful to his former master King Desiderius. Cf. G. Falco, "Voci Cassinesi nell'alto medioevo," *Il monachesimo nell'alto medioevo e la formazione della civiltà occidentale* (Spoleto, 1957), 24.

7. M. Becker, pp. 236–38.

8. I wish to thank J. Banker and R. Weissman for information on the confraternities at Borgo San Sepolcro and in sixteenth-century Florence.

9. For a useful survey of Florentine merchant culture and its chroniclers, see the by-now-classic account by A. Sapori, *The Italian Merchant in the Middle Ages*, trans. P. Kennen (New York, 1970). Cf. also R. Goldthwaite, *Private Wealth in Renaissance Florence: A Study of Four Families* (Princeton, 1968).

10. G. Pinto, *Il libro del biadaiolo: Carestie e annona a Firenze* (Florence, 1978), pp. 108–49.

11. M. Bloch, *Feudal Society*, trans. L. Manyon (Chicago, 1964), I, pp. 85 ff., and his *Rois et serfs* (Paris, 1920). Cf. also R. Southern's incisive discussion in *Western Society and the Church in the Middle Ages* (Baltimore, 1970), pp. 28–32.

12. For a useful survey of recent scholarship on these questions, see L. Roth-

krug, "Popular Religion and Holy Shrines," *Religion and the People 800–1700*, ed. J. Obelkevich (Chapel Hill, N.C., 1979), 36–40. For some original insights into relationships between the decline of "translations" and the theft of relics, see R. Lopez, "The Practical Transmission of Medieval Culture," *By Things Seen: Reference and Recognition in Medieval Thought* (Ottawa, 1979), 125–28.

13. Sarah White's soon-to-be-published "Some Literary Consequences of the Anatomical Distinction: Genital Imagery in Old French Fabliaux" has been most helpful in formulating hypotheses.

14. G. Argan's *Storia dell'arte italiana* (Florence, 1968), I, pp. 255–301, is a most excellent survey of that complex zone between art and society.

15. D. Herlihy, "L'economia della città e del distretto di Lucca secondo le carte private nell'alto medioevo," *Atti del 5° Congresso internazionali di studi sull'alto medioevo* (Spoleto, 1973), 370–83.

16. E. Sareni, "Agricoltura e mondo rurale," *Storia d'Italia* (Turin, 1972), I, 176 ff., gives a summary of the data on population figures. On "les générosités nécessaires," see G. Duby, *The Early Growth of the European Economy*, trans. H. Clarke (Ithaca, N.Y., 1974), p. 56. On the changing character of *libri memoriales*, see K. Schmid, "Über der Verhältnis von Person und Gemeinschaft im frühreren Mittelalter," *Früh mittelalterliche Studien*, I (1967), 96–134. For changes in the language of politics, see E. Kantorowicz's now classic *The King's Two Bodies: A Study in Political Theology* (Princeton, N.J., 1957), pp. 87 ff. For an illuminating discussion of conceptions of cultural change, see D. Sperber, "Claude Lévi-Strauss," *Structuralism and Since*, ed. J. Sturrock (Oxford, 1979), 19–31.

17. M. Bloch's still valuable "Les invasions: Deux structures économique: Occupation du sol et peuplement," *Annales d'Histoire Sociale*, I (1945), 33–46; II (1946), 13–28. For a thoughtful appraisal of the historian's use of dream literature, see J. LeGoff, *Time, Work and Culture in the Middle Ages*, trans. A. Goldhammer (Chicago, 1980), pp. 201–4, 347–50. For an illuminating discussion of Peirce's ideas, see N. Chomsky, *Language and Responsibility* (New York, 1977), pp. 70–80. For a comparison of the Venerable Bede and St. Anselm of Aosta, see J. de Ghellinck, *Le mouvement théologique du XIIᵉ siècle*, 2nd ed. (Brussels, 1948), p. 88.

18. For an informed and lively discussion of Dante's views on language and grammar, see G. Mazzotta, *Dante, Poet of the Desert: History and Allegory in the Divine Comedy* (Princeton, N.J., 1979), pp. 81–109, 295 ff. Fundamental to any consideration of the relationship between word and thing is F. Cranz, "Cusanus, Luther and the Mystical Tradition," *The Pursuit of Holiness in Late Medieval and Renaissance Religion*, ed. C. Trinkaus and H. Oberman (Leiden, 1974), pp. 93–102.

1. RELIGION AND SOCIAL CHANGE

1. Particularly useful for background on these developments are the following: L. White, *Medieval Technology and Social Change* (Oxford, 1962); G. Duby, *Rural Economy and Country Life in the Medieval West* (Columbia, S.C., 1968), and *The Early Growth of the European Economy* (Ithaca, N.Y., 1974); R. Lopez, *The Commercial Revolution of the Middle Ages* (Englewood Cliffs, N.J., 1971); P. J. Jones, "La storia economica: Dalla caduta dell'Impero Romano al secolo XIV," *Storia d'Italia* (Turin, 1974), II, part 1, 1469–1810 (this masterful survey contains an extensive bibliography for all regions of Italy); C. Violante, "Storia ed economia dell'Italia medievale," *Rivista Storica Italiana*, LXXII (1961), 513–35; D. Herlihy, "The Agrarian Revolution in Southern France and

Italy, 801–1150," *Speculum*, XXXIII (1958), 23–41; I. Imberciadori, *Mezzadria classica toscana con documentazione inedita dal sec. 9 al sec. 14* (Florence, 1951); E. Fiumi, "Fioritura e decadenza dell'economia fiorentina," *Archivio Storico Italiano*, CXV (1957), 385–439; D. Hughes, "Urban Growth and Family Structure in Medieval Genoa," *Past and Present*, LXVI (1975), 3–28; C. Klapisch, "Villaggi abbandonati ed emigrazioni interne," *Storia d'Italia* (Turin, 1973), V, part 1, 311–69; M. Pegna, *Firenze dalle origini al medioevo* (Florence, 1962); J. Plesner, *L'émigration de la compagne à la ville libre de Florence au 13e siècle* (Copenhagen, 1934); "The Tenth Century: A Symposium," in *Mediaevalia et Humanistica*, IX (1955).

2. For a recent summary of remarkable insights into the problem of credit, see R. Lopez's introduction to *The Dawn of Modern Banking* (New Haven, 1979), pp. 3–22; see also his comments in *Artigianato nella società dell'alto medioevo occidentale* (Spoleto, 1971), II, 245–46, and "Moneta e monetieri nell'Italia barbarica," *Moneta e scambi nell'alto medioevo* (Spoleto, 1961); P. Grierson, "Symbolism in Medieval Charters and Coins," *Simboli e simbologia nell'alto medioevo* (Spoleto, 1976), II, 609–25, and his *Numismatics and History* (London, 1951). For a general discussion of money and credit, see C. Cipolla, *Studi di storia della moneta, I* (Pavia, 1948). For a translation of pertinent documents, see R. Lopez and I. Raymond, *Medieval Trade in the Mediterranean World* (New York, 1965), pp. 41–48. For the Latin documents of the Lombard period, see L. Schiaparelli, ed., *Codice diplomatico longobardo*, (Rome, 1929–33), 2 vols.

3. Of course, the classic work on gift culture is M. Mauss, *The Gift: Form and Function of Exchange in Archaic Societies*, trans. I. Cunnison (New York, 1967). On the application of Mauss's theories to early European history, see G. Duby, *The Early Growth of the European Economy* (Ithaca, N.Y., 1974), P. Grierson, "Commerce in the Dark Ages: A Critique of the Evidence," *Transactions of the Royal Historical Society*, 5th ser., IX (1959), 123–40, and L. Little, *Religious Poverty and the Profit Economy in Medieval Europe* (Ithaca, N.Y., 1978), pp. 3–6. For the general history of ties of obligation, see the magisterial survey by F. Schupfer, *Il diritto delle obbligazioni in Italia nell'età del Risorgimento* (Turin, 1921), 3 vols. On *launegeld* in Tuscany, see G. Masi, " 'La defensio' nel diritto prerinascementale," *Rivista di Storia del Diritto Italiano*, XXIV (1951), 95–147.

4. G. Astuti's "Influssi romanistici nelle fonte del diritto longobardo," in *La cultura antica nell'occidente latino dal VII all'XI secolo* (Spoleto, 1975), II, 653–95, presents a nuanced discussion of the theme of composition, with an extensive bibliography. Peter Brown, "Society and the Supernatural: A Medieval Change," *Daedalus*, CLV (1975), 133–51, discusses the ordeal from an anthropological perspective. On *wergeld*, see the recent study by G. Fasoli, *Scritti di storia medievale* (Bologna, 1974), pp. 17–19. For a consideration of the religious dimension of composition, see C. Vogel, "Composition légale et commutation dans le système de la pénitence tarifée," *Revue de Droit Canonique*, VII (1958), 289–318; IX (1959), 1–30, 341–55.

5. For a discussion of *mund*, see C. Giardina, "Sul mundualdo della donna," *Rivista di Storia del Diritto Italiano*, XXXV (1962): 41–51; cf. also G. Salvioli, *Storia del diritto italiano* (Turin, 1921), pp. 506 ff.; A. Tagliaferri, "Fasi dell'-economia longobarda," *Problemi dell'economia longobarda* (Milan, 1964), 254–55. For a general discussion of these questions, see R. Doehaerd, *Le haut moyen âge occidental: Économies et sociétés* (Paris, 1971), pp. 219–47. For a recent discussion of evidence on these problems in contemporary chronicles, see A. Murray, *Reason and Society in the Middle Ages* (Oxford, 1978), pp. 32–33, and L. Little, pp. 4–5, 25. F. Graus's "Le funzioni del culte dei santi e della leggenda," *Agiografia altomedioevale*, ed. S. Boesch Gajano (Bologna, 1976), 145–60, is a

useful recent discussion of religious developments, with valuable bibliographical references.

6. On the religious dimension of this exchange system, see G. Miccoli, *Chiesa Gregoriana: Ricerche sulla riforma nel secolo XI* (Florence, 1960), pp. 56 ff. E. Besta, *Le obbligazione nella storia del diritto italiano* (Padua, 1936), deals with the complex topic of changing ties of obligations; see especially pp. 193 ff. for the spiritual implications. For leading features of Tuscan legacies in the eighth and ninth centuries, see L. Nanni, *La parrocchia studiata nei documenti lucchesi dei secoli VIII–XIII* (Rome, 1948), pp. 28–46. A textured source providing documentation on the religious sensibility of benefactors is *Il regesto di Farfa di Gregorio di Catino*, ed. I. Giorgi and U. Balzani (Rome, 1879–88), particularly volumes 2–4. On penance as a long-term *guidrigildo*, see E. Rocca, "Considerazioni giuridiche sulla regola e sul 'penitenziale di San Colombano,'" *Contributi dell'istituto di storia medioevale* (Milan, 1972), 449.

7. For a general discussion of salvation and the role of monks, see G. Miccoli, pp. 47–54. For the bequests of Lombard kings and Carolingian rulers, see R. Morghen, *Gregorio VII e la riforma della chiesa nel secolo XI* (Palermo, 1974), pp. 31–32. On the dispensation of charity on a ritual basis, see L. Nanni, p. 78, and documents in *Codice diplomatico longobardo*, I, nos. 28, 48; II, nos. 127, 140, 194, and 204; *Memorie et documenti per servire all'istoria del Ducato di Lucca* (Lucca, 1836), IV, part 2, passim, and V, nos. 231, 907; C. Boyd, *Tithes and Parishes in Medieval Italy* (Ithaca, N.Y., 1952), pp. 36–37. For an extensive bibliography on spiritual preoccupations and developments, see *Agiografia altomedioevale*, pp. 261–300. On wills and donations, see G. Vismara, *Storia dei patti successori* (Milan, 1941), I, pp. 211 ff.; A. Pertile, *Storia del diritto italiano* (Turin, 1896–1903), IV, pp. 10 ff.; E. Besta, *Le successioni nella storia del diritto italiano* (Milan, 1936), pp. 2, 144–388.

8. For numerous instances of this sensibility, see documents in *Il regesto di Farfa*, II, pp. 46, 60, 69, 75, 79, 126–28. A general discussion of the intellectual dimension of this theme is found in J. Leclercq, *La spiritualité du moyen âge* (Aubier, 1961), pp. 38–51; A. Bush, "An Echo of Christian Antiquity in Saint Gregory the Great," *Traditio*, III, (1965), 369–90; R. Manselli, "L'escatologismo di S. Gregorio Magno," *Atti del Primo Congresso Internazionali di Studi Longobardi* (Spoleto, 1952), 383–87, and his *La 'lectura super Apocalipsim' di Pietro di Giovanni Olivi. Ricerche sull'escatologismo medioevale* (Rome, 1955), pp. 5–16.

9. P. Ariès, in his *L'homme devant la mort* (Paris, 1977), pp. 41–114, outlines the nature of the problem, and, though one could disagree with particulars and even points of interpretation, the aperçus are suggestive. E. Delaruelle, *La piété populaire au moyen âge* (Turin, 1975), pp. 94–95, considers changing rituals. Cf. D. Bullough, "Early Medieval Social Groupings: The Terminology of Kinship," *Past and Present*, XLV (1969), 3–18. On the casual attitude toward children and the theme of affective family ties, see D. Herlihy, "Medieval Children," *The Walter Prescott Webb Memorial Lectures: Essays on Medieval Civilization* (Austin, Tex., 1978), 115–16; M. McLaughlin, "Survivors and Surrogates: Children and Parents from the Ninth to the Thirteenth Centuries," *The History of Childhood*, ed. L. deMause (New York, 1974), 101–81. Seldom do we find a personal note in legacies and benefactions. L. Nanni, p. 33, observes, after having reviewed extensive documentation for Lucca, that instances of the personal are exceedingly rare. For examples of commonplace, detached statements, see *Codice diplomatico longobardo*, I, pp. 35, 42, 109, 165; II, pp. 4–5 passim.

10. For an analysis of juridical symbols employed in contractual arrangements and legal procedures, see J. LeGoff, "Les gestes symboliques dans la vie sociale," *Simboli e simbologia nell'altomedioevo*, II, 778–82; M. Thevenin, *Textes relatifs*

aux institutions merovingiennes et carolingiennes (Paris, 1887), pp. 263–68. On the nature of pledges and guarantees, see P. Leicht, *Il diritto privato preirneriano* (Bologna, 1933), pp. 194–98. It is interesting to note that documents registering debts had a penitential character during early medieval times. Cf. E. Besta, *Le obbligazione*, p. 126. For the material aspect of political and social arrangements, see G. Barni and G. Fasoli, *L'Italia nell'alto medioevo: Società e costumi* (Turin, 1971), pp. 121–25. On the role of the notary, see T. Blomquist's review of M. Amelotti and G. Costamagna, *Alle origini del notariato italiano* (Rome, 1975), in *Speculum*, LII (1977), 912–13; cf. also C. Mor, "Simbologia e simboli nella vita guiridica," *Symboli e simbologia*, I, 24–25; Barni and Fasoli, p. 505.

11. On the twilight zone between folklore and law, see E. Carusi, "Folkloristica giuridica e storia del diritto," *Rivista di Storia del Diritto Italiano*, II (1929), 129–54. On the theme of symbolism, see the comments of A. Tenenti in *Simboli e simbologia*, II (Spoleto, 1976), 854–55. On the question of boundaries, see D. Werkmüller, "Recinzioni, confini e sengi terminali," ibid., 640–78. On ritual and Italian law, see G. Salvioli, pp. 581–82; E. Cortese, "Per la storia del mundio in Italia," *Revista Italiana per le Scienze Giuridice*, LXXXI (1955–56), 465 ff.

12. For background, see C. Violante, *La pataria milanese e la riforma ecclesiastica* (Rome, 1955); G. Miccoli, "Per la storia della pataria milanese," *Bullettino dell'Istituto Storico Italiano per il Medio Evo*, LXX (1958), 43–123. (This source will henceforth be abbreviated as *B.I.S.I.*) Cf. also the chronicler Landolfo di San Paolo, *Historia mediolanensis*, *R.I.S.*, V, part 3 (Bologna, 1934), p. 6. (*R.I.S.* is an abbreviation for *Rerum Italicarum Scriptores*.)

13. R. Rough, *The Reformist Illuminations in the Gospels of Matilda: A Study in the Art of Gregory VII* (The Hague, 1973), p. 13. For annotations on the Canossa codex of the *Vita Mathildis* by a contemporary who indicated sympathy with reformist ideals, see C. Violante, *Studi sulla cristianità medioevale* (Milan, 1972), p. 338. The text of St. Matthew (21:12), in which he describes Christ driving the buyers and sellers from the temple of the Lord, was widely cited during this turbulent period; cf. J. Gilchrist, *The Church and Economic Activity in the Middle Ages* (New York, 1969), pp. 51–52.

14. G. Miccoli, "Aspetti di monachesimo toscano nel secolo XI," *Il romanico pistoiese nei suoi rapporti con l'arte romanica dell'occidente* (Pistoia, 1966), 53 ff.; W. Goez, "Reformpapstum, Adel und Monastische Erneuerung in der Toscana, *Investitur und Reichsversassung*, ed. J. Fleckenstein (Sigmaringen, 1973), 295–319.

15. For a discussion of the new rapport among men, see G. Tabacco, "Privilegium amoris," *Il Saggiatore*, IV (1954), 1–20. On Peter Damiani's ideal of monastic perfection highlighting solitary battle and freedom from traditional rigidity, see O. Capitani, "San Pier Damiani e l'istituto eremitico," *L'eremitisimo in occidente nei secoli XI e XII* (Milan, 1965), 122–63. On the holy man in earlier times, see P. Conti, *Devotio viri devoti in Italia da Diocleziano ai Carolinghi* (Padua, 1971). For a discussion of the less austere spirituality in the century preceding the Gregorian Reforms, see L. Zoepf, *Das Heiligen Leben im 10 Jahrhundert* (Leipzig, 1908), pp. 125–31. For documents pertaining to Marchesa Willa, see L. Schiaparelli, ed., *Le carte del monastero di S. Maria in Firenze (Badia)* (Rome, 1913), I, pp. 10–11. For further documentation pertaining to other great Tuscan feudatories, see G. Miccoli, *Chiesa Gregoriana*, pp. 50–61. For an explication of the theme of "social space," see M. D. Chenu, "Fraternitas: Evangile et condition socio-culturelle," *Revue d'Histoire de la Spiritualité*, XLIX (1973), 385–400. It is worth noting that not until the prose description of the twelfth century do the inhabitants of Italian towns commence to figure prominently; previously, the stage was dominated by saints and edifices. Cf. D. Bullough, "Social and Economic Structure in the Early Medieval City," *Topografia*

urbana e vita cittadina nell'alto medioevo in occidente (Spoleto, 1974), I, 358.

16. G. Miccoli, pp. 58–60. Cf. also G. Miccoli, *Pietro Igneo: Studi sull'età gregoriana* (Rome, 1960).

17. C. Violante, "Riflessioni sulla povertà nel secolo XI," *Studi sul medioevo cristiano offerti a Raffaello Morghen* (Rome, 1974), II, 1060–62. Cf. also the recent monograph by L. Little previously cited. For additional bibliography, see C. Violante, "Vescovi e diocesi in Italia nel medioevo," *Atti del II Convegno di Storia della Chiesa in Italia* (Padua, 1964), 193–217.

18. These observations are based upon a reading of documents housed in the *Archivio di Stato* in Florence, particularly the *Diplomatico of San Salvatore di Camaldoli; Badia di San Lorenzo a Coltibuono; Strozzioni Uguccioni; Società di S. Maria del Bigallo; Badia di Ripoli; Dono Rinuccini; San Spirito; Vescovado di Pistoia; Monastero degli Olivetani; Patrimonio Ecclesiastico di Firenze; Badia di San Fidele di Poppi; Crociferi di Firenze; Diplomatico Pistoia; San Lorenzo di Pisa; Spoglio dalle Cartapecore dei Cistercensi; Santa Croce; Santa Maria Novella.* Conclusions drawn from such an array of documents are of the nature of hypotheses. The run of documents for the monastery of Farfa (outside Rome) lends support to observations for Tuscany. The earliest charters contain the greatest incidence of references to hell fire. Though materials are scanty for the ninth century, it does appear that a break occurs at mid-tenth century. The future life appears to be less fraught with spiritual perils, and remedies for sin are increasingly mild. Such impressions support the conclusions advanced by R. Southern in his *The Making of the Middle Ages* (New Haven, Conn., 1953). His generalizations stem from a reading of materials in a variety of sources ranging from feudal romances to theological tracts. If the Tuscan experience is valid, the changes that he describes have their origins in renewed confidence expressed by a considerable segment of the will-maker and benefactor populations.

19. R. Southern notes that in Italy hospitals and hermitages, "harbingers of later religious ideals grow up side-by-side presenting an alternative to the corporate life of the Benedictine monastery"; cf. *St. Anselm and His Biographers* (Cambridge, 1963), p. 29. Cf. also L. Nanni, pp. 31–43; G. Richa, *Notizie delle chiese fiorentine* (Florence, 1757), V, p. 286.

20. For a discussion of the heightened concern with family evidenced in the Bolognese Glossa, see R. Trifone, "Fedecommesso," *Nuovissimo digesto italiano* (Turin, 1961), VII, 196. Cf. also D. Hughes, "Struttura familiare e del suo funzionamento nella società medievale," *Quaderni Storici*, XXXIII (1976), 936–47; N. Tamassia, *La famiglia italiana nel secoli XV e XVI* (Palermo, 1910), pp. 130–36. On the influence of Roman law upon the disposition of property in Tuscany and Lombardy, see F. Niccolai, *La formazione del diritto successorio negli statuti communali del territorio lombardo-tosco* (Milan, 1940), pp. 325–44.

21. For a survey of the role of executor, with an extensive bibliography, see P. Fedele, "Esecutore testamentario," *Enciclopedia del diritto* (Varese, 1966), XV, 383–89. On the complex issue of inheritance, see M. Bellomo, "Erede," ibid., 184–94, and his *Ricerche sui rapporti patrimoniali tra coniugi. Contributo alla storia delle familie medievali* (Milan, 1961), pp. 163–85. For practices during the earlier period, see F. Schupfer, *Il diritto privato dei popoli germanici con speciale riguardo all'Italia* (Città di Castello, 1909) IV, pp. 254–64; G. Vismara, "La successione voluntarie nelle leggi barbariche," *Studi di storia e diritto in onore di A. Solmi* (Milan, 1941), II, 183–270.

22. G. Miccoli's "La storia religiosa," in *Storia d'Italia* (Turin, 1974), II, part 1, 472–507, provides an excellent summary of religious change over the eleventh century. Cf. also his *Pietro Igneo*, pp. 134 ff. On the influential San Nilo, see G. Pepe, *Da san Nilo all'umanesimo* (Bari, 1966), pp. 9–14.

23. For changes in canon law, with a bibliography, see O. Giacchi, "Matrimonio (diritto canonico)," *Enciclopedia del diritto* (Varese, 1975), XXV, 887–901. In considering these changes it is useful to recall that the Gregorians placed the highest priority on restricting marriage between family members. This was not, as G. Ladner has concluded, a negative act. Damiani maintained that marriage was a most appropriate means of repairing the sacred cords of charity. In the early Middle Ages endogamy kept patrimony within the same household. When Damiani argued, at the request of the Florentines, before the judges of Ravenna, in favor of more severe medieval consanguinity provisions, he was working in fact to enhance prospects for sociability among humankind. G. Ladner,"Medieval and Modern Understanding of Symbolism: A Comparison," *Speculum*, LIV (1979), 247–49, views these structural changes within the context of the history of ideas, whereas I fix them in the domain of social experience.

24. On the spiritualization of the conjugal union, see G. Duby, "Le mariage dans la société du haut moyen âge," *Il matrimonio nella società altomedievale* (Spoleto, 1977), 34–37, and his *Medieval Marriage: Two Models from Twelfth-Century France*, trans. E. Forster (Baltimore, 1978). For a discussion of the evolution of a rich vocabulary pertaining to marital relationships, see P. Toubert, *Les structures du Latium médiéval* (Rome, 1973), I, pp. 709 ff. On new spiritual possibilities open to men and women living within the family circle, see G. Meersseman and E. Adda, "Pénitents ruraux communautaires en Italie aux XIIe siècle," *Revue d'Histoire Écclésiastique*, XLIX (1954), 343–90. On preaching, see M. H. Vicaire, *L'imitation des apôtres. Moines, chanoines et mendiants IVe–XIIIe siècles* (Paris, 1963), pp. 54–61.

25. A. Falce, *Ugo di Tuscia* (Florence, 1921), pp. 113–33; I. Mittarelli and A. Costadoni, *Annales Camaldulenses* (Venice, 1755), I, c. 145; F. Schneider, ed., *Regestum Senese* (Rome, 1911), I, p. 9. For other references, see G. Miccoli, *Chiesa Gregoriana*, pp. 50–57.

26. See D. Hughes, "From Brideprice to Dowry in Mediterranean Europe," *Journal of Family History*, September 1978, 262–96, for a recent discussion of the changing character of the family, with a bibliography. For Tuscany, see D. Herlihy, "Land, Family and Women in Continental Europe, 701–1200," *Traditio*, XVIII (1962), 89–120; Herlihy and C. Klapisch-Zuber, *Les toscans et leurs familles* (Paris, 1978), pp. 526–51. Cf. also P. J. Jones, "Florentine Families and Florentine Diaries in the Fourteenth Century," *Papers of the British School at Rome*, XXIV (1956), 183–205.

27. A. Del Vecchio, *Le seconde nozze coniunge superstite* (Florence, 1885), pp. 237 ff. P. Toubert estimates an increase in provisions "sub conditione viduitatis" in the wills of husbands during this period; cf. *Les structures du Latium médiéval*, pp. 778–79. Though it is not possible to estimate the effect of the persistence of the Lombard tradition of partible inheritance, it was not possible for primogeniture to triumph to the extent that it did in France; cf. G. Duby, "Structures de parenté et de noblesse, France du Nord IXe–XIIe siècle," *Miscellania mediaevalia in memoriam J. Frederik Niermeyer* (Groningen, 1967), 149–65. Cf. also J. LeGoff, "The Usurer and Purgatory," *The Dawn of Modern Banking* (New Haven, Conn., 1979), 25–52.

28. C. Cipolla, "Introduzione," *Storia dell'economia italiana* (Turin, 1959), I, 7–8, and his *Before the Industrial Revolution: European Society and Economy, 1000–1700* (New York, 1976), pp. 182–87. For a bibliography, see C. Violante, "Storia ed economia dell'Italia medievale," 513–35. Cf. P. J. Jones, "La storia economica," 1496–98. For a discussion of the emergence of a language for complex economic transactions, see P. Toubert, *Les structures*, pp. 609–24.

29. For a critique of the theory of the release of the treasure hoard, see P. Toubert, "Histoire de l'Italie médiévale (Xe–XIIIe siècles)," *Revue Historique*,

CCXXVII (1960), 168–70; D. Herlihy, "Treasure Hoards in the Italian Economy, 960–1139," *The Economic History Revue*, 2nd ser., X (1957), 1–14. On the paucity of documents pertaining to *cambiatores, prestatores*, and other monetary specialists, see R. Lopez, "Moneta e monetieri nell'Italia barbarica," *Moneta e scambi nell'alto medioevo* (Spoleto, 1961), 59. For a full discussion of the theme of credit in north and central Italy, see Lopez's *The Commercial Revolution of the Middle Ages, 950–1350* (Englewood Cliffs, N.J., 1971).

30. Cf. note 10. A new interest in the conservation of documents was manifested with the switch from papyrus to parchment; cf. R. Lopez, "Still Another Renaissance," *American Historical Revue*, LVII (1951), 1–21. On the elaboration of new notarial formulas, see P. Leicht, *Storia del diritto italiano* (Milan, 1937), pp. 96–98, and G. Cencetti, "Studium fuit Bononie," *Le origini dell'Università*, ed. G. Arnaldi (Bologna, 1974), 113. For a recent summary of scholarship and bibliography on the notary, see G. Costamagna, "Notaio," *Enciclopedia del diritto* (Varese, 1978), XXVIII, 561–65.

31. E. Besta, *Fonti: Legislazione e scienza giuridica* (Milan, 1923), I, pp. 378–94; G. Astuti, *I contratti obligatori nella storia del diritto italiano* (Milan, 1952), pp. 125 ff.; P. Leicht, *Il diritto privato preirneriano* (Bologna, 1933), pp. 20–21; G. Dahm, *Das Strafrecht Italiens im ausgehenden Mittelalter* (Berlin, 1931), pp. 520 ff.; E. Besta, *Le obbligazioni*, pp. 36, 141; G. Mor, *L'età feudale* (Milan, 1952), II, p. 59.

32. For a discussion of the particulars of these transformations, see G. Meersseman, *Ordo fraternitatis: Confraternitate e pietà dei laici nel medioevo* (Rome, 1977), I, chap. 1, especially pp. 7–145. M. D. Chenu, in his *Nature, Man, and Society in the Twelfth Century: Essays on New Theological Perspectives in the Latin West*, ed. and trans. J. Taylor and L. Little (Chicago, 1968), pp. xvii, 265 ff., deals with general questions pertaining to the formation of evangelical brotherhoods. He integrates them into the burgeoning of associative life with the rise of communes, guilds, business partnerships, etc. These new forms of solidarity expressed a more vivid sense of equality; cf. note 15.

33. E. Cortese, "Errore," *Enciclopedia del diritto* (Varese, 1966), XV, 236–40; G. Salvioli, pp. 593–95; R. Bloome, *La doctrine du péché dans les écoles théologiques de la première moitié du XIIe siècle* (Louvain, 1958); C. Vogel, "Le rites de la célébration du mariage," *Il matrimonio nella società alto-medievale* (Spoleto, 1977), I, 453–71. Such important figures as Arialdo, the Patarine leader of Milan, were strong in their opposition to marriage between kin of a forbidden degree of relationship; cf. C. Violante, *Studi sul cristianità medioevale* (Milan, 1972), p. 179.

34. A. Pertile, IV, pp. 27–28, 494–548, 554–73; E. Besta, pp. 500–540; G. Post, *Studies in Medieval Legal Thought* (Princeton, 1961), pp. 6–24, and his "Philosophy and Citizenship in the Thirteenth Century," *Order and Innovation in the Middle Ages*, ed. W. C. Jordan, B. McNab, and T. Ruiz (Princeton, 1976), 400–402; A. D'Amia, *Rinascenza pisani del diritto e di cultura e d'arte* (Pisa, 1975).

35. D. Osheim, *An Italian Lordship. The Bishropric of Lucca in the Late Middle Ages* (Berkeley, Cal., 1977), p. 21; J. Plesner, *L'émigration de la campagne a la ville libre de Florence au XIIIe siècle* (Copenhagen, 1934), pp. 2–3; E. Conti, *La formazione della struttura agraria moderna nel contado fiorentino* (Rome, 1965), I, p. 107.

36. G. Mollat, *Études sur l'histoire de la pauvreté* (Paris, 1974), p. 25; and his "La notion de la pauvreté au Moyen Âge," *Revue d'Histoire de l'Église de France*, LII (1966), 5–19. E. Conti observes changes in the pattern of donations in the Tuscan countryside at the time of agitation against the simoniacs; cf. *La formazione*, pp. 157 ff. D. Herlihy, "Church Property on the European con-

tinent," 96, indicates that the climax in lay donations was reached at the time of Gregory VII.

37. G. Meersseman, pp. 95–145. For a full discussion of Franciscanism and Florentine involvement in charitable activity, see Meersseman's *Dossier de l'ordre de la pénitence au XIIIe siècle, Spicilegium Friburgense*, VII (Fribourg, Switzerland, 1961).

38. A. Hibbert's "The Origins of the Medieval Town Patriciate," originally published in *Past and Present* (1953) and republished in E. Wrigley and P. Abrams, eds., *Town in Societies* (Cambridge, 1978), pp. 91–104, is the classic study dealing with the aristocratic foundation of cities. For a detailed treatment of Italian nobility, with a massive bibliography, see P. J. Jones, "Economia e società nell'Italia medievale: La leggenda della borghesia," *Storia d'Italia. Annali I* (Turin, 1978), 187–372. In his "From Manor to Mezzadria," *Florentine Studies: Politics and Society in Renaissance Florence* (London, 1968), 193–241, especially 206–13, Jones indicates that the most conspicuous of all changes in the Tuscan agrarian regime was to result in the transfer of land and rights to a "new middle class of land holders or 'great *libellari.*' " R. Lopez, *The Commercial Revolution of the Middle Ages*, p. 72, observes that the commercial revolution did not occur in Germany, where new silver mines began their activity, but in Italy, where the gulf between agrarian proprietors and merchants was narrowed.

39. V. Fumagalli, *Le origini de una grande dinastia feudale Adalberto-Atto di Canossa* (Tubingen, 1971). For a comparable situation in Lombardy, see G. Rosetti, *Società e istituzioni nel contado lombardo durante il medioevo* (Milan, 1968); for a series of trenchant generalizations, see P. J. Jones, "Economia e società," 233–58.

40. D. Herlihy, "Family Solidarity in Medieval Italian History," *Economy, Society and Government in Medieval Italy* (Kent, Ohio, 1969), 173–84; G. Prunai, "Il 'Breve Dominorum de Cerreto del 1216,' " *Archivio Storico Italiano*, CXVI (1958), 75–85. For the nobility in Pisa, see E. Cristiani, *Nobiltà e popolo nel Comune di Pisa dalle origini del podestariato alla signoria del Donoratico* (Naples, 1962), pp. 370–440. For nobility in San Gimignano, see E. Fiumi, *Storia economica e sociale di San Gimignano* (Florence, 1961), pp. 231–80. On the participation of great Genoese families in commerce, see E. Byrne, "Genoese Trade with Syria in the Twelfth Century," *American Historical Review*, XXV (1920), 191–219; E. Sayons, "Aristocratie et noblesse à Gênes," *Annales d'Histoire Économique et Sociale*, IX (1937), 366–72.

41. M. Martini, "La vita di San Giovanni Gualberto in una antica laude inedita," *La Bibliografia*, XXVIII (1926), 161–77. In judgments rendered by Beatrice and Matilda, countesses of Tuscany over the last half of the eleventh century, names of *boni homines*, judges, and assessors included men from new families, such as the Ughi, Lamberti, Giuochi, and Caponsachi, along with old-line nobles, such as the Sichelmi, Suarizzi, Uberti, and Visdomini.

42. D. Waley, *The Italian City-Republics* (New York, 1969), pp. 138–40; H. Schwarzmaier, *Lucca und das Reich bis zum Ende des XI Jahrhunderts* (Tubingen, 1972). Among the earliest Florentine communal documents are the peace pacts entered into by leading families to terminate vendettas. Cf. G. Masi, ed., *Collectio chartarum pacis privatae medii aevi ad regionem Tusciae pertinentium* (Milan, 1943), pp. 10 ff., with numerous citations of Florentine notaries.

43. For the Lucca region documentation is particularly ample; approximately eighteen hundred documents survive for the early Middle Ages, and many are published in the *Codice diplomatico longobardo*, of which two-thirds are from Lucca. G. Rossetti, "Il matrimonio del clero nella società altomedioevo," *Il matrimonio nella società altomedievale* (Spoleto, 1977), I, 533–45, offers a statistical analysis of the impact of eleventh-century reforms on ecclesiastical concubinage.

For the Florentine *contado*, see E. Conti, pp. 150–58. For a discussion of the social forces arrayed against married clergy and the part played by youth in France, see G. Duby, "Dans la France du nord-ouest au XIIᵉ siècle les 'Jeunes' dans la société aristocratique," *Annales. E.S.C.*, XIX (1964), 838–44. For Milan, see C. Violante, *Studi*, pp. 195–96.

44. For a balanced discussion of these themes, see G. Miccoli, "La storia religiosa," 480–516. Cf. also B. Quilici, *La chiesa di Firenze nei primi decenni del secolo undecimo* (Florence, 1940), pp. 42–80; R. Davidsohn, *Storia di Firenze* (Florence, 1956), I, pp. 168–202.

45. S. Boesch Gajano, "Giovanni Gualberto e la vita comune del clero nelle biografie di Andrea da Strumi e di Azzo da Vallombrosa," *La vita comune del clero nei secoli XI e XII* (Milan, 1962), II, 228–35; G. Penco, *Storia del monachesimo in Italia* (Rome, 1961), pp. 186 ff.; H. Cowdrey, *The Cluniacs and the Gregorian Reform* (Oxford, 1970), pp. 120–87. In Tuscan documents pertaining to religious bequests the pastoral ministry is not mentioned until after the early eleventh century; cf. L. Nanni, p. 57.

46. For an assessment of spiritual change, see J. Leclercq, *La spiritualità del medioevo da San Gregorio a San Bernardo (secoli VI–XII)* (Bologna, 1972), pp. 311 ff. On politics, see the justly celebrated G. Tellenbach, *Church, State and Christian Society at the Time of the Investiture Contest*, trans. R. F. Bennett (New York, 1970). In documents of the earlier period we seldom hear a personal voice, and only in rare instances can motives be adduced. Cf. L. Nanni, p. 33.

47. Tuscan documents of the twelfth century reveal a marked increase in the incidence of the conception of salvation as something to be earned, with merits of donor and testator highlighted. Further, the likelihood of requesting prayers for all Christians increased exponentially with the eleventh century. The pessimism of the earlier period is discussed by J. Leclercq, *La spiritualité du moyen âge* (Aubier, 1961), pp. 43–55. Cf. also P. Ariès, pp. 100–104; G. Meersseman, *Ordo fraternitatis*, I, pp. 11–15.

48. On the battle against obscure language in notarial documents, see P. Toubert, I, pp. 1240–48. For a discussion of the changing nature of Florentine bequests and charitable acts, see A. Benvenuti, "Fonti e problemi per la storia dei penitenti a Firenze nel secolo XIII," *L'ordine della penitenza da San Francesco*, ed. O. Schmucki (Rome, 1973), pp. 281–98; R. Franci, "L'ospedale di San Paoli a Firenze e i terziari francescani," *Studi Francesci*, VII (1921), 52–70. For evidence of the changing round of Florentine pious activity, see *San Paolo dei Convalescenti*, filze 547–49, 616, 647, 886, 967–68, 971–74.

49. G. Meersseman, "I penitenti nei secoli XI e XII," *I laici nella 'società christiana' dei secoli XI e XII* (Milan, 1968), 306–39. On the restitution of usury in Florence, see A. Sapori, "La beneficenza delle compagnie mercantili del Trecento," *Studi di storia economica* (Florence, 1955), II, 839–58, and his "I precedenti della previdenza sociale nel medioevo," *ibid.*, I, pp. 427–41; C. Gargiolli, ed., *Il libro segreto di Gregorio Dati* (Bologna, 1869), pp. 69–73; R. Davidsohn, *Firenze ai tempi di Dante*, trans. E. Theseider (Florence, 1929), pp. 169, 193, and *Forschungen zur Geschichte von Florenz* (Berlin, 1912), III, pp. 36–39. For a general treatment of this topic, see B. Nelson, "The Usurer and the Merchant Prince: Italian Businessmen and the Ecclesiastical Law of Restitution, 1100–1550," *Journal of Economic History*, VII (1947), 104–22. On the theme of *metanoia*, see G. Meersseman, *Ordo fraternitatis*, I, pp. 518 ff., and especially p. 526, where he quotes this line from Dante's *Convivio*: "Dio non volse religioso di noi se non lo cuore."

50. C. Picasso, "I fondamenti del matrimonio nelle collezioni canoniche," *Il matrimonio nella società altomedievale* (Spoleto, 1977), I, 192–231, but espe-

cially 218–19. For Tuscany, see Herlihy and Klapisch-Zuber, pp. 525–37. On the general question of the influence of canon law on reformers, see P. Fournier, "Un tournant de l'histoire du droit 1060–1140," *Nouvelle Revue Historique de Droit Français et Étranger*, XLI (1917), 129–80. G. Duby's central insight into the changing character of the institution of marriage during this period might be summarized thus: there were two radically opposed models of marriage: one laic, created to safeguard the social order, and the other ecclesiastical, created to protect the divine order. These two now moved toward an accommodation; cf. *Medieval Marriage*, p. 3.

51. M. Becker, "Aspects of Lay Piety in Early Renaissance Florence," *The Pursuit of Holiness*, ed. C. Trinkaus with H. Oberman (Leiden, 1974), 177–99.

52. I wish to thank my student Carol Lansing for allowing me to benefit from her researches into the question of changing norms for female sanctity in Tuscany. For the earlier period, see R. Manselli, "Vie familiale et éthique sexuelle dans les pénitentes," *Famille et parenti* (Rome, 1977), 363–78.

53. G. Petrocchi, "Inchiesta sulla tradizione manoscritti dei *Fioretti*," *Filologia Romanza* (1957), III, 311–25; P. Kristeller, *Studies in Renaissance Thought and Letters* (Rome, 1956), pp. 100–102; M. Becker, 181–85; G. Meersseman, I, pp. 507–9.

54. M. Becker, "Individualism in the Early Renaissance: Burden and Blessing," *Studies in the Renaissance*, XIX (1972), 273–97, and "Towards a Renaissance Historiography," *Renaissance Studies in Honor of Hans Baron*, ed. A. Molho and J. Tedeschi (De Kalb, Ill., 1971), 151–53.

55. M. D. Chenu, pp. 264–67; cf. also general comments of C. Violante, "Discorso di chiusura," *Il matrimonio nella società altomedievale* (Spoleto, 1977), II, 986–87. On symbolism, see G. Ladner, "Medieval and Modern Understanding of Symbolism: A Comparison," *Speculum*, LIV (1979), 223–56. One should not forget that many were displaced, even uprooted, by economic change in the eleventh and twelfth centuries. It is worth recalling that the ideal community extolled by Gregorian reformers appears to have exercised a special attraction for the wealthier elements of the population who were in fact married; cf. the recent work of P. Toubert, Chenu, and Duby.

56. E. Delaruelle, *La piété populaire au moyen âge* (Turin, 1975), pp. 27–38, 328 ff.; A. Vauchez, *La spiritualité au moyen âge occidental VIIIe–XIIe siècles* (Paris, 1953), pp. 83–106; P. Riche, "Le Psautier, livre de lecture élémentaire d'après les vies des saints mérovingiens," *Études mérovingiennes* (Paris, 1953), 253–56; J. Leclercq, *La spiritualità del medioevo*, pp. 98–114. For a general discussion of spirituality in "The Primitive Age, ca. 700–1050," see R. Southern, *Western Society and the Church in the Middle Ages* (Baltimore, 1970), pp. 24–34.

57. C. Mor, "Simbologia e simboli nella vita giuridica," *Simboli e simbologia nell'alto medioevo*, I, p. 18. Paul the Deacon's writings reveal many features of the mentality we have been describing: he harbored intense feeling for discrete events, lacked concern for developments over long periods of time, had a taste for anecdote even if it interrupted his discourse, and was passionate for etymology. Cf. E. Sestan, "La storiografia dell'Italia longobarda," *La storiografia alto-medievali* (Spoleto, 1970), I, pp. 365–85. For an analysis of literary texts and their stylistic relationship to historical developments in medieval Italy before 1000, see the sensitive appraisals of G. Vinay, *Alto medioevo latino* (Naples, 1978), pp. 378–463. E. Besta, in his *L'opera d'irnerio* (Turin, 1896), argues that archaic culture placed a high value on the simple materiality of an act and that this began to change in the time of Irnerius.

58. For a judicious discussion of leading ideas of Claude Lévi-Strauss, see E. Leach, *Claude Lévi-Strauss* (New York, 1970). Particularly relevant to our dis-

cussion is Lévi-Strauss's *La pensée sauvage* (Paris, 1962), translated as *The Savage Mind* (London, 1966); cf. also *The Raw and the Cooked* (New York, 1969) and *Structural Anthropology* (New York, 1963). It is not my intention to consider distinctions between synchronic and diachronic structures at this time; however, the reader will be struck by the transition from associative and simultaneous-ahistorical structures to syntagmatic and sequential-historical structures. Clearly, strategies from linguistics could be applied to generate further hypotheses, but as Judge Learned Hand once said to a young lawyer who argued interminably, "Some concession must be made to the brevity of human life." For further discussion of the work of F. de Saussure and R. Jakobson, see H. V. White, *Metahistory* (Baltimore, 1973); G. Ladner, 227–30.

59. R. Southern's periodization is a useful guide for charting changes (*Western Society and the Church*, pp. 34–44). On the theme of heightened self-consciousness on the use of symbols, see J. Le Goff, "Les gestes symboliques dans la vie sociale," *Simboli e simbologia*, II, 679–788. On possible implications of these changes for the history of science, see T. Gregory, "La nouvelle idée de nature au XII siècle," *The Cultural Context of Medieval Learning* (Boston, 1975), 183–212, and his *Filosofia della natura nel medioevo* (Milan, 1966). For implications of change for politics, see W. Ullmann, *The Growth of Papal Government in the Middle Ages*, 3d ed. (London, 1970), pp. 262–412.

60. C. Lévi-Strauss, *Totemism* (Middlesex, England, 1973), pp. 38, 41–42, 140–42, and the introduction by Roger Poole. Cf. also C. Geertz, *The Interpretation of Cultures* (New York, 1974); M. Sahlins, *Culture and Practical Reason* (Chicago, 1976), especially pp. 223–40 for a bibliography.

61. See the many essays in *Il monachesimo nell'alto medioevo e la formazione della civiltà occidentale* (Spoleto, 1957). For a discussion of changing meanings of the idea of spirituality, see articles by G. Vinay, J. Leclercq, and others in *Studi Medievali*, ser. 3, II (1961).

62. For background, see A. Vauchez, pp. 15–20; E. Cattaneo, *Il culto cristiano in occidente* (Rome, 1978). On Benedict of Aniane, see D. Schmitz, "L'influence de S. Benoît d'Aniane dans l'histoire de L'Ordre de S. Benoît," *Il monachesimo nell'alto medioevo e la formazione della civiltà occidentale* (Spoleto, 1957), 401–15. On Carolingian civilization as "une civilisation de la liturgie," see E. Delaruelle, "La pietà popolare nel secolo XI," *Storia del Medioevo, Atti X. Congresso Internazionale Scienze Storiche* (Florence, 1955), 318. For Amalarius and liturgy, see I. Haussens, *Amalarii episcopi opera liturgica omnia* (Città del Vaticano, 1948), II, pp. 209–36.

63. E. Cattaneo, pp. 220–36; C. Leonardi, "Spiritualità di Ambrogio Autperto," *Studi Medievali*, ser. 3, IX (1968), 1–131. For the life of Italian clergy in the tenth century, see an old but useful monograph by A. Dresdner, *Kultur und Sittengeschichte der italienischen Geistlichkeit in X und XI Jahrhundert* (Breslau, 1890). On the theme of poverty, see the essays of K. Bosl, F. Graus, and J. Devisse in *La concezione della povertà nel medioevo* (Bologna, 1974), 35–151.

64. For the interpretations that follow, I am much indebted to F. Cranz, particularly his unpublished paper "New Dimensions of Thought in Anselm and Abelard as Against Augustine and Boethius." Cf. also R. Javelet, *Image et ressemblance au douzième siècle* (Paris, 1967), II, xvii–xxx, for a bibliography; R. Markus, in *The Cambridge History of Later Greek and Early Medieval Philosophy*, ed. A. Armstrong (Cambridge, 1967), 341–425. For an assessment of Erigena's role in the history of science, see B. Stock, "Science, Technology, and Economic Progress in the Early Middle Ages," *Science in the Middle Ages*, ed. D. Lindberg (Chicago, 1978), 35–36. On general philosophic questions, see G. Leff, *Medieval Thought: St. Augustine to Ockham* (Baltimore, 1958), pp. 65–68; P. Chevallier, "Denys L'Areopagite," *Dictionnaire de spiritualité*, III, col. 319–24.

65. B. Smalley, *The Study of the Bible in the Middle Ages* (South Bend, Ind., 1970), passim; B. Fischer, *Die Alkuin-Bibel* (Fribourg-en-Brisgau, 1953), pp. 13 ff.; C. Nordenfalk, "An Early Medieval Shorthand Alphabet," *Speculum*, XIV (1939), 443–47. The writings of Paul the Deacon again prove instructive on this subject. G. Bognetti proposes that in writing such important works as *Gesta episcoporum mettensium*, Paul utilized intellectual processes that might be described as "hypothetically rational." In composing the lives of three of the bishops of Metz, about whom he knew nothing other than their names, he will say, "quorum omnium studio certum est, crevisse Dei ecclesiam, quamvis eorum nobis specialiter occulta sunt gesta." Cf. Bognetti, "Processo logico e integrazioni delle fonti nella storiografia di Paolo Diacano," *Miscellanea di studi muratori* (Modena, 1951), 357–81.

66. B. Smalley, pp. 43–48; J. Leclercq, *L'amour des lettres et le désir de Dieu* (Paris, 1957), pp. 19–30, 71–73, and his "Contemplation," *Dictionnaire de spiritualité* (Paris, 1953), II, col. 1937–48; J. Jungman, *Missarum sollemnia* (Paris, 1964), I, pp. 106–26.

67. F. Cranz, "1100 A.D.: A Crisis for Us?" *Occasional Papers in the Humanities* (Connecticut College Library, New London, Conn., 1978), 84–108; M. Cappuyns, "Note sur le problème de la vision béatifique au IX siècle," *Recherches de Théologie Ancienne et Médiévale*, I (1929), 98–107.

68. F. Cranz, 99–108. On the crisis of Augustinian symbolism, see O. Capitani, "Studi per Berengario di Tours," *B.I.S.I.*, LXIX (1951), 154–69; M. Cristiani, "La controversia eucharistica nella cultura del secolo IX," *Studi Medioevali*, 3rd ser., IX (1968), 167–233.

69. F. Cranz, 97; A. Koyré, *L'idée de Dieu dans la philosophie de Saint Anselm* (Paris, 1923); J. Leclercq, *La spiritualità del medioevo*, 279–82. In both the *Proslogium* and *Monologium*, Anselm attempted a philosophical transposition of a psychological argument advanced by Augustine in respect to the Trinity. J. Leclercq notes that the "immagine" of Augustine became "analogia" in Anselm. Of course, there are no precise ways of describing a transformation such as this, and jargon is most tiresome; still, it is useful to call attention to recent writings in linguistics and anthropology. The distinctions between *sign* relationships and *symbol* relationships are important. The latter are "arbitrary assertions of similarity and therefore mainly *metaphoric*," whereas the former are "contiguous and thus mainly *metonymic*." Cf. E. Leach, *Culture and Communication: The Logic by Which Symbols Are Connected* (Cambridge, 1976), p. 15. The historical shift we witness could be viewed as a movement from symbol to sign; we could follow R. Jakobson's *metaphor-metonymy* usage, F. de Saussere's *paradigmatic-syntagmatic* distinction, or that of Lévi-Strauss, with his elegant discriminations between *melody* and *harmony*. Each would illuminate an aspect of the transition from literal to abstract ties. In this context it is interesting to note possible parallels between social change and linguistic shifts. See R. Jakobson and M. Halle, *Fundamentals of Language* (The Hague, 1956); F. Saussure, *Course in General Linguistics*, ed. C. Bally (New York, 1966).

70. G. Leff, pp. 95–97, 104; B. Smalley, pp. 40–50; O. Capitani, *Studi sul Berengario di Tours* (Lecce, 1966).

71. In discussing these matters, the unpublished lectures of N. Haring, Pontifical Institute, University of Toronto, have been of great assistance. See R. Southern, "Lanfranc of Bec and Berengar of Tours," *Studies in Medieval History Presented to F. M. Powicke* (Oxford, 1948), 27 ff. The crisis of Augustinian symbolism was revealed not only in the arguments of Berengarius but also in those of his adversaries.

72. J. Leclercq, pp. 157–63; M. Cristiani, 167–233.

73. For a general discussion of developments associated with the "twelfth-century Renaissance," see R. Lopez, "Still Another Renaissance," *American His-*

torical Review, LVIII (1951), 1–22; C. Haskins, The Renaissance of the Twelfth Century (Cambridge, 1927), and Studies in Medieval Culture (New York, 1929). For a treatment of Alberic of Monte Casino, author of the first medieval handbook on rhetoric, see I. Robinson, Authority and Resistance in the Investiture Contest: The Polemical Literature of the Late 11th Century (Manchester, 1978), pp. 28–29, and "The 'Colores rhetorici' in the Investiture Contest," Traditio, XXXII (1976), 209–38.

74. A. Cantin, Les sciences seculières et la foi (Spoleto, 1975), pp. 535–632, provides an informed discussion of intellectual developments and personalities in Italy during this period.

2. CHALLENGES IN THE ELEVENTH CENTURY

1. For a full discussion of agrarian developments, see P. J. Jones, "Medieval Agrarian Society in its Prime: Italy," Cambridge Economic History of Europe, 2d ed. (Cambridge, 1966), I, 340–431, and "L'Italia agraria nel alto medioevo," Agricoltura e mondo rurale in occidente nell'alto medioevo (Spoleto, 1966), 57–92. Cf. also G. Pepe, Il medio evo barbarico d'Italia (Turin, 1959), pp. 182–86; R. Lopez, The Birth of Europe (New York, 1967), pp. 139–45; G. Falco, La Sancta Romana Repubblica: Profilo storico del Medio Evo, 9th ed. (Milan-Naples, 1973), pp. 194–210, 403–6; G. Fasoli, Le incrusioni ungare in Europa nel secolo X (Florence, 1945), pp. 132–55.

2. P. Toubert, Études sur l'Italie médiévale (London, 1976), pp. 400–503; P. J. Jones, "From Manor to Mezzadria," 193–241; R. de Roover, "The Organization of Trade," Cambridge Economic History of Europe (Cambridge, 1963), III, 42–118; F. Niccolae, "I consorzi nobiliari ed il comune nell'alta Italia," Rivista di Storia del Diritto Italiano, XIII (1940), 304–9; G. Fasoli, "Ricerche sulla legislazione antimagnatizia nei comuni dell'alta e media Italia," ibid., XII (1939), 86–133, 240–309. On true contracts of alienation, with right of usufruct, see G. Fasoli, Scritti di storia medievale (Bologna, 1974), pp. 552–54.

3. For background on the medieval commune, see P. Brezzi, I comuni medioevali nella storia d'Italia, 2d ed. (Turin, 1970); cf. also G. Fasoli and F. Bocchi, La città medievale italiana (Florence, 1973), pp. 52–78; D. Hughes, "Kinsmen and Neighbors in Medieval Genoa," The Medieval City, ed. H. Miskimin, D. Herlihy, and A. Udovitch (New Haven, Conn., 1977), 95–111; R. Lopez, pp. 262–75.

4. For a general discussion of these themes, see T. Gregory, La filosofia della natura nel medioevo (Milan, 1966), pp. 27–65; P. Delhaye, "L'enseignement de la philosophie morale au XIe siècle," Medieval Studies, XI (1949), 77 ff.; M. D. Chenu, "Naturalisme et théologie au XIIe siècle," Recherches de Science Religieuse, XXXVII (1950), 5–12; A. Forest, F. van Steenberghen, and M. de Gandillac, "Le mouvement doctrinal du IX au XIV siècle," Histoire de l'église, ed. A. Fliche and V. Martin (Paris, 1951), XIII, 73–78; F. Simone, "La reductio artium ad sacram scripturam fino al secolo XII," Convivium, XX (1949), 887–927.

5. For a recent introduction to these changes, see M. Gibson, Lanfranc of Bec (Oxford, 1978); cf. also A. Cantin, pp. 192 ff.; D. Bullough, "Urban Change in Early Medieval Italy," Papers of the British School at Rome, XXXIV (1966), 116 ff.; B. Stock, pp. 23–37. On the Carolingian renaissance, see L. Wallach, Alcuin and Charlemagne: Studies in Carolingian History and Literature (Ithaca, N.Y., 1959). L. Little points out that Duby is not consistent and will diverge from his views on the eleventh and twelfth centuries as an amplification or re-

newal of earlier developments in order to use the term *renaissance* to apply to the later period. Cf. L. Little, "Pride Goes before Avarice: Social Change and the Vices in Latin Christendom," *American Historical Review*, LXXVI (1971), 28.

6. S. Thrupp, "The Gilds," *Cambridge Economic History* (Cambridge, 1963), III, 230–80; G. Luzzato, *Storia economica d'Italia* (Florence, 1948), pp. 102–5; E. Ennen, *Storia della città medievale* (Bari, 1978), p. 83; A. Tagliaferri, "Fasi dell'economia longobarda," *Problemi della civiltà e dell'economia longobarda* (Milan, 1964), 249–52.

7. For judicious observations on these complex developments in north Italy, see B. Bullough, "Le scuole cattedrali e la cultura dell'Italia settentrionale prima dei comuni," *Italia Sacra* (Padua, 1964), 140–42, and *English Historical Review*, LXXV (1960), 487–91. On pressure to produce men who could argue in a public forum, see M. Gibson, p. 18. On the practical needs of Italian urban society, see Anselm of Besate, *Rhetorimachia*, ed. K. Manitius (Weimar, 1958), pp. 61–86. G. Duby, in *The Early Growth of the European Economy*, calls attention to the importance of the mint at Pavia and the role it played in the continuous expansion of a money economy throughout north Italy after 1000; cf. p. 151.

8. It is important to note that Roman law ceased to be conceived of as the law of a particular Latin people or of clergy. The process by which this transformation took place was gradual, but over the eleventh century its generalized status was effectively championed by jurists of north Italy. Cf. G. Cencetti, 105–13; H. Grundmann, "La genesi dell'Università nel medioevo," *Le origini dell'Università*, ed. G. Arnaldi (Bologna, 1974), 90–94; J. Gaudement, "Le droit romain dans la pratique et chez les docteurs aux XIe et XIIe siècles," *Cahiers de civilisation médiévale*, VIII (1965), 365–80. On foreign observers' comments on the Italian scene, see L. Rockinger, *Briefsteller und Formelbücher eilfsten bis vierzehnten Jahrhunderts* (Munich, 1863), pp. xx–xxi. For a bibliography and discussion of cultural developments, see C. Violante, "Anselmo da Besate," *Dizionario biografico degli Italiani* (Rome, 1961), III, 401–9.

9. A. Cantin, pp. 35 ff.; cf. also J. Migne, ed., *Patrologia Latina* (Paris, 1841–), CXLV, col. 614–16 (henceforth abbreviated as *P.L.*); G. Vinay, *Alto medioevo latino*, pp. 397–431.

10. The central work for the interpretation of Anselm is, of course, R. Southern, *Saint Anselm and His Biographers* (Cambridge, 1963). The most recent work, G. Evans, *Anselm and Talk About God* (Oxford, 1978), is most useful.

11. J. de Montclos, *Lanfranc et Berenger. La controverse eucharistique du XIe siècle* (Louvain, 1971).

12. R. Southern, pp. 14–16; D. Henry, *A Commentary on the 'De Grammatica' of St. Anselm* (Dordrecht, 1974).

13. For a summary of these intellectual developments, see R. Moore, *The Origins of European Dissent* (London, 1977), pp. 22–25. Cf. also K. Manitius, "Magie und Rhetorik bei Anselm von Besate," *Deutsches Archiv für Erforschung des Mittelalters*, XII (1956), 52 ff.; A. Cantin, p. 189.

14. A. Cantin, p. 418; Lanfranc of Pavia, *P.L.*, CL, col. 416D; R. Southern, pp. 24 ff.; H. Grundmann, 98.

15. R. Southern, pp. 82–102; D. de Clerck, "Droit du démon et nécessité de la rédemption dans les écoles d'Abelard et de Pierre Lombard," *Recherches de Théologie Ancienne et Médiévale*, XIV (1947), 33–64.

16. Works on this topic are legion, but particularly illuminating is G. Ladner's "The Life of the Mind in the Christian West Around the Year 1200," *The Year 1200: A Symposium* (Dublin, 1975), 1–23. The tendency of lawyers, both canon and civil, was to spiritualize material relations by using a very passionate

and figurative language. This observation is relevant to the basic hypothesis of this book. Cf. also R. Southern, *Medieval Humanism and Other Studies* (New York, 1970), pp. 29–105.

17. We are well informed about Anselm's way of life through Eadmer's *The Life of St. Anselm, Archbishop of Canterbury*, ed. and trans. R. Southern (London, 1962), pp. 141 ff.; R. Southern, *St. Anselm and His Biographers*, pp. 103–7.

18. G. Tellenbach, pp. 164 ff.; A. Vauchez, pp. 89–95. Gregory summoned laity to resist the concubinary clerics "even by force if necessary." Cf. *Epistolae vagantes*, ed. H. Cowdrey (Oxford, 1972), pp. 22–24; *Registrum*, ed. E. Caspar, *Monumenta Germaniae Historica, Epistolae* (1920–23), II, 49, p. 188; IV, 10, p. 309. Gregory's letters indicate that he perceived society as a field of battle on which the disciples of Christ must overcome the forces of evil. No longer would it be sufficient for the pope to pray for the spiritual health of the world. Laity participated directly in the work of reform.

19. E. R. Labande, *Spiritualité et vie littéraire de l'occident Xᵉ–XIVᵉ siècle* (London, 1974), pp. 41–43. For a general discussion of the intellectual odyssey of Damiani, see F. Dressler, *Petrus Damiani Leben und Werke* (Rome, 1954). On the subject of penance and flagellation, see C. Vogel, *Le pécheur et la pénitence au moyen âge* (Paris, 1968), pp. 154–55; *P.L.*, CXLV, col. 679–82.

20. E. R. Labande, pp. 34–40; R. Southern, *The Making of the Middle Ages* (New Haven, Conn., 1977), pp. 225–28; P. Damiani, *Vita beati Romualdi*, ed. G. Tabacco (*Fonti per la storia d'Italia*, XCIV) (1957), pp. 75–80; *P.L.*, CXLIV, col. 1014–79.

21. G. Tabacco, "Privilegium amoris. Aspetti della spiritualità Romualdina," 1–70; L. Little, *Religious Poverty*, pp. 71–72, 83; R. Moore, *The Origins of European Dissent*, p. 47; N. Hunt, *Cluny under St. Hugh* (London, 1967), pp. 99–109; A. Wilmart, "Le manuel de prières de Saint Jean Gualbert," *Revue Bénédictine*, XLVIII (1936), 259–99; *P.L.*, CXLIV, col. 380.

22. Raterio, *Praeloquiorum*, in *P.L.*, CXXXVI, col. 149 ff.; S. Boesch Gajano, "Storia e tradizioni Vallombrosane," 133 ff. For an exposition of theories concerning the laic order and its position in the Church, see A. Frugoni, "Momenti e problemi dell'ordo laicorum nei secoli X–XII," *Nova Historia*, XIII (1961), 3–22.

23. For a full discussion of historical evidence on the religious life of Milan in the eleventh century and a textured narrative of the history of the Patarine movement, see C. Violante, *La Pataria milanese e la riforma ecclesiastica* (Rome, 1955); G. Miccoli, *Chiesa gregoriana*, pp. 101–61. On the economic background, see R. Lopez, "An Aristocracy of Money in the Early Middle Ages," *Speculum*, XXVIII (1953), 39–43; C. Violante, *La società milanese nell'età precomunale* (Bari, 1953), pp. 144 ff.

24. H. Cowdrey, "The Papacy, the Patarenes, and the Church of Milan," *Transactions of the Royal Historical Society*, 5th ser., XVIII (1968), 25–48; R. Moore, pp. 55–71. On the canonization of laity, see A. Vauchez, p. 131; L. Little, p. 215.

25. C. Violante, *Studi sulla cristianità medievale*, pp. 145–246 (this is a republication of an article appearing in *I laici nella 'societas christiana' dei secoli XI e XII* [Milan, 1968]). Cf. also Damiani's comments on the Florentine situation, *P.L.*, CXLV, col. 528. Milan did not have the reformed monasteries that in other places, notably Florence, offered a starting point for the gradual dissemination of new spiritual teachings. See C. Violante, *La società milanese*, pp. 178–79.

26. See R. Moore, p. 56, for germane comments on the Ambrosian tradition permitting marriage for Milanese clerks; this was an essential part of the pattern of an archaic society, as was the exaction of standard tariffs for entry into the Church, including ordination and benefices. These were not abuses to be casti-

gated by reformers. Cf. also G. Meersseman, *Ordo fraternitatis*, I, p. 219; D. Herlihy, "L'economia della città e del distretto di Lucca secondo le carte private nell'alto medioevo," *Atti del Ve Congresso Internazione di Studi sul Medioevo* (Spoleto, 1973), 363–88.

27. For numerous citations of contemporary views and a persuasive analysis of reformers, see again the works of G. Miccoli, especially, "La storia religiosa," 489–647. Cf. also A. Murray, *Religion and Society in the Middle Ages* (Oxford, 1978), p. 72; *P.L.*, CXLVI, cols. 671–83.

28. C. Erdmann, *The Origin of the Idea of Crusade*, trans. M. Baldwin and W. Goffart (Princeton, N.J., 1977), pp. 140–44; H. Cowdrey, 35–39; P. Toubert, *Études*, pp. 60–66; G. Meersseman, pp. 230–33; C. Brakel, "Die vom Reformpapsttum geförderten Heiligenkulte," *Studi Gregoriani*, IX (1972), 239–312.

29. G. Duby, in *The Growth of the European Economy*, p. 150, notes that only in Italy was the Church being denied the right to display her worldly power and accumulate precious metals in her sanctuaries in order to magnify the glory of God. *The Cronica fiorentina, compilata nel sec. XIII, detta dello Pseudo-Brunetto*, in P. Villari, *I primi due secoli della storia di Firenze* (Florence, 1905), pp. 515, 529, 536–37, contains a record of events considered noteworthy by an anonymous annalist of the late thirteenth or early fourteenth century. Special attention is given by this Florentine to the deposing of simoniac clerics. He speaks of the sad fate of a certain preacher upholding apostolic poverty and condemning riches who converted many "gentili huomini e gran possenti" of Rome. So great was the clerics' hatred of him that he was imprisoned and had his eyes poked out. Cf. T. Panaro and L. Pruneti, *Opposizione religiosa nel Medioevo* (Florence, 1977), pp. 153–57, for appropriate citations.

30. E. Delaruelle, "Les ermités et la spiritualité populaire," *L'eremitismo in occidente nei secoli XI e XII* (Milan, 1965), 228 ff.; C. Violante, "I Vescovi dell'Italia centro-settentrionale e lo sviluppo dell'economia monetaria," *Vescovi e diocesi in Italia nel medioevo* (Padua, 1961), 193–217.

31. G. Tellenbach, pp. 126–64; O. Blum, *Saint Peter Damian* (Washington, D.C., 1947), pp. 126–27; D. Meade, "From Turmoil to Solidarity: The Emergence of the Vallombrosan Monastic Congregation," *The American Benedictine Review*, XIX (1968), 323–51; R. Duvernay, "Vallombrose, Citeaux et Étienne Harding," *Analecta S. O. Cisterciensis*, VIII (1958), 428 ff. For a recent discussion of intellectual developments, see W. Patt, "Early 'Ars Dictaminis,'" *Viator*, IX (1978), 133–52.

32. See comments on Gratian's *sic et non*: two lists were made, one in favor of the judgment of God and one opposed; the former was Germanic in origin, whereas the latter was Roman. On Bologna and the notaries, see G. Cenetti, "Studium fuit Bononie," 113–14. Symptomatic of change was the great increase in the number of notaries in the Florentine *contado* of the twelfth century; E. Conti, pp. 101 ff. On the economic background for the decline of labor services and the rise of contractual relationships ("the formal attributes of ownership") in Tuscany, see P. J. Jones, "From Manor to Mezzadria," 210–15.

33. P. Fournier, "Les collections canoniques romaines de l'époque de Grégoire VII," *Mélanges de l'Académe des Inscriptions et de Belles Lettres*, XLI (1918), 271–394. J. Batany, "L'église et le mépris du monde," *Annales, E.S.C.*, XX (1965), 218–28. C. Dereine, "Vie commune règle de Saint Augustin et chanoines réguliers au XIe sècle," *Revue d'Histoire Écclésiastique*, XLI (1946), 395.

34. A. Vauchez, pp. 44–46; G. Tabacco, "Eremo e cenobio," *Spiritualità cluniacense* (Todi, 1960), 326–35. For a general treatment of spiritual life as combat, see B. Rosenwein, "Feudal War and Monastic Peace: Cluniac Liturgy as Ritual Aggression," *Viator*, II (1971), 17 ff.

35. L. Little, pp. 70 ff.; G. Tabacco, "Romualdo di Ravenna a gli inizi dell'-eremitismo camaldolese," *L'eremitismo in occidente nei secoli XI e XII*, 73-120; J. Leclercq, "The Monastic Crisis of the 11th and 12th Centuries," *Cluniac Monasticism in the Central Middle Ages*, ed. N. Hunt (London, 1971), 204 ff.

36. L. Little, "The Personal Development of Peter Damiani," *Order and Innovation in the Middle Ages: Studies in Honor of Joseph Strayer*, ed. W. C. Jordan, B. McNab, and T. Ruiz (Princeton, 1976), 317-41. For background, see R. Davidsohn, *Storia di Firenze*, I, pp. 170 ff.

37. *P.L.*, CXLVI, cols. 671-73; L. Little, *Religious Poverty*, pp. 75-76; G. Penco, *Storia del monachesimo in Italia* (Turin, 1961), pp. 230-33.

38. A. Wilmart, "Le recueil des poèmes et des prières de Saint Damien," *Revue Bénédictine*, XLI (1929), 342-57; R. Southern, *The Making of the Middle Ages*, pp. 246-54.

39. P. Brown, 133-51; R. Southern, pp. 246-49; G. Miccoli, "La storia religiosa," 494-98. For the culture and religious sensibilities of Damiani, see J. Leclercq, *Saint Pierre Damien, ermite et homme d'église* (Rome, 1960); J. Ryan, *Saint Peter Damiani and His Canonical Sources: A Preliminary Study in the Antecedents of the Gregorian Reform* (Toronto, 1956).

40. R. Southern, pp. 246, 251-56.

41. A. Vauchez, pp. 150-54. For detailed studies of influential eleventh-century spiritual figures, whose teachings and writings expressed the new sensibility with its personal note (Giovanni di Fécamp from Ravenna and Guglielmo da Volpiano), see J. Leclercq and J. Bonnes, *Un maître de la vie spirituelle au XIe siècle, Jean de Fécamp* (Paris, 1946). Leclercq, in discussing the Psalms, observes that in the earlier Middle Ages hymns were regarded as having been written by Christ or by those with foreknowledge of His redemptive works. For a discussion of the change, see J. Leclercq, *La spiritualità*, pp. 196-222; A. Wilmart, *Auteurs spirituels et textes dévots du moyen âge latin* (Paris, 1932), pp. 72-79; *P.L.*, CXLIX, cols. 971-80.

42. On the theme of credit, see the classic studies of R. Lopez, particularly *The Commercial Revolution of the Middle Ages*. On business practices, see R. de Roover, "The Organization of Trade," *Cambridge Economic History* (Cambridge, 1963), III, 42-153, especially 48-77. See also the observations of C. Cipolla, *Before the Industrial Revolution: European Society and Economy, 1000-1700* (New York, 1976), passim; J. Noonan, *The Scholastic Analyses of Usury* (Cambridge, Mass., 1957).

43. R. Lopez, pp. 63-79; M. Becker, "Nota dei processi riguardanti prestatori di denaro del 1343 al 1379," *Archivio Storico Italiano*, CXIV (1956), 93-104, and *Florence in Transition. Vol. I: The Decline of the Commune* (Baltimore, 1967), pp. 5-8, 13, 15-21.

44. On the complexity of distinctions between manifest and occult usury in Florence, see A. Sapori, *Studi di storia economica* (Florence, 1955), I, pp. 181-89. For canonist theory on usury, see T. McLaughlin, "The Teachings of the Canonists on Usury," *Mediaeval Studies*, I (1939), 81-147, and II (1940), 1-22; G. Le Bras, *Dictionnaire de théologie catholique* (Paris, 1950), XV, part 2, 2336-72; J. Baldwin, *Masters, Princes and Merchants: The Social Views of Peter the Chanter and His Circle* (Princeton, 1970), I, pp. 306 ff., and *The Medieval Theories of the Just Price* (*Transactions of the American Philosophical Society*, XLIV, part 4 (1959).

45. For the quotation from writings of Damiani, see L. Little, p. 74. On Damiani's response to the new and old learning of his times, see A. Cantin, especially pp. 262-79. For new directions in the study of logic, see L. Minio-Paluello, "Nuovi impulsi allo studio della logica," *La Scuola nell'Occidente latino dell'alto medioevo* (Spoleto, 1972), 743-66.

46. See C. Verzár Bornstein, "Matilda of Canossa, Papal Rome and the Earliest Italian Porch Portals," to be published in *Atti del Convegno Romanico Mediopadano*. I wish to thank the author for allowing me to read this paper. On the shrinking area of vengeance, the extension of the idea of justice, and the growing belief in the possibility of cures for mental and physical disease, see R. Southern, p. 255. For general comments, see P. Geary, *Furta Sacra: Thefts of Relics in the Central Middle Ages* (Princeton, N.J., 1978), pp. 158–63.

47. See D. Waley, *The Italian City-Republics*, pp. 49–51, for illustrations of the Arthurian legend on the Duomo at Modena. For the text of Anselm's *Proslogium*, see *St. Anselm: Basic Writings*, trans. S. Deane, with intro. by C. Hartshorne (La Salle, Ill., 1962), pp. 3–7. For telling comments on Paul the Deacon, see G. Vinay, "Paolo Diacono e la poesia," *Convivium* I (1950), 97 ff.

48. In dealing with the art of the period, I have drawn heavily from the works of R. Salvini and his conceptual vocabulary, especially *Wiligelmo e le origini della scultura romanica* (Milan, 1956). On the conscious archaism of the early Middle Ages, see A. Romanini, "Problemi di scultura e plastica altomedioevo," *Artigianato e tecnica nella società del alto medioevo occidentale* (Spoleto, 1971), II, 447–55.

49. A. Quintavalle, "Questioni medievali," *Critica d'Arte*, XV (1968), 61–76; "La cattedrale di Cremona, Cluny, la scuola de Lanfranco e Wiligelmo," *Storia dell'Arte*, XVIII (1973), 117–72; "Piacenza Cathedral, Lanfranco and the School of Wiligelmo," *Art Bulletin*, LV (1973), 46–57; C. Verzár Bornstein, *Die romanischen Skulpturen der Abtei Sagra di San Michele* (Berne, 1968). For a discussion of individual artists mentioned in the text, see appropriate entries in McGraw Hill's *Encyclopedia of World Art*, I (1959).

50. A. Quintavalle, *Wiligelmo e la sua scuola* (Florence, 1967); D. Robb, "Niccolò, A North Italian Sculptor of the Twelfth Century," *Art Bulletin*, XII (1930), 374–412; G. de Francovich, *Benedetto Antelami* (Milan-Florence, 1952); C. Verzár Bornstein, "The Capitals of the Porch at Sant'Eufemia," *Gesta*, XIII (1974), 19–24; P. Toesca, *Storia dell'arte italiana: Il medioevo* (Turin, 1927), II, pp. 743–82; G. Rosati, "Antelami," *Encyclopedia of World Art*, I (1959), 466; XII (1960), R. Salvini, "Romanesque," *Encyclopedia*, XII, 402–7; R. Salvini, "Wiligelmo," *Encyclopedia*, XIV (1967), 844–47.

51. A. Vasina, *Romagna medievale* (Ravenna, 1970), pp. 168 ff.; P. J. Jones, "Medieval Agrarian Society," 354–55; *P.L.*, CXLIV, col. 454. On population growth in Tuscany, see J. Russell, "Thirteenth-Century Tuscany as a Region," *Taius. Texas Agricultural and Industrial University: Studies*, I (1968), 42–52. According to Russell, the ten principal cities of Tuscany contained approximately one-quarter of the population at the end of the thirteenth century. This he regards as a very substantial figure. In comparison, in England in 1377 only 10 percent of the population lived in boroughs or cities of more than thirty-two hundred inhabitants. If one used this figure as a criterion, then the figure for Tuscany could stand at perhaps 40 percent of the population. On the high ratio of rural to urban population, see P. J. Jones, 245–47; D. Herlihy, *Medieval and Renaissance Pistoia* (New Haven, Conn., 1967), pp. 76–77, 112–14, and *Pisa in the Early Renaissance* (New Haven, Conn., 1958), pp. 42–43. E. Cristiani, pp. 166 ff.; K. Beloch, *Bevolkerungsgeschichte Italiens* (Berlin, 1939), II, pp. 165–66; C. Meek, *Lucca 1369–1400: Politics and Society in an Early Renaissance City-State* (Oxford, 1978), pp. 24–27.

52. For an enumeration of the establishment of fortified settlements, see R. Davidsohn, I, p. 451. On the theme of colonization in general, see the two volumes by P. Toubert, *Les structures du Latium médiéval*. For Passignano, see J. Plesner, *L'emigration de la compagne à la ville libre de Florence au XIIIᵉ siècle* (Copenhagen, 1934). Cf. also P. J. Jones, "A Tuscan Lordship in the Later

Middle Ages: Camaldoli," *Journal of Ecclesiastical History*, V (1954), 176 ff., and "Per la storia agraria italiana nel Medio Evo. Lineamenti e problemi," *Rivista Storica Italiana*, LXXVI (1964), 300–348; D. Herlihy, "Santa Maria Impruneta," *Florentine Studies: Politics and Society in Renaissance Florence*, ed. N. Rubinstein (London, 1968), 254–56.

53. On grain shortages and dependency of Florence on importation, see G. Pinto, *Il libro del Biadaiolo: Carestie e annona a Firenze della metà del '200 al 1348* (Florence, 1978), pp. 78–88. On the question of deserted villages, see C. Klapisch, "Villaggi abbandonati ed emigrazioni interne," *Storia d'Italia* (Turin, 1973), V, part 1, 311–69. E. Fiumi estimates the total population of Tuscany before the Black Death as standing at "not less than" two million people; for purposes of comparison, we can suggest that the population of England for the fourteenth century has been reckoned at about three million. For the citation of Fiumi's figure, see D. Herlihy, "Santa Maria Impruneta," 250.

54. P. J. Jones, "Medieval Agrarian Society in Its Prime: Italy," 421 ff.; J. Plesner, *L'emigration de la compagne*, pp. 51–59; G. Luzzato, "L'inurbamento delle populazione rurali in Italia nei secoli XII e XIII," *Studi di storia e diritto in onore di Enrico Besta* (Milan, 1939), I, 183–203.

55. D. Herlihy, "Family Solidarity in Medieval Italian History," *Economy, Society and Government in Medieval Italy* (Kent, Ohio, 1969), 173–84; O. Bratto, *Studi di antroponimia fiorentina: Il Libro di Montaperti*, 1260 (Göteborg, 1953), and *Nuovi studi di antroponimia fiorentina. I nomi meno frequenti del Libro di Montaperti* (Göteborg, 1955).

56. Tuscany was very precocious in the intelligent use of notarial cartularies and the *Liber Papiensis*; P. Leicht, "Leggi e capitolari," *Bullettino Senese di Storia Patria*, XIV (1907), 536–57. Cf. also E. Conti, I, pp. 107 ff.; J. Plesner, pp. 181 ff. E. Fiumi estimates that 60 percent of all notaries in Florence during this period were immigrants from the *contado;* "Fioritura e decadenza dell'economia," *Archivio Storico Italiano*, CXVI (1958), 497. For a discussion of the replacement of clerics by lay notaries, see A. Petrucci, *Notarii: Documenti per la storia del notariato italiano* (Milan, 1958), pp. 3–13. For the role of the notary in the formation of thirteenth-century civic culture, see J. Hyde, *Padua in the Age of Dante* (Manchester, 1966), pp. 162 ff.

57. R. Davidsohn, I, pp. 207–302, regards all evidence of the ties between ecclesiastics and feudatories as symptomatic of corruption. The data presented are invaluable,, although one may disagree entirely with the interpretation.

58. C. Boyd, *Tithes and Parishes in Medieval Italy*, p. 105; *P.L.*, CXXXVI, cols. 585–86; *P.L.*, CXLVIII, cols. 981–82; D. Herlihy, "The History of the Rural Seigneury in Italy, 751–1200," *Agricultural History*, XXXIII (1959), 58–71, especially 66.

59. C. Boyd, p. 105, for the quotation; *P.L.*, CXLIV, cols. 323–24; *P.L.*, CXLV, cols. 445–46.

60. For a historical account of the recovery of property in the Arezzo region, see R. Southern, *The Making of the Middle Ages*, pp. 128–130; C. Boyd, p. 102, for references to appropriate documents in *Documenti per la storia della città di Arezzo nel Medio Evo*, ed. P. Santini, (Florence, 1889), I, docs. 95, 278.

3. LAY PIETY

1. W. Kurze, "Monasteri e nobiltà nella Tuscia altomedievale," *Atti del 5° Congresso Internazionale di Studi sull'Alto Medioevo* (Spoleto, 1973), 344–48; D. Osheim, pp. 20–21; L. Nanni, pp. 14–21; R. Davidsohn, *Storia di Firenze*, I, pp. 188, 230, 288, 366.

2. For gifts to such monasteries as Coltibuono by small proprietors and women, see E. Conti, pp. 107 ff.; on the increase of donations to Passignano, which doubled between 1011 and 1040 over those of the preceding century and a quarter, see E. Conti, p. 160. In subsequent decades of the eleventh century the rate of increase accelerated. Cf. P. J. Jones, "From Manor to Mezzadria," 209; D. Herlihy, "Church Property on the European Continent, 701–1200," *Speculum,* XXXVI (1961), 96; D. Osheim, p. 6.

3. C. Bynum, "The Spirituality of Regular Canons in the 12th Century," *Medievalia et Humanistica,* n.s., IV (1973), 3–24; G. Miccoli, *Pietro Igneo,* pp. 120–23; *P.L.,* cols. 684–85; R. Volpini, "Giovanni Gualberto," *Bibliotheca Sanctorum,* VI (1965), 1012–29.

4. M. Mollat, "La notion de la pauvreté au Moyen Âge: Positions des problèmes," *Revue d'Histoire de l'Église de France,* LII (1966), 5–23; C. Boyd, pp. 34–36; G. Tabacco, "Canoniche aretine," *La vita comune del clero nei secoli XI e XII* (Milan, 1962), 245 ff.; G. Miccoli, *Chiesa Gregoriana,* p. 60.

5. See the *Vita* of Giovanni Gualberto in *M.G.H., SS. (Monumenta Germaniae Historica Scriptores),* XXX, part 11, 1087: "Quae usque ad suum tempus per Tusciam erant hospitalia? . . . Hospitalia tot et tanta huius exemplo et exortatu iam videmus nunc per Tusciam edificata et ecclesias vertustissimas tot renovatas ut nos cogant dicere: 'Ecce vetera transierunt et facta sunt omnia nova.' " L. Bertelli, "L'ospizio e il paese di Altopascio in Italia," *Atti del Primo Congresso Italiano di Storia Ospitaliera* (Reggio Emilia, 1957), 151–67; D. Osheim, pp. 19–22; G. Villani, *Cronica,* ed. F. Dragomanni (Florence, 1844–45), bk. XI, chap. 92.

6. Fundamental to a discussion of demographic and economic expansion in Tuscany is J. Plesner, "Una rivoluzione stradale nel dugento," *Acta Jutlandica,* X (1938), 1–102. Cf. also E. Fiumi, "La demografia fiorentina nelle pagine di Giovanni Villani," *Archivio Storico Italiano,* CVIII (1950), 78–158, and "Sui rapporti economici tra città e contado nell'età communale," ibid., CXIV (1956), 20 ff.; D. Osheim, pp. 21–22; J. Plesner, *L'émigration,* pp. 20–23; L. Nanni, pp. 56–58.

7. See the figures presented for Tuscany by E. Conti, I, pp. 157–58. For the Latium and Sabine regions, see P. Toubert, *Les structures,* I, pp. 776–87. Toubert notes the progressive abandonment of individual Germanic names for those of saints during the tenth and eleventh centuries; he also observes that the religious expansion was modeled after the agricultural reconquest; cf. I, p. 699, and II, p. 856. The role of the commune was much enhanced in the twelfth and thirteenth centuries as it intervened to strengthen the authority of the family; cf. *Statuti di Volterra,* ed. E. Fiumi (Florence, 1952), I, 10.

8. By the end of the thirteenth century the number of baptismal churches (*pieve*) had increased to three score in the Florentine *contado;* D. Herlihy, "Santa Maria Impruneta," 242. On the work of reclamation, see P. J. Jones, "Medieval Agriculture in Its Prime: Italy," 356 ff. Cf. also A. Sorbelli, *La parrochia dell'Appenino emiliano nel Medio Evo* (Bologna, 1910), pp. 30–83; P. Toubert, *Études,* pp. 501–3; R. Romeo, "La signoria del abate di Sant'Ambrogio di Milano sul comune rurale di Origgio nel secolo XIII," *Rivista Storica Italiana,* LXIX (1957), 340–77, 473–507; P. Sambin, "Studi di storia ecclesiastica medioevale," *Deputazione di storia patria per le Venezie miscellanea* (Venice, 1954), IX, 53–60; D. Hay, *The Church in Italy in the Fifteenth Century* (Cambridge, 1977), pp. 23–24.

9. C. Boyd, pp. 154 ff.; D. Zema, "Reform Legislation in the 11th Century and Its Economic Import," *Catholic Historical Review,* XXVII (1941), 16–18; B. Kurtscheid, *Historia Iuris Canonici: Historia Institutorum* (Rome, 1941), I, pp. 270 ff.; P. J. Jones, "An Italian Estate, 900–1200," *Economic History Review,*

2d ser., VII (1954), 18–32; C. Violante, *Studi sulla cristianità medioevale*, pp. 336–37.

10. Cf. the works of E. Fiumi in note 6 and his *Demografia movimento urbanistico e classi sociali in Prato* (Florence, 1968), pp. 83, 135, 139–52. Cf. also F. Sznura, *L'espansione urbana di Firenze nel dugento* (Florence, 1975), pp. 60–90; P. Santini, *Studi sull'antica costituzione del Comune di Firenze* (Rome, 1972), p. 23; G. Pampaloni, *Firenze al tempo di Dante* (Rome, 1973), pp. xvi–xviii. On the Florentine army, see D. Waley, "The Army of the Florentine Republic from the 12th to the 14th Century," *Florentine Studies*, ed. N. Rubinstein (1968), 70–108. On citizen participation in rural communal life, see *Archivio di Stato Firenze, Notarile Anticosimiano*, A981, fol. 88r; A983, fols. 15r, 26v, 44v, 85r (henceforth abbreviated as *ASF, Notarile*). For a keen observation of rural activity and farm life, one of course recalls Ambrogio Lorenzetti's frescoes (1338–39) in the Palazzo Pubblico in the Sala della Pace in Siena; G. Rowley, *Ambrogio Lorenzetti* (Princeton, N.J., 1958), 2 vols.

11. E. Delaruelle, *La piété populaire*, pp. 463 ff.; cf. also p. 325. E. Cattaneo, *Il culto cristiano*, pp. 238 ff.; G. Spinelli, "Il sacerdozio ministeriale nella predicazione della pataria milanesi," *Benedictina*, XXII (1975), 91–110; *P.L.*, CXLIV, cols. 1009–29.

12. C. Derein, "Vie commune règle de Saint Augustin et chanoines réguliers au Xᵉ siècle," *Revue d'Histoire Écclésiastique*, XLI (1946), 371–72; M. Guisti, "Le canoniche della città e diocese di Lucca al tempo della riforma Gregoriana," *Studi Gregoriani*, III (1948), 321–67; C. Boyd, pp. 110–24; C. Fonesca, "Le canoniche regolari riformate del Italia nord-occidentale," *Monasteri in alta Italia dopo le invasioni saracene a magiare* (Turin, 1966), 345–63.

13. For Damiani, see A. Cantin, pp. 315–38; on Romualdo, see H. de Lubac, *Exégèse médiévale* (Paris, 1959), pp. 571–86. Cf. also G. Giovannelli, "Nilo di Rossano fondature dell'abbazia greca di Grottaferrata santo," *Bibliotheca Sanctorum*, IX (1967), 995–1108.

14. G. Rosati, "Antelami," 467; R. Tassi, *Duomo di Parma: Il tempo romanico* (Parma, 1966), I, pp. 12–14. G. Miccoli, *Chiesa Gregoriana*, pp. 60–68, on the changing nature of bequests; cf. also the comments of C. Violante, "Discussione," *Il movimento dei disciplinati* (Perugia, 1960), 387; M. D. Chenu, "La fin des temps dans la spiritualité médiévale," *Lumière et vie*, II (1953), 101–16.

15. On the general subject of wills, see the very useful discussion by A. Pertile, *Storia del diritto italiano* (Turin, 1893), IV, pp. 27 ff.; V, pp. 42 ff. For examples of legacies and donations from the earlier period, see C. Troya, *Storia d'Italia del Medio Evo* (Naples, 1839–59), IV, part 5B, pp. 384–98, 467–717. For examples from the later period, see P. Ildefonso, *Delizie degli eruditi toscani* (Florence, 1770), X, pp. 220–81. For a recent discussion of the complex question of succession, see P. Cammarosano, "Aspetti delle structure familiari nelle città dell'Italia comunale (secoli XII–XIV)," *Studi Medievali*, XVI (1975), 417–35. We observe a decline in punitive clauses and penalties for heirs in Tuscan documents over the eleventh and twelfth centuries; for earlier examples, see C. Troya, p. 388; on this general topic, see L. Little, "Formules monastiques de malédiction au IXᵉ et Xᵉ siècles," *Revue Mabillon*, LVIII (1975), 377–99. On the theme of affective family ties, see E. Cattaneo, "Il battistero in Italia dopo il mille," *Italia Sacra*, XV (1970), 171–95, where he discusses baptism as a sacrament to be administered shortly after birth; cf. also D. Hay, p. 23; P. Ariès, pp. 77–85; J. Le Goff, "The Usurer and Purgatory," 25–52.

16. C. de La Roncière, *Florence: Centre économique régional au XIVᵉ siècle* (Aix-en-Provence, 1976), I, pp. 310–17, and "Pauvres et pauvreté à Florence au XIVᵉ siècle," *Études sur l'histoire de la pauvreté*, ed. M. Mollat, VIII (Paris, n.d.), 661–745.

17. A. Vauchez, p. 60; L. Little, *Religious Poverty*, p. 76; *P.L.*, CXLIX, col. 637; K. Hallinger, "Woher kommen die Laienbruder," *Analecta Sacri Ordini Cisterciensis*, XII (1956), 1–104. On *conversi* in Florence, see F. Dal Pino, *I Frati Servi di S. Maria dalle origini all'approvazione* (Louvain, 1972), I, pp. 515–31. For additional studies, see *I laici nella 'societas christiana' dei secoli XI e XII* (Milan, 1968).

18. G. Meersseman, *Ordo fraternitatis*, I, pp. 35–40; A. Vauchez, 23–25; P. Riché, *La vie quotidienne dans l'Empire Carolingien* (Paris, 1973), pp. 215–26; R. Manselli, *La religione popolare nel medioevo* (Turin, 1974), pp. 68–69. For Sta. Maria in Gradis, see U. Pasqui, *Documenti per la storia di Arezzo nel medio evo* (Florence, 1899), I, pp. 384 ff. For Florence, see M. Lami, *Ecclesiae florentinae monumenta* (Florence, 1759), II, pp. 955–56.

19. On the differences between Cathars in France and Italy, see L. Little, *Religious Poverty*, pp. 166 ff. On the confraternity at San Appiano, see G. Monti, *La confraternite medievali dell'alta e media Italia* (Venice, 1927), II, pp. 140–43; G. Meersseman, *Ordo fraternitatis*, I, pp. 55–67.

20. Bonizone di Sutri, *Liber de vita christiana*, ed. E. Perels (Berlin, 1930); see especially Perels's introduction to Bonizone's *Vita*, pp. xii ff.; cf. also G. Miccoli, "Bonizone," *Dizionario biografico degli Italiani* (Rome, 1970), XII, 246–59; I. Robinson, "Gregory VII and the Soldiers of Christ," *History*, LVIII (1973), 169–92; C. Erdmann, *The Origin of the Idea of Crusades*, pp. 249–55; P. Fournier and G. Le Bras, *Histoire des collections canonique en occident depuis les fausses décrétales jusqu'au décret de Gratien* (Paris, 1932), II, pp. 139–50.

21. L. Prosdocimi, "Chierici e laici nella società occidentale del secolo XII," *Annali della Facoltà di Giurisprudenta dell'Università di Genoa*, III (1964), 241–62; republished in *Proceedings of the Second International Congress of Medieval Canon Law* (Città del Vaticano, 1965), 105–22. Cf. also E. Friedberg, ed., *Corpus Juris Canonici* (Leipzig, 1879–81), I, p. 678.

22. R. Moore, *The Birth of Popular Heresy* (London, 1975), p. 17. For background on heresy and religious dissent in this period, see G. Cracco, "Riforma ed eresia in momenti della cultura Europea tra X e XI secolo," *Rivista di Storia e Letteratura Religiosa*, VII (1971), 411–77; I. da Milano, "Le eresie popolari del secolo XI nell'Europa occidentale," *Studi Gregoriani*, II (1947), 43–89; J. Russell, "À propos du synode d'Arras," *Revue d'Histoire Écclésiastique*, LVII (1962), 66–87. Cf. also *P.L.*, CXLII, cols. 1269–1312.

23. R. Moore, pp. 19–20. For background on this episode, see C. Violante, *La società milanese nell'età precomunale* (Bari, 1953), pp. 1,6–85; J. Russell, *Dissent and Reform in the Early Middle Ages* (Los Angeles, 1965), pp. 276 ff.; cf. also Landulfus Senior, *Historia mediolanensis libri quatuor, M.G.H., Scriptores VIII* (Hanover, 1848), pp. 65–66.

24. R. Moore, pp. 9–10. For background, see B. Quilici, *La chiesa di Firenze nei primi decenni del secolo undecimo* (Florence, 1940), pp. 52–80; L. Little, p. 76. On Adhermar, see G. Duby, *L'anno mille: Storia religiosa e psicologia collettiva* (Turin, 1976), pp. 100–103; cf. also *P.L.*, CXLV, col. 528, and CXLVI, col. 675.

25. S. Boesch Gajano, "Giovanni Gualberto e la vita comune del clero nelle biografie di Andrea da Strumi e di Atto da Vallombrosa," *La vita comune del clero nei secoli XI e XII* (Milan, 1962), II, 278–335; G. Borino, "L'investitura laica dal decreto di Niccolo II al decreto di Gregorio VII," *Studi Gregoriani*, V (1956), 345–55; A. Sticker, "Il potere coattivo materiale della chiesa nella riforma gregoriana secondo Anselmo di Lucca," ibid., II (1947), 235–85. Damiani was torn between the exemplary and prophetic functions of monasticism on the one hand and the attraction of direct appeal and preaching to laity on the other; cf. *P.L.*, CXLV, cols. 525 ff., and A. Cantin, passim.

26. C. Violante, "I laici nel movimento patarino," *I laici nella 'societas christiana' dei secoli XI e XII* (Milan, 1968), 596–687; Y. Congar, *Lay People in the Church* (Westminster, 1957), pp. 309–90; W. Ullmann, "Cardinal Humbert and the Ecclesia Romana," *Studi Gregoriani*, IV (1952), 123 ff.; C. Erdmann, pp. 17–19, 141–83; cf. also *P.L.*, CVI, cols. 121–24; CXXV, cols. 953–57; CXXXIV, cols. 102–4; CXXXVI, cols. 149–55; CXLIV, col. 463.

27. For a discussion of the conflict over the role of laity in Christian society, see A. Frugoni, "Momenti e problemi dell'ordo laicorum nei secoli X–XI," *Nova Historia*, XII (1961), 2–22; G. Meersseman, "Chiesa e 'ordo laicorum' nel secolo XI," *Chiesa e riforma nella spiritualità del secolo XI* (Todi, 1968), 51–68. On crusades as pilgrimage, see E. Delaruelle, "Le croisade comme pèlerinage," *Mélanges Saint Bernard* (Dijon, 1964), 60–64; P. Alphandery and A. Dupront, *La christienté et l'idée de croisade. Les premières croisades* (Paris, 1954), I, pp. 18–31; cf. G. Miccoli's review in *Bullettino della Scuola Normale Superiore di Pisa* XXVI (1957), 294–305. On the crusade and remission of sin, see C. Vogel, *Le pécheur et la pénitence au moyen âge* (Paris, 1968), p. 162.

28. On Ivo and the transvaluation of the word *humanitas*, see C. Morris, *The Discovery of the Individual 1050–1200* (London, 1972), p. 10. Of course, Ivo's delight in humanity was theologically directed: the grandeur of man lay in his divine vocation, his calling, and in the possibilities open to him. But the opportunities were circumscribed by a profound sense of sin and an understanding of the misery to which the human condition was liable. Cf. R. Spandrel, *Ivo von Chartres und seine Stellung in der Kirchengeschichte* (Stuttgart, 1962).

29. G. Miccoli, "La storia religiosa," 512–18; L. Little, *Religious Poverty*, p. 179; J. Baldwin, *Masters, Princes, and Merchants*, I, pp. 288–90; J. Noonan, *The Scholastic Analysis of Usury* (Cambridge, Mass., 1957), pp. 133–53. Cf. also *P.L.*, CLXII, cols. 260–64.

30. R. Spandrel, pp. 141 ff.; G. Morin, "Rainaud l'ermite et Ives de Chartres: Un episode de la crise du cenobitisme au XIᵉ–XIIᵉ siècle," *Revue Bénédictine*, XL (1928), 99–113. Cf. also *P.L.*, CLXII, cols. 196–202.

31. G. Morin, 101 ff.; L. Little, pp. 77, 108; G. Miccoli, *Chiesa Gregoriana*, pp. 285 ff. On Urban II, see C. Derein, "L'élaboration du statut canonique des chanoines réguliers spécialement sous Urban II," *Revue Historique Écclésiastique*, XLVI (1951), 550 ff.; *P.L.*, CLI, cols. 338–39.

32. R. Southern, *Saint Anselm and His Biographers*, p. 102. Cf. also Saint Anselm, *Basic Writings*, p. 179: "It seems to me a case of negligence if, after becoming firm in our faith, we strive not to understand what we believe"; St. Anselm, *Opera omnia* (Edinburgh-Rome, 1938–68), III, p. 211; J. Leclercq, "Sur la dévotion a l'humanité du Christ," *Revue Bénédictine*, LXIII (1953), 128–30.

33. R. Southern, p. 262; C. Vogel, pp. 58–59; St. Anselm, *Basic Writings*, pp. 207–12.

34. On the later works of Anselm, see G. Evans, *Anselm and Talking about God*, pp. 195 ff. For a balanced discussion of interpretations of the philosophic, mystical mix in Anselm's outlook, see J. Leclercq, *La spiritualità*, pp. 280–81.

35. On Anselm of Lucca and Gregory VII's reactions to mercenary impulses, see C. Erdmann, pp. 157–58, 177; H. Cowdrey, "Pope Gregory VII and the Anglo-Norman Church," *Studi Gregoriani*, IX (1972), 77–114; cf. also J. Leclercq, "The Monastic Crisis of the 11th and 12th Centuries," *Cluniac Monasticism in the Central Middle Ages*, ed. N. Hunt (London, 1971), 204 ff.; J. Baldwin, II, p. 44.

36. R. Blomme, *La doctrine du péché dans les écoles théologiques de la première moitié du XII siècle* (Louvain, 1958); C. Hugueny, "Gratien et la confession," *Revue des Sciences Philosophiques et Théologique*, VI (1912), 81–88;

R. Debil, "La première distinction du 'De poenitentia' de Gratien," *Revue d'Histoire Écclésiastique*, XV (1914), 251–73, 442 ff.; P. Lombard, *Sententiarum Liber* (Quaracchi, 1916), I, pp. 533–35; II, 580. On the force of love and charity, see B. Calati, "Alcuni aspetti della monastica di S. Bernardo," *Camaldoli*, VII (1953), 101–18, and of course E. Gilson, *La théologie mystique de Saint Bernard* (Paris, 1932).

37. Hersey was almost, though not quite, unknown in medieval Italy since the conversion of the Lombards from Arianism in the late seventh century. Cf. R. Moore, p. 6. For background on the relationship between lay piety and heresy, see R. Morghen, *Medioevo Cristiano* (Bari, 1951), pp. 212–86. Repeatedly and effectively, Morghen has challenged the contentions of H. C. Lea and S. Runciman that there is sufficient evidence for establishing a connection between the outbreak of heresy in the eleventh century and the preachings of such sects as the Bogomils. The weight of scholarly opinion is clearly on the side of interpretations emphasizing the indigenous roots of religious heterodoxy in the West; cf. R. Morghen, "Problèmes sur l'origine de l'hérésie au moyen-âge," *Hérésies et sociétés dans l'Europe pré-industrielle 11e–18e siècles* (Paris, 1968), 120–32. For a general discussion, see A. Vauchez, pp. 52 ff.; L. Little, pp. 136 ff.; on Arialdo, see C. Violante, *Studi sulla Cristianità*, pp. 149 ff.; on Monforte, see C. Violante, *La società milanese*, pp. 176–85. Landulfus Senior's *Historia mediolanensis*, ed. A. Cutolo, *Rerum Italicarum Scriptores*, IV, part 2 (Bologna, 1932), pp. 67–69, is a more recent edition of the chronicle.

38. R. Moore, *The Origins of Religious Dissent* (London, 1977), pp. 55–71; C. Violante, "I laici nel movimento patarino," 597–640. For a discussion of the historiography of church reform, see O. Capitani, "Storiografia e riforma della chiesa in Italia," *La storiografia altomedievale* (Spoleto, 1970), II, 557–629.

39. G. Miccoli, *Chiesa Gregoriana*, pp. 285 ff.; R. Morghen, *Gregorio VII*, pp. 32–34; S. Boesch Gajano, "Storia e tradizione Vallombrosane," 111 ff.; G. Miccoli, *Pietro Igneo*, pp. 120–27.

40. P. Zerbi, "Pasquale II e l'ideale di povertà della chiesa," *Annuario dell'Università Cattolica del Sacro Cuore* (Milan, 1965), 207–29; G. Miccoli, "La storia religiosa," p. 514.

41. For historical background on Rome in the twelfth century, see P. Partner, *The Lands of St. Peter: The Papal State in the Middle Ages and the Early Renaissance* (Berkeley, Cal., 1972), pp. 158–202. For a discussion of historical sources treating the life and times of Arnold of Brescia, see A. Frugoni's *Arnaldo da Brescia nelle fonti del secolo XII* (Rome, 1954); cf. also John of Salisbury, *Historia Pontificalis*, trans. M. Chibnall (London, 1956), pp. 59–65.

42. Relevant passages from John of Salisbury's *Historia Pontificalis*, cited in R. Moore's *The Birth of Popular Heresy*, pp. 67–68, as well as in M. Chibnall's edition (London, 1956). Cf. also A. Frugoni, pp. 107–38.

43. For the letter of Wenzel, see R. Moore, pp. 69–70; cf. also A. Frugoni, pp. 15–33; L. Little, pp. 139 ff.; *P.L.*, CLXXXII, col. 135; CLXXXIII, col. 1094.

44. For the views of Otto of Freising, see A. Frugoni, pp. 163–70; P. Brezzi, "Ottone di Frisinga," *B.I.S.I.*, LIV (1939), 129–328. For the pertinent selections from Otto of Freising, see *The Deeds of Frederick Barbarossa by Otto of Freising and His Continuator, Rahewin*, trans. C. Mierow, with the collaboration of R. Emery (New York, 1953), pp. 61, 142–44; W. Wakefield and A. Evans, *Heresies of the High Middle Ages* (New York, 1969), p. 147.

45. For the development of the *ars dictaminis*, see Q. Skinner, *The Foundations of Modern Political Thought* (London, 1978), I, pp. 28–35; J. Banker, "The *Ars Dictaminis* and Rhetorical Textbooks at the Bolognese University in the 14th Century," *Medievalia et Humanistica*, n.s., V (1974), 153–68. On lit-

eracy, see C. Cipolla, *Literacy and Development in the West* (London, 1969), p. 41.; cf. also Otto of Freising, *The Deeds of Frederick Barbarossa*, pp. 127–28.

46. D. Waley, *The Italian City Republics*, pp. 138–39; H. Cowdrey, "Archbishop Ariberto II of Milan," *History*, LI (1966), 12; M. Martorati, "Ariberto," *Dizionario biografico degli Italiani* (Rome, 1962), 144–51.

47. E. Battisti, "I interstizi profani nell'arte figurativa," *Il contributo dei giullari alla drammaturgia italiana delle origini* (Viterbo, 1977), 70–88; C. Ragghianti, "L'arte bizantina e romanica," *L'arte in Italia* (Rome, 1968), II, cols. 820–22; H. Wieruszowski, *Politics and Culture in Medieval Spain and Italy* (Rome, 1971), pp. 331–45, 359–77, 387–474, 589–627; A. Grabar, *Romanesque Painting from the 11th to the 13th Century* (New York, 1958), p. 30.

48. Otto of Freising, pp. 142–44; W. Wakefield and A. Evans, p. 150.

49. Otto of Freising, p. 274; M. D. Chenu, *Nature, Man, and Society*, pp. 240 ff.; L. Delaruelle, *La piété populaire*, pp. 331 ff. G. Duby, in "Les chanoines réguliers et la vie économique des XIe et XIIe siècles," *La vita comune del clero nei secoli XI e XII* (Milan, 1962), I, 72–81, makes the point that canons professing the regular life, according to the rule attributed to St. Augustine, and who renounced the possession of citizen property came, for the most part, from new merchant families of citizen origin. There also were recruits from seigneurial families; cf. R. Lopez, "An Aristocracy of Money," 41–42; C. Derein, "La 'vita apostolica' dans l'ordre canonial du Xe au XIIe siècle," *Revue Mabillon*, LI (1961), 47–53.

50. J. Leclercq, " 'Eremus' et 'eremità'. Pour l'histoire du vocabulaire de la vie solitaire," *Collectanea Ordinis Cistercensium Reformatorum*, XXV (1965), 8–30; P. Delhaye, "L'organisation secolaire au XIIe siècle," *Traditio*, V (1947), 211–68. On lay initiatives in Florence, see G. Meersseman, *Dossier de l'ordre de la pénitence*, pp. 11–14, 205–9; M. Becker, "Aspects of Lay Piety," 177–99. For a discussion of the extension of conceptions of *fraternitas* in the Italian context, see P. Zerbi and A. Ambrosini, *Problemi di storia medioevo* (Milan, 1977), pp. 68–170. On realizing those ideals of brotherhood and equality that characterized the Church of the Apostles, see J. R. Smith, *The Knights of St. John in Jerusalem and Cyprus* (London, 1967), pp. 40 ff. For an emphasis on manual labor, see A. Borst, *Die Katharer* (Stuttgart, 1953), pp. 124 ff. On the heightened influence of classical ethical teachings upon laity, see E. Curtius, *European Literature and the Middle Ages* (London, 1953), pp. 519–29.

51. M. D. Chenu, pp. 222–23; L. Little, *Religious Poverty*, pp. 110–12; Anna L. Del Grosso, "Povertà e ricchezza nel pensiero di Gerhoch de Reichersberg," *Annali della Facoltà di Giurisprudenza dell'Università di Genova*, VIII (1969), pp. 146–93. On Gerhoh's reaction to the slaying of Arnold, see A. Frugoni, *Arnoldo da Brescia*, pp. 147–62. Cf. also R. Manselli, *La "lectura super Apocalipsim" di Pietro di Giovanni Olivi: Ricerche sull'escatologismo medioevale* (Rome, 1955), pp. 62–64; *P.L.*, CLXXXXIV, col. 1302; *De investigatione Antichristi*, I, 40 in *M.G.H., Libelli de lite imperatorum et pontificum*, III, pp. 347–48.

52. P. Classen, *Gerhoch von Reichersberg* (Wiesbaden, 1960), pp. 291–98; R. Manselli, pp. 63–66. With Gerhoh medieval eschatology became more ductile and capable of explicating the contours of history; cf. P. Vauchez, p. 112. *De quarta vigilia noctis, M.G.H., Libelli de lite imperatorum et pontificum*, III, pp. 503–25.

53. E. Buonaiuti, *Gioacchino da Fiore* (Rome, 1930), pp. 204–36; R. Manselli, pp. 98–101. For background and the relationship between Joachim and his contemporaries, see M. Reeves, *The Influence of Prophecy in the Later Middle Ages: A Study in Joachimism* (Oxford, 1969), pp. 4–15; for his view of history, see pp. 16–27.

Notes for Pages 135–39

4. TOWARD ACCEPTANCE OF THE PROBLEMATIC AND AMBIGUOUS

1. P. Ilarino da Milano, "La spiritualità evangelica anteriore a San Francesco," *Quaderni di Spiritualità Francescana*, VI (1963), 61–70; G. Miccoli, "Dal pellegrinaggio alla conquista," *Povertà e ricchezza nella spiritualità dei secoli XI e XII* (Todi, 1969), 74 ff. On Otto III, see the classic account by G. Falco, *The Holy Roman Republic*, trans. K. Kent (London, 1964), pp. 169–75; P. Partner, pp. 87–92. On the question of the followers of Arnold, see A. Frugoni, "Filii Arnaldi," *B.I.S.I.*, LXX (1958), 521–24. For a critical note on the use of Otto of Freising as a source, see R. Moore, *The Origins of European Dissent*, p. 300.

2. H. Poschmann, *Poenitentia secunda* (Bonn, 1940), p. 143; T. Oakley, "The Cooperation of Medieval Penance and Secular Law," *Speculum*, VII (1932), 515–24; E. Rocca, "Considerazioni giuridiche," 449–50; G. Pepe, *Da San Nilo all'umanesimo*, pp. 9–14; A. Vauchez, p. 156.

3. G. Meersseman, "Chiesa e 'ordo laicorum' nel secolo XI," *Chiesa e riforma nella spiritualità del secolo XI* (Todi, 1968), 57, and "I penitenti nei XI e XII secoli," 331–36.

4. G. Meersseman, *Dossier de l'ordre de la pénitence*, pp. 1–38, and *Ordo fraternitatis*, I, pp. 520 ff. On the creation of new forms of piety distinct from those of clergy, see A. Pompei, "Il movimento penitenziale nei secoli XII–XIII," *L'ordine della penitenza di San Francesco*, ed. O. Schmucki (Rome, 1973), 32–35. The quest for laity's spiritual perfection became increasingly dramatic and far-reaching; it was encouraged by such figures as Pier Giovanni Olivi, whose stay in Florence contributed to the ferment of the times. F. Ehrle, "Petrus Johannis Olivi, sein Leben und seine Schriften," *Archiv für Literatur und Kirchengeschichte des Mittelalters*, III (1887), 409–552. M. Reeves, *The Influence of Prophecy in the Later Middle Ages*, p. 291, suggests that the distinctive element in the faith of *viri spirituales* (followers of Joachite teachings) sprang from a "myth of the future, not the past. . . . Their models might be drawn from the past, but their belief was that the life of the future would far exceed that of the past. It was not so much a recapturing of the life of the first Apostles that they expected as the creating of the life of new apostles."

5. For an example of the persistence of public penance for a gross crime, such as the murder of a *converso*, see *Archivio di Stato, Firenze* (henceforth abbreviated as *ASF*). *Diplomatico, Badia di S. Lorenzo a Coltibuono* (23 December 1284). For background on penitential practice, see C. Vogel, *Il peccatore e la penitenza nella chiesa antica* (Turin, 1967). On the proclivity of Florentines for supporting religious establishments in which penitential intentions were strong, see F. Dal Pino, *I Frati Servi di S. Maria dalle origini all'approvazione (1233–1304)* (Louvain, 1972), I, pp. 714 ff. On devotion to the Virgin, see G. Petrocchi, *Scrittori religiosi del Duecento* (Florence, 1974), pp. 125 ff.; *ASF* (Compagnia Laudi di Sta. Maria Novella), *Diplomatico, Sta. Maria Novella* (15 April 1285, 20 February 1288); *Conventi Soppressi*, CII, nos. 281, 292.

6. For the civic role of the penitent in the Italian city, see G. Meersseman, *Dossier*, pp. 17 ff.; A. Benvenuti, "Fonti e problemi per la storia dei penitenti a Firenze," *L'ordine della penitenza di San Francesco*, ed. O. Schmucki (Rome, 1973), 290 ff. On the establishment and naming of the chief magistracy of Florence, see G. Villani, *Cronica*, VII, 79. For archival materials on the penitential movement in Florence, see *ASF, Archivio dell'Arcispedale di Sta. Maria Nuova, San Paolo dei convalescenti*, filze 972–77; *Biblioteca Nazionale Centrale di Firenza*, Ms. mglb. XXXVII, cod. 200; *ASF, Corporazioni religiose soppresse*, F103, n. 109.

7. M. Reeves, *Joachim of Fiore and the Prophetic Future* (New York, 1977).

8. G. Monti, *Le confraternite medievali*, I, pp. 7–10, 150–65; G. Meersseman, pp. 56 ff.; P. Santini, *Documenti dell'antica costituzione di Firenze* (Florence, 1895), p. 493.

9. For Salimbene, see G. Coulton, *From St. Francis to Dante* (London, 1907), pp. 21–22. On Salimbene's reactions to the Alleluia, see *Cronica*, ed. G. Scalia (Bari, 1966), I, pp. 99–100; cf. also V. Fumagalli, "In margine all'Alleluja del 1233," *B.I.S.I.*, LXXX (1968), 257–72. For a balanced discussion of penitential confraternities in the year 1260, see J. Henderson, "The Flagellant Movement and Flagellant Confraternities in Central Italy," *Studies in Church History*, XV (1978), 147–60.

10. I wish to thank John Henderson for permitting me to read his "The Religious Confraternities of Florence" (a dissertation to be submitted to the University of London). On lay confraternities and the Dominicans, see L. Little, *Religious Poverty*, pp. 206–10; G. Meersseman, "Les confréries des disciplinés de Saint-Dominique," *Archivum Fratrum Praedicatorum*, XX (1950), 21–63. For an examination of the penitential movement in rural areas, see G. Meersseman and E. Adda, "Pénitents ruraux communautaires en Italie au XIIᵉ siècle," *Revue d'Histoire Écclésiastique*, XLIX (1954), 343–90. For the growth of the confraternal movement in the Florentine *contado*, see C. De la Roncière, "La place des confréries dans l'encadrement religieux du contado florentin au XIVᵉ siècle," *Mélanges de l'École Française de Rome*, LXXXV (1973), 31–77.

11. P. Meloni, "Topografia, diffusione e aspetti delle confraternite," *Risultati e prospettive della ricerca sul movimento dei disciplinati* (Perugia, 1972), 26–30. The *anonimo* of Padua wrote that it was not a preacher, learned man, or ecclesiastical authority of any type who moved the people to flagellate themselves in public "sed a simplicibus sumpsit initium." Cf. R. Manselli, "L'anno 1260 fu anno giochimitico?" *Il movimento dei disciplinati* (Perugia, 1962), 100–108; A. Frugoni, "Sui flagellanti del 1260," *B.I.S.I.*, LXXV (1963), 220.

12. V. Ansidei, ed., *Regestum reformationum comunis perusii ab anno MCCLVI ad annum MCCC* (Perugia, 1935), I, pp. xvii, 180; G. Meersseman, *Ordo fraternitatis*, I, p. 454; J. Henderson, "The Flagellant Movement," 150.

13. On Fasani, see U. Nicolini, "Nuove testimonianze su Raniero Fasani e suoi disciplinati," *Bollettino della Deputazione di Storia Patria per l'Umbria*, LX (1963), 334–38. This holy man had a wife and children and initiated the founding of a hospital. G. Mazzatini, "Legenda de fra Rainero Faxano," *ibid.*, II (1896), 561–63; A. Gaudenzi, *Statuti delle società del popolo di Bologna* (Rome, 1896), II, pp. 421–36; these statutes of a Società dei Devoti state that they were written at the time of the "general devotion" (1260). In their early years flagellants were known officially as *devoti*, and in Imola as well as Perugia their first grand public manifestations were called "devotions." Of course Raniero was a penitent, and in Pisa the statutes of a flagellant confraternity fixed the name day of the company on the day of St. Raniero. Cf. G. Meersseman, I, p. 463; II, p. 966; cf. A. Frugoni, 223–34. For possible Joachite influences at mid-thirteenth century, see M. Reeves, *The Influence of Prophecy*, pp. 45–58.

14. G. Meersseman, "Nota sull'origine delle compagnia dei laudesi," *Rivista Storica della Chiesa in Italia*, XVII (1963), 395 ff.; E. Pasquini, "La Lauda," *Il Duecento: Dalle origini a Dante*, ed. E. Pasquini and A. Quaglio, in *La letteratura italiana storia e testi* (Bari, 1970), I, part 1, 481–548.

15. The paper of my former student M. Northrup on the theme of Last Judgments in medieval Italian art was most useful in my formulations; cf. also A. Frugoni, "I temi della morte," *B.I.S.I.*, LXIX (1957), 187 ff.; J. White, *Art and Architecture in Italy 1250 to 1400* (Baltimore, 1966), p. 46; R. Romano, *Tra due crisi: L'Italia del Rinascimento* (Turin, 1971), pp. 100–115; M. Meiss, *Painting in Florence and Siena after the Black Death* (New York, 1964), pp. 84 ff. For

a general discussion of the spiritual milieu and its relationship to suffering and death, see the many excellent articles in *Il dolore e la morte nella spiritualità dei secoli XII e XIII* (Todi, 1967).

16. If one considers such an important text as *De miseria humane condicionis*, by Lotario di Segni (the future Innocent III), this seemingly most pessimistic of widely popular arguments centers on not death but punishment. The reader is summoned to meditate on fire and eternal darkness rather than on death itself. The frailty and corruption of man demonstrate his abiding need for church hierarchy; cf. A. Frugoni, 187–88. At the same time other texts equally prominent emphasized the capacity of laymen to resolve human and moral questions; see P. Kristeller, *Renaissance Thought II: Papers on Humanism and the Arts* (New York, 1965), pp. 25 ff.; C. Segre, *Volgarizzamento del Due e Trecento* (Turin, 1935); G. Folena, "Cultura poetica dei primi fiorentini," *Giornale Storico della Letteratura Italiana*, CXLII (1970), 1–42.

17. W. Wakefield and A. Evans, p. 159, for a translation from *Chronicon universale anonymi Laudunensis*, in *M.G.H., Scriptores*, XXVI, 449–50. On the Humiliati, see G. Tiraboschi, *Vetera Humiliatorum Monumenta* (Milan, 1767), II, pp. 127 ff.; L. Zanoni, *Gli umiliati nei loro rapporti con l'eresia, l'industria della lana, ed i comuni nei secoli XII e XIII* (Milan, 1911). On Humbert of Romans, see L. Little, *Religious Poverty*, 200–203.

18. J. Mundy, *Europe in the High Middle Ages 1150–1309* (New York, 1973), p. 550; cf. also J. Hinnebush, ed., *Historia Occidentalis of Jacques of Vitry* (Fribourg, 1972), p. 145.

19. W. Wakefield and A. Evans, pp. 200–202; L. Little, p. 122; G. Miccoli, "La storia religiosa," 687. On the subject of St. Alexis, that most laic of all medieval saints, see E. Delaruelle, *La piété populaire*, pp. 453–54. For another celebrated account of the Waldensians by a contemporary, see W. Map, *De Nugis Curialium*, trans. M. James (London, 1923), pp. 65–68.

20. A. Dondaine, "Aux origines du Valdeisme," *Archivum Fratrum Praedicatorum*, XVI (1946), 191–235, and his "Le hierarchie cathare en Italie," ibid., XIX (1949), 280–312; XX (1950), 234–324; A. Borst, pp. 231–39. For a translation of pertinent sections of the tract of Raniero Sacchoni, see R. Moore, *The Birth of Popular Heresy*, pp. 132–45.

21. On differences between Italian Cathars and those of south France, see W. Wakefield and A. Evans, pp. 269–78; J. Mundy, p. 288; L. Little, pp. 125–26. For Bonvesin de la Riva, a Humiliato and married, see S. Pasquini, "La letteratura didattica e allegorica," *Il duecento*, ed. E. Pasquini and A. Quaglio, I, part 2, 52–55. He was the first authentic dialect poet of Milan.

22. For an illuminating view of spirituality in the earlier society, see E. Delaruelle, "Style de vie héroïque," *Comitato Internazionale di Scienze Storiche. X Congresso* (Florence, 1955), III, 322–31. Cf. J. Mundy, p. 293; B. Bolton, "Old Wealth and New Poverty in the Twelfth Century," *Studies in Church History*, XIV (1977), 99 ff.; A. Vauchez, "Une campagne de pacification en Lombardie autour de 1233," *Mélanges d'Archéologie et d'Histoire*, LXXVIII (1966), 534 ff. On Damiani, see E. Delaruelle, *La piété populaire*, pp. 454–58.

23. Numerous Florentines from patrician houses were to embrace the penitential life in the thirteenth century. Cf. G. Meersseman, *Dossier*, pp. 51–54; V. Fineschi, *Memorie istoriche che possono servire alle vite degli uomini illustri convento di S. Maria Novella di Firenze* (Florence, 1790), I, 360–63. Boncompagno da Signa, eminent teacher of rhetoric in Bologna in the late twelfth century, composed a set of norms for redacting statutes of the innumerable associations recently formed (Cedrus). He indicated that these societies were much more numerous in Tuscany than elsewhere in Italy; among them were, of course, the confraternity. In Florence one such confraternity, the Disciplinati di San

Domenico, was to have 240 members, among whom were wool workers, rope makers, stationers, hosiers, painters, and the ubiquitous Medici and Strozzi; confraternities were among the most democratic of all communal organizations, and their membership could exceed 700. Also, restitution of usury was democratic in that it was not solely the prerogative of merchants; though they predominated, nobles too restored ill-got gains. The affluent were responsive, and the period, coinciding with Dante's lifetime, was indeed to be the statistical high point for restitution. See G. Meersseman, *Ordo fraternitatis*, I, 18–20; II, 707–12.

24. E. Panofsky, *Early Netherlandish Painting* (Cambridge, Mass., 1953), pp. 22–25; on Giotto, see B. Cole, *Giotto and Florentine Painting 1280–1375* (New York, 1976); M. Meiss, pp. 15–26; cf. also E. Cataneo, "La partecipazione dei laici alla liturgia," *I laici nella societas christiana dei secoli XI e XII* (Milan, 1968), 403 ff.

25. Social problems and historical questions tended to be viewed in the literature of the thirteenth century within a generalized, even universal, context. For example, the problem of poverty was itself regarded as being amenable to a universal solution, as was the eradication of "corruption" in the Church. Cf. R. Manselli, "De Dante à Coluccio Salutati discussions sur la pauvreté a Florence au XIVe siècle," *Études sur l'histoire de la pauvreté*, ed. M. Mollat (Paris, 1974), II, 633–42. What is at base appears to be a buoyant optimism that society's major problems could indeed be resolved. Cf. M. Becker, *Florence in Transition: Vol. I: The Decline of the Commune* (Baltimore, 1967), pp. 11–64. Just as the advocacy of voluntary poverty and mendicancy depended upon the fiscal resources of an expanding urban economy, so St. Francis's call for global penance allowed no scarcity of grace: his message was one of sociability, courtesy, courtliness, kindness, and good nature, to be responded to by a commercially active community. M. D. Chenu makes the telling point that writers of history during those times were becoming increasingly sensitive to the universalism of humanity as it existed in time; their sense of human continuity intensified. Cf. *Nature, Man, and Society*, p. 178. In the Italian cities we observe how the chroniclers shift focus from the explication of urban history, through the narrative of great families, powerful officials, and monunmental events, to a vivid and full portrayal of an integrated urban scene. Giovanni Villani is exemplary of this trend in historical writing as Boccaccio is in prose fiction and Dante in poetry.

26. H. Boehner, *Analekten zur Geschichte des Franciscus von Assisi* (Tubingen, 1930), II, p. 24. For an English translation of "The Testament of St. Francis," see M. Habig, ed., *St. Francis of Assisi: Writings and Early Biographies: English Omnibus of the Sources for the Life of St. Francis* (Chicago, 1972), pp. 67–73 (henceforth abbreviated as *St. Francis of Assisi: Writings*).

27. G. Miccoli, "La 'conversione' di San Francesco secondo Tommaso da Celano," *Studi Medievali*, 3rd ser., V (1964), 775–92; R. Hostie, *Vie et mort des ordres religieux. Approches psychosociologiques* (Paris, 1972), pp. 132–37.

28. P. Willibrord, "Rapport de Saint François de'Assise avec le mouvement spirituel du XIIe siècle," *Études Franciscaines*, XII (1962), 129–43, and "Signification sociale du Franciscanisme naissant," *ibid.*, XV (1965), 84–95. On the Eucharist, see H. De Lubac, *Corpus Mysticum* (Paris, 1948). For a discussion of the response to the French visitor to Assisi, see J. Hubert, "La place fait aux laics dans les églises monastiques," *I laici nella societas christiana dei secoli XI e XII* (Milan, 1968), 473 ff. The cycles of the life of St. Francis depict a countryside and urban scene complete with decor and costume appropriate to the contemporary world. The deeds performed are not those of remote times (*gesta*), and the values and customs honored are those of townsmen and peasants. See E. Delaruelle, pp. 273 ff. Perhaps the leading characteristic of Italian

art in Umbria and Tuscany was a "softening of the symbol" in the service of a new ideal of humanity; this sensibility is expressed by every major artist from Coppo di Marcovaldo and Cimabue to Giotto. See J. White, pp. 117 ff.

29. *Regula prima*, in *Opuscula sancti patris Francisci*, 2d ed. (Quaracchi, 1941), I, chap. 21; J. Jörgensen, *St. Francis of Assisi* (New York, 1953), p. 67; M. Lambert, *Franciscan Poverty: The Doctrine of the Absolute Poverty of Christ and the Apostles in the Franciscan Order, 1210–1323* (London, 1961), pp. 39 ff.

30. *St. Francis of Assisi: Writings*, pp. 926–28.

31. Ibid., pp. 1601–2; L. Lemmens, *Testimonia minora saeculi XIII de S. Francisco Assisiensi* (Quaracchi, 1926), p. 10; R. Manselli, *La religione popolare nel medioevo (secoli VI–XII)* (Turin, 1974), pp. 119–20.

32. R. Manselli, *La 'lectura,'* p. 107; *Scripta Leonis*, ed. and trans. R. Brooke (Oxford, 1970), p. 93.

33. *St. Francis of Assisi: Writings*, p. 1089; J. Moorman, *The Sources for the Life of St. Francis of Assisi* (Manchester, 1940), p. 29; G. Miccoli, "La storia religiosa," 741.

34. For a penetrating discussion of the theme of "reversal" and "carnival," see C. Ginzburg, "Folklore, magia, religione," *Storia d'Italia* (Turin, 1972), I, 615 ff.

35. *The Divine Comedy*, trans. D. Sayers and B. Reynolds (Baltimore, 1966), pp. 150–51. Speculation as to whether Dante was a member of a Third-Order Franciscan confraternity in his early years may indeed have a basis; cf. G. Meersseman, *Ordo fraternitatis*, I, pp. 519–20, for quotations from authorities from Trecento commentators on Dante to twentieth-century literary historians, such as V. Branca.

36. J. Jörgensen, p. 128, records the anecdote reported in L. Wadding, the Franciscan annalist. Cf. also *St. Francis of Assisi: Writings*, p. 507.

37. As mentioned in note 23, the restitution of usury reached its heights between the decades of the 1250s and 1320s. There were, of course, large-scale restitutions after that date, but in terms of the percentages in relationship to the number of wills and benefactions, the figure is highest for the period between the 1250s and 1320s. In the 1330s and '40s there were restitutions by the Peruzzi, Strozzi, and others. Cf. *ASF, Diplomatico, S. Maria Novella* (12 July 1345). Further, the number of tertiaries and penitents making charitable bequests and restitutions was also at its peak during those decades. The following were important notaries redacting documents for this clientele: *ASF, Notarile Anticosimiano*: Attaviano di Chiaro, Bartolo di Ser Lapo Amici, Arrigo Benintendi, Lando di Ubaldino, Opizzo da Pontremoli, Uguccione di Bondone, Ranieri di Cione da Petrognano. Commencing with the second half of the Trecento, we find a change in the nature of bequests. A subsequent book will consider these developments in detail.

38. M. Reeves, *Joachim of Fiore*, pp. 29–31; C. Davis, *Dante and the Idea of Rome* (Oxford, 1957), pp. 242 ff.

39. See notes 41 and 42 in Chapter 3 and T. Panaro and L. Pruneti, *Opposizione religiosa medioevo* (Florence, 1977), pp. 105–7; *Polycraticus*, bk. VI, chap. 24, ed. C. Webb (London, 1932), II, p. 67. On Florence, the Church, and the Cathars, see B. Quilici, *Il Vescovo Ardingo e la chiesa di Firenze nel quarto e quinto decennio del secolo XIII* (Florence, 1965).

40. Tertiaries and penitents, and even the moderately orthodox, did not suffer the fate of the Beguines in north Europe; they were protected by communal government. Cf. A. Inni, "Nuovi documenti sugli Spirituali in Toscana," *Archivum Franciscanum Historicum*, LXVI (1972), 305–77, especially 359. On the

Third Order membership of tradesmen and lesser guildsmen, see J. Moorman, *A History of the Franciscan Order: From Its Origins to the Year 1517* (Oxford, 1968), p. 221.

41. On St. Bernard, see L. Little, pp. 139–40; cf. also *P.L.*, CLXXXII, cols. 434–36; CLXXXV, cols. 410–16; *The Letters of St. Bernard*, trans. B. James (London, 1953), pp. 388–91.

42. D. Lesnick, "Popular Dominican Preaching in Early Fourteenth-Century Florence" (Ph.D. dissertation, University of Rochester, 1975), and "Dominican Preaching and the Creation of Capitalist Ideology in Late Medieval Florence," *Memorie Domenicane*, n.s., VIII–IX (1977–78), 204–41. Cf. L. Little, pp. 145, 200–203; for a translation of pertinent writings of Jacques de Vitry, see *St. Francis of Assisi: Writings*, pp. 1608–15; *The Historia Occidentalis*, pp. 165 ff.; G. Meersseman, *Ordo fraternitatis*, I, p. 374.

43. G. Miccoli, "La storia religiosa," 803 ff.; H. Baron, "Franciscan Poverty and Civic Wealth as Factors in the Rise of Humanistic Thought," *Speculum*, XIII (1938), 1–35. G. Olsen, in "The Idea of the Ecclesia Primitiva in the Writing of the Twelfth-Century Canonists," *Traditio*, XXV (1969), 85–86, notes that the term *primitive church* had practically disappeared by the tenth century but was to be revived by the Gregorian reformers in the middle of the eleventh century.

44. For an analysis of merchant sensibilities, see A. Sapori, *The Italian Merchant in the Middle Ages*, trans. P. Kennen (New York, 1970), and "Il giusto prezzo nella dottrina di San Tommaso e nella pratica del suo tempo," *Studi di storia economica (secoli XIII, XIV, XV)* (Florence, 1955), 189 ff. C. Cipolla, "The Italian and Iberian Peninsulas," *Cambridge Economic History*, III, 399–419; R. Lopez and I. Raymond, *Medieval Trade*, pp. 409–26.

45. A. Prandi, "Arte figurativa per le confraternité dei disciplinati," *Risultati e prospettive della ricerca sul movimento dei disciplinati* (Perugia, 1972), 266–73; F. Savini, "Sui flagellanti sui fraticelli, sui bizochi nel secoli XIII e XIV," *Archivio Storico Italiano*, XXXV (1905), 82 ff.; I. Magli, *Gli uomini della penitenza* (Rocca San Casciano, 1967), pp. 106 ff.; B. Bolton, "Innocent III's Treatment of the Humiliati," *Studies in Church History*, VIII (1971), 73–82.

46. J. Henderson, "The Flagellant Movement," 144–60; J. Leclercq, "Disciplina," *Dictionnaire de spiritualité* (1957), III, 1291–1302. Tuscan crucifixes illustrate well the movement in the arts from the depiction of an open-eyed and triumphant Christ in the late twelfth century to the pathetic, swaying figure of the dead Christ in the thirteenth century. See J. White, p. 110.

47. G. Lami, *Lezioni di antichità Toscana e spezialmente di Firenze* (Florence, 1762), II, pp. 613–17; G. Meersseman, "Les confréries de Saint Pierre Martyr," *Archivum Fratrum Praedicatorum*, XXI (1951), 51–196; F. Tocco, *Quel che non c'e nella Divina Commedia o Dante e l'eresia* (Bologna, 1900), pp. 34–57. Cf. also *ASF, Diplomatico, S. Maria Novella* (12 November 1221); V. Fineschi, *Memorie istoriche che possono servire alle vite degli uomini illustri del Convento di Santa Maria Novella* (Florence, 1790), I, pp. 118–19. For an additional bibliography, see J. Stephens, "Heresy in Medieval and Renaissance Florence," *Past and Present*, LIV (1972), 25–32.

48. C. Ginzburg, 617–19; R. Davidsohn, *Storia di Firenze*, II, pp. 525 ff.

49. H. Grundmann, *Movimento religiosi nel medioevo*, trans. M. Ausserhofer and L. Santini (Bologna, 1974), p. 448, observes that the radical pauperism of the Franciscans was to be found almost exclusively in Italy, Provence, and Spain. Cf. also W. Hinnebush, "Poverty in the Order of the Preachers," *Catholic Historical Review*, XLV (1960), 436 ff.

50. S. Orlandi, *Il VII centenario della predicazione e ricordi di S. Pietro Martire in Firenze* (Florence, 1946–47), pp. 96–113; G. Meersseman, *Ordo fraterni-*

tatis, I, pp. 455–70. Religious confraternities of the thirteenth century were frequently taking the names of new saints (St. Dominic, Francis, Anthony, Peter Martyr); this suggests something of the contemporaneity of religious movements. Cf. also A. Benvenuti, "Fonti e problemi per la storia dei penitenti a Firenze nel secolo XIII," *L'ordine della penitenza di San Francesco*, ed. O. Schmucki (Rome, 1973), 281–98.

51. B. Geremek, "Il pauperismo nell'età preindustriale," *Storia d'Italia* (Turin, 1973), V, 672–79.

52. On collective norms and sumptuary legislation, see M. Becker, *Florence in Transition*, I, pp. 228 ff., and "La esecuzione della legislazione contro le pratiche monopolistiche," *Archivio Storico Italiano*, CXVII (1959), 8–28. On the decline of wages and increase in grain prices, see G. Pinto, pp. 50–100; R. Goldthwaite, "I prezzi del grano a Firenze dal XIV al XVI secolo," *Quaderni Storici*, X (1975), 15–36.

53. In a subsequent book I will describe some of the leading features of Florentine wills and pious legacies of the fourteenth and fifteenth centuries. That the latter-day bequests were increasingly egoistic is disclosed by a comparison with earlier testaments.

54. Important evidence is to be found in the numerous vernacular sermons extant for Florence; cf. C. Delcorno, ed., *Giordano da Pisa. Quaresimale fiorentino, 1305–1306* (Florence, 1974), and articles by the same author published in *Studi di Filogia Italiana*, XXII (1964), 25 ff.; XXIV (1966), 39 ff.; XXVI (1968), 81 ff.; cf. also D. Lesnick, 199 ff. For a consideration of such influential preachers as Jacopo Passavanti and Cavalca, see M. Meiss, pp. 83 ff.; G. Miccoli, "La storia religiosa," 814–36; C. Ginzburg, 619–27.

55. G. Ristori, "I paterini in Firenze nella prima metà del secolo XIII," *Rivista Storico-Critica delle Scienze Teologiche*, I (1905), 10–23, 328–41, 754–60; L. Fiumi, "I paterini in Orvieto," *Archivio Storico Italiano*, XXI (1875), 65 ff.; S. Orlandi, pp. 54–55; F. Tocco, pp. 45–50; N. Ottokar, "La condanna postuma di Farinata degli Uberti," *Archivio Storico Italiano*, LXVII (1919), 162 ff.

56. As persecution intensified and the inquisition was set in place, the targeted sects closed ranks and distanced themselves yet further from society. Cf. C. Cipolla, "Il patarenismo a Verona nel secolo XIII," *Archivio Veneto*, XIII (1883), 278 ff.; M. da Alatri, "L'inquisizione francescana nell' Italia centrale nel secolo XIII," *Collectanea Franciscana*, XXIII (1953), 148 ff.

57. Perhaps one of the most telling expressions of this heightened solidarity is to be found in the writings of Italian notaries of the late twelfth and early thirteenth centuries. Boncompagno da Signa provided models for drafting legislation on all matter of civic concern, from the regulation of gambling to prostitution to knightly participation in tournaments. If one follows successive redactions of statutes, one can discern the extent to which economic activities and social life in the cities of north and central Italy were becoming regulated in ever-greater detail. Further, the sensitivities of civil servants, lawyers, judges, and notaries, as well as teachers, were heightened on the vexing question of whether one could sell those skills and talents that were God-given. The debate on this matter suggests a dimension of the conflict concerning legitimation of the new laic professions and an economy where wealth was not regarded as a reward for virtue. Cf. G. Post and K. Giocarinis, "The Medieval Heritage of a Humanistic Ideal: 'Scientia Donum Dei Est, Unde Vendi Non Potest,' " *Traditio*, XI (1955), 196–220. On the role of civil servants and notaries, see H. Wieruszowski, "Arezzo as a Center for Learning and Letters in the Thirteenth Century," ibid., IX (1953), 321–91. For a further discussion of this theme, see R. Rosenwein and L. Little, "Social Meaning in Monastic and Mendicant Spiritualities," *Past and Present*, LXIII (1974), 20–25.

58. The basic thrust of vernacular literature during the first half of the thirteenth century was markedly didactic. Leading poets, such as Gerardo Patecchio of Cremona and Uguccione da Lodi, vividly represented the infernal penalties besetting those on the road to salvation. In the second half of the century this Giacomino da Verona's *De Babylonia civitate infernali,* and, of course, Dante's didactic literature gained force with Bonvesin da Riva's *Libro delle tre scritture, Commedia.* The personal, autobiographical, and evocative qualities of vernacular writing at that time have been discussed in depth by Italian literary historians. Cf. G. Petrocchi, *Scrittori religiosi del Duecento* (Florence, 1974), pp. 1–27, with a bibliography.

59. P. Mercier, trans. and ed., *XV homeliés du IXᵉ siècle d'un auteur inconnu de l'Italie du nord* (Paris, 1970). On the numerous vernacular versions of Innocent III's tract on human misery, see C. Segre, *Volgarizzamenti del Due e Trecento* (Turin, 1935), pp. 193 ff.

60. Studies on these topics are legion, but see especially *Sacrum commercium sancti Francisci cum domina Paupertate,* in *Le origini,* ed. A. Viscardi and others (Milan-Naples, 1955), pp. 914–23; G. Gasca Queirazza, "Per sora nostra morte corporale," *Giornale Storico della Letteratura Italiana,* CXLIX (1972), 195–206; U. Cosmo, "Le mistiche nozze di frate Francesco con Madonna Povertà," *Giornale Dantesco,* VI (1898), 48–82.

61. Particularly relevant are the comments of M. Lambert, "The Motives of the Cathars," *Studies in Church History,* XV (1978), 52–54, and *Medieval Heresy (Popular Movements from Bogomil to Hus)* (London, 1977), pp. 14–23, 108–13. Cf. also G. Leff, *Heresy in the Later Middle Ages: The Relation of Heterodoxy to Dissent, c.1250–c.1450* (Manchester, 1967), I, pp. 55 ff.

62. Mary Douglas's *Purity and Danger: An Analysis of Concepts of Pollution and Taboo* (Baltimore, 1966) is a textured discussion of the theme of contamination and its risks. Her perspective is, of course, anthropological, with its focus on tribal society; ours is historical, and we observe that as society moves from archaic to communal, obligations become more abstract and human ties less literal. With an emphasis on love, charity, credit, etc., human arrangements become more problematic and therefore prone to engender guilt. As the claims of community grow more apparent and commanding, unwelcome contradictions surface. At the most basic level these contradictions require the individual to be disloyal to parents. In the melodramatic language of the anthropologist, sons must replace fathers and daughters betray mothers. We hide this crucial fact from human consciousness because it runs counter to our morality. Cf. E. Leach, *Claude Lévi-Strauss* (New York, 1967), pp. 82 ff., and *Culture and Communication: The Logic by Which Symbols Are Connected* (Cambridge, 1976), pp. 61–67.

63. Of course, Tuscany was to become the center for a protracted and creative debate on the exchange system in general and usury in particular. Further, such themes as "just wage" and "just price" were to receive their most sensitive treatment at the hands of influential preachers concerned with economic theory—not the least of which were Sant'Antonino and San Bernardino. For a full discussion of this theme, see R. de Roover, "Labor Conditions in Florence around 1400; Theory, Policy, and Reality," *Florentine Studies,* ed. N. Rubinstein (London, 1968), 277–313, and *San Bernardino of Siena and Sant'Antonino of Florence: The Two Great Economic Thinkers of the Middle Ages* (Boston, 1967).

64. M. Apollonio, *Jacopone da Todi e la poetica delle confraternitè religiose nella cultura preumanistica* (Milan, 1946); N. Sapegno, *Frate Iacopone da Todi* (Turin, 1926). For Dante's fundamentally laic conception of *metanoia,* see *Convivio,* IV, xxviii: "And no one ought to excuse himself by reason of the marriage tie which still binds him in extreme age: for not only does he who assumes

a habit and rule of life like that of St. Augustine, or St. Francis, or St. Dominic, join the ranks of the professed, but a man may also become truly and properly professed while married, for God does not require us to be professed save in heart." For a translation, see Dante's *Convivio*, ed. W. Jackson (Oxford, 1909), p. 293. Cf. also G. Meersseman, "Dante e la cultura Veneta," *Atti del Congresso Internazionale di Studi Danteschi* (Florence, 1965), I, 177 ff. On the passionate affirmation of laic moralism, see A. Monteverdi, "Arrigo da Settimello," *Dizionario biografico degli Italiani* (Rome, 1962), IV, 315 ff. Cf. also C. Trinkaus, "Petrarch's Views on the Individual and His Society," *Osiris*, XI (1954), 172 ff.

65. Religious writers of the fourteenth century, with only a few notable exceptions, did not put reform of church and society at the center of their thought. Even Catherine of Siena, who did favor sweeping reform, readily transmitted doctrine into personal religiosity. The message of St. Francis was likewise being converted into a series of edifying anecdotes as popular religious sentiment blunted ideology. Cf. A. Tartaro, "Scrittori devoti," Vol. II: *Il Trecento*, ed. C. Muscetta and A. Tartaro, in *La letteratura italiana* (Bari, 1972), part 2, 438–81; R. Manselli, *La religione popolare*, pp. 313–15.

66. Giovanni Villani's *Cronica* is, of course, the telling instance of the emergence of guild associative life into full historical consciousness. This chronicle, however, is but a single expression of the hold exercised on historical imagination by a highly articulated guild world. Dino Compagni, Stefani, Matteo Villani, and others were to establish a tradition of social history unique to the European city. Cf. M. Becker, "Towards a Renaissance Historiography in Florence," *Studies in Honor of Hans Baron*, ed. A. Molho and J. Tedeschi (De Kalb, Ill., 1971), 143–71. For the implications of this tradition, see A. Brown, *Bartolomeo Scala, 1430–1497* (Princeton, N.J., 1979), pp. 257 ff.

67. G. Contini, *Poeti del Duecento* (Milan-Naples, 1962), pp. 189–253; A. Tartaro, "La conversione letteraria di Guittone," *Rivista di Cultura Classica e Medioevale*, VII (1965), 1057–67; C. Davis, "Education in Dante's Florence," *Speculum*, XL (1965), 426 ff., and "Brunetto Latini and Dante," *Studi Medievali*, 3d ser., VIII (1967), 424–28.

68. A. Quaglio, "Retorica, prosa e narrativa del Duecento," *Il Duecento: Dalla origini a Dante*, I, part 2, 101–6; C. Segra and M. Marti, eds., *La prosa del Duecento* (Milan-Naples, 1952), pp. 187–345.

69. A. Quaglio, 393–401. The capacity of the vernacular to achieve high levels of conceptual expression is evidenced in an early example of a doctrinal treatise in Tuscan. Cf. Ristoro d'Arezzo's *Composizione del mondo*; P. Kristeller, *Studies in Renaissance Thought and Letters* (Rome, 1956), pp. 479–80.

70. For the application of Jean Piaget's child psychology to the study of medieval history, see C. Radding, "Evolution of Medieval Mentalities," *American Historical Review*, LXXXIII (1978), 577–97. On credit, see the frequently-referred-to works of R. Lopez, particularly *La prima crisi della banca di Genoa (1250–59)* (Milan, 1956), and his introduction to *The Dawn of Modern Banking*, pp. 4–22. Cf. also R. de Roover, "The Commercial Revolution of the 13th Century," *Bulletin of the Business Historical Society*, XVI (1942), 34 ff., and *The Rise and Decline of the Medici Bank, 1397–1494* (New York, 1966), pp. 8–15.

71. The mastery referred to was no longer based on the belief that words had inherent power. Thomas Aquinas, when treating the subject of witchcraft, made a clear distinction between "words as symbols and as things efficacious in themselves." Cf. C. Radding, "Superstition to Science: The Medieval Ordeal," *American Historical Review*, LXXXIV (1979), 967. Aquinas says: "Now words, in so far as they signify something, have no power except as derived from the intellect; either of the speaker, or of the person to whom they are spoken. . . . Now

it cannot be said that these significant words uttered by magicians derive efficacy from the intellect of the speaker. . . . Moreover, man's intellect is invariably of such a disposition that its knowledge is caused by things, rather than it is able by its mere thought to cause things" (*Summa contra Gentiles*, bk. 3, part 2, chap. 105). Cf. C. Radding, "Superstition to Science." This hard-won conviction was to lead to a quest for mediation between word and thing through theories of causality and demonology.

BIBLIOGRAPHY

ABBREVIATIONS

ASF	Archivio di Stato in Firenze
BISI	*Bullettino del'Istituto Storico Italiano*
BNF	Biblioteca Nazionale in Firenze
MGH	*Monumenta Germaniae historica* (Hanover, 1826–). The most frequently cited series are the *Scriptores*, abbreviated as *SS*.
PL	*Patrologia Latina*, ed. J. P. Migne (Paris, 1844–64).
RIS	*Rerum Italicarum Scriptores*. New edition by G. Carducci and V. Fiorini (Città di Castello-Bologna, 1900–).

ARCHIVAL SOURCES
Diplomatico

Archivio di Stato in Firenze

Arte dei Mercatanti
Arte del Cambio
Badia di S. Lorenzo a Coltibuono
Passignano
San Salvatore di Camaldoli
Santa Maria d'Acquabella di Vallombrosa
Santa Maria degli Angioli
Santa Maria del Bigallo
Santa Maria del Fiore
Santa Maria della Badia
Santa Maria Novella
Santa Maria Nuova
Santissima Annunziata
Santo Spirito
Strozziane-Uguccione, acquisto

Notarile Anticosimiano

A. 981–83	Attaviano di Chiaro
B. 1262	Bencivenni di Gianni
B. 1340	Benintendi di Guittone
B. 1426	Bernardi Buonaccorso

B. 1462	Benvenuto di Alberto della Castellina
B. 1473	Bernardo di Rustichello
B. 1948	Biagio Boccadibue (recently published as *Biagio Bocca-dibue* (1298–1314), ed. L. De Angelis, E. Gigli, and F. Sznura (Pisa, 1978).
B. 2166	Bonizzi Bonizzo
B. 2527	Buonaccorso da Firenze
C. 102	Cantapochi Giovanni
C. 568ª	Ciuffoli Bonavere
D. 45	Dietaiuti di Simone
F. 66	Faccioli Buonaccorso
G. 364	Giovanni di Buoninsegna da Rignano
L. 76	Lapo Gianni
M. 293	Matteo di Biliotto
O. 3	Opizzo da Pontremoli
R. 40	Rinieri Baldesi
R. 150	Ricevuto d'Andrea
R. 192	Rinuccio di Piero
S. 733	Simone di Dino

Archivio Arcispedale di Santa Maria Nuova, San Paolo dei Convalescenti, filze 972–81.

Biblioteca Nazionale, Firenze, Magliabechi Collection XXV, 43.

PRIMARY SOURCES

I Capitoli del Comune di Firenze, ed. C. Guasti (Florence), I, 1866.

Carte della Badia di Firenze (*sec. X–XI*), ed. L. Schiaparelli (Rome), I, 1913.

Le carte della canonica della cattedrale di Firenze, ed. R. Piattoli (Rome), 1938.

Le carte del monastero di S. Maria in Firenze (Badia), ed. L. Schiaparelli (Rome), I, 1913.

Castellani, A. *Nuovi testi fiorentini del Dugento* (Florence), 1952, 2 vols.

Codice diplomatico longobardo, ed. L. Schiaparelli (Rome,), 1929–33, 2 vols.

Collectio chartarum pacis privatae medii sevi ad regionem Tusciae pertinentium, ed. G. Masi (Milan), 1943.

Contini, G. *Poeti del Duecento* (Milan-Naples), 1962.

La Cronica fiorentina, compilata nel sec. XIII, detta dello Pseudo-Brunetto, in *I primi due secoli della storia di Firenze*, ed. P. Villari (Florence,), 1905.

The Deeds of Frederick Barbarossa by Otto of Freising and His Continuator, Rahewin, trans. C. Mierow, with the collaboration of R. Emery (New York), 1953.

Diplomatico, Badia di S. Lorenzo a Coltibuono (23 December 1284).

Diplomatico, Sta. Maria Novella (15 April 1285), (20 February 1288).

Documenti per la storia della città di Arezzo nel Medio Evo, ed. P. Santini (Florence), I, 1889.

Documenti per la storia della città di Arezzo nel Medio Evo, ed. U. Pasqui (Florence), II, 1889.

Epistolae vagantes, ed. H. Cowdrey (Oxford,), 1972.

St. Francis of Assisi: Writings and Early Biographies. English Omnibus of the Sources for the Life of St. Francis, ed. M. Habig (Chicago), 1972 (abbreviated as *St. Francis of Assisi: Writings*).

John of Salisbury. *Historia Pontificis*, trans. M. Chibnall (London), 1956.

Lami, G. *Sanctae ecclesiae florentinae monumenta* (Florence), III, 1758.

Landolfo di San Paolo. *Historia mediolanensis, RIS*, V, part 3 (Bologna), 1934.
Landulfus Senior. *Historia mediolanensis libri quatuor, MGH, Scriptores,* VIII (Hanover), 1848.
Il libro segreto di Gregorio Dati, ed. C. Gargiolli (Bologna), 1869.
Memorie et documenti per servire all'istoria del Ducato di Lucca (Lucca), 1836, IV, parts 2 and 5.
Mittarelli, G. B., and Costadoni, A. *Annales camaldulenses ordinis Sancti Benedicti* (Venezia), I, 1755–73.
La prosa del Duecento, ed. C. Segra and M. Marti (Milan-Naples), 1952.
XV homeliés du IXe siècle d'un auteur inconnu de l'Italie du nord, trans. and ed. P. Mercier (Paris), 1970.
Il regesto della chiesa di Pisa, ed. N. Caturegli (Rome), 1938.
Regesto di Coltibuono, ed. L. Pagliai (Rome), IV, 1909.
Il regesto di Farfa di Gregorio di Catino, ed. I. Giorgi and U. Balzani (Rome), 1879–88, vols. 2–4.
Regestum reformationum comunis perusii ab anno MCCLVI ad annum MCCC, ed. V. Ansidei (Perugia), I, 1935.
Regestum Senense, ed. F. Schneider (Rome), I, 1911.
Rhetorimachia, ed. K. Manitius (Weimar), 1958.
Salimbene. *Cronica,* ed. G. Scalia (Bari), I, 1966.
Scripta Leonis, ed. and trans. R. Brooke (Oxford), 1970.
Statuti delle società del popolo di Bologna, ed. A. Gaudenzi (Rome), II, 1896.
Statuti di Volterra, ed. E. Fiumi (Florence), I, 1952.
Villani, Giovanni. *Cronica,* ed. F. Dragomanni (Florence), 1844–45, 4 vols.

SECONDARY SOURCES

Alphandery, P., and Dupont, A. *La christienté et l'idée de croisade. Les premières croisades* (Paris), 1954, I.
Ariès, P. *L'homme devant la mort* (Paris), 1977.
Astuti, G. *I contratti obligatori nella storia del diritto Italiano* (Milan), 1952.
———. "Influssi romanistice nelle fonte del diritto longobardo," *La cultura antica nell'occidente latino dal VII all' XI secolo* (Spoleto), 1975, II, 653–95.
Baldwin, J. *The Medieval Theories of the Just Price (Transactions of the American Philosophical Society)* XLIV, bk. 4, 1959.
———. *Masters, Princes, and Merchants: The Social Views of Peter the Chanter and His Circle* (Princeton), 1970, I.
Banker, J. "The *Ars Dictaminis* and Rhetorical Textbooks at the Bolognese University in the 14th Century," *Medievalia et Humanistica,* n.s., V, 1974, 155–68.
Barni, G., and Fasoli, G. *L'Italia nell'alto medioevo. Società e costume* (Turin), 1971, 121–25.
Baron, H. "Franciscan Poverty and Civic Wealth as Factors in the Rise of Humanistic Thought," *Speculum,* XIII, 1938, 1–35.
Batany, J. "L'Église et le mépris du monde," *Annales, E.S.C.,* XX, 1965, 218–28.
Becker, M. "Nota dei processi riguardanti prestatori di denaro del 1343 al 1379," *Archivio Storico Italiano,* CXIV, 1956, 95–104.
———. "La esecuzione della legislazione contro le pratiche monopolistiche," *Archivio Storico Italiano,* CXVII, 1959, 8–28.
———. *Florence in Transition. Vol. I: The Decline of the Commune* (Baltimore), 1967.
———. "Towards a Renaissance Historiography in Florence," *Studies in Honor*

of Hans Baron, ed. A. Molho and J. Tedeschi (De Kalb, Ill.), 1971, 143–71.

————. "Individualism in the Early Renaissance: Burden and Blessing," *Studies in the Renaissance*, XIX, 1972, 273–97.

————. "Aspects of Lay Piety in Early Renaissance Florence," *The Pursuit of Holiness*, ed. C. Trinkaus with H. Oberman (Leiden), 1974, 177–99.

Bellomo, M., *Ricerche sui rapporti patrimoniali tra coniugi. Contributo alla storia delle famiglie medievale* (Milan), 1961.

————. "Erede," *Enciclopedia del diritto* (Varese), 1966, XV, 184–94.

Beloch, K. *Bevolkerungsgeschichte Italiens* (Berlin), 1939, II.

Benvenuti, A. "Fonti e problemi per la storia dei penitenti a Firenze nel secolo XIII," *L'ordine della penitenza di San Francesco*, ed. O. Schmucki (Rome), 1973, 281–98.

Bertelli, L. "L'ospizio e il paese di Altopascio in Italia," *Atti del Primo Congresso Italiano di Storia Capitaliera* (Reggio Emilia), 1957, 151–67.

Besta, E. *L'opera d'irnerio* (Turin), 1896.

————. *Fonti: Legislazione e scienza giuridica* (Milan), 1923, I.

————. *Le obbligazione nella storia del diritto italiano* (Padua), 1936.

————. *Le successione nella storia del diritto italiano* (Milan), 1936.

Bloome, R. *La doctrine du péché dans les écoles théologiques de la première moitié du XII siècle* (Louvain), 1958.

Blum, C. *Saint Peter Damian* (Washington), 1947.

Boehmer, H. *Analekten zur Geschichte des Franciscus von Assisi* (Tubingen), 1930, II.

Boesch Gajano, S. "Giovanni Gualberto e la vita comune del clero nelle biografie di Andrea da Strume e di Azzo da Vallombrosa," *La vita comune del clero nei secoli XI e XII* (Milan), 1962, II, 228–35.

————. "Storia e tradizioni Vallombrosane," *BISI, LXXVI*, 1964, 99–215.

Bognetti, G. "Processo logico e integrazioni delle fonti nella storiografia di Paolo Diacano," *Miscellanea di studi muratori* (Modena), 1951, 357–81.

Bolton, B. "Innocent III's Treatment of the Humiliati," *Studies in Church History*, VIII, 1971, 73–82.

————. "Old Wealth and New Poverty in the Twelfth Century," *Studies in Church History*, XIV, 1977, 99 ff.

Bonizone di Sutri. *Liber de vita christiana*, ed. E. Perels (Berlin), 1930.

Borino, G. "L'investitura laica dal decreto di Niccolo II al decreto di Gregorio VII," *Studi Gregoriana*, V, 1956, 354–55.

Bornstein, C. V. *Die romanischen Sculpturen der Abtei Sagra di San Michele* (Berne), 1968.

————. "The Capitals of the Porch at Sant'Eufemia," *Gesta*, XIII, 1974, 19–24.

————. "Matilda of Canossa, Papal Rome and the Earliest Italian Porch Portals," *Atti del Convegno Romanico Mediopadano*, in press.

Borst, A. *Die Katharer* (Stuttgart), 1953.

Bosl, K., Graus, F., and Devisse, J. Essays in *La concezione della povertà nel Medioevo*, ed. O. Capitani (Bologna), 1974, 35–151.

Boyd, C. *Tithes and Parishes in Medieval Italy* (Ithaca, N.Y.), 1952.

Brakel, C. Die vom Reformpapattum geförderten Heiligenkulte," *Studi Gregoriani*, IX, 1972, 239–312.

Bratto, O. *Studi di antroponimia fiorentina: Il Libro di Montaperti, 1260* (Göteborg), 1953.

————. *Nuovi studi di antroponimia fiorentina: I nomi meno frequenti del Libro di Montaperti* (Göteborg), 1955.

Brezzi, P. "Ottone di Frisinga," *BISI*, LIV, 1939, 129–328.

————. *I comuni medioevali nella storia d'Italia* (Turin), 1970, 2nd ed.

Brown, Peter. "Society and the Supernatural: A Medieval Change," *Daedalus*, CLV, 1975, 133–51.

Bullough, D. "Le scuole cattedrali e la cultura dell'Italia settentrionale prima
dei comuni," *Italia Sacra* (Padua), 1964, 140–42, and *English Historical
Review*, LXXV, 1960, 487–91.
———. "Urban Change in Early Medieval Italy," *Papers of the British School
at Rome*, XXXIV, 1966, 116 ff.
———. "Early Medieval Social Groupings: The Terminology of Kinship," *Past
and Present*, XLV, 1969, 3–18.
———. "Social and Economic Structure in the Early Medieval City," *Topografia
urbana e vita cittadina nell'alto medioevo in occidente* (Spoleto), 1974, I,
358, ff.
Buonaiuti, E. *Gioacchino da Fiore* (Rome), 1930.
Bush, A. "An Echo of Christian Antiquity in Saint Gregory the Great," *Traditio*,
III, 1965, 369–90.
Bynum, C. "The Spirituality of Regular Canons in the 12th Century," *Medievalia et Humanistica*, n.s., IV, 1973, 3–24.
Byrne, E. "Genoese Trade with Syria in the Twelfth Century," *American Historical Review*, XXV, 1920, 191–219.
Calati, B. "Alcuni aspetti della monastica di S. Bernardo," *Camaldoli*, VII, 1953,
101–18.
Cammarosano, P. "Aspetti delle structure familiari nelle città dell'Italia comunale (secoli XII–XIV)," *Studi Medievali*, XVI, 1975, 417–35.
Cantin, A. *Les sciences seculières et la foi* (Spoleto), 1975.
Capitani, C. "San Pier Damiani e l'istituto eremitico," *L'eremitisimo in occidente
nei secoli XI e XII* (Milan), 1965, 122–63.
Capitani, O. "Studi per Berengario di Tours," *BISI*, LXIX, 1951, 154–69.
———. *Studi sul Berengario di Tours* (Lecce), 1966.
———. "Storiografia e riforma della chiesa in Italia," *La storiografia altomedievale* (Spoleto), 1970, II, 557–629.
Cappuyns, M. "Note sur le problème de la vision béatifique au IX siècle,"
Recherches de Théologie Anciènne et Médiévale, I, 1929, 98–107.
Carusi, E. "Folkloristica giuridica e storia del diritto," *Rivista di Storia del
Diritto Italiano*, II, 1929, 129–54.
Cattaneo, E. "La partecipazione dei laici alla liturgia," *I laici nella societas
christiana dei secoli XI e XII* (Milan), 1968, 403 ff.
———. "Il battistero in Italia dopo il mille," *Italia Sacra*, XV, 1970, 171–95.
———. *Il culto cristiano in occidente* (Rome), 1978.
Cencetti, G. "Studium fuit Bononie," *Le origini dell'Università*, ed. G. Arnaldi
(Bologna), 1974, 101–51.
Chenu, M. D. "Naturalisme et théologie au XII siècle," *Recherches de Science
Religieuse*, XXXVII, 1950, 5–12.
———. "La fin des temps dans la spiritualité médiévale," *Lumière et Vie*, II,
1953, 101–16.
———. *Nature, Man, and Society in the Twelfth Century: Essays on New
Theological Perspectives in the Latin West*, ed. and trans. J. Taylor and L.
Little (Chicago), 1968.
———. "Fraternitas: Evangile et condition socio-culturelle," *Revue d'Histoire
de la Spiritualité*, XLIX, 1973, 385–400.
Chevallier, P. "Denys L'Aréopagite," *Dictionnaire de spiritualité* (Paris), 1957,
III, cols. 319–24.
Cipolla, C. *Studi di storia della moneta* (Pavia), 1948, I.
———. "Introduzione," *Storia dell'economia italiana* (Turin), 1959, I, 2–8.
———. *Literacy and Development in the West* (London), 1969.
———. *Before the Industrial Revolution: European Society and Economy, 1000–
1700* (New York), 1976.
Classen, P. *Gerhoch von Reichersberg* (Wiesbaden), 1960.

Cole, B. *Giotto and Florentine Painting 1280–1375* (New York), 1976.

Congar, Y. *Lay People in the Church* (Westminster), 1957.

Conte, P. *Devotio viri devoti in Italia da Diocleziano ai Carolinghi* (Padua), 1971.

Conti, E. *La formazione della struttura agraria moderna nel contado fiorentino* (Rome), 1965, I.

Cortese, E. "Per la storia del mundio in Italia," *Rivista Italiana per le Scienze Giuridice*, LXXXI, 1955–56, 465 ff.

———. "Errore," *Enciclopedia del diritto* (Varese), 1966, XV, 236–40.

Costamagna, G. "Notaio," *Enciclopedia del diritto* (Varese), 1978, XXVIII, 561–65.

Coulton, G. *From St. Francis to Dante* (London), 1907.

Cowdrey, H. "The Papacy, the Patarenes, and the Church of Milan," *Transactions of the Royal Historical Society*, 5th ser., XVIII, 1968, 25–48.

———. *The Cluniacs and the Gregorian Reform* (Oxford), 1970.

———. "Anglo-Norman Church," *Studi Gregoriani*, IX, 1972, 77–114.

Cranz, F. "1100 A.D.: A Crisis for Us?" *Occasional Papers in the Humanities* (Connecticut College Library, New London, Conn.), 1978, 84–108.

———. "New Dimensions of Thought in Anselm and Abelard as Against Augustine and Boethius" (unpublished).

Cristiani, E. *Nobiltà e popolo nel Comune di Pisa delle origini del podestariato alla Signoria del Donoratico* (Naples), 1962.

Cristiani, M. "La controversia eucharistica nella cultura del secolo IX," *Studi Medioevali*, 3d ser., IX, 1968, 167–233.

Curtius, E. *European Literature and the Middle Ages* (London), 1953.

Cutolo, A. *Rerum Italicarum Scriptores* (Bologna), 1932.

Dahm, G. *Das Strafrecht Italiens im ausgehenden Mittelalter* (Berlin), 1931.

Dal Pino, F. *I Frati Servi di S. Maria dalle origini all'approvazione* (Louvain), 1972, I.

D'Amia, A. *Rinascenza pisani del diritto e di cultura e d'arte* (Pisa), 1975.

Damiani, P. *Vita beati Romualdi*, ed. G. Tabacco, *Fonti per la storia d'Italia*, XCIV, 1957.

da Milano, I. "Le eresie popolari del secolo XI nell'Europa occidentale," *Studi Gregoriana*, II, 1947, 43–89.

Dante. *The Divine Comedy*, trans. D. Sayers and B. Reynolds (Baltimore), 1966.

Davidsohn, R. *Forschungen zur Geschichte von Florenz* (Berlin), 1912, III.

———. *Firenze ai tempi di Dante*, trans. E. Theseider (Florence), 1929.

———. *Storia di Firenze* (Florence), 1956, I.

Davis, C. *Dante and the Idea of Rome* (Oxford), 1957.

———. "Education in Dante's Florence," *Speculum*, XL, 1965, 426 ff.

———. "Brunetto Latini and Dante," *Studi Medievali*, 3d ser., VIII, 1967, 424–28.

Debil, R. "La première distinction du 'De poenitentia' de Gratien," *Revue d'Histoire Écclésiastique*, XV, 1914, 251–73, 442 ff.

de Clerck, D. "Droit du démon et nécessité de la redemption dans les écoles d'Abelard et de Pierre Lombard," *Recherches de Théologie Ancienne et Médiévale*, XIV, 1947, 33–64.

De La Roncière, C. "La place des confréries dans l'encadrement religieux du contado florentin au XIVᵉ siècle," *Mélanges de l'École Française de Rome*, LXXXV, 1973, 31–77.

———. *Florence: Centre économique régional au XIVᵉ siècle* (Aix-en-Provence), 1976, I.

Delaruelle, E. "La pietà popolare nel secolo XI," *Storia del Medioevo, Atti X: Congresso Internazionale Scienze Storiche* (Florence), 1955, 318.

———. "Style de vie héroïque," *Comitato Internazionale di Scienze Storiche.* X *Congresso* (Florence), 1955, III, 322–31.

———. "Les ermités et la spiritualité populaire," *L'eremitismo in occidente nei secoli XI e XII* (Milan), 1965, 228 ff.

———. *La piété populaire au moyen âge* (Turin), 1975.

Delhaye, P. "L'enseignement de la philosophie morale au XIe siècle," *Mediaeval Studies,* XI, 1949, 77 ff.

de Lubac, H. *Corpus Mysticum* (Paris), 1948.

———. *Exégèse médiévale* (Paris), 1959.

Del Vecchio, A. *Le seconde nozze coniunge superstite* (Florence), 1885.

de Montclos, J. *Lanfranc et Berenger: La controverse eucharistique du XIe siècle* (Louvain), 1971.

Derein, C. "L'elaboration du statut canonique des chanoines réguliers spéciale- ment sous Urban II," *Revue Historique Écclésiastique,* XLVI, 1951, 550 ff.

———. "La 'vita apostolica' dans l'ordre canonial du Xe au XIIe siècle," *Revue Mabillon,* LI, 1961, 47–53.

Dereine, C. "Vie commune règle de Saint Augustin et chanoines réguliers au XIe siècle," *Revue d'Histoire Écclésiastique* XLI, 1946, 395.

de Roover, R. "The Organization of Trade," *Cambridge Economic History of Europe* (Cambridge), 1963, III, 42–153.

———. "Labor Conditions in Florence around 1400: Theory, Policy, and Real- ity," *Florentine Studies,* ed. N. Rubinstein (London), 1968, 277–313.

Doehaerd, R. *Le haut moyen âge occidental. Économies et sociétés* (Paris), 1971.

Dondaine, A. "Aux origines du Valdeisme," *Archivum Fratrum Praedicatorum,* XVI, 1946, 191–235.

———. "Le hierarchie cathare en Italie," *Archivum Fratrum Praedictatorum,* XIX, 1949, 280–312; XX, 1950, 234–324.

Douglas, M. *Purity and Danger: An Analysis of Concepts of Pollution and Ta- boo* (Baltimore), 1966.

Dresdner, A. *Kultur und Sittengeschichte der italienischen Geistlichkeit in X und XI Jahrhundert* (Breslaw), 1890.

Dressler, F. *Petrus Damiani Leben und Werke* (Rome), 1954.

Duby, G. "Les chanoines réguliers et la vie économique des XIe et XIIe siècles," *La vita comune del clero nei secoli XI e XII* (Milan), 1962, I, 72–81.

———. "Dans la France du nord-ouest au XIIe siècle les 'Jeunes' dans la so- ciété aristocratique," *Annales, E.S.C.,* XIX, 1964, 838–44.

———. "Structures de parenté et de noblesse, France du nord IXe–XIIe siècle," *Miscellania mediaevalia in memoriam J. Frederik Niermeyer* (Groningen), 1967, 149–65.

———. *Rural Economy and Country Life in the Medieval West* (Columbia, S.C.), 1968.

———. *The Early Growth of the European Economy* (Ithaca, N.Y.), 1974.

———. *L'anno mille: Storia religiosa e psicologia collettiva* (Turin), 1976.

———. "Le mariage dans la société du haut moyen âge," *Il matrimonio nella società altomedievale* (Spoleto), 1977, 34–37.

———. *Medieval Marriage: Two Models from Twelfth-Century France,* trans. E. Forster (Baltimore), 1978.

Duvernay, R. "Vallombrose, Citeaux et Étienne Harding," *Analecta S. O. Cis- terciensis,* VIII, 1958, 428 ff.

Eadmer. *The Life of St. Anselm, Archbishop of Canterbury,* ed. and trans. R. Southern (London), 1962.

Ehrle, F. "Petrus Johannis Olivi, sein Leben und seine Schriften," *Archiv für Literatur und Kirchengeschichte des Mittelalters,* III, 1887, 409–552.

Encyclopedia of World Art, 1959, I.

Ennen, E. *Storia della città medievale* (Bari), 1978.

Erdmann, C. *The Origin of the Idea of Crusade*, trans. M. Baldwin and W. Goffart (Princeton, N.J.), 1977.

Evans, G. *Anselm and Talk about God* (Oxford), 1978.

Falce, A. *Ugo di Tuscia* (Florence), 1921.

Falco, G. *La Sancta Romana Repubblica: Profile storico del Medio Evo* (Milan-Naples), 1973, 9th ed., trans. K. Kent (London), 1964.

Fasoli, G. "Ricerche sulla legislazione antimagnatizia nei comuni dell'alta e media Italia," *Rivista di Storia del Diritto Italiano*, XII, 1939, 86–133, 240–309.

———. *Le incrusioni ungare in Europa nel secolo X* (Florence), 1945.

———. *Scritti di storia medievale* (Bologna), 1974.

Fasoli, G., and Bocchi, F. *La città medievale italiana* (Florence), 1973.

Fedele, P. "Esecutore testamentario," *Enciclopedia del diritto* (Varese), 1966, XV, 383–89.

Fischer, B. *Die alkuin-Bibel* (Fribourg-en-Brisgau), 1953.

Fiumi, E. "La demografia fiorentina nella pagine di Giovanni Villani," *Archivio Storico Italiano*, CVIII, 1950, 78–158.

———. "Sui rapporti economici tra città e contado nell'età comunale," *Archivio Storico Italiano*, CXIV, 1956, 20 ff.

———. "Fioritura e decadenza dell'economia fiorentina," *Archivio Storico Italiano*, CXV, 1957, 385–439.

———. *Storia economica e sociale di San Gimignano* (Florence), 1961.

———. *Demografia movimento urbanistico e classi sociali in Prato* (Florence), 1968.

Fonesca, C. "Le canoniche regolari riformate del Italia nord-occidentale," *Monasteri in alta Italia dopo le invasioni saracene e magiare* (Turin), 1966, 345–63.

Fournier, P. "Un tournant de l'histoire du droit 1060–1140," *Nouvelle Revue Historique de Droit Français et Étranger*, XLI, 1917, 129–80.

———. "Les collections canoniques romaines de l'époque de Grégoire VII," *Mélanges de l'Académe des Inscriptions et de Belles Lettres*, XLI, 1918, 271–394.

Fournier, P., and Le Bras, G. *Histoire des collections canonique en occident depuis les fausses decrétales jusqu'au décret de Gratien* (Paris), 1932, II.

Franci, R. "L'ospedale di San Paoli a Firenze e i terziari francescani," *Studi Francesci*, VII, 1921, 52–70.

Freising, Otto of. *The Deeds of Frederick Barbarosa*, trans. C. Miero (New York), 1953.

Frugoni, A. *Arnaldo da Brescia nelle fonti del secolo XII* (Rome), 1954.

———. "I temi della morte," *BISI*, LXIX, 1957, 175–222.

———. "Filii Arnaldi," *BISI*, LXX, 1958, 521–24.

———. "Momenti e problemi dell'ordo laicorum nei secoli X–XII," *Nova Historia*, XIII, 1961, 3–22.

———. "Sui flagellanti del 1260," *BISI*, LXXV, 1963, 210–37.

Fumagalli, V. "In margine all'Alleluja del 1233," *BISI*, LXXX, 1968, 257–72.

———. *Le origini di una grande dinastia feudale Adalberto-Atto di Canossa* (Tubingen), 1971.

Gaudement, J. "Le droit romain dans la pratique et chez les docteurs aux XIe et XIIe siècles," *Cahiers de Civilization Médiévale*, VIII, 1965, 365–80.

Geary, P. *Furta Sacra: Thefts of Relics in the Central Middle Ages* (Princeton, N.J.), 1978.

Geertz, C. *The Interpretation of Cultures* (New York), 1974.

Giacchi, O. "Matrimonio (diritto canonico)," *Enciclopedia del diritto* (Varese), 1975, XXV, 887–901.

Giardina, C. "Sul mundualdo della donna," *Rivista di Storia del Diritto Italiano*, XXXV, 1962, 41–51.

Gibson, M. *Lanfranc of Bec* (Oxford), 1978.

Gilchrist, J. *The Church and Economic Activity in the Middle Ages* (New York), 1969.

Ginzburg, C. "Folklore, magia, religione," *Storia d'Italia* (Turin), 1972, I, 615 ff.

Giordano da Pisa. *Quaresimale fiorentino, 1305–1306*, ed. C. Delcorno (Florence), 1974.

Giovannelli, G. "Nilo di Rossano fondature dell'abbazia greca di Grottaferrata santo," *Bibliotheca Sanctorum*, IX, 1967, 995–1108.

Goez, W. "Reformpapatum, Adel und Monastiche Erneuerung in der Toscana," *Investitur und Reichaversassung*, ed. J. Fleckenstein (Sigmaringen), 1973, 295–319.

Goldthwaite, R. "I prezzi del grano a Firenze del XIV al XVI secolo," *Quaderni Storici*, X, 1975, 15–36.

Grabar, A. *Romanesque Painting from the 11th to the 13th Century* (New York), 1958.

Graus, F. "Le funzioni del culte dei santi e della leggenda," *Agiografia altomedioevale*, ed. S. Boesch Gajano (Bologna), 1976, 145–60.

Gregory, T. *La filosofia della natura nel medioevo* (Milan), 1966.

———. "La nouvelle idée de nature au XII siècle," *The Cultural Context of Medieval Learning* (Boston), 175, 183–212.

Grierson, P. *Numismatics and History* (London), 1951.

———. "Commerce in the Dark Ages: A Critique of the Evidence," *Transactions of the Royal Historical Society*, 5th ser., IX, 1959, 123–40.

———. "Symbolism in Medieval Charters and Coins," *Simboli e simbologia nell'alto medioevo* (Spoleto), 1976, II, 609–25.

Grundmann, H. "La genesi dell'Università nel medioevo," *Le origini dell'Università*, ed. G. Arnaldi (Bologna), 1974, 90–94.

———. *Movimento religiosi nel medioevo*, trans. M. Ausserhofer and L. Santini (Bologna), 1974.

Guisti, M. "Le canoniche della città e diocese di Lucca al tempo della riforma Gregoriana," *Studi Gregoriani*, III, 1948, 321–67.

Haskins, C. *Studies in Medieval Culture* (New York), 1929.

———. *The Renaissance of the Twelfth Century* (Cambridge, Mass.), 1972.

Haussens, I. *Amalarii episcopi opera liturgica omnia* (Città del Vaticano), 1948, II.

Hay, D. *The Church in Italy in the Fifteenth Century* (Cambridge), 1977.

Henderson, J. "The Flagellant Movement and Flagellant Confraternities in Central Italy," *Studies in Church History*, XV, 1978, 147–60.

Henry, D. *A Commentary on the 'De Grammatica' of St. Anselm* (Dordrecht), 1974.

Herlihy, D. "Treasure Hoards in the Italian Economy, 960–1139," *The Economic History Revue*, 2d ser., X, 1957, 1–14.

———. "The Agrarian Revolution in Southern France and Italy, 801–1150," *Speculum*, XXXII, 1958, 23–41.

———. *Pisa in the Early Renaissance* (New Haven, Conn.), 1958.

———. "The History of the Rural Seigneury in Italy, 751–1200," *Agricultural History*, XXXIII, 1959, 58–71.

———. "Church Property on the European Continent, 701–1200," *Speculum*, XXXVI, 1961, 81–102.

————. "Land, Family and Women in Continental Europe, 701–1200," *Traditio*, XVIII, 1962, 89–120.

————. *Medieval and Renaissance Pistoia* (New Haven, Conn.), 1967.

————. "Santa Maria Impruneta," *Florentine Studies: Politics and Society in Renaissance Florence*, ed. N. Rubinstein (London), 1968, 242–76.

————. "Family Solidarity in Medieval Italian History," *Economy, Society and Government in Medieval Italy* (Kent, Ohio), 1969, 173–84.

————. "L'economia della città e del distretto di Lucca secondo le carte private nell'alto medioevo," *Atti del 5° Congresso internazionale di studi sull'alto medioevo* (Spoleto), 1973, 363–88.

————. "Medieval Children," *The Walter Prescott Webb Memorial Lectures: Essays on Medieval Civilization* (Austin, Tex.), 1978, 115 ff.

Herlihy, D., and Klapisch-Zuber, C. *Les toscans et leurs familles* (Paris), 1978.

Hibbert, A. "The Origins of the Medieval Town Patriciate," *Past and Present*, 1953. Republished in *Town in Societies*, ed. E. Wrigley and P. Abrams (Cambridge), 1978, 91–104.

Hubert, J. "La place fait aux laics dans les églises monastiques," *I laici nella societas christiana dei secoli XI e XII* (Milan), 1968, 473 ff.

Hughes, D. "Urban Growth and Family Structure in Medieval Genoa," *Past and Present*, LXVI, 1975, 3–28.

————. "Struttura familiare e del suo funzionamento nella società medievale," *Quaderni Storici*, XXXIII, 1976, 936–47.

————. "Kinsmen and Neighbors in Medieval Genoa," *The Medieval City*, ed. H. Miskimin, D. Herlihy, and A. Udovitch (New Haven, Conn), 1977, 95–111.

————. "From Brideprice to Dowry in Mediterranean Europe," *Journal of Family History*, Sep. 1978, 262–96.

Hugueny, C. "Gratien et la confession," *Revue des Sciences Philosophiques et Théologiques*, VI, 1912, 81–88.

Hunt, N. *Cluny under St. Hugh* (London), 1967.

Hyde, J. *Padua in the Age of Dante* (Manchester), 1966.

Ilarino da Milano, P. "La spiritualità evangelica anteriore a San Francesco," *Quaderni di Spiritualità Francescana*, VI, 1963, 61–70.

Ildefonso, P. *Delizie degli eruditi toscani* (Florence), 1770, X.

Imberciadori, I. *Mezzadria classica toscana con documentazione inedita dal sec. 9 al sec. 14* (Florence), 1951.

Inni, A. "Nuovi documenti sugli Spirituali in Toscana," *Archivum Franciscanum Historicum*, LXVI, 1972, 305–77.

Jakobson, R., and Halle, M. *Fundamentals of Language* (The Hague), 1956.

Javelet, R. *Image et ressemblance au douzième siècle* (Paris), 1967, II.

Jones, P. J. "An Italian Estate, 900–1200," *Economic History Review*, 2nd ser., VII, 1954, 18–32.

————. "A Tuscan Lordship in the Later Middle Ages: Camaldoli," *Journal of Ecclesiastical History*, V, 1954, 176 ff.

————. "Florentine Families and Florentine Diaries in the Fourteenth Century," *Papers of the British School at Rome*, XXIV, 1956, 183–205.

————. "Per la storia agraria italiana nel Medio Evo. Lineamenti e problemi," *Rivista Storica Italiana*, LXXVI, 1964, 300–48.

————. "L'Italia agraria nell'alto medioevo," *Agricoltura e mondo rurale in occidente nell'alto medioevo* (Spoleto), 1966, 57–92.

————. "Medieval Agrarian Society in Its Prime: Italy," *Cambridge Economic History of Europe* (Cambridge), 1966, 2d ed., I, 340–431.

————. "From Manor to Mezzadria," *Florentine Studies: Politics and Society in Renaissance Florence* (London), 1968, 193–241.

————. "La storia economica. Dalla Caduta, dell'Impero Romano al secolo XIV," *Storia d'Italia* (Turin), 1974, II, part 1, 1469–1810.

————. "Economia e società nell'Italia medievale: La leggenda della borghesia," *Storia d'Italia, Annali I* (Turin), 1978, 187–372.

Jorgensen, J. *St. Francis of Assisi* (New York), 1953.

Jungman, J. *Missarum sollemnia* (Paris), 1964.

Klapisch-Zuber, C. "Villaggi abbandonati ed emigrazioni interne," *Storia d'Italia* (Turin), 1973, V, part 1, 311–69.

Koyré, A. *L'idée de Dieu dans la philosophie de Saint Anselm* (Paris), 1923.

Kristeller, P. *Studies in Renaissance Thought and Letters* (Rome), 1956.

————. *Renaissance Thought II: Papers on Humanism and the Arts* (New York), 1965.

Kurtscheid, B. *Historia Iuris Canonici: Historia Institutorum* (Rome), 1941, I.

Kurze, W. "Monasteri e nobiltà nella Tuscia altomedievale," *Atti del 5° Congresso Internazionale di Studi sull'Alto Medioevo* (Spoleto), 1973, 344–48.

Labande, E. R. *Spiritualité et vie littéraire de l'occident X^e–XIVe siècle* (London), 1974.

Ladner, G. "The Life of the Mind in the Christian West around the Year 1200," *The Year 1200: A Symposium* (Dublin), 1975, 1–23.

————. "Medieval and Modern Understanding of Symbolism: A Comparison," *Speculum*, LIV, 1979, 223–56.

Lambert, M. *Franciscan Poverty: The Doctrine of the Absolute Poverty of Christ and the Apostles in the Franciscan Order, 1210–1323* (London), 1961.

————. *Medieval Heresy: Popular Movements from Bogomil to Hus* (London), 1977.

————. "The Motives of the Cathars," *Studies in Church History*, XV, 1978, 52–54.

Lami, M. *Ecclesiae florentinae monumenta* (Florence), 1759, II.

Leach, E. *Claude Lévi-Strauss* (New York), 1970.

————. *Culture and Communication: The Logic by Which Symbols are Connected* (Cambridge), 1976.

Le Bras, G. *Dictionnaire de Théologie Catholique* (Paris), 1950, XV, part 2, 2336–72.

Leclercq, J. "Contemplation," *Dictionnaire de Spiritualité* (Paris), 1953, II, cols. 1937–48.

————. *L'amour des lettres et le désir de Dieu* (Paris), 1957.

————. *La spiritualité du Moyen Âge* (Aubier), 1961.

————. "The Monastic Crisis of the 11th and 12th Centuries," *Cluniac Monasticism in the Central Middle Ages*, ed. N. Hunt (London), 1971, 204 ff.

————. *La spiritualità del medioevo da San Gregoria a San Bernardo (secoli VI–XII)* (Bologna), 1972.

Leff, G. *Medieval Thought: St. Augustine to Ockham* (Baltimore), 1958.

————. *Heresy in the Later Middle Ages: The Relation of Heterodoxy to Dissent, c.1250–c.1450* (Manchester), 1967, I.

Le Goff, J. "Les gestes symboliques dans la vie sociale," *Simboli e simbologia nell'altomedioevo* (Spoleto), 1976, II, 679–88.

————. "The Usurer and Purgatory," *The Dawn of Modern Banking* (New Haven, Conn.), 1979, 25–52.

Leicht, P. *Il diritto privato preirneriano* (Bologna), 1933.

————. *Storia del diritto italiano* (Milan), 1937.

Lemmens, L. *Testimonia minora saeculi XIII de S. Francisco Assisiensi* (Quaracchi), 1926.

Leonardi, C. "Spiritualità di Ambrogio Autperto," *Studi Medievali*, 3d ser., IX, 1968, 1–131.

Lesnick, D. "Popular Dominican Preaching in Early Fourteenth-Century Florence." Ph.D. dissertation, University of Rochester, 1975.

————. "Dominican Preaching and the Creation of Capitalist Ideology in Late Medieval Florence," *Memorie Domenicane*, n.s., VIII–XIX, 1977–78, 204–41.

Lévi-Strauss, C. *Structural Anthropology* (New York), 1963.

————. *La pensée sauvage* (Paris), 1962, trans. as *The Savage Mind* (London), 1966.

————. *The Raw and the Cooked* (New York), 1969.

————. *Totemism* (Middlesex, England), 1973; introduction by R. Poole.

Little, L. "Pride Goes before Avarice: Social Change and the Vices in Latin Christendom," *American Historical Review*, LXXVI, 1971, 16–49.

————. "Formules monastiques de malediction au IXe et Xe siècles," *Revue Mabillon*, LVIII, 1975, 377–99.

————. "The Personal Development of Peter Damiani," *Order and Innovation in the Middle Ages: Studies in Honor of Joseph Strayer*, ed. W. C. Jordan, B. McNab, and T. Ruiz (Princeton, N.J.), 1976, 317–41.

————. *Religious Poverty and the Profit Economy in Medieval Europe* (Ithaca, N.Y.), 1978.

Lombard, P. *Senteniarum Liber* (Quaracchi), 1916, I.

Lopez, R. "Still Another Renaissance," *American Historical Revue*, LVII, 1951, 1–22.

————. "An Aristocracy of Money in the Early Middle Ages," *Speculum*, XXVIII, 1953, 1–43.

————. *La prima crisi della banca di Genoa (1250–59)* (Milan), 1956.

————. "Moneta e monetieri nell'Italia barbarica," *Moneta e scambi nell'alto medioevo* (Spoleto), 1961, 59–73.

————. *The Birth of Europe* (New York), 1967.

————. *The Commercial Revolution of the Middle Ages 950–1350* (Englewood Cliffs, N.J.), 1971.

————. Introduction, *The Dawn of Modern Banking* (New Haven, Conn.), 1979, 3–22.

Lopez, R., and Raymond, I. *Medieval Trade in the Mediterranean World* (New York), 1965.

Luzzato, G. "L'inurbamento delle populazione rurali in Italia nei secoli XII e XIII," *Studi di storia e diritto in onore di Enrico Besta* (Milan), 1939, I, 183–203.

————. *Storia economica d'Italia* (Florence), 1948.

McLaughlin, M. "Survivors and Surrogates: Children and Parents from the Ninth to the Thirteenth Centuries," *The History of Childhood*, ed. L. de Mause (New York), 1974, 101–81.

McLaughlin, T. "The Teachings of the Canonists on Usury," *Mediaeval Studies*, I, 1939, 81–147, and II, 1940, 1–22.

Magli, I. *Gli uomini della penitenza* (Rocca, San Casciano), 1967.

Manitius, K. "Magic und Rhetorik bei Anselm von Besate," *Deutsches Archiv für Erforschung des Mittelalters*, XII, 1956, 52 ff.

Manselli, R. "L'escatologismo di S. Gregorio Magno," *Atti del Primo Congresso Internazionali di Studi Longobardi* (Spoleto), 1952, 383–87.

————. *La 'lectura super Apocalipsim' di Pietro di Giovanni Olivi. Ricerche sull'escatologismo medioevale* (Rome), 1955.

————. "L'anno 1260 fu anno giochimitico?" *Il movimento dei disciplinati* (Perugia), 1962, 100–108.

————. "De Dante à Coluccio Salutati discussions sur la pauvreté à Florence au XIVe siècle," *Études sur l'histoire de la pauvreté*, ed. M. Mollat (Paris), 1974, II, 633–42.

————. *La religione popolare nel medioevo (secoli VI–XII)* (Turin), 1974.

————. "Vie familiale et éthique sexuelle dans les pénitentes," *Famille et parenti* (Rome), 1977, 363–78.

Map, W. *De Nugis Curialium*, trans. M. James (London), 1923.

Markus, R. *The Cambridge History of Later Greek and Early Medieval Philosophy*, ed. A. Armstrong (Cambridge), 1967, 341–425.

Martini, M. "La vita di San Giovanni Gualberto in una antica laude inedita," *La Bibliografia*, XXVIII, 1926, 161–77.

Masi, G. "La 'defensio' nel diritto prerinascementale," *Rivista di Storia del Diritto Italiano*, XXIV, 1951, 95–147.

Mauss, M. *The Gift: Form and Function of Exchange in Archaic Societies*, trans. I. Cunnison (New York), 1967.

Meade, D. "From Turmoil to Solidarity: The Emergence of the Vallombrosan Monastic Congregation," *The American Benedictine Review*, XIX, 1968, 323–51.

Meek, C. *Lucca 1369–1400: Politics and Society in an Early Renaissance City-State* (Oxford), 1978.

Meersseman, G. "Les confréries des disciplinés de Saint-Dominique," *Archivum Fratrum Praedicatorum*, XX, 1950, 21–63.

————."Les confréries de Saint Pierre Martyr," *Archivum Fratrum Praedicatorum*, XXI, 1951, 51–196.

————. *Dossier de l'ordre de la pénitence au XIIIᵉ siècle, Spicilegium Friburgense*, VII (Fribourg, Switzerland), 1961.

————. "Nota sull'origine delle compagnia dei laudesi," *Rivista Storica della Chiesa in Italia*, XVII, 1963, 395 ff.

————. "Dante e la cultura Veneta," *Atti del Congresso Internazionale di Studi Danteschi* (Florence), 1965, I, 177 ff.

————. "Chiesa e 'ordo laicorum' nel secolo XI," *Chiesa e riforma nella spiritualità del secolo* XI (Todi), 1968, 57 ff.

————."I penitenti nei secoli XI e XII," *I laici nella 'società christiana' dei secoli XI e XII* (Milan), 1968.

————. *Ordo fraternitatis: Confraternite e pietà dei laici nel medioevo* (Rome), 1977, I.

Meersseman, G., and Adda, E. "Pénitents ruraux communautaires en Italie aux XIIᵉ siècle," *Revue d'Histoire Ecclésiastique*, XLIX, 1954, 343–90.

Meiss, M. *Painting in Florence and Siena after the Black Death* (New York), 1964.

Meloni, P. "Topografia, diffusione e aspetti delle confraternite," *Risultati e prospettive della ricerca sul movimento dei disciplinati* (Perugia), 1972, 26–30.

Miccoli, G. "Per la storia della pataria milanese," *Bullettino dell'Istituto Storico Italiano per il Medio Evo*, LXX, 1958, 43–123.

————. *Chiesa Gregoriana: Richerche sulla riforma nel secolo* XI (Florence), 1960.

————. *Pietro Igneo. Studi sull'età gregoriana* (Rome), 1960.

————. "La 'conversione' di San Francesco secondo Tommaso da Celano," *Studi Medievali*, 3d ser., V, 1964, 775–92.

————. "Aspetti di monachesimo toscano nel secolo XI," *Il romanico pistoiese nei suoi rapporti con l'arte romanica dell'occidente* (Pistoia), 1966, 53 ff.

————. "Dal pellegrinaggio alla conquista," *Povertà e ricchezza nella spiritualità dei secoli XI e XII* (Todi), 1969, 74 ff.

————. "Bonizone," *Dizionario biografico degli Italiani* (Rome), 1970, XII, 246–59.

————. "La storia religiosa," *Storia d'Italia* (Turin), 1974, II, part 1, 472–507.

Minio-Paluello, L. "Nuovi impulsi allo studio della logica," *La Scuola nell'Occidente latino dell'alto medioevo* (Spoleto), 1972, 743–66.

Mittarelli, I., and Costadoni, A. *Annales Camaldulenses* (Venice), 1755, I.

Mollat, M. "La notion de la pauvreté au Moyen Âge: Positions des problèmes," *Revue d'Histoire de l'Église de France*, LII, 1966, 5–23.

Monti, G. *Le confraternitè medievali dell'alta e media Italia* (Venice), 1927, II.

Moore, R. *The Birth of Popular Heresy* (London), 1975.

————. *The Origins of European Dissent* (London), 1977.

Moorman, J. *The Sources for the Life of St. Francis of Assisi* (Manchester), 1940.

————. *A History of the Franciscan Order: From Its Origins to the Year 1517* (Oxford), 1968.

Mor, C. *L'età feudale* (Milan), 1952, II.

————. "Simbologia e simboli nella vita Giuridica," *Simboli e simbologia* (Spoleto,) 1976, I, 18–27.

Morghen, R. *Medioevo Cristiano* (Bari), 1951.

————. Problèmes sur l'origine de l'hérésie au Moyen-Âge," *Hérésies e sociétés dans l'Europe préindustrielle 11e–18e siècles* (Paris), 1968, 120–32.

————. *Gregorio VII e la riforma della chiesa nel secolo XI* (Palermo), 1974.

Morin, G. "Rainaud l'ermite et Ives de Chartres: Un épisode de la crise du cenobitisme au XIe–XIIe siècle," *Revue Bénédictine*, XL, 1928, 99–113.

Morris, C. *The Discovery of the Individual 1050–1200* (London), 1972.

Mundy, J. *Europe in the Middle Ages 1150–1309* (New York), 1973.

Murray, A. *Reason and Society in the Middle Ages* (Oxford), 1978.

Nanni, L. *La parrocchia studiata nei documenti lucchesi dei secoli VIII–XIII* (Rome), 1948.

Nelson, B. "The Usurer and the Merchant Prince: Italian Businessmen and the Ecclesiastical Law of Restitution, 1100–1550," *Journal of Economic History*, VII, 1947, 104–22.

Niccolai, F. "I consorzi nobiliari ed il comune nell'alta Italia," *Rivista di Storia del Diritto Italiano*, XIII, 1940, 304–9.

————. *La formazione del diritto successorio negli statuti communali del territorio lombardo-tosco* (Milan), 1940.

Nicolini, U. "Nuove testimonianze su Raniero Fasani e suoi disciplinati," *Bullettino della Deputazione di Storia Patria per l'Umbria*, LX, 1963, 334–38.

Nordenfalk, C. "An Early Medieval Shorthand Alphabet," *Speculum*, XIV, 1939, 443–47.

Olsen, G. "The Idea of the Ecclesia Primitiva in the Writing of the Twelfth-Century Canonists," *Traditio*, XXV, 1969, 85 ff.

Orlandi, S. *Il VII centenario della predicazione e ricordi di S. Pietro Martire in Firenze* (Florence), 1946–47.

Osheim, D. *An Italian Lordship. The Bishopric of Lucca in the Late Middle Ages* (Berkeley, Cal.), 1977.

Pampaloni, G. *Firenze al tempo di Dante* (Rome), 1973.

Panaro, T., and Pruneti, L. *Opposizione religiosa nel Medioevo* (Florence), 1977.

Partner, P. *The Lands of St. Peter: The Papal State in the Middle Ages and the Early Renaissance* (Berkeley, Cal.), 1972.

Pasqui, U. *Documenti per la storia di Arezzo nel Medio Evo* (Florence), 1899, I.

Pasquini, E. "La Lauda," *Il Duecento: Dalle origini a Dante*, ed. E. Pasquini and A. Quaglio, in *La letteratura italiana storia e testi* (Bari), 1970, I, part 1, 481–548.

————. "La letteratura didattica e allegorica," *Il Duecento: Dalle origini a Dante*, ed. E. Pasquini and A. Quaglio, in *La letteratura italiana storia e testi* (Bari), 1971, I, part 2, 3–111.

Patt, W. "Early 'Ars Dictaminis,' " *Viator*, IX, 1978, 133–52.

Pegna, M. *Firenze dalle origini al medioevo* (Florence), 1962.

Penco, G. *Storia del monachesimo in Italia* (Rome), 1961.

Pepe, G. *Il Medio Evo barbarico d'Italia* (Turin), 1959.

———. *Da San Nilo all'umanesimo* (Bari), 1966.

Pertile, A. *Storia del diritto italiano* (Turin), 1896–1903, IV, V.

Petrocchi, G. "Inchiesta sulla tradizione manoscritti dei *Fioretti,*" *Filologia Romanza*, III, 1957, 311–25.

———. *Scrittori religiosi del Duecento* (Florence), 1974.

Petrucci, A. *Notarii: Documenti per la storia del notariato italiano* (Milan), 1958.

Picasso, C. "I fondamenti del matrimonio nelle collezioni canoniche," *Il matrimonio nella società altomedievale* (Spoleto), 1977, I, 192–231.

Pinto, G. *Il libro del Biadaiolo: Carestie e annona a Firenze della metà del '200 al 1348* (Florence), 1978.

Plesner, J. *L'émigration de la compagne à la ville libre de Florence au XIIIe siècle* (Copenhagen), 1934.

———. "Una rivoluzione stradale nel Dugento," *Acta Jutlandica*, X, 1938, 1–102.

Poschmann, H. *Poenitentia secunda* (Bonn), 1940.

Post, G. *Studies in Medieval Legal Thought* (Princeton, N.J.), 1961.

———. "Philosophy and Citizenship in the Thirteenth Century," *Order and Innovation in the Middle Ages: Studies in Honor of Joseph Strayer*, ed. W. C. Jordan, B. McNab, and T. Ruiz (Princeton, N.J.), 1976, 400 ff.

Post, G., and Giocarinis, K. "The Medieval Heritage of a Humanistic Ideal: 'Scientia Donum Dei Est, Unde Vendi Non Potest,'" *Traditio*, XI, 1955, 196–220.

Prandi, A. "Arte figurativa per le confraternite dei disciplinati," *Risultati e prospettive della ricerca sul movimento dei disciplinati* (Perugia), 1972, 266–73.

Prosdocimi, L. "Chierici e laici nella società occidentale del secolo XII," *Annali della Facoltà di Giurisprudenta dell'Università di Genoa*, III, 1964, 241–62.

Prunai, G. "Il 'Breve Dominorum di Cerreto del 1216,'" *Archivio Storico Italiano*, CXVI, 1958, 75–85.

Quaglio, A. "Retorica, prosa e narrativa del Duecento," *Il Duecento: Dalle origini a Dante*, ed. E. Pasquini and A. Quaglio, in *La letteratura italiana e testi* (Bari) 1970, I, part 2, 101–106.

Quilici, B. *La chiesa di Firenze nei primi decenni del secolo undecimo* (Florence), 1940.

———. *Il Vescovo Ardingo e la chiesa di Firenze nel quarto e quinto decennio del secolo XIII* (Florence), 1965.

Quintavalle, A. *Wiligelmo e la sua scuola* (Florence), 1967.

———. "Questioni medievali," *Critica d'Arte*, XV, 1968, 61–76.

———. "La cattedrale di Cremona, Cluny, la scuola de Lanfranco e Wiligelmo," *Storia dell'Arte*, XVIII, 1973, 117–72.

———. "Piacenza Cathedral, Lanfranco and the School of Wiligelmo," *Art Bulletin*, LV, 1973, 46–57.

Radding, C. "Evolution of Medieval Mentalities," *American Historical Review*, Review, LXXXIII, 1978, 577–97.

———. "Superstition to Science: The Medieval Ordeal," *American Historical Review*, LXXIV, 1979, 945–69.

Reeves, M. *The Influence of Prophecy in the Later Middle Ages: A Study in Joachimism* (Oxford), 1969.

———. *Joachim of Fiore and the Prophetic Future* (New York), 1977.

Richa, G. *Notizie delle chiese fiorentine* (Florence), 1757, V.

Riché, P. "Le Pasutier, livre de lecture élémentaire d'après les vies des saints

mérovingiens," *Études mérovingiennes* (Paris), 1953, 253–56.
Robb, D. "Niccolò, A North Italian Sculptor of the Twelfth Century," *Art Bulletin*, XII, 1930, 374–412.
Robinson, I. "Gregory VII and the Soldiers of Christ," *History*, LVIII, 1973, 169–92.
———. "The 'Colores rhetorici' in the Investiture Contest," *Traditio*, XXXII, 1976, 209–38.
———. *Authority and Resistance in the Investiture Contest: The Polemical Literature of the Late 11th Century* (Manchester), 1978.
Rocca, E. "Considerazioni giuridiche sulla regola e sul 'penitenziale di San Colombano,'" *Contributi dell'istituto di storia medioevale* (Milan), 1972, 449–60.
Rockinger, L. *Briefsteller und Formelbücher eilfsten bis vierzehnten Jahrhunderts* (Munich), 1863.
Romanini, A. "Problemi di scultura e plastica altomedioevo," *Artigianato e tecnica nella società del alto medioevo occidentale* (Spoleto), 1971, II, 447–55.
Romans, R. *Tra due crisi: L'Italia del Rinascimento* (Turin), 1971.
Romeo, R. "La signoria del abate di Sant'Ambrogio di Milano sul comune rurale di Origgio nel secolo XIII," *Rivista Storica Italiana*, LXIX, 1957, 340–77, 473–507.
Rosenwein, B. "Feudal War and Monastic Peace: Cluniac Liturgy as Ritual Aggression," *Viator*, II, 1971, 17 ff.
Rosenwein, B., and Little, L. "Social Meaning in Monastic and Mendicant Spiritualities," *Past and Present*, LXIII, 1974, 20–25.
Rosetti, G. *Società e istituzioni nel contado lombardo durante il medioevo* (Milan), 1968.
———. "Il matrimonio del clero nella società altomedioevo," *Il matrimonio nella società altomedievale* (Spoleto), 1977, I, 533–45.
Rough, R. *The Reformist Illuminations in the Gospels of Matilda: A Study in the Art of Gregory VII* (The Hague), 1973.
Rowley, G. *Ambrogio Lorenzetti* (Princeton, N.J.), 1958, 2 vols.
Russell, J. *Dissent and Reform in the Early Middle Ages* (Los Angeles), 1965.
———. "Thirteenth-Century Tuscany as a Region," *Taius. Texas Agricultural and Industrial University: Studies*, I, 1968, 42–52.
Sahlins, M. *Culture and Practical Reason* (Chicago), 1976.
Salvini, R. *Wiligelmo e le origini della scultura romanica* (Milan), 1956.
Salvioli, G. *Storia del diritto italiano* (Turin), 1921.
Sambin, P. "Studi di storia ecclesiastica medioevale," *Deputazione di storia patria per le Venezie miscellanea* (Venice), 1954, IX, 53–60.
Santini, P. *Documenti dell'antica costituzione di Firenze* (Florence), 1895, I.
———. *Studi sull'antica costituzione del comune di Firenze* (Rome), 1972.
Sapegno, N. *Frate Iacopone da Todi* (Turin), 1926.
Sapori, A. "La beneficenza delle compagnie mercantili del Trecento," *Studi di storia economica* (Florence), 1955, II, 1–20.
———. "Il giusto prezzo nella dottrina di San Tommaso e nella pratica del suo tempo," *Studi di storia economica (secoli XIII, XIV, XV)* (Florence), 1955, 189 ff.
———. "I precedenti della providenze sociale nel medioevo," *Studi di storia economica* (Florence), 1955, I, 427–41.
———. *Studi di storia economica* (Florence), 1955, I.
———. *The Italian Merchant in the Middle Ages*, trans. P. Kennen (New York), 1970.
Saussure, F. *Course in General Linguistics*, ed. C. Bally (New York), 1966.

Sayons, E. "Aristocratie et noblesse à Gênes," *Annales d'Histoire Économique et Sociale*, IX, 1937, 366–72.

Schmitz, D. "L'influence de S. Benoît d'Aniane dans l'histoire de l'Ordre de S. Benoît," *Il monachesimo nell'alto medioevo e la formazione della civiltà occidentale* (Spoleto), 1957, 401–15.

Schupfer, F. *Il diritto privato dei popoli germanici con speciale riguardo all'Italia* (Città di Castello), 1909, IV.

———. *Il diritto delle obbligazioni in Italia nell'età del Risorgimento* (Turin), 1921, 3 vols.

Schwarzmaier, H. *Lucca und das Reich bis zum Ende des XI Jahrhunderts* (Tubingen), 1972.

Segre, C. *Volgarizzamenti del Due e Trecento* (Turin), 1955.

Sestan, E. "La storiografia dell'Italia longobarda," *La storiagrafia altomedievale* (Spoleto), 1970, I, 365–85.

Smalley, B. *The Study of the Bible in the Middle Ages* (South Bend, Ind.), 1970.

Sorbelli, A. *La parrochia dell'Appenino emiliano nel Medio Evo* (Bologna), 1910.

Southern, R. "Lanfranc of Bec and Berengar of Tours," *Studies in Medieval History Presented to F. M. Powicke* (Oxford), 1948, 27 ff.

———. *St. Anselm and His Biographers* (Cambridge), 1963.

———. *Medieval Humanism and Other Studies* (New York), 1970.

———. *Western Society and the Church in the Middle Ages* (Baltimore), 1970.

———. *The Making of the Middle Ages* (New Haven, Conn.), 1953.

Spandrel, R. *Ivo von Chartres und seine Stellung in der Kirchengeschichte* (Stuttgart), 1962.

Spinelli, G. "Il sacerdozio ministeriale nella predicazione della pataria milanesi," *Benedictina*, XXII, 1975, 91–110.

Sticker, A. "Il potere coattivo materiale della chiesa nella riforma gregoriana secondo Anselmo di Lucca," *Studi Gregoriani*, II, 1947, 235–85.

Stock, B. "Science, Technology, and Economic Progress in the Early Middle Ages," *Science in the Middle Ages,* ed. D. Lindberg (Chicago), 1978, 1–50.

Sznura, F. *L'espansione urbana di Firenze nel Dugento* (Florence), 1975.

Tabacco, G. "Privilegium amoris," *Il Saggiatore*, IV, 1954, 1–70.

———. "Eremo e cenobio," *Spiritualità cluniacense* (Todi), 1960, 326–35.

———. "Canoniche aretine," *La vita comune del clero nei secoli XI e XII* (Milan), 1962, 245 ff.

———. "Romualdo di Ravenna e gli inizi dell'eremitismo camaldolese," *L'eremitismo in occidente nei secoli XI e XII* (Milan), 1965, 73–120.

Tagliaferri, A. "Fasi dell'economia longobarda," in *Problemi della civiltà e dell'economia longobarda* (Milan), 1964, 245 ff.

Tamassia, N. *La famiglia italiana nel secoli XV e XVI* (Palermo), 1910.

Tartaro, A. "Scrittori devoti," *Il Trecento*, ed. C. Muscetta and A. Tartaro, in *La letteratura italiana* (Bari), 1972, II, part 2, 438–81.

Tellenbach, G. *Church, State and Christian Society at the Time of the Investiture Contest*, trans. R. F. Bennet (New York), 1970.

"The Tenth Century: A Symposium," *Mediaevalia et Humanistica*, IX, 1955.

Thevenin, M. *Textes relatifs aux institutions mérovingiennes et carolingiennes* (Paris), 1887.

Thrupp, S. "The Gilds," *Cambridge Economic History* (Cambridge), 1963, III, 230–80.

Toubert, P. "Histoire de l'Italie médiévale (X^e–XIIIe siècles)," *Revue Historique*, CCXXVII (1960), 168 ff.

———. *Les structures du Latium médiéval* (Rome), 1973, 2 vols.

———. *Études sur l'Italie médiévale* (London), 1976.

Trifone, P. "Fedecommesso," *Nuovissimo digesto italiano* (Turin), 1961, VII, 196.

Trinkaus, C. "Petrarch's Views on the Individual and His Society," *Osiris*, XI, 1954, 168–98.

Troya, C. *Storia d'Italia del Medio Evo* (Naples), 1839–59, IV, part 5B.

Ullmann, W. "Cardinal Humbert and the Ecclesia Romana," *Studi Gregoriani*, IV, 1952, 111–27.

———. *The Growth of Papal Government in the Middle Ages* (London), 1970, 3d ed.

Vasina, A. *Romagna medievale* (Ravenna), 1970.

Vauchez, A. *La spiritualité du Moyen Âge occidental VIIIᵉ–XIIᵉ siècles* (Paris), 1975.

Vicaire, M. H. *L'imitation des apôtres. Moines, chanoines et mendiants IVᵉ–XIIIᵉ siècles* (Paris), 1963.

Villani, G. *Cronica*, ed. F. Dragomanni (Florence), 1844–45, bk. XI, chap. 92.

Vinay, G. "Paolo Diacano e la poesia," *Convivium*, I, 1950, 97 ff.

———. *Alto medioevo latino* (Naples), 1978.

Violante, C. *La società milanese nell'età precomunale* (Bari), 1953.

———. *La pataria milanese e la riforma ecclesiastica* (Rome), 1955.

———. "Discussione," *Il movimento dei disciplinati* (Perugia), 1960, 387.

———. "Anselmo da Besate," *Dizionario biografico degli Italiani* (Rome), 1961, III, 401–9.

———. "Storia ed economia dell'Italia medievale," *Rivista Storica Italiana*, LXXII, 1961, 513–35.

———. "Vescovi e diocesi in Italia nel medioevo," *Atti del II Convegno di Storia della Chiesa in Italia* (Padua), 1964, 193–217.

———. "I laici nel movimento patarino," *I laici nella 'societes christiane' dei secoli XI e XII* (Milan), 1968, 596–687.

———. *Studi sulla cristianità medioevale* (Milan), 1972.

———. "Riflessioni sulla povertà nel secolo XI," *Studi sul medioevo cristiano offerti a Raffaello Morghen* (Rome), 1974, II, 1060–62.

———. "Discorso di chiusura," *Il matrimonio nella società altomedievale* (Spoleto), 1977, II, 986–87.

Vismara, G. *Storia dei patti successori* (Milan), 1941, I.

———. "La successione voluntarie nelle leggi barbariche," *Studi di storia e diritto in onore di A. Solmi* (Milan), 1941, II, 183–270.

Vogel, C. "Composition légale et commutation dans le système de la pénitence tarifée," *Revue de Droit Canonique*, VII, 1958, 289–318; IX, 1959, 1–30, 341–55.

———. *Il peccatore e la penitenza nella chiesa antica* (Turin), 1967.

———. *Le pécheur et la pénitence au Moyen Âge* (Paris), 1968.

———. "Les rites de la celebration du mariage," *Il matrimonio nella società alto-medievale* (Spoleto), 1977, I, 453–71.

Volpini, R. "Giovanni Gualberto," *Bibliotheca Sanctorum*, VI, 1965, 1012–29.

Wakefield, W., and Evans, A. *Heresies of the High Middle Ages* (New York), 1969.

Waley, D. "The Army of the Florentine Republic from the 12th to the 14th Century," *Florentine Studies*, ed. N. Rubinstein (London), 1968, 70–108.

———. *The Italian City-Republics* (New York), 1969.

Werkmüller, D. "Recinzioni, confini e sengi terminali," *Simboli e simbologia* (Spoleto), 1976, 640–78.

White, H. V. *Metahistory* (Baltimore), 1973.

White, J. *Art and Architecture in Italy 1250 to 1400* (Baltimore), 1966.

White, L. *Medieval Technology and Social Change* (Oxford), 1962.

Wieruszowski, H. "Arezzo as a Center for Learning and Letters in the Thirteenth Century," *Traditio*, IX, 1953, 321–91.

———. *Politics and Culture in Medieval Spain and Italy* (Rome), 1971.

Willibrord, P. "Rapport de Saint François d'Assise avec le mouvement spirituel du XIIᵉ siècle," *Études Franciscaines*, XII, 1962, 129–43.

———. "Signification sociale du Franciscanisme naissant," *Études Franciscaines*, XV, 1965, 84–95.

Wilmart, A. "Le recueil des poèmes et des prières de Saint Damien," *Revue Bénédictine*, XLI, 1929, 342–57.

———. *Auteurs spirituels et textes dévots du moyen âge latin* (Paris), 1932.

———. "Le manuel de prières de Saint Jean Gualbert," *Revue Bénédictine*, XLVIII, 1936, 259–99.

Zema, D. "Reform Legislation in the 11th Century and Its Economic Import," *Catholic Historical Review*, XXVII, 1941, 16–18.

Zerbi, P. "Pasquale II e l'ideale di povertà della chiesa," *Annuario dell'Università Cattolica del Sacro Cuore* (Milan), 1965, 207–29.

Zerbi, P., and Ambrosini A. *Problemi di storia medioevo* (Milan), 1977.

Zoepf, L. *Das Heiligen Leben im 10 Jahrhundert* (Leipzig), 1908.

INDEX

235